Ron Calcutt's
COMPLETE BOOK OF
FISHING

Ron Calcutt's
COMPLETE BOOK OF
FISHING

The essential reference for everyone who loves to fish

SIMON & SCHUSTER
AUSTRALIA

RON CALCUTT'S COMPLETE BOOK OF FISHING

First published in Australia in 1991 by Simon & Schuster
an imprint of Simon & Schuster (Australia) Pty Limited
20 Barcoo Street, East Roseville NSW 2069
This revised edition published in 2003

A Viacom Company
Sydney New York London Toronto

Visit our website at www.simonsaysaustralia.com

National Library of Australia
Cataloguing-in-Publication data:

Calcutt, Ron.
Ron Calcutt's complete book of fishing:
the essential reference for everyone who loves to fish.

New ed.
Includes index.
ISBN 0 7318 1206 9.

1. Fishing – Australia. 2. Fishes – Australia.
I. Title.
II. Title: Complete book of fishing.

799.10994

Cover design by Jason van Genderen, Treehouse Creative
Internal design by Gravity AAD
Typeset in 11 on 14 Berkeley Book
Printed in China by Leefung-Asco

Cover photography by Ron Calcutt (main picture and centre inset); and Rick Huckstepp
(left and right insets). Internal photography by Ron Calcutt, except for the following: pages
2, 3, 14 (right), 18, 27, 31, 39 (right), 41, 42, 52, 90–91, 182, 208, 237 by Rick
Huckstepp; pages 6, 13, 14 (left), 54, 58, 78–79, 81, 85, 126, 127, 154, 170 by Gil Schott;
pages 12, 16, 19, 21, 24, 36, 53, 103, 110, 125, 132, 136, 137, 138, 207, 210 (left) by
Tim Simpson. Screen shots on pages 8, 20 and 66 courtesy of Lowrance Australia.

Contents

Chapter Six

Fishing tackle 107

Chapter Seven

Skills and techniques 187

Chapter Eight

Handling and cooking fish 213

Chapter Nine

Hints for safe fishing, family fishing and travel 229

Acknowledgements

The knowledge of fishing that has allowed me to produce this book is the sum total of personal experience over 50 years of fishing, plus all the things I have learned from the people I have fished with over the years; and that includes a lot of people.

I am fortunate to be able to count master fishermen Rod Harrison and Alex Julius as both friends and teachers, and a lot of their wisdom has found its way into these pages. Dave Harrigan made a major contribution by working with me on previous projects that led to this book. My good friend from the Wild West, Ross Cusack, deserves special thanks for his invaluable assistance in getting all of this information into some sort of order that works. The men from Lowrance who hung in over the years to give me an understanding of the finer points of sonar and GPS also deserve a vote of thanks for making available their immense fund of knowledge.

Tom Bethurem's absolute mastery of threadline gear made me aware of the great potential of that equipment as serious hog-stopping tackle. I also have to thank him for putting up with my antics on some of the best fishing trips I've ever had.

Gil Schott, Tim Simpson and Rick Huckstepp all provided wonderful pictures for this book, and I owe a special vote of thanks to Tim for allowing me into his head to find out just about everything anyone ever knew about fishing tackle. Many people from the tackle trade have also contributed with access to their gear for photography.

Over the past 20 years I have edited literally hundreds of thousands of words for *Fishing World* and *Power Boat* magazines, learning something from every article I have ever worked on. I thank all those fishermen and writers I have worked with over the years for the privilege of working with them and learning from their adventures, experiments and experiences.

Finally, and perhaps this should have come first, I acknowledge the role my family plays in the big projects of my life – the films, the magazines, and now this book, which has taken up so much time I might have spent with them: Lynette, Mitch, Benny and Alex, my present fishing companion and good mate. My wife, Jan, must also come in for a great deal of credit for encouraging me and keeping me going when I am in serious states of despair – which is a lot of the time.

Introduction

The human creature was not designed yesterday, and while we may have become creatures of sophistication, whim and fashion over the years, the original blueprint is embedded deep inside every one of us. The blueprint inside our genes is that of a primitive animal, designed to function inside a tribal group.

A successful tribal group will need a variety of personality types. It will need brutal, aggressive types to defend it from invading tribal groups. It will need individuals with a natural interest and inclination to understand the trees and plants that can provide fruit and when that is likely to be available. It will need types who can invent and construct things, such as shelter and tools. It will need individuals with exceptional memories to be the storytellers and historians, pacifists to be the adjudicators and peacekeepers, and it will need strong females to produce the healthy offspring necessary to maintain the strength of a group with a naturally high mortality rate and short life span. But the future of the tribe will always depend absolutely on the skills of one type within the group: the hunters and gatherers.

The gatherers may or may not need specific individual skills, but the hunters need to be a unique type. Courage and stamina would be essential, as would a total understanding and rapport with the animals they hunt. They would have a mind-set that made them alert to every nuance of the forest, every opportunity presented by the world of water. To others the moon would be a source of light, but to the hunters the moon would be the clock of nature, dictating cycles of activity within the varying worlds of their prey. A plant would just be a plant to other members of the group, but to the hunter it would be the plant favoured as food by an animal they hunt and kill. Its presence would announce the presence of their prey.

Stark naked, clad in an animal skin or a pin-striped executive suit, the genes of the hunter are still there in a high percentage of human beings. In this modern world very few people need to hunt in order to survive, but a great many of us need to hunt because there is a program inside us that says we are only ever complete and okay with ourselves when we hunt. Anglers today are modern people with a highly active, but very primitive element in their individual blueprint. This book was designed for the primitive in many of us.

The first edition of this book went to print in 1991, and at that time it could claim to represent cutting edge thinking about the world of sportfishing. When the time came along for a major revision, I was surprised, and pleased, to discover how much of it was still relevant. The fish have not changed, so that gives us solid foundations to build on.

There have been some profound changes, though, some to do with technology moving ahead at breakneck speed, some to do with our response to a declining saltwater fishery in many heavily populated and developed areas.

The freshwater fishery was always the poor cousin of the saltwater fishery, partly because the fish were not as good to eat, and possibly because they were located away from the major centres of population and tended to be a bit harder to find and catch. Many inland anglers migrated to the coast for their holidays for a taste of 'real fishing'.

Beautiful country, calm waters and good fishing have combined to make stocked impoundment fishing enormously popular in recent years.

But as anglers began to find themselves working harder for their saltwater fish, some began working with local councils and state governments to look into the idea of stocking some of our impoundments with freshwater sportfish, most particularly the Australian bass. To cut a long story short, the Queensland government got right behind the idea, which has proved to be a great success.

So far, Queensland anglers have had the best of it, with many dams being stocked with bass, Mary River cod, yellowbelly, silver perch, saratoga, sooty grunter, barramundi and more. New South Wales was quick to see the value in what was happening, and then Victoria came on board. The number of stocked impoundments and the quality of the fishing they provide is pretty much in line with the length of time the various programs have been in place.

Anglers have taken to this new freshwater fishery in a big way, and they now even have a Bass Tournament circuit, which has been a great success. So much of a success that it has spawned a look-alike Bream Tournament circuit for dedicated saltwater anglers.

It would be impossible to speak for all anglers when trying to explain what is behind this great acceptance of the new-look freshwater fishery, but I am sure that as a recent convert myself, my reasoning may well represent the views of many others.

The quality of the fishing has to be the first consideration, and there can be no doubt that a majority of the stocked waters do provide good to outstanding fishing. Most of the fish readily take lures, so there is a high skill and sporting content involved. To my mind, active fishing with lures beats soaking baits any day.

The environment is usually attractive, and some of the areas are downright beautiful, with an abundance of wildlife adding a lot to the overall experience. The fact that most of these waters are protected, and therefore fishable in quite strong winds, means that all in all they are a powerful magnet for anglers, particularly fishing families who camp or take the onsite cabins and caravans that are available in most areas.

This style of fishery has seen the rapid growth of a whole new way of angling with lures that had previously seen little use in Australia: spinner baits, every kind of diving and surface-running minnow you could imagine and, of course, soft plastics. Soft plastics have been around for as long as I have been involved in serious fishing, and they seem to have been something of a fashion item over the years. As with fashions of every kind, they would come and go from time to time the way yo-yos have cyclic seasons with kids.

But this time the soft plastics have not only stayed around, they have revolutionised the fishing world. They stormed though the freshwater fishery, then

The introduction of gelspun (GSP) lines, such as this braid, have turned sportfishing on its head.

spread rapidly into the saltwater, where they are catching everything that eats lures and a whole lot of other things, like whiting, that are not supposed to be lure targets.

The other significant change is the introduction of gelspun (GSP) lines. These lines have the breaking strains of monofilament (mono) lines, but are a half to a third the diameter of the equivalent strength mono line. They are also inert and lifeless lines, which means that they create only a tiny fraction of the friction produced by mono lines passing through rod guides.

These characteristics have had a huge bearing on the role various types of fishing tackle play in the overall scheme of things. The impact seems to have been greatest on threadline outfits, where line coming away from the reel in coils created distance reducing friction, the friction increasing with the breaking strain and diameter of the line. Now anglers are using higher breaking strains in finer inert gelspun lines and casting further than they ever have before.

Fish-finding and position-finding electronics have undergone extraordinary development over the last 10 years, and today's entry-level sounders were yesterday's mid-range models.

These are all major changes to our fishing world, and the impact they have had across the whole spectrum of sportfishing has been significant.

With the technology sections updated, this book still sets out to do the job I envisioned it doing when I wrote the first edition. Back then I wrote the following introduction, and am happy to feel I am offering you the same quality reference in this latest edition.

'To take short cuts in fishing is to reduce the amount of success you can expect to enjoy. It is an incredibly complicated subject, made even more so by the fact that this huge continent of ours encompasses a vast range of fishing environments, from tropical fishing in the north to high-altitude alpine lake fishing in the south. There is very little overlap in the way the fish of the various regions behave, and the angling techniques are as varied as the fish.

'Clearly, knowing all there is to know about a subject so vast is the work of a lifetime, and then some. The trick is to clearly identify your own situation, and the fishing environment available to you, and then learn as much as you can about those matters that will concern you the most.

'All fishing is serious, because all anglers are serious about catching fish. The only difference between an experienced game angler squinting into the sun, looking down a berley trail for the first surface swirl that will announce the presence of hundreds of kilos of white shark, and a six-year-old trying to get a toad to bite is their age and environmental circumstance. I am not convinced that there is any real variation in the level of passion each experiences in the thrill of the hunt.

'The information in this book, then, is for people who are serious about catching fish, and it recognises that the hardest part of the task is identifying the right starting point. Once you've done that, progress is rapid, for you quickly become aware of what you need to know next.

'You don't have to read all this book to get a lot out of it. In fact, once you become familiar with the range of information it contains – and that won't take long at all – you should be able to learn enough to go fishing this afternoon. If things go well you can then turn to the back for information on the best way to clean and cook your catch. If you missed out, you can look up sections on the style of fishing you were working on to obtain advice on ways to improve your luck. In due course you might even find that you can eliminate the need for luck altogether, and become master of your own fishing fate.

'Ultimately, I want this book to be that old fishing friend you always wished you had; a friend well informed from a lifetime of practical experience, with the infinite patience required to answer your questions and solve your problems.'

I finished this introduction in the original book with a portrait of myself and my then six-year-old son exploring the rocks together. He's a young man now, but another one has moved up the ladder to take his place. Two days ago we were fishing a quiet coastal creek, casting soft plastic lures off high-tech rods and reels while watching magnificent Brahminy kites in their white and chestnut plumage circle against a pure blue backdrop.

Suddenly Al's rod buckled and the line hissed through the water as something took off at incredible speed. It's adrenalin time. This fish turns on 5 cents and seems to be swimming in ten directions at once, all at the same breathtaking speed. Al's razor-sharp 13-year-old reflexes are right there with every twist and turn, and finally the fish is on its side alongside the boat. He is a 60 cm giant herring with more metallic hues flashing through his scales than you could imagine in a holograph. He is beautiful – perfect in every way. We release him to get on with his role in the workings of the creek. The magic is alive and well. It always is for the angler.

Chapter One

The essentials of fishing

Anglers love to collect, and play with, fishing tackle. It has often been said that collecting and playing with tackle is more than half the fun of fishing, and that is probably quite true.

Later in this book we will deal with fishing tackle in depth, but for the moment we want to identify those things that are absolutely fundamental to successful fishing, and in this sense the only really *essential* items of tackle are a length of fishing line and a sharp hook.

No matter where you go in Australia, or the world for that matter, the success or failure of every fishing expedition you undertake will rest on your ability to find fish. As obvious as that may sound, very few people who fish make finding fish their number one priority.

Finding fish is not just a matter of being in a particular place, either. In 20 m of water, finding fish may mean knowing whether fish are on the top or the bottom. If they are on the top and you don't know it,

you might anchor over a big school and go without a bite all day because you are fishing on the bottom.

A great deal of the Earth's surface is covered in water of one sort or another, but only a very small amount of that water is populated with fish. Obviously, you could waste a great deal of time, effort and money prospecting for fish on a trial-and-error basis, so it's fortunate that we know enough about the fish we seek to be able to eliminate a lot of the guesswork from the process.

Chapter 3 of this book will look into the subject of finding fish in more detail, but before we do that there is one more fundamental to consider, and that is the business of getting the fish to bite when you do find them.

A lot of people go all day without a bite, then come home declaring that the place has been 'fished out'. Often they have been dangling their line right in the

There are plenty of trophy fish like this snapper swimming around, but to catch one you first have to find where the fish are.

middle of a school of fish the whole time, and the fish simply haven't been interested in the bait on the hook. If they are hungry enough, fish will eat almost anything, but most of the time they are extremely selective feeders. A prawn is not just a prawn to a fish. It is a Clarence River prawn, a Sydney Harbour prawn, a Hawkesbury River prawn, a fresh prawn, a rotten prawn, or a prawn sold as bait that has been treated with chemicals so that it will retain its colour and appeal to anglers after being frozen for long periods of time. What you choose for bait, and your understanding of what fish are most likely to eat in any given area, often provides the key to success.

If you eat scraps out of the garbage bin you may have trouble grasping this, but if you are particular about what you put in your own stomach, you'll understand. We all eat very ordinary food without interest at times, just because it is available when we are hungry. If we are hungry enough, seriously hungry, we might even eat things we would normally consider revolting. At other times we will travel some distance, then pay a great deal of money, to eat food we love in a favourite restaurant.

Fish, too, have this approach to food. Given enough competition for a limited supply of food, most fish will eat anything and gulp it down before they are beaten to it, but when they are not pressed by aggressive competition, and there is an abundance of food available, only the most tempting morsel will get them to bite.

This is the bottom line of fishing – finding the fish and getting them to bite! Everything else is secondary.

Fishing with purpose

On a recent estuary outing we came across a school of tailor working the surface, and cast lures to them. We caught some and found them to be stuffed full of frogmouth pilchards. In an effort to throw the hooks the tailor regurgitated the baitfish, and we soon had small pilchards all over the floor of the boat.

An experienced angler in the boat had a lure on his line that was much the same size as the pilchards, and he let his next cast sink to the bottom, then bounced it back towards the boat. He soon got a good strike and eventually landed a big flathead.

Depending how you choose to look at things, this could be the prize or the bait.

This is an excellent example of an experienced person fishing with purpose by actually targeting a fish. First off he targeted and used the appropriate technique for fish we could see on the surface, then he took things a step further by targeting a fish he suspected might be working *under* the bait school. Tailor chop baitfish to shreds when they work a school, and particles falling to the bottom act as berley. If there are enough tailor working an area, it is a safe bet that bream, flathead, snapper and other species could be under the bait, picking up the scraps and a few of the baitfish themselves. There's also a good chance that a major predator, such as a jewfish, may be taking advantage of the tailor's preoccupation with the bait to catch a few of the tailor. A live tailor returned to the water on a large hook would be quite irresistible to a big jewfish shadowing the action.

On another occasion we arrived at a river we'd never fished before. It was flathead season so we went to the river entrance and started to work our way upstream, looking for sand flats cut by channels and gutters where flathead would normally be waiting in ambush for the run-off tide to push the smaller fish off the flats and out into the channels. We found great-looking territory and fished with just about every kind of lure in three well-stocked tackle boxes, without much luck.

Heading back to the ramp, one jig dropped in a deep and featureless part of the river produced a good flathead. The next morning we went back to what had looked to be the best territory and once again caught very little, so we decided to try where the single good fish had been taken the day before. This time we hit paydirt and found flathead in residence in great numbers. The thing was that they were only eating soft plastic lures of 6–7 cm in length, and then only in a narrow range of colours.

The next morning we returned to the hot spot early and went for an hour without a single bite. Then the tide turned and began to run in, and once again the flathead went berserk but would only take a narrow range of lures. In those two sessions we hooked and released around 100 fish.

The interesting thing about that exercise is that the fish were biting on the opposite tide from that normally associated with feeding flathead, and the size and colour of our offering played a crucial part in our success. An open mind and our willingness to try different things allowed us to unlock what was a very difficult situation.

Knowing what to offer, where, and when, is a major part of the angler's art, and to acquire knowledge in this aspect of the game there is no better way to start than to study the fish themselves.

Some fish seem to exist for the sole purpose of being eaten by other fish. Whenever garfish, whitebait, pilchards, prawns, mullet and so on school up or cluster in any numbers, it will only be a matter of time before they are under attack. By finding the bait, you have found a potential hot spot.

The fish most commonly found working shoals of small baitfish are the minor predators. Some species not normally grouped under the predator heading are aggressive predators all the same – flathead, sole and flounder are good examples. These fish hunt as individuals, and most often ambush from hiding, but they will come out of the sand and move when stimulated by an abundance of bait or berley.

Tailor, salmon, kingfish, the larger trevally, queenfish and tuna of all kinds are good examples of the more mobile predators that hunt in schools. When these schools become dense enough, they in turn become bait for the major predators. It is common for jewfish to hunt tailor that are eating a minor baitfish, and it is not uncommon at sea to find huge yellowfin tuna and marlin slashing their way through a school of striped tuna that in turn are feeding on pilchards.

Another dimension to this bait-and-predator scenario is the layering effect that often applies when bait of any kind is under attack. Often a school of bait under attack by predators will have the smaller predators in among the bait at the surface, while larger predators will be well under the bait, or working around the edge of the action. A live bait of any kind that is isolated, either by being dropped in at the edge of the school or allowed to swim deep under the school, will soon become a prime target for something bigger.

Living in a totally different world, with completely different behaviour patterns from the predators, is another group of fish that can be roughly categorised as browsers, or opportunists. Many of these fish will turn into active predators when stimulated by an abundance of bait in the area, but their basic feeding pattern involves mooching about over a variety of terrain for whatever they can find.

OPPOSITE A typical bluewater chain-reaction feeding situation. A dense shoal of bait is moving deep enough under the surface to be protected from seabirds. A school of small tuna attacks the bait, driving it to the top where the birds can reach it. The noise and smell created as the bait is attacked attracts larger predators such as big yellowfin tuna, then larger predators again in the form of sharks and marlin. Like the other predators, anglers will be drawn to the scene by observing the actions of the birds, or perhaps because they have been sharp enough to spot the bait before it comes under attack. Some anglers will aim to exploit the obvious targets in the shape of the minor predators working right at the surface, while others will try for the unseen major predators they know could be working under the surface activity.

This lovely aft luderick is normally considered a vegetarian, but from time to time they can get very interested in bread, worms and prawns.

The bream is the ultimate scavenger, and anyone who has ever cleaned a few bream will testify that the stomach contents are a lucky dip of just about anything not firmly fixed to the ocean floor. Wheat and chook pellets are among the best berley for bream, and the same fish is partial to a little cheddar cheese and garlic sausage from time to time – hardly natural foods for a fish.

Sand flats and ribbon weed beds in shallows and channels are happy hunting grounds for bream, whiting, trevally and leatherjacket, to name a few, who all browse about for a crab, yabby, worm, hermit crab or any edible shellfish. Almost anything encrusted with growth also attracts browsers like a magnet, and pylons, reefs, wrecks and just about any kind of underwater structure will have the colonies of moochers looking for a titbit.

Snapper, groper and rock blackfish (black drummer) are all good examples of reef browsers; fish that eat the prawns, crabs and crustaceans associated with the reef, and also a considerable amount of vegetable matter. The snapper eats absolutely everything at one time or another, becoming a serious predator of other fish when its own size demands more substantial meals than are available through foraging.

The final group in this highly unscientific categorisation of marine life is the vegetarians. There are, in fact, very few strict vegetarians in the sea, and those that do eat vegetable matter most of the time still seem to eat a certain amount of crustaceans and worms. Probably the most important vegetarian in angling terms is the luderick, and 90 per cent of the angling done for this fish is done with weed of one kind or another.

When you consider the vast spectrum of environments, feeding patterns and preferred foods represented in this essentially superficial overview, one thing becomes obvious. You will do better by understanding a few fish very well, and targeting them with the most suitable presentation in the most likely location, than you will with any kind of 'general purpose' approach to fishing. Many techniques and locations will cover quite a variety of species sharing similar habitat and diet, but you still need to be able to identify both the species and the right presentation under the prevailing circumstances if you are going to produce consistent results.

There is no such thing as a general-purpose rig for the common bream. In the white water around the rocks you would fish for bream with only a very small lead running right down onto the hook, or you might use a small float of some kind. Fishing a rising tide over a sand flat you would fish a reasonable length of trace with just enough lead to reach the bottom without anchoring the bait. You might use a straight unweighted bait around some rugged structure, and to fish a fast run in a channel you might have to resort to feeding a considerable amount of line out into the current, then dropping a picker's doom sinker over the side to slowly work its way right down to the hook. All these methods, and more, are employed at various times to catch the same fish.

Fish-finding skills

In the next chapter you will find an extensive section on fish-finding techniques, dealing in detail with the preferred environments of fish. For the moment I will take a broad look at some of the principles of finding fish.

The example of the tailor and the flathead deals with a situation where there are visual clues. You can actually see fish working, determine what they are, and employ tactics appropriate to the situation. This often happens at sea, where anglers are able to see surface fish working on bait.

Sometimes the signs may not be apparent to a novice, but they will be clear to an experienced angler. A person with good eyes might just spot the bait itself, and bargain on it being attacked sooner or later by larger fish. Bait

may make its presence obvious by exploding from the water as something attacks the lower levels of the school, or the signs may be a little more subtle, such as a 'rippler', when all you see at the surface is a shimmer, a pattern that is at odds with the surrounding surface.

Seabirds are a good indicator, and it pays to familiarise yourself with the different birds and their movements. Seagulls are not much of an indicator at all, but all varieties of tern are absolutely reliable fish spotters. Mutton-birds are also reasonable indicators, as are the gannets. You can use frigate birds and terns to determine how deep bait is swimming by observing how high the birds suspend themselves off the water. They stay high to see bait that is swimming deep, then drop down as the bait comes towards the surface. By watching terns and frigate birds closely you can sometimes anticipate when predators are closing in on bait and about to come to the surface.

Echo sounders can be valuable aids to finding fish, but you need to understand their limitations and not become too reliant on them. For instance, they are no good at all over the shallows, when the presence of your boat will be pushing the fish away as you pass. They are also not much use when fishing the run in a channel where you are not relying on fish to congregate.

Sounders are worth their weight in gold when you are trying to locate a reef, or a bottom feature of any kind, and when you are looking for concentrations of fish. I use sounders a good deal to explore new territory, patiently working an area over at dead low speed, cataloguing bottom features, deep holes and concentrations of fish. A sounder will sometimes show up a spot where fish regularly congregate for no apparent reason, something you would never find without one.

Selecting fishing tackle

Keeping in mind what you have just read, you can start to look at fishing tackle as a tool kit. You need one sort of tool kit to make a wooden box, and another sort altogether to fix a motorbike. Likewise, you need one sort of tackle to catch whiting in the surf, and another to troll for yellowfin on the open sea.

Fishing rods are tools for lifting, throwing and reaching, whereas a reel can either be just a convenient place to store fishing line or a complex precision braking system with variable gearing and many other engineering refinements.

When you know your fish, where it lives, what sort of bait you are going to need and just how you will need to present it, and have some idea of how the fish is going to react to the hook, you will know what tools you are going to need for the job.

When people first come into fishing, and begin to appreciate that specialist tackle is required for most fishing environments, they sometimes make the mistake of trying to put a tackle collection together in one hit. That's not the way to do it. Identify the type of fishing that is most available to you, and put a concentrated effort into such fishing over a reasonable period of time. Put your money into developing a specialty kit for the particular place where you are going to invest most of your fishing time and effort.

By doing the one thing in the one place for a while you will begin to establish a knowledge base. Rather than learning a small amount about a good many places and fish, you will learn a great deal about one place and the fish that live there, or move through. Some days you may fail to catch fish on one bait and see someone else succeed fishing another bait. You will make mistakes and correct them. Fish may pick your bait but refuse to run with it, giving you second thoughts about the big sinker you have been using. When you try to use a lighter one, maybe you will find the line on your reel is too heavy for a light lead, or perhaps your rod is too stiff for a lighter line. Under such circumstances you will have grasped some fundamental truths about fishing and tackle, and the next time you walk into the tackle store you will be searching for the tools you know you need, rather than running blind and asking for advice. Better still, when you are eventually confronted with new water and a new fishing situation, you will have a base of proven routines, rigs and baits to put to work.

You simply won't gain this fundamental knowledge by jumping from one thing to another. Working this way, as you move on to new challenges, the original tool kit will remain an asset, rather than being something you've outgrown. In time you will develop a second complete kit for another type of environment, and so on, until in years to come you will have the gear to fish any one of a number of locations, and not have to run down to the tackle shop for a big spend every time you set out to fish some new territory. Cheap short cuts in the early days often result in tackle that fails to measure up to your maturing skills.

In 8 metres of water those distinct arches on an echo sounder screen would indicate fish well worth catching.

Which brings us to the question of just how much we should be spending on our tackle. This can be a real problem when we look in the showcase in a tackle store and see that there are a dozen models of threadline on show, all the same size but being offered at a surprising range of prices. How do you make sense of this?

Modern fishing reels are required to be high-performance machines, and at the heart of the performance is the drag system (or internal clutch), the gearing, and the ability of the external casing to withstand the ravages of corrosion.

At the bottom end of the price range you will find reels that don't perform well (or don't perform at all) in any of these areas. At the top of the range you will find reels that are built to fine tolerances with multiple ball bearings and high-tech metals that will last forever. They probably exceed the average person's requirements by a long shot, and are priced accordingly. In the middle to upper-middle ranges you will find a nice selection of reels that are very well made, have excellent drag systems and offer an impressive working life. If money is no object, always buy at the top end of the range, but most anglers will find good hardworking tackle at a respectable price in the mid to three-quarter level of the price range.

The complex subject of buying fishing tackle is covered in detail in Chapter 6, starting on page 106.

Chapter Two

The fish

Basic fish types

There are a number of ways you could choose to group the various types of fish inhabiting our waters, but until fairly recently anglers generally divided them into those fish you could eat and those that you couldn't. This simple division still works just fine for many anglers, but the real growth in amateur fishing these days is in the area of sportfishing, where completely inedible fish may rate very highly, simply because they are an exceptional sporting proposition and a challenge to the angler.

Catch-and-release fishing, where fish are carefully tagged and then released, is gaining in popularity too, but the mainstream trend is for anglers to look for the best of both worlds by adopting a sporting approach to fish that are good to eat.

It is in the long-term interest of all anglers, and of all of us for that matter, given that the produce of the sea is an important food source, to also be aware of another category of marine life: those creatures of the sea that are of no *direct* value to us, but are of great importance as a food source for other fish. These are the baitfish, squid, prawns and plankton – the stuff of which the ocean's foundations are made. When this end of the food chain fails, the whole structure collapses. When there is abundance at this level, there is abundance at every level.

BAITFISH

Bait comes in all shapes, forms and sizes. Bait may be shimmering square kilometres of fish, a school packed so densely as to have almost become a single life form, or it may be the extraordinary diversity of life found in a bed of ribbon weed anywhere around our coastline. If you can get hold of one of those fine mesh nets with a flat leading edge, walk through a bed of ribbon weed pushing the scoop through the weed ahead of you, and you will turn up an astonishing harvest of bait after just a few minutes of effort: shrimp, prawns, bottle squid, crabs and tiny fish.

The oceans are loaded with what appear to be unfortunate creatures, existing for the sole purpose of creating more of their own kind as fast as they can, so that other fish can eat them and their offspring at a tremendous rate. Some are tiny creatures the size of a match head; others may be quite substantial fish of a kilogram or more in weight. What they have in common is that they school in prodigious numbers, and this is the way things need to be in the sea, for the bait schools are virtual floating supermarkets, providing the larger fish with their food supply.

When there is an abundance of food available the predators will demonstrate accelerated growth and there will be a high survival rate from their spawning. The new generations of fish will grow and mature

At **LEFT** bursts of spray and the presence of birds make bait under attack obvious to even the inexperienced eye. On the **RIGHT**, a rippler is less obvious. The bait is not yet under attack but it represents great fishing potential.

quickly, spawning early and further accelerating the cycle of abundance. The system is geared to prolific consumption and replacement levels, and it is possible to see the dynamics of all this at work whenever something goes awry and affects any one link in the chain.

Many years ago, Lake Michigan in the US had a healthy population of steelhead trout flourishing on an equally prolific population of tiny baitfish known as alewives.

Pollution levels were allowed to build up in the lake system to the point where the steelhead ranks were decimated. With the natural predator removed from the scene, the population of alewives blew out to the point where they ran out of food, dying in their millions. The resulting stench as the dead fish washed up onto the beaches convinced the people of Chicago that they had gone too far, and a massive clean-up of the lake resulted. Today, good numbers of steelhead are back in the Great Lakes again. The fish are quite toxic, and it is extremely dangerous for pregnant women to eat even a small amount of this fish, but at least the alewives are under control again.

Obviously it is vital to the health of any marine system that the environment suits the bait species, so that they reproduce at their usual prolific rate. Anglers and conservationists should be paying greater attention to the petfood industry, for important bait species are being harvested on a large scale to fill pet-food cans. By doing this we are removing from the sea the only form of food available to many varieties of fish, and are passing it on to animals that have lived happily for years on table scraps that now go into the garbage bin instead. Nothing will prove more destructive to fish stocks than this sort of tampering with the natural order.

EDIBLE FISH

FORAGERS

Foragers are those fish that feed on vegetable matter and the smaller life forms. Many of the reef dwellers fall into this category, browsing on shellfish, various weeds, and the small crustaceans encountered on the reef. This group also includes those fish that work the sandbars of the rivers and beaches, feeding on worms and small shellfish.

Leatherjacket (**TOP**) and whiting (**ABOVE**) are opportunist browsers with a widely varied diet.

Bream, dart, herring, leatherjacket, groper and whiting are excellent examples of this group, with fish like the luderick representing the largely vegetarian segment. Garfish hover somewhere between this group and the baitfish, as do some of the larger mullet. Offshore species in this group would be the nannygai and morwong.

FORAGER/PREDATORS

A little way up the ladder from the peaceful foragers we find a group of fish that forms something of a bridge between them and the full-blown predators. These are opportunists who will make the most of a wide variety of available foods.

The silver trevally is mostly a forager in the early stages of life, but will become increasingly predatory as it grows. Such diverse species as snapper, red emperor and fingermark all follow a similar pattern of becoming more predatory as they grow. This is simply a matter of requiring more fuel to run a bigger engine as the fish grows, and is in line with the natural law that the best food is that which delivers maximum return for minimal expenditure of energy.

MINOR PREDATORS

Minor predators are interesting little fish that are not normally thought of when the word 'predator' is used, but they do aggressively prey on other fish to survive. In this group the flounder, flathead and John dory are good examples.

The flounder and flathead employ similar ambush techniques, burying themselves in the sand at the bottom with just the eyes clear to spot their prey, then bursting forth for a short lunge at the unsuspecting passer-by. The John dory does its ambushing from right out in the open, simply hanging about in places where small fish congregate, such as the pylons of wharves and around boat moorings. It is a very thin fish, and so can approach other fish head-on without presenting a specially threatening profile. Its major advantage is its ability to project its mouth forward for an extraordinary distance, thus putting in range targets made careless by their conviction that they are just out of range.

Silver trevally have great growth potential and their appetite grows accordingly. They are an extremely aggressive fish.

Schooling tailor can behave like a pack of mad dogs when the mood takes them, continuing to kill long after they are stuffed with food.

MAJOR PREDATORS

The category of major predators includes most of our big fish, along with quite a few smaller species that tend to congregate in large numbers. The major predators fall into two loose groups, the first being fish that associate themselves with some sort of structure that attracts bait, and the second being those wide-ranging fish that work the oceanic bait schools. Most of the predatory species will, however, comfortably switch roles from time to time to take advantage of an abundance of food available outside their normal field of operation.

The schooling fish include tailor, salmon, barracouta and barracuda, all of the tunas and wahoo.

The mulloway, or jewfish, slips comfortably between the role of solitary hunter and school fish, although it is most commonly encountered in numbers away from inshore rocks and beaches. The mulloway also moves from being a predator working a fixed structure, such as a reef or shipwreck, to a free-roaming predator when an abundance of food opens up opportunities. A good example of the latter situation is when the tailor are schooling in great numbers and the mulloway move with the schools, attacking from below. They do much the same thing when flood conditions concentrate mullet around river mouths.

In the north, queenfish, all the mackerel, threadfin salmon and, of course, the barramundi are the major predators that are also good table fish.

Many fish are highly valued for their sporting appeal, but have no value whatsoever as a table fish. Probably the best example of this category is the legendary bonefish. Although comparatively rare in Australia, these fish have an international reputation as a sportfish, based on the difficulty of getting close enough to them – on the shallow flats they normally inhabit – to make a cast, and the mind-boggling speed and endurance they demonstrate when hooked.

The queenfish and giant trevally also fall into this category. The queenfish is prized for its willingness to take surface lures and perform spectacular aerobatics on the line, the giant trevally for its legendary strength and staying power. Neither species makes a good table fish.

The yellowfin tuna comes into this category for most people. Admired for its great strength and speed, the average fish captured by yellowfin specialists is quite big by any standards. The 90 kg fish is the one every angler is after, and such trophy-sized specimens are not all that uncommon. Even those who love sashimi are hard put to eat a whole large tuna, however, and most of the big fish are being tagged and released these days. Lovers of Japanese-style raw fish prefer the flesh of the larger fish, but few Australians can tell the difference between prime and mediocre yellowfin, as long as the fish is fresh and the flesh has been well cared for.

It is hardly surprising that the barramundi is considered by many to be Australia's premier fish, as it combines many of the most desirable characteristics of an outstanding sportfish with superb table qualities

when it is in salt water. But in fresh water, especially when it has been in it for some time – when land-locked in a billabong, for instance – the barra too won't rate as a table fish.

BIG GAME

Many of the fish we have talked about already are classified as game fish, but when most people think game fish, they are thinking of the big game fish – the predators right at the top of the tree, the supreme hunters of the ocean.

At the bottom of this group, between sportfish and big game fish in status, are the yellowfin and bluefin tunas. These are fish of enormous strength and potentially great size. The true lightweight in the big-game category is the sailfish, the ballerina of the ocean, a fish of great beauty that is in the air more than in the water.

Billfish are excellent big game, the most important species being the striped, blue and black marlin. The black marlin has hogged the billfish spotlight for many years in this country, mainly due to the publicity given to the short breeding season captures north of Cairns, where giant female blacks attract world record seekers from all corners of the globe. It is the blue marlin, however, that provides the bulk of large fish captures around the country, and we are only just beginning to appreciate the true quality and extent of blue marlin stocks in our waters.

The broadbill swordfish remains the trophy fish that every true big-game angler wants to capture, and although we know that they are present in good numbers around our coastline, they remain stubbornly elusive.

Depending on your point of view, the sharks could either be at the top or the bottom of the big-game list. Species such as the grey nurse probably don't deserve to be there at all, and the various whalers are a dubious sporting proposition at the best of times.

The hammerhead is a better sporting fish than it is given credit for, and a light-line tussle with a good hammerhead will give most anglers a solid workout.

There is absolutely no doubt as to the mako's qualifications as a true game species, and although not a man-eater, the mako's habit of going completely berserk when hooked makes it a dangerous fish to deal

Sharks have lost much of their popularity as game fish in recent times, but the larger specimens such as this big tiger shark are still very impressive critters.

with from any size of boat. Most who have had dealings with makos will have a tale to tell of a leaping, cartwheeling fish that ended up in the cockpit of the boat. I had a small mako miss my head by centimetres as it bounced off the cabin bulkhead on its way back into the water once. These are not fish to tackle lightly from small boats!

The tiger shark is one of the true heavyweights of the game fish world, and the great white is the greatest predator in the ocean. There is no shortage of those willing to condemn sharks for their lack of fighting ability, but I am yet to meet the person who can remain unmoved when one of the true monsters of this group comes cruising up. I once had a white shark over 5 m long come storming to within a few metres of a small aluminium boat I was fishing from at the time, and that day I experienced a few feelings of apprehension!

At present, most shark species are in serious decline worldwide, so given the alternatives readily available to us in Australian waters, it might be a good idea to leave them alone altogether.

Understanding fish behaviour

A fish thinks the way you might think if you'd been left alone by educators, all the way through from your parents and teachers to your partners and bosses.

If you'd been left completely alone you would have the needs of a baby, but you would be very much better than a baby at satisfying those needs. You would need food, shelter, a way of protecting yourself from harm, and eventually you would manifest strong basic instincts about procreation. That's all there would be to life, and if all those needs were being met to your complete satisfaction, you might doze off in the sun with absolutely nothing on your mind. And if you were a fish and you gave in to that human instinct to doze off, you would probably soon be killed and eaten.

As we are not like fish at all, we have a good deal of trouble understanding their behaviour. Human behaviour and the thought patterns required to control that behaviour have evolved to become an incredibly complex business; the fish, on the other hand, is still

operating in survival mode, the most basic mode there is. The whole thrust of our education, both formal and informal, makes us rationalise everything we do and deny our instincts. This is why 90 per cent of the fish are caught by 10 per cent of the people who go fishing; the 10 per cent who work in an instinctual way and actually learn what it means to think like a fish.

When people joke about a good fisherman and say, 'He practically thinks like a fish', they are probably making a very astute observation about the person in question. While it is highly unlikely that he actually goes around thinking fishy thoughts, he at least knows how to recognise those basic signs in the natural environment that are meaningful to his quarry.

If you want to learn how to think like a fish, you first need to understand something about the world of the fish, and the way various species of fish have developed specific physical and behavioural characteristics in order to survive and flourish in their particular niche in the marine environment.

You also have to learn that everything about the behaviour of fish is surprisingly, and often annoyingly, flexible. Unlike humans, whose upbringing and experience leads them to believe that a set of circumstances always works in a particular way, fish won't keep banging their heads against the same wall when the circumstances have a different outcome. Nor will they waste a lot of valuable time trying to work out why things have changed, or stand around complaining about it. They will simply make the quickest and easiest adaptation available to them to accommodate and survive in the new situation. When all your proven baits and techniques at your best fishing hole stop working for a while, the explanation is nearly always as simple and straightforward as that. Nine times out of ten, the fish have simply changed their behaviour pattern to accommodate some environmental prerogative that you, as a rational human, simply cannot begin to comprehend. The following story about mangrove jack offers an excellent example of this sort of flexibility at work.

Long before I caught my first mangrove jack, I had read dozens of accounts of fishing for jack, all of which stressed the degree of difficulty associated with catching this fish, commonly known as the 'mangrove marauder'. According to those accounts, you had to cast the lure to within a thin whisker of a mangrove root or snag, then after making two or three hundred such precise casts, a jack would finally appear as a copper blur, taking the lure on the way back into cover it seemed hardly to have left, tying your line and lure up in the snags before you were even completely sure you'd had a strike! I have actually experienced jack fishing like this, but compare it with the following Northern Territory experience.

We were primarily fishing for barramundi in a system of creeks we had never visited before. The area was remote, and was lightly, if ever, fished. Close to the mouth of the main creek we came across the first little tidal arm, and there was a big snag complex right in

The behaviour patterns of mangrove jacks are shaped by environmental considerations and fishing pressure. They become so cunning in heavily fished areas that a lot of people come to believe they are no longer there, when in fact the fish are abundant but supercautious.

the opening of the mouth. The first cast landed a metre or two away from the snag, but mangrove jack and a couple of small barra bolted out to chase the lure in open water. After a number of casts had hooked both barra and jack, I had a fish come off the hooks just a metre or so from the boat, and as I wound the lure slowly to the side of the boat and allowed it to rest in the water for a moment, a big jack came out from under the boat and crashed the stationary lure right on the surface. He had obviously moved off the snag and taken up residence under the boat.

As we worked our way up the creek, every snag was the same: mangrove jacks everywhere and all of them prepared to come out into open water chasing lures.

When we reached the last navigable section of this small creek it narrowed right down, opening into a relatively large shallow pool before forking to a rock bar on one side. A very narrow offshoot, not much wider than our punt, went off for a short distance in the other direction. As we entered the pool we could clearly see a number of mangrove jack and small barramundi swimming about in the open, and we hooked several before the fish moved under cover.

But the real surprise this tiny creek had in store for us was up that narrow little arm, where mangrove jack were lined up along the bank like a picket fence of fish. They were all out in the open, and happy to bolt out from the bank in hot pursuit of anything even remotely resembling edible life of any kind.

Now there was precious little resemblance between the mangrove jack of this creek and the fish of those Queensland creeks I'd been reading about over the years. So little resemblance, in fact, that you might think you were dealing with a different species of fish altogether. They were all mangrove jack, though; it was just that their behaviour had been shaped by dramatically differing environments and population levels.

The behaviour of the southern fish had been shaped by extreme fishing pressure over a long period of time, probably coupled with the presence of fairly constant boat traffic on the waterways. Up north, the dominant factor was the overcrowding of the creek by fish. There were more jack in that creek than there were suitable stations for the fish, so some had been left with no choice but to accept whatever was left —

thus the picket fence of jacks lining the last little offshoot of the creek.

For all I know those jack are still all there, lined up along that bank. We let dozens of fish go that day, and took only the handful that had swallowed lures and so made successful release an impossibility.

This story presents an extreme example of behaviour conditioned by environment and circumstances, but most fish demonstrate similar flexibility in their day-to-day behaviour as environmental conditions vary.

Along our coastline, when strong offshore winds push the warm surface waters of the shallows out to sea, this water is replaced by water welling up from below – colder, clearer water. The fish that normally inhabit the shoreline reefs suddenly find the water too cold for their liking, and they also find themselves exposed by water clarity to which they are unaccustomed. They therefore move out to sea some distance, probably just far enough to find a comfort zone between the surface and the bottom, suspending there at a level deep enough to miss the worst effects of the wind on the surface but not deep enough for the sort of cold they are trying to escape. There is no natural food for them in this environment, so when the first onshore winds return conditions at their regular habitat to normal and the fish go back, an angler smart enough to be there for the first few days will enjoy spectacular fishing.

Obsessive feeding can also change normal behaviour patterns dramatically. This occurs from time to time when an abundance of some form of food suddenly becomes available, as when vast shoals of a tiny fish such as whitebait move inshore. Big fish feeding on these tiny baits become absolutely obsessive in their feeding behaviour – anything that is not exactly the same size as the bait, and preferably a member of the bait community itself, will be ignored.

Big tuna feeding on plankton have the ability to send anglers crazy at times. They see the great fish exploding through the surface, obviously feeding but oblivious to anything the angler can present, including large live baits that should offer the tuna a much more satisfying return for energy expended than a mouthful of tiny plankton.

The three things that commonly have the greatest effect on the behaviour of fish are the tides, the water

Big tuna like these can be hot to trot or distressingly sensitive at times.

temperature and the atmospheric (barometric) pressure. I am not ruling out the influence of the moon, but am taking a short cut by accepting that tidal movement is a direct result of the state of the moon. If you consult the moon chart it will only tell you what the phase of the moon is and when it rises and sets. If you consult the tide chart, you can measure the intensity of the moon's influence by noting the difference between high and low tides for the day. A great deal more water moves around on some days than on others, and depending on the nature of the spot you want to fish, you should look for days with the maximum, or minimum, water movement.

It would seem, then, that the effect of the moon would only be felt where water is directly associated with the easily measurable tidal ebb and flow of the oceans – in a coastal estuary, for example. But when you consider that tidal movement can be measured in a teacup, and that tiny birds migrating more than halfway around this planet do so by navigating directly off the same magnetic fields of the Earth that influence our compasses, you will understand that it is highly likely that the moon's effect can be felt by a native fish in a freshwater impoundment.

Freshwater fish will not experience the same effects of tidal movements as saltwater fish, which actually gain access to new food sources in periods of major water movement, but they may well be affected in the same way as a giant billfish cruising many kilometres offshore. The bright moon brings small life forms to the surface of the sea at these times, starting off a chain reaction of feeding which affects the billfish. A similar thing could well take place in a dam or stream.

I know anglers who say they don't go much by tides, but concentrate their fishing in the week preceding the dark of the moon and the week preceding the full moon. Take a look at your tide chart and note the periods of maximum and minimum tidal movement. Right – they are the week preceding the dark of the moon and the week preceding the full moon.

Do not, however, assume that the big spring tides or the small neap tides will work wonders everywhere. Different tides suit different locations, and you also need to have some feeling for the stage of that particular tide that will see the fish on the job. No matter how good conditions are, fish rarely bite well 24 hours a day. Since many fish take up to half a day to digest their food, it follows that if you are able to be at a spot when the majority of fish are feeding, the fishing will be a lot better than in the next 12 hours, when they are digesting that meal. It is no accident that late morning through to late afternoon, then from midnight through to dawn, tend generally to be the least productive fishing hours.

A big creek with extensive areas of sand flats and mangroves would benefit from large tides. The big flush-out would deny fish access to food for the whole period at the bottom of the tide, so they would take advantage of the run-in to get to the food on the flats, and then to access the mangrove areas on towards the top of the tide. The very best time to fish such a creek would be on the early run-in tide, when the fish are

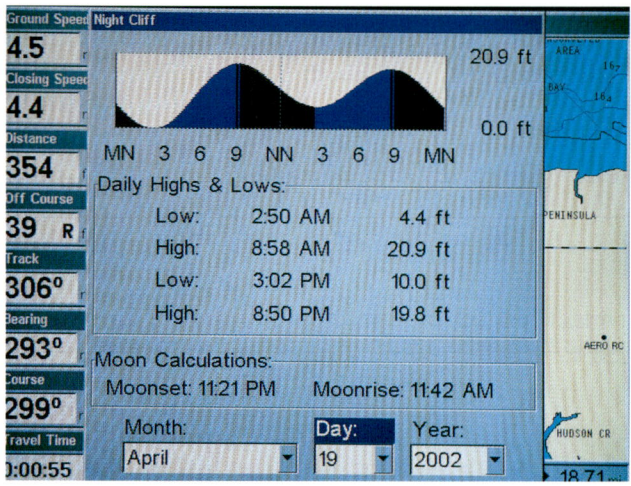

This graphic illustration of tide tables as displayed on a GPS mapping unit shows that not only are there two tides in the day, but that those two tides will also vary in height.

hungry and concentrated in the front of the tidal run, anxious to get at the food. Once the main body of water is into the system the fish will be too widely dispersed to be effectively targeted.

Very large estuaries, like the Hawkesbury River just north of Sydney, fish well on the big tides in places where the river is wide enough for some of the force of the current to be dissipated, but in other areas the hour either side of the tide change is the time to fish, when the water flow is reduced and the fish can move about without burning up too much energy. It pays to remember that a fish can only eat what it catches, and if it burns more energy hunting than it replaces with what it catches, it is actually starving to death. A fish will always choose the easiest feeding option available. In narrow confines, where water is pressuring through at speed, fish will take cover and feed aggressively between tides, but out in the big stretches they will take advantage of the enormous amount of food and life being transported along in that great body of moving water, often lying close to the bottom where an uneven surface tends to break down the main force of the water movement.

This is really what the tides are all about: water movement either giving fish easy access to rich new food sources or denying them access to food. In a very general way it can be said that the run-in tide produces the best fishing, but there are exceptions.

Flathead anglers, for example, like the run-out tide, for this is when flathead congregate in those channels the baitfish have to use when receding water forces them to leave the safety of the shallow sand flats.

Fish are also directly susceptible to atmospheric pressure. A sharp rise or fall, regardless of other factors, will cause them to feed, and a sustained period of low pressure will send them right off the bite. In my part of the world you will hear anglers say you can't catch fish in this wind or that wind, and these are invariably winds associated with a low-pressure system.

The final factor, water temperature, often overrides all others. Many fish have comfort zones of just one or two degrees within which they function normally, and within that comfort zone there is often an even narrower zone where they are at their most active. To better understand this, think of yourself getting up on a dark, cold winter's morning, and that revolting sensation of placing your warm feet on an ice-cold floor! Alternatively, visualise a stinking hot day, the kind that saps your energy to the point where even a trip to the fridge is almost too much effort. Contrast these examples with those perfect mornings when the air is clean and beautifully warm and you can't wait to get on with life. Now you can understand what a comfort zone is all about.

We frequently ignore all the sensible advice our minds and bodies give us, staying out in the cold in winter, running the risk of catching flu, and playing tennis in the heat of summer, also putting our health at risk.

Fish are nowhere near as silly as we are. They know what their comfort zones are and they pursue them. When they are stuck in a situation where the temperature is far from comfortable, they simply suspend themselves and do nothing until things come good again.

Strong current lines can indicate a path well travelled by fish and probably indicate the meeting of two temperature zones.

While humans are stuck with whatever weather the season presents us with, fish are more flexible. In summer, a fish living in a dam only has to go deeper to find its preferred temperature, and in cool weather it moves to the warmer surface layers. On the open sea you can imagine great water highways and massive pools that slowly move and spin in unpredictable patterns. These highways and pools are of a specific temperature, and they are capable of flowing through larger bodies of water of quite a different temperature without mixing. Just as a paved road flows through a forest, retaining its character and clearly defined edges, so a current of 24°C water can flow through a body of 22°C water and retain its character and defined edges. In fact, the edges of a strong current are so clearly defined that fish on either side will treat the demarcation zone much the same way you would a solid concrete wall.

Anglers out for big game work these current lines to great effect, as fish tend to travel along the edges. The same strong currents are often a matter of make or break for rock anglers, producing a bonanza when onshore winds bring a warm current right into the rocks, bringing all those game fish normally only found well offshore, but breaking hearts when the same fish-rich current sits just out of casting range with a band of cold water between it and the shore.

Tropical fish can sometimes get caught up in a massive pool of warm water slowly spinning southward, and anglers who have never seen such fish before suddenly find themselves catching exotic tropical species for a few days. By the same token, pools of cold water drifting northwards can shut fishing down overnight, as fish simply suspend all activity, using all their energy to maintain body temperature until the cold spell moves on.

Most fish with bodies designed for long-range swimming come and go according to water temperature, moving in all directions to find the aquatic season they prefer. These temperature fluctuations all have their influence on the quality of fishing you enjoy in the one spot from day to day, and are some of the reasons why even the best spots in the world shut down from time to time, and why some fishing days are better than others. When you can only fish on fixed days off work, knowing about all these factors is of academic interest only, but if you can choose your fishing times, and you can't afford to be out there all the time, you can certainly recognise periods that are going to offer you your best fishing opportunities.

For example, look at your chart for the periods before both the full moon and the dark of the moon, then look for the days in those periods where the change of tide, or the run-in tide, coincides with daybreak or dusk into dark, or the early part of the night. If the barometric pressure stays high during these periods, fishing should be good.

However, there are a number of factors which can blow much of this theory to the winds; the most influential of these are intense storm activity and periods of very heavy and flooding rain.

Very heavy to flood rain has a major effect on fish movement. In some estuaries and freshwater streams, very heavy rain will discolour the water to the point where the fish stop feeding altogether, if they can't actually leave the area. It could be that they simply can't breathe well enough to support much activity with the amount of suspended silt that is in the water (much like us trying to breathe in a sandstorm). In many cases the run-off of fertilisers and other chemicals used on farm lands produces sickness, and sometimes major fish kills. When you consider this, it is not surprising that some freshwater fish tend to go crazy as the barometer plummets in the period immediately preceding a major weather change. They know they could be in for a tough time of it in the immediate future, and will eat everything they can get into their mouths as insurance against the possibility of a long lean spell.

Conversely, situations also arise where flooding allows fish to gain access to new food sources and they go on a feeding spree. As water inundates grassland, worms are forced up out of the ground and freshwater fish go on a rampage for a time.

In times of flooding, those estuarine fish that can move do so, heading downstream in search of deeper bodies of water where the fresh and salt will separate, with the fresh on the top and the salt on the bottom. The bigger the flush-out, the further they are pushed downstream. In true floods, the fish are forced all the way down to the river entrance.

Obviously, this concentrates fish to a great extent, and the predators know it and move in. Prawns and mullet

Rough seas can be caused by local or distant weather systems. The wind on the ocean's surface means that local weather will have more effect on fishing than swell generated by far-off storms.

are the major targets, and if you can locate the areas where those creatures brought downstream are starting to concentrate, you can enjoy great fishing. In flood times, when our big coastal rivers are muddy torrents, everything is flushed out into the sea at first. Then, as the run-off settles, each incoming tide will force clean sea water in under the floodwaters at the surface. All the mullet that were formerly spread out over many, many kilometres of river now try to re-enter the system at the same time in huge schools, and as they mass in the front of the tidal surge, every jewfish and shark within swimming distance of the river is there to greet them.

Some overseas research indicates that pelagic (ocean) fish swimming 100 km or more offshore in a totally different weather pattern from that prevailing on the mainland know when flood rain falls on the mainland coast and head inshore.

Superb angling for billfish off Sydney in the very wet 1989–90 season tends to support this, particularly given that in the summer of 1990, Lord Howe Island, some 300 km off the Australian east coast, had superb weather and no billfish.

On the open ocean, storm wind also concentrates food inshore. It does this in a couple of ways. High winds produce breaking seas that actually move surface water inshore. This can bend currents inshore, along with all the food moving in that current. Up to a point, rough seas pounding the coastline also break considerable amounts of food away from inshore rocks and reef, and this, too, concentrates fish inshore.

There comes a time when the seas become too rough, and massive water movement creates a situation where fish are using more energy to work the environment than they are taking in from the food they find there. Under such conditions, look for the nearest coastal shelter and see if you can fish the area of protected water closest to the unprotected coastline. This will often be an area inside a point, and usually one where a heavy break at the point is producing a protected lee immediately inside.

Remember that a fish's concept of rough water is very different from yours. You will be looking at spectacular action as waves roar and explode against rocks, but underneath, where the fish lives, things could be quite pleasant. Fish can remain happy in incredibly rough conditions at times, and if you check the armoured scales and heavy slime on a groper or drummer (rock blackfish), it's not hard to see how such fish can operate right up on the rocks in the worst of the rough and tumble without too many problems. As a rule of thumb, however, when it looks as if the white water is solid all the way to the bottom out off the rocks most of the time, it is probably too rough for the fish.

Keep in mind that there are two kinds of rough seas – those that are produced locally and those that come in from distant storm systems. You know all about local storms because you experience the wind and rain that creates the rough water, but there are times when huge swells roll inshore in a period of calm weather, and these may have travelled a great distance from a violent weather system far out at sea. Although it is possible to experience good fishing in a heavy swell, such conditions don't do nearly as much to promote good fishing as a local storm system with a strong wind behind it.

These are just a few of the major variables affecting fish behaviour. There are also variables common to specific types of fish, and others common to localities. You can't expect to find all of these listed in a book, and they are lessons best learned through observation of your local area. The best anglers tend to be very observant people.

The senses

SIGHT

A fish may detect its prey through the use of sight, sonar, smell, or by tasting the water, but in the great majority of cases, the final attack or rejection will be

sight guided. This suggests that no matter what your basic approach to the fish might be, the way it sees your offering will have a great deal to do with the degree of success you ultimately enjoy.

The eye of a fish is not very different from our own eye, especially with regard to its ability to cope with light changes. One variation is that most fish have two systems for receiving an image: one designed for low light, the other for bright light. The bright light system is colour capable, while the low light system sees in black and white. The black and white system is far more sensitive than the bright light colour system, enabling the fish to see quite well in the dark.

The shift from the bright light system to the low light system takes two to three hours to complete in some species, though many of the game fish are capable of much faster system shifts. This may account for the fact that most game fish go on feeding sprees at first and last light, when they may well have a sight advantage over their prey. The fact that less adjustment time is required to cope with shifts in marginal light situations might also explain why overcast, rainy days are often very good days for catching surface fish, when predatory species can comfortably work close to the surface, and calm, bright days are usually the least productive for catching surface fish.

The large eyes of the mangrove jack indicate that sight plays an important part in its hunting activities. You can also see the nostrils just ahead of the eyes.

The fact that the low light to bright light shift generally takes more than three hours may also explain why fishing the second half of the night is usually less productive than fishing the first half. People fishing for tailor, working floating baits, often find that the dead period immediately before first light can be brought to life by keeping the bait moving. This gives the tailor a sonic target to home in on before the arrival of light.

Sudden light shifts produce a state of temporary blindness in fish, along with some discomfort, but a constant light actually attracts fish. Night anglers would do well to keep this in mind. Beach and rock anglers might give some thought to setting up a screen so they can do their baiting and rigging without having their torch or lantern beam shining directly onto the water.

It is interesting to speculate on whether the two sight systems might have something to do with the fact that the big billfish are said to prefer a cruising depth of around 35 m. Is this a constant twilight zone where the fish can easily swing to either sight system as required? Might it also explain why marlin often hang about behind a boat, moving from bait to bait before striking? Perhaps the fish is simply short-sighted after being drawn up from cruise depth by the sound of the boat.

On one occasion when I was lure fishing from the rocks for Spanish mackerel, I observed that the mackerel appeared to zigzag rapidly in the final approach to the lure. Later, watching frigate mackerel feeding, from the height advantage of a 13-storey building, I was able to clearly observe the way the fish moved about the bait school in large circling movements, then tore in to feed in a series of lightning-fast zigzags. This rather odd behaviour made some sense later when I actually understood how a fish sees things.

Fish have their eyes on the sides of their heads, which gives them the ability to scan almost 180° either side of their body. Looking forward there is a limited area in which the field of sight of both eyes overlaps to deliver a narrow band of binocular vision, and this is the only area in its entire field of sight where the fish has accurate depth perception. Although they are able to accurately judge distance in this zone, a certain amount of sharpness of vision is lost, as the sharpest vision is only available to each eye when the target object is observed at right angles to the eye.

Blending perfectly into the surroundings, this school of mullet uses reflective silver scales to mirror the light and colour around them. Out of the water they are just a bright silver fish. Never assume that fish under the water look the way they do in sunlight.

Looking back on those mackerel and their movements, did the zigzag allow those fish to switch between a clear image of the target and the depth perception necessary in order to home in effectively in a high-speed attack? Such a system would work well for a lightning-fast fish like the mackerel, which has its two eyes placed relatively close together, on either side of a fine, tapered snout, but what of a fish like the Murray cod, which has a very broad head and eyes set well apart? Clearly, everything would have to be slowed down considerably in a presentation suited to the cod. Relying on sight in an atmosphere that is poorly lit and often murky, fish are unusually sensitive to contrast and movement. When the water is relatively clean and the fish get a clear look at a lure near the surface, colour alone might provide sufficient contrast to excite their interest. In a less clear environment, colour with tonal contrast will be more effective. In almost any situation, a flash will probably be the most efficient attractor, but there's an interesting point to consider here. When you see a fish roll and flash in the water, bright though that fish may be, the flash is always limited to the side of the fish. Contrast this with some of the materials being used to produce

Is one of these examples a better colour than the others? The answer is no. They will vary in value according to where you are fishing and the quality of the water in which you are fishing.

flash on lure sides today, where light beams are fired off in all directions like a laser light show. Depending on the size of the fish you are trying to attract, if you're not careful, you might just convince it that your lure is large enough to be a predator! There is potential here to have too much of a good thing.

The never-ending argument about colour and its effectiveness in fishing will not be settled here, but a couple of worthwhile observations can be made. Fish *can* see colour, although some see colour better than others. The thing the angler needs to keep in mind is this: colour as the angler sees it only remains true in the surface layers of clear water. As depth increases, so the intensity and accuracy of colour are lost.

Red is pretty much a lost cause by 4 m, and at 6 to 7 m you might as well be using a black lure. Since red and the combination of red and white are very productive colours at times, you have to ask yourself whether it is the colour red or the contrast value involved that is attracting attention and making the lure work. Might not black and white be just as effective, since red and white virtually becomes black and white at quite a shallow depth? Well, it might, but anglers will not buy black and white lures, although they will buy and swear by black and yellow in freshwater situations!

In terms of being seen as a colour, red is the first colour to be lost as depth increases; at 10 m, orange is 480 times more visible than red, yellow is 3.3 times more visible than orange, and green is 1.7 times more visible than yellow, or 2760 times more visible than red. All the colours except red work pretty well down to around 6 m. Yellow through blue and green are the colours least affected by depth, with only a 30 per cent fall-off for yellow and a mere 19 per cent fall-off for green between 3 and 10 m. A fall-off does not mean that the object itself loses visibility, only that the colour loses identity.

White remains the most visible colour at depth, and black through purple and red affords the greatest contrast. For deepwater anglers, a case might be made in favour of going against traditional prejudice to stock up with these basics.

Shallow-water fish are said to have much better perception of colour than deepwater fish, so perhaps freshwater anglers might be well advised to stay with the technicolour tackle box.

Almost all top-rank anglers agree that the actual size and silhouette of a lure is at least as important as colour, perhaps more so. Shape may play an important role, but the actual overall size of the lure can be critical. Having 300 colours in the box won't help an angler much if all those lures are 8 cm long and the fish are feeding on bait 3 cm long. If you really want to convince yourself about the silhouette issue, try getting under some bait with a face mask on and see how it looks from below – the angle from which most of your target fish will be viewing it. The overwhelming importance of contrast and silhouette size will very quickly be brought home to you.

One final aspect of vision to consider is the ability of the fish to see you, and perhaps your fishing line. None of this matters much when the surface of the water is broken by wind, but when the surface is calm it may become a critical factor.

When you poke a stick into the water, it will seem to break at the level of the surface and the section of stick under the water will appear to spear off in a new direction at quite a sharp angle. This is happening because water refracts light waves. In the reverse situation, a fish near the bank, a fish that you can't yet see as you approach the water, may have an excellent view of you, because as it looks up at an angle of 40° it can actually see objects above the water at an angle of 10°. The fish will be long gone before you make your first cast. When approaching calm water there is much to be said for working low, well back from the water, and with the rod tip kept as close to the ground as is practicable.

HEARING

A fish has ears just like us, although these ears are inside the head rather than outside. Not only does the fish have very much better primary hearing than we do, it also has a secondary hearing system based on the lateral line. This system interprets low-frequency vibrations in water in much the same way we would use sonar. The lateral line is more distinct in some species than in others, but it is usually plainly visible as a fine line that starts at the shoulder of the fish just over the pectoral fin.

Sound travels at around 1.6 km per second in water, five times faster than it does in air, which means that hearing may be the most important of all the senses to a fish. By the same token, the noise factor might also be the most important element for the angler to consider. The right sort of sound might attract a fish, but the wrong sort of sound could send it running in fright. When you drop a tackle box on the floor of the boat, the hull amplifies the sound and belts it out into the water to travel at 1.6 km per second – you won't do your fishing prospects for the next couple of hours a whole lot of good. However, your mate who never stops talking at the top of his voice is only annoying you – the fish can't hear a word of it, as the surface of the water deflects almost all above-water sound.

While the fish hears sounds as sounds through its ears, and can hear sounds made some distance away, the low-frequency vibrations received through the lateral line are restricted to a range of around 10 m. The great value of this sonar system is that the fish can use it to accurately pinpoint the position of the sound source, and also to estimate the size and possibly the shape of the target.

Combined, these two hearing systems allow the fish to locate and attack prey that it cannot see, either because of light conditions, or because the sound source is a long way off. The fish initially hears the sound with its ears and moves in the general direction of the source. When it gets closer to the sound source it locks in on the target through its lateral line, then

can make the final approach using either lateral line sonar or vision, if there is sufficient light.

All sound is created by vibrations travelling through the elements of water or air, but when we think in terms of water we can also be thinking about pressure waves as vibrations. A fish moving quietly through the water displaces the molecules of the element about it, that then radiate out in a series of pressure waves. These are 'heard' by other fish through their lateral lines.

When we use live bait, putting a hook through that bait, no matter how carefully we do it, inhibits its normal swimming action, and that fish will broadcast the fact that it is crippled and distressed through the type of vibrations it emits as it tries to swim. It is

The lateral line can be clearly seen on this fish. This acts as a form of sonar with which the fish can literally feel movement about it.

the distress signal rather than the presence of the fish itself that attracts the predator.

The sonic value of a lure should never be underestimated. Every lure has its own sonic factor, and in some cases this may be far more effective than the way the lure looks.

The most obvious examples of sonic lures are those with rattles of some kind built in, and all the surface lures. Surface lures demonstrate a wide range of sonic effects that work. A fizzer needs only to have its little propeller blades turning to bring a fish up ready for action; a concave-faced blooper produces a sudden explosive 'pop' that is just as effective.

In the late 1980s there was something of a craze for barramundi lures with built-in rattles, after a pattern called the 'Rattlin' Spot' did well in a major barramundi competition. The original 'spots' were in short supply for a time, and distributors conjured up an extraordinary range of rattlers from around the world to meet the demand. But interestingly enough, out of the dozens of lures with built-in rattles offered, only a few actually worked. Obviously, it wasn't enough for the lure to rattle – it had to rattle in a particular way.

Anglers have interesting attitudes to sound. Some of the old-school Murray cod anglers believed that it helped to roar a boat around a hole in the river a few times to 'wake the cod up' before fishing. Some anglers don't like to walk along the bank, for fear of frightening the fish with the vibrations of their footsteps transmitted through the earth into the water; others advocate stamping along the bank to get the attention of barramundi when night fishing with surface poppers or sonic lures.

I have seen instances where engine noises have frightened fish off, and other cases when the same noises have attracted them. Trolling for both bass and barramundi in half a metre to a metre of water, particularly along the edge of a weed bank, I have been intrigued at the way the fish will still be there to hit a lure trolled only a short distance behind the boat. My educated guess about this is that the fish know the boat's engine will work in their favour, perhaps by stirring the bottom with the propellor which flushes bait out of cover, or maybe because the noise of the engine has the same effect, and they are working behind the boat knowing that its passing produces an opportunity for easy pickings.

Professional game charter skippers talk about boats having sound 'signatures', and so do professional submarine hunters. Apparently the sound and sonic waves given off by seemingly identical vessels are as uniquely different from one another as the fingerprints of humans. So identifiable, in fact, are their signatures that sub hunters are able to put the sound print of a submarine into a computer, then have the computer recognise and identify that particular vessel the next time it 'hears' it. Gamefishing skippers claim that some fishing boats have a sound 'signature' that will actually draw fish up from their cruising depth to look at the boat. The sound of a diesel engine certainly seems to be more attractive to fish than the higher revving sound of a petrol engine, although the real sound enthusiasts go on to claim that even the propeller signature can be important.

Four-stroke motors have taken the fishing world by storm. A recent survey showed that only 60 per cent of 2-stroke owners would purchase another 2-stroke motor, while 100 per cent of 4-stroke owners indicated that they would stay with 4-strokes.

In recent years, outboard companies have focused on the production of 4-stroke outboard motors, believing that the time is not far away when environmental legislation in the US will outlaw the use of polluting 2-strokes. Many anglers took to the 4-strokes because they did not produce the smelly clouds of exhaust fumes common to the 2-strokes, and because they were extremely fuel efficient.

As more 4-strokes appeared on the back of fishing boats, some sharp fishermen noticed that fishing results, particularly when trolling, improved out of sight with the introduction of the 4-stroke motor. The bigger EFI engines in particular have been specially effective in this area. You might hear different explanations as to why the fours are having this effect, but for my money it all comes down to the harmonics set up in the hull of the boat, especially aluminium boats, as 2-strokes bounce and jitter on the transom at low trolling speeds. The 4-strokes generally produce far less vibration, and some of the new 4-strokes in the top end of the horsepower range are as vibration-free as it is possible to make a machine with working parts.

Professional tuna fishermen play hoses onto the water to simulate the sound of a nervous bait school at the surface, and old-time anglers always used to put the first kingfish they caught back in the water on a tether, knowing that this struggling fish would keep the school close by.

Although it is difficult for us to know what sounds will attract fish, what sounds will repel them, and what sounds will have no effect, the successful angler will be aware that sound may sometimes be what is needed to fire up a quiet session.

SMELL

The third important sense to consider is the sense of smell. In some fishing situations, and for some species of fish, this is the most important sense of all to exploit.

The olfactory system actually forms the largest portion of the fish's brain, and it would not be occupying so much space if it were not fundamental to survival.

To begin to appreciate just how powerful a tool the sense of smell is to a fish, bear in mind that fish react

Some people have problems with the smell of fish, but all fish have problems with the smell of people.

to odour traces in water that are too small for scientific instruments to detect. The sockeye salmon is said to be able to sense the scent of shrimp in water at a level of one part to 100 million parts of water, and eels can do a lot better even than that.

Not only can fish smell out the normal odours you would expect them to be familiar with; they are also sensitive to such odours as the specific smell associated with fear or injury in other fish. Eels and salmon know the scent of particular waterways so intimately that they are capable of finding their way across hundreds, even thousands of kilometres of open sea to the streams they were spawned in, by scent alone.

One of the odours many fish find particularly revolting is a substance called L-serine. This is rather unfortunate, because it occurs in our skin. On the brighter side of things, fish are quite taken with the scent of human spit, so if you have been wondering how you were going to tie your lure on, or bait your hook, without sending the fish into a dead faint, you now know how to cover up your own disgusting odour.

On a more serious note, people who handle objects made from polished metals such as silver or stainless steel, and are responsible for keeping such objects nice and shiny, are well aware that some individuals leave much stickier fingerprints than others, and that this occurs even when the hands appear to be clean and dry. This might explain why two people fishing exactly the same bait and tackle, in exactly the same place, will turn up significantly different results. It could also account for that 'lucky' individual in the group who always catches the most fish. It is entirely possible that they are simply excreting less of the offensive substance than other people.

Another interesting thing to consider in this respect is the use of bottled bait scents. These are said to enhance the attractiveness of lures and baits, and are seen as being a little suspect by a majority of anglers. But if you happen to be the person who is always out-fished in the boat, it would certainly pay to try these scents, not only on your bait and lures, but also on your hands before you touch anything. This is a fertile field for experimentation.

Once aware of the fish's extreme sensitivity to smells, coupled with a similar level of sensitivity in the taste department, little more needs to be said about the role bait quality plays in a fishing situation – fresh is great, but alive and kicking will always be better. Nor do I need to emphasise the immense importance of berley. If this is the only thing you remember out of the entire book, and you go on to build a berley routine into your fishing system, you are well on your way to getting the price of the book back in increased catches.

Berley is the ingredient that turns dead spots into top-secret hot spots. Because fish have this extraordinary sense of smell, a berley trail will attract and concentrate them, pulling fish in from far and wide. If you berley continuously into a 2-knot current, at the end of 2 hours you will have extended an irresistible invitation 3.7 km downstream from your anchored boat. This will bring within fishing range every single fish, or school of fish, that crosses the trail in that distance. A berley trail is an awesomely powerful tool.

Body types

The body shape of a fish can tell you a great deal about how and where it lives, what it is likely to favour in the way of food, and how it's likely to behave.

PREDICTING BEHAVIOUR BY BODY TYPE

Shown a species of fish you have never seen before, you should be able to tell a great deal about it by simply looking at the way it has been designed. There are no accidents in nature – even the oddest animals have been put together specifically to exploit a very particular niche in the overall scheme of things.

Fish wear scales the way knights wore armour. Scales protect the body of the fish as it feeds against cover. The more hostile the environment, the tougher the scales. Whiting and garfish, which work over sand and soft weed, have fine scales that come away easily. The groper, on the other hand, which works around reefs and in rough water, has very heavy scales that are firmly embedded in its flesh, and coated in a thick layer of protective slime to minimise the effect of impacts against rock.

Both the bream and the groper will at times feed off the same reef, but the bream will work clear of the rock, while the groper is able to get right into crevices to root out hiding crustaceans.

The placement of a species' eyes is another useful clue to behaviour. Most of the pelagic predators have eyes set towards the top of the head, telling us that they will normally seek to approach their prey from below.

Clearly it pays to know why fish are made the way they are, as this can often be an important clue as to where you are likely to find the various species. Conversely, when confronted with new territory, a careful study of the characteristics of the terrain should enable you to accurately assess the type of fish most likely to be found there, and thus employ the appropriate techniques to produce results. You won't get many fish dinners by angling for tuna in an oyster lease, but it does help to know that bream are capable of crushing oyster shells.

DESIGNED FOR SPEED

Most, although not all, of the predators are designed for speed. Their bodies are designed to move through a great deal of water at relatively high cruise speeds, and then to deliver a dazzling sprint when the quarry is sighted. Tuna fall into this category; they have the ability to cruise at up to 50 km/h, then cut loose with a burst of speed to 80 km/h to run down prey.

The fat body of the cod (**ABOVE**) is not all that hydrodynamic, but the big tail and large anterior fins will probably give it useful speed over a short distance. Just enough to swallow quite large prey whole. The saratoga (**RIGHT**) is more streamlined, but note how the anterior dorsal and anal fins are placed so far back as to almost become an addition to the tail fin. This gives the fish so much leverage on the water it is capable of making spectacular and frequent jumps. The barracuda (**BELOW**) is virtually a swimming mouth full of teeth. The head and jaws are huge and capable of taking on very large prey. They are very fast over a short distance.

The yellowfin tuna (**ABOVE LEFT**) and the wahoo (**BELOW LEFT**) are both built for speed, with the wahoo taking out the short sprints and the yellowfin excelling at high-speed endurance swimming. The luderick (**ABOVE RIGHT**) is built to move about at a sedate pace, and the fins and tail are designed to stabilise it and allow it to hold station while feeding. The whiting (**BELOW RIGHT**) is another browser, but this time the body is low and long, allowing the fish to feed on the shallowest sand flats, an area denied to most other fish.

A tuna has a body mass of muscle, a relatively small head, and a tail assembly reminiscent of the propellers on racing powerboats. Its body represents near perfection in hydrodynamic form, and is even vented so that the comparatively small fins can tuck down inside the body line to totally eliminate drag at top speed.

Wahoo and mackerel are longer, thinner fish, and are even more streamlined, but they lack the bulk muscle to be long-distance performers. They too have super-efficient propulsion systems, however, so they are blindingly fast over 100 to 200 m.

DESIGNED FOR AMBUSH

The tuna, wahoo and mackerel are fish of the open sea, and so have no need for the skin protection offered by heavy scales. The barracuda, on the other hand, is also a long, tapered, streamlined fish capable of fairly high

speeds in short bursts, but its association with reef and weed as part of its ambushing way of life sees it fitted out with scales. The barracuda also has the soft, wedge style of tail more useful in slow-speed manoeuvring than the tuna's strictly high-performance sickle tail.

The classic ambushers are the flathead and the true flatfish: the flounder and sole. The body design of these fish gives absolute priority to concealment. Because they are flat, they only have to place themselves on the bottom and give a bit of a wriggle to bed into the sand; the sand displaced then settles on top of them and affords perfect camouflage. Eyes placed on the top of the flathead allow them to see everything passing by.

The flatfish are capable of surprising bursts of speed over short distances; the flathead uses a snake-like wriggling action, and the sole and flounder use a combination of jet-assisted take-off, firing water against the bottom from the gills and following that with a

This flathead has been on dark sand, so its colouring is dark. When the fish moves over light-coloured sand it will turn a very pale colour and virtually disappear into the background. The eyes on the top of the head allow the fish to wriggle into the sand until just the eyes are showing, ready to pounce on any unwary fish that ventures within range of its snake-like strike.

strange head-to-tail body undulation. Anyone who has walked along a sandy channel edge will have seen puffs of sand burst up as flathead take off in alarm, but few people actually see the fish itself. The short sprint capacity of the flatfish is most impressive, but they have little to offer in the way of sustained performance.

DESIGNED TO BROWSE

The browsing species have body and fin shapes designed for buoyancy and low-speed performance. The bodies are often quite deep, with pectoral and anal fins long and well developed, and they have large paddle-style tails. This sort of body design has nothing to do with high-

speed performance, and everything to do with balance and control, with power at ultra-low speeds.

The luderick fits this picture well. It is a vegetarian schooling fish that spends most of its life pottering about close to areas where abundant food supplies are readily accessible, with the odd leisurely short migration (or spawning) jaunt at sea, all taken at a very sedate pace.

The luderick feeds on weed growing on hard cover, sometimes in the steady flow of a river current, at other times in the turbulent wash associated with a rocky coastal shoreline. Its greatest need is to be able to hold station in the water flow and retain vertical orientation without forward speed, so its body is deep like a keel, with well-developed pectoral fins that provide balance and also allow it some movement in reverse gear. The big paddle tail provides considerable thrust, with little forward movement, like a car in low gear.

The whiting is another browser. It is uniquely designed to exploit the shallowest water on the sand flats, a food source denied to all but the tiniest members of other families. Its body shape lies somewhere between the flatfish and the faster-bodied fish, allowing it to get up into just a few centimetres of water, yet have the power for a dazzling burst of speed when threatened in this very exposed position. The colouration of the whiting is such that it blends into the sandy background perfectly. Even anglers using polaroid sunglasses sometimes find it easier to see the shadow of the fish than the fish itself.

DESIGNED TO SURVIVE

For some fish, survival revolves largely around being able to find enough to eat, while for others the main business of life is to get through each day without being eaten. Whitebait, pilchards and other small schooling fish are good examples of this latter category. Everything about these fish is designed to make each of them an effective part of a group rather than a totally self-sufficient entity.

A bait can smell a predator from a distance, hear them at a distance, and sense and see them at medium to short range, but none of this does it much good when its top speed is not even one-tenth that of the predator. For this reason these small fish are designed primarily to pool resources, making the most of the old adage that there is 'safety in numbers'. By joining forces, a school identity is produced. The baitfish virtually link senses in a tight school, so that an attack on one side of the school is known of on the other side, and so on. When you consider that a bait school might cover 100 square metres, the fish on one side has certainly extended its sonar range significantly if it can tune into the reactions of the fish on the opposite side.

An electrical field can be measured around most life forms; this is commonly known as our 'aura'. Some researchers have speculated about this electrical charge actually linking individual fish within a school, so that an action or reaction at any point in that school will occur simultaneously throughout the school.

It would appear to our logical minds that fish massed together like this would just be making things easier for predators, but in fact the massing effect works in favour of the baitfish. Predators hunt baitfish one fish at a time, and they target and chase the bait as individual fish. When the bait mass together it makes it more difficult for the predator to isolate targets. With only odd exceptions to the rule, predators pick off those fish not conforming to the school identity – those that are hanging off the edge or trailing behind.

A notable exception applies in the case of sailfish, which work together to ball bait so that a slash with the bill will stun a few baits that can then be eaten individually. Even then you could say that the basic principle still applies, and that the sailfish are artificially creating stragglers.

Colour

You can find every colour there is in one fish or another, and you can also find the drabbest mix of mud tones through to dazzling explosions of the most vivid colours imaginable all jumbled up along the sides of the one fish. Every fish is coloured the way it is for good reasons, only some of which we can fully understand and appreciate.

I am not, by the way, talking about the colour of dead fish in the fish shop here; I am talking about the colour of fish in, or just out of, the water. You also need to keep in mind that the colours you see when a deepwater fish is on the surface, or when it is photographed by divers using a flash, have little to do with the way the fish is seen in its normal habitat.

You will never see a better illustration than this of the way a fish can use colour to its advantage. This little wrasse has outrageous colouring out of its environment, but in the second picture you see how the colour disappears in the water. In the third shot the little wrasse is close to its normal environment, the darker beginnings of reef to the right of the picture. Once in that environment it is virtually invisible.

COLOUR FOR CAMOUFLAGE

All fish have one common element in their colour schemes: bodies are counter shaded. In other words, they are darker on the top of the body than they are on the bottom. In some of the deepwater fish, and also in many of the more flamboyant coral reef dwellers, this counter shading may be marginal, but it is still there.

Counter shading is the basic ingredient in the camouflage of all fish. It is a response to the fact that the major light source is always above, that secondary light comes in from the sides when the fish swims near the surface, and that little or no light comes from below the fish. Thus the back is normally dark, so that when viewed from above the fish will blend into what would usually be a dark background. The lower sides to the belly will be a light colour, so that when viewed from below the fish will blend into the light from above.

The degree of counter shading apparent varies according to the regular habitat of the fish, and most fish can vary their colours and shading to some degree. A whiting, ghosting over the sunlit shallows of a sand flat, will have the palest combination of white and olive on its back, white sides, and white with a silver sheen on its belly. By contrast, the rock blackfish often takes the black from its back two-thirds of the way down its body, and only fades to a heavy grey on the lower portion. The whiting not only wants to blend into the sand when viewed from below; it also wants to reflect the bottom on its sides as much as possible. The rock blackfish, living over and amidst reef and weed, has only a marginal need to blend against the light, and a light belly would simply make it stand out when viewed against the rock backdrop. Interestingly enough, when the same fish moves off the rocks and goes out over the sand or gravel in the late winter months, it takes on a pale, mottled appearance on the back and sides and develops a very pale belly.

Flathead and flounder rely on a pale, mottled upper surface with plenty of white spots to help them blend perfectly into a sand background. This is the basic colouration of the dusky flathead, although the same fish can be almost black when that colour scheme works with its environment.

Many of the tiny baitfish are a bright reflective silver all over, which makes them stand out like a

Almost everything in the water is counter shaded to some degree, even a crocodile such as this huge beast.

beacon when they break away from the school. But when they are in the midst or on the outskirts of thousands of similar fish in a school, the constant reflection tends to minimise outlines, making it harder for predators to identify a single fish in order to launch a successful attack.

A great deal of the camouflage effect in fish colouration has to do with breaking down outlines. Fish that work close to cover of any kind are often marked with bars, spots, splotches, circles, marbling or stripes of some kind, with the colours quite strong and the patterns quite complex. Most of the reef and weed species are like this, as are trout.

Fish that live near the surface have wonderfully transparent colour schemes, often involving a reflective base covered in stripes or bars. The mackerel, wahoo and many of the tunas fit into this group. Just think of how these fish must appear from below or from the sides as they swim close to the surface, where light shafts through a pulsing, undulating mirror, frequently confused by sparkling bubbles as waves crest and break. Could there be anything more perfect than such colour schemes?

COLOUR TO BE SEEN

All the tunas and marlin are coloured in a similar manner, but with an interesting variable in the form of the inclusion of either a little or a considerable amount of bright yellow. Remembering that yellow is one of the last colours to be lost as we travel further and further down away from the light source, clearly this colouring is intended to be seen.

Anyone who has had the good fortune to find themselves over a big school of yellowtail kingfish at sea will vividly recall the way the school shows up below as a mass of yellow. Yellowfin tuna have a good deal of bright yellow in their fins, and other tunas have it on lesser fins. Marlin don't have any yellow showing when they are in a placid frame of mind, but as soon as they get excited they 'light up', and one of the dominant colours in that display is at least a patch of bright yellow or gold.

Even the invisible whiting, swimming along over the sand flat, has a single patch of bright yellow right at the base of the pectoral fin. The colour must be there to be seen. Probably it is for the benefit of other school members.

If you go to a tourist destination where guided tour groups are commonplace, especially Japanese groups, you will see tour leaders with little coloured flags, and all the people with that particular group will be wearing a little badge of the same colour. They do this because it makes it easier for the group to keep together. It is reasonable to assume that fish wear their identifying colours for the same reason.

COLOUR TO REPEL AND ATTRACT

Other examples of using colour in underwater advertising are the colour displays of trout at spawning time, and the outrageous colour schemes of some of the most poisonous species, which obviously want to be seen for what they are: 'Here I am, leave me alone!' Although I have never been able to get my hands on one for a close look, at Lord Howe and Norfolk islands a bright yellow fish can often be seen milling about in the middle of schools of silver drummer, salmon and bluefish. The locals call these 'dream fish', and say that they have a powerful narcotic effect if eaten. The colour is obviously there to tell the world that they are different from the rest of the school, but your guess is as good as mine as to what this is all about.

Breathtaking as the colours of a snapper or jewfish may be at the surface, the only thing you would see as colour when down below would be the row of tiny blue or light-reflecting spots along the sides. The flamboyant colourings of coral trout, and of all the cod and perch associated with the coral reef, actually reduce back to even less colourful patterns than those seen in the surface fish when they are viewed at the reef fish's normal operating depth. Remember, you only see all those brilliant colours in coral when the reef is lit by bright lights used for filming, or close to the surface, where sunlight still penetrates. The reef colours the fish is most often trying to blend with are those found lower down in the water – grey, soft blues, drab olive and black.

Understanding the way colour actually appears in the water can go a long way towards helping you make intelligent lure selections. On the open sea, when the surface is rough and the penetrating light is broken, high-contrast colour schemes containing reds, black or purple would be obvious choices.

On a quiet, bright day, hunting fish would expect their targets to be blending well into the background, so combinations of blue, green and white, broken with soft bars and stripes, would be best. Blue and white with some dark areas would be a good combination for a deep runner or a deepwater jig.

In some freshwater and creek fishing, the face value of colour is far more important, as the water being worked is less deep. The high contrast value of yellow and black can be exploited to the full in murky water,

The dolphinfish has the ability to change colour rapidly, using an amazing range of brilliant hues.

and the shock value of the fluorescent pinks and oranges can be used to great effect on fish with territorial natures. Metallic flash is an important element in the bladed spinners too, although the sonic value of that little metal blade should never be overlooked. The angler should always remember that the only way a fish can check out something quite new and strange is to take it into its mouth. This may help explain why some of the more outrageous colour schemes work so well – they might simply be very good at arousing the curiosity of fish.

How fish feed

The majority of fish are specialised feeders, with teeth and mouths designed specially to cope with their favoured foods. The angler is well advised to study this particular part of the fish's anatomy, for the nature of the mouth will often determine the ideal size and shape of the hook to use.

BROWSERS

Probably the best examples of the browsers are the popular herbivores such as the luderick and the rock blackfish. Weeds of various kinds form the bulk of their diet, so they are equipped with quite a small mouth and fine, close-set teeth. The teeth are located well forward in the mouth and are protected by a rubbery, slightly prominent top lip. The lip is very tough, and probably offers some protection to the teeth when the fish is cropping weed off a rock base.

The leatherjacket is an interesting little browser, with a protruding mouth backed by plate-like teeth that are as effective as side-cutter pliers, and quite capable of nipping through a fine wire hook at times (although nowhere near as good at this as the toadfish).

The whiting has very little in the way of teeth, but it has a protruding mouth backed by a concertina-like membrane which allows for surprising extension. With soldier crabs, yabbies and worms at the top of its list of dietary preferences, it seems likely that the whiting uses this extension to work into the sand for its food.

All of the wonderful wrasse family of fishes are browsers, poking about the reefs eating crustaceans, shellfish, vegetable matter, and even the reef itself in tropical coral regions. They use a variety of dental equipment for their work, ranging from reasonably fine, sharp teeth well suited to vegetable matter and small crustaceans all the way through to the groper's heavy-duty protective upper lip, large cropping pegs of teeth situated at the front of the mouth and crushing plates in the back of the throat.

SCAVENGERS

A great many fish can be called scavengers from time to time; almost anything that is willing to eat a dead bait would qualify. However, there are a few species that are true scavengers, and none suit this classification better than the various bream.

There is some similarity between the teeth of a bream and our own teeth, in that the front ones are suitable for biting or tearing, while the back teeth are dedicated to pulping and grinding. The interesting thing about the bream, though, is that when you take a close look inside the mouth, almost the entire area is studded with teeth. You can't help but wonder how a hook ever finds purchase in there. Obviously the bream is well equipped to handle anything it can fit into its mouth. The actual size of its mouth is probably the only limiting factor in its diet. I once caught a bream that had swallowed a large turban shell whole, its intestine bulging where the point of the shell was wedged. I could see no way that the fish could have swallowed anything so large. Since it was still feeding, I assumed that the shell was causing it no great discomfort.

Having nominated the bream as a scavenger willing to eat just about anything that will fit in its mouth, including garlic sausage and cheddar cheese (as I mentioned earlier), it is also true that the same fish can drive anglers crazy at times by being totally single-minded about food. I once caught a good bag of bream while fishing side by side with other anglers who caught nothing. I had beach worms and they had live blood worms, and we were fishing an area where blood worms are considered to be the top bait.

PREDATORS THAT BITE

There is a distinction to be made between those predators that bite and those that swallow their prey whole. Both types will, in the main, take much the same sort of offerings; it is the way in which they take the bait that determines how anglers need to rig terminal tackle and how they need to react to a strike.

Classic biters are the tailor, Spanish mackerel and wahoo. Each of these fish has slightly different dental equipment. The tailor, for example, quite closely resembles some of the sharks with its close-set triangular teeth. These teeth have razor-sharp edges and needle-like points, and any angler whose finger has inadvertently found its way into the mouth of a tailor is sure to be able to give you a colourful account of the amount of damage they can do. I gave myself a good cut once just feeling a dead tailor's teeth to see how sharp they were.

What makes the biters particularly tricky customers to hook is the speed at which they operate their jaws when attacking. I have removed small whitebait from the stomach of a tailor to find the tiny fish cut into several neat chunks. Biters don't just bite, then take the bait into their mouths – they bite their way along the bait with their jaws operating at great

speed, and it is this that sometimes makes them difficult to hook. During the attack, the jaws are open as often as they are closed on the bait, and any strike only stands a fifty-fifty chance of connecting.

When you combine this characteristic with the swimming speed of the fish, which probably enables it to get a good look at even a fast-trolled bait when attacking, it is not so surprising that wahoo and mackerel are able to snip off bait after bait within a whisker of the most cunningly placed hooks. Most sharks also bite very large prey, but if they can swallow a fish whole they do so. When taking a chunk out of a large carcass they open wide, clamp down onto the meat and/or bone, then twist back and forth using their jaws as a sort of primitive but highly effective circular saw.

Barracuda, especially very large ones, are interesting, as they are armed with the dog-like teeth that normally adorn the jaws of fish that either tear prey or swallow it whole, yet they are capable of slicing through quite large carcasses with apparent ease. I once saw a barracuda of around 10 to 12 kg brought

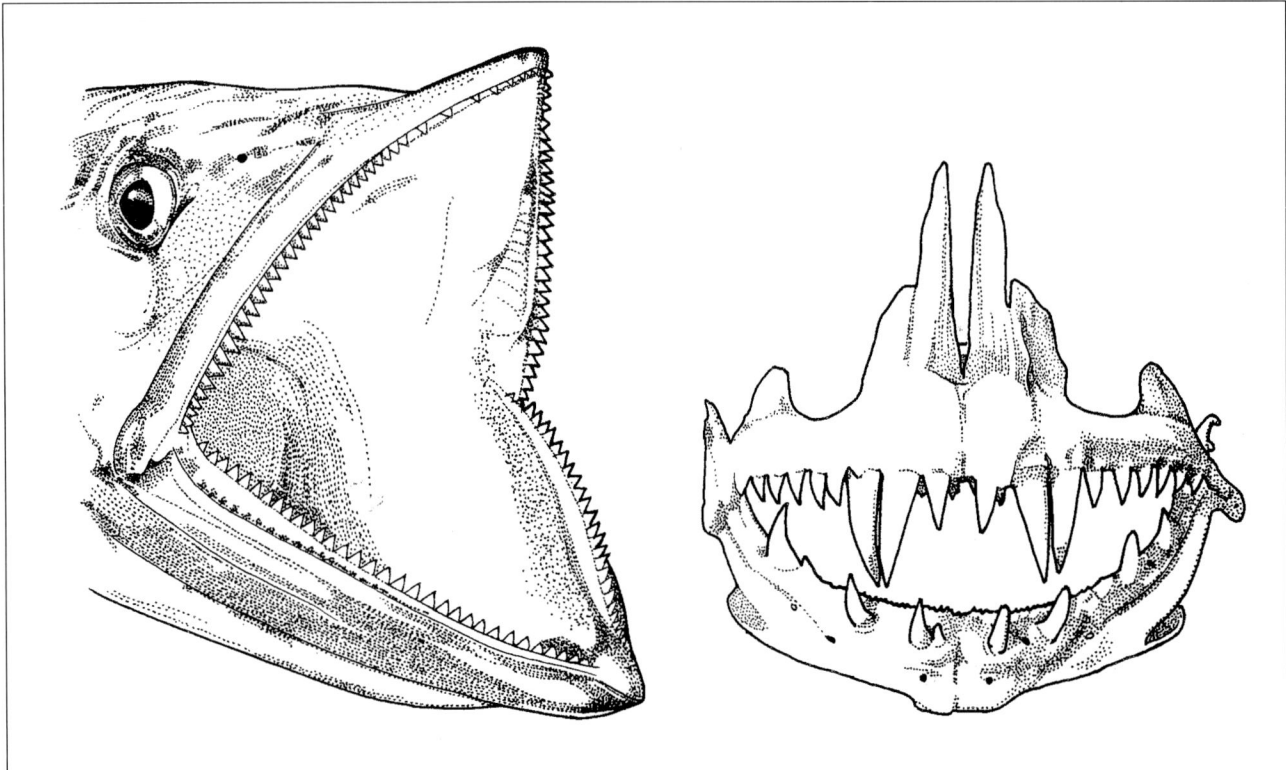

LEFT The triangular-shaped teeth of the Spanish mackerel are very sharp and cut with surgical precision. **RIGHT** The teeth of the mangrove jack are designed to hold and cripple or kill prey prior to turning it and swallowing it whole.

up alongside a small aluminium dinghy, and just as it was about to be gaffed, another huge barracuda slid up out of the depths and closed its mouth over the hooked fish, which promptly became not much more than a head left on the hook and a tail section drifting off towards the bottom. That big barra did not shake its head or body as much as a centimetre to either side – it simply sliced a big chunk out of the middle of the fish with surgical precision. Just consider the backbone it had to cut through in order to do that!

PREDATORS THAT SWALLOW WHOLE

This category could be used to describe just about every fish that eats other fish, starting with small creek fish like the mangrove jack and going all the way up to the largest marlin.

Obviously, the prey must fit into the predator's mouth, but some fish are able to swallow fish of almost their own size. Having said that, it does take a fish quite some time to swallow an over-large bait. This makes it very difficult to hook the fish, as there is a good chance that the hook is well and truly outside its mouth when the angler tries to set the hook.

Even when the bait is in proportion to your target fish, you need to allow time for the fish to take the bait across the body, or tailfirst, then turn it around in its mouth before swallowing. You always slide your hand

down the fish from the head to lay the spines of the pectoral, pelvic and dorsal fins flat so that you don't get spiked – the predator does the same thing. If it tries to swallow the bait tailfirst, the fin spines will jam in its throat, so it has to turn the bait and slide it down headfirst.

Most fish that swallow their prey whole are equipped with quite small teeth. These are used for gripping the bait on initial capture, then during the process of turning. Many of the smaller predators have quite pronounced canine teeth, or a single protruding spike of a tooth from the lower jaw. These are probably used to impale and kill the bait before turning and swallowing it.

So with the biters your job is to get the hook to take hold in a long, tapered jaw which is opening and closing like the shutter of a motor-drive camera; with the fish that swallow their prey whole you need to develop the feel to know when the bait has been turned and taken down. Either way, you really need to have your mind on the job.

HOW FISH EAT

It is important to understand how a fish actually ingests its food if you are to have any chance of a decent hookup rate. If you have access to a good aquarium where large fish are fed at regular times, a little time spent watching the way they take in food can pay big dividends.

What will a big barra eat? Everything, including smaller barra like this one removed from the stomach of the larger fish.

No doubt as to what the mouth of this cod was designed to do. Everything goes down whole.

You have to keep in mind that the fish has no means of assistance in actually getting the food into its mouth. All the handling of the food actually has to be done by the mouth. A dog can use its paws to hold down the end of a large piece of meat while it tears chunks away with its mouth. In other words, it can use leverage. You also see birds doing something similar. But the fish has to either use its mouth alone to break down a large piece of food, or swallow the entire offering whole.

Many fish have the capacity to extend their mouth or jaw to make feeding a little easier. The great white shark actually projects its jaw and teeth beyond the mouth-line as it closes in to attack, and many fish have a concertina-like membrane behind the lips that enables them to project and extend their mouths. Trevally are outstanding exponents of the extended-mouth trick: if you can, try to see some being fed.

Apart from fish that browse and have the opportunity to place themselves adjacent to a static meal, most other fish feed by one of two methods. They either run the prey down and grasp it with their jaws prior to swallowing, or they inhale the morsel along with a mouthful of water.

The first group grasp the prey, tailfirst in many cases, then have to turn it and swallow it. There must be a tricky moment when the captive is transferred from the first firm grip to a crosswise position, then turned again to be swallowed. It would clearly be a lot easier if the prey were killed in that first position, before it had to be released to be turned, so the live bait angler should not only anticipate a significant delay after the initial take, but also be keenly aware of the need to keep tension off the line while the bait is still largely outside the fish's mouth.

Fish like jewfish, with their cavernous mouths, give novice (and experienced) anglers nightmares as they roar off with baits, apparently locked up solid on the hook, then manage to spit the bait out after quite a long period of contact. It has occurred to me that the jewfish might have a real problem with small baits, in that there might be simply too much room inside its mouth to easily turn them. It could be taking all that time just because it is hard for it to get the bait organised in its mouth. With its relatively fine teeth for a fish of its size, the jewfish is not terribly well placed to chew on anything other than a large bait. This could be why the bait sometimes comes back completely scaled after a missed strike.

Kingfish don't have much in the way of teeth, but they have rough jaws capable of exerting enormous power. When we were spinning for surface fish from the rocks at Jervis Bay, huge resident kingfish that holed up under the rock ledges would come up sniffing about like a pack of hunting dogs when captured fish were brought in close for gaffing. A bonito held kicking at the surface would always prove to be too much for these hoodlums to resist, and one of the monsters would always storm up and simply crush the bonito with a single nip. This ability to more or less instantly kill prey is probably essential to the kingfish if it is to hang onto anything it catches. Other fish in the school will soon be after anything dangling from the mouth of another fish – you frequently see kingfish trying to attack a lure dangling from the jaws of another hooked fish. The kingfish has to kill its prey and get it down fast. The ease with which anglers are able to hook kingfish certainly suggests that they bolt their food.

The group of fish that inhale their food with water present fewer problems to the angler, but there are still things you need to know. These fish take the food in with a great amount of water, which is then expelled through the gills. This expulsion of water does not happen immediately, so, for a short time at least, your offering could be floating around with no contact at all with the inside of the fish's mouth. Allowing for the fact that the fish can blow that water back out of its mouth just as quickly as it sucked it in, this is a time when you need to be on the ball.

Once, while fishing a Flopy lure in the little creek at Hat Head, on the north coast of New South Wales, I was watching the lure as it wobbled back into the clear shallow water when three big flathead homed in on it from behind. The biggest of the three inhaled the lure, and then, while my knees were still shaking at the size of the fish, opened its mouth and fired the lure right back out again. It was a powerful demonstration of the way the bigger fish, inhaling a substantial amount of water along with a lure, have a definite advantage if they are sharp enough to recognise that all is not as it should be with the easy meal. They can just unload it.

Fishing barramundi on lures with Alex Julius on one of my early trips to the Northern Territory, Alex noted that I was missing strikes, and advised me to

Lures can come back out just as quickly as they go in when you deal with a large-mouthed fish.

just hold back a fraction – after feeling the take and before trying to set the hook. I might have ignored that seemingly silly advice from anyone other than Alex, but I did as I was told and went straight to a ten out of ten hookup rate. The barra, with its great bellows of a gill structure and huge mouth, probably takes in far more water than any other fish, and since nearly all barra lures are floaters, the lure probably floats about in its mouth quite harmlessly until the water is ejected.

The flathead is another classic inhaler of baits, and once again you can be looking at quite an extensive mouth and throat area into which the bait is ingested before it is organised and passed back into the top of the throat for swallowing.

There is a good case to be made for large gape hooks when dealing with fish that feed this way. A big, round hook will have much more chance of finding the side of that cave than a small one.

As you can see, getting a fish to bite is only the beginning of the hooking process. Your understanding of the way the fish you are after handles a bait will have influenced your choice of hook to start with, and will have an even more significant effect on the way you handle the seconds, or fraction of a second, after that take.

Spend some time looking at the next fish you catch, taking a good, critical look at the mouth and tooth design. *Always* check what the fish has been eating when you clean it. That is the sort of knowledge that can make a big difference to your end result.

One last thing to mention here. There are times when a fish will simply take something into its mouth to see what it is. They can't pick it up, so they have to test it with the mouth. A television documentary dealing with the recovery of snapper stocks in New Zealand, in an area where all fishing had been banned for a number of years, showed a biologist sitting on the bottom making notes on a slate. The writing implement was attached to the slate with what looked like a thick white plastic cord that wiggled about as the diver wrote. A quite large snapper had suspended itself just 20 cm from the cord and was eyeballing it with such intense interest I was fully expecting it to charge in and try to make off with the cord. Instead, it slowly drifted over to the cord, took it into its lips in the most gentle fashion imaginable, held it for a moment, then released the cord and backed away. It was the best demonstration of a fish checking out a strange object the way we would use our hands that you could ever hope to see.

Do fish think?

Fish certainly do think, but it is highly unlikely that a fish ever settles down for an hour or two of quiet contemplation. Most of the thinking a fish does is of an instantaneous nature, and is probably more correctly labelled a reflex action than the result of any sort of conscious thought.

Fish do have the ability to learn, and this learning provides the soil out of which the creature's reflex actions will spring. This translates roughly into barren soil equals short life, fertile soil equals long life.

An easy example every angler will recognise is the one involving lures. Why is this year's red-hot lure next year's dead stock in the tackle shop, and why is it that with literally hundreds of fish-catching lures going out of fashion every year, some patterns just go on catching fish year in, year out?

The first factor you have to eliminate is the human one. Many good and bad lures come and go simply because we are creatures of fashion. We talk ourselves into, and out of, all sorts of good and bad ideas every day, sometimes to our benefit, at other times to our detriment.

With human quirks out of the way, the fact remains that some very good lures do just stop catching fish. I recall some years ago suggesting to a fisheries biologist that fish obviously learned about lures, because every new lure that came along seemed to start off well and would then become less and less effective as the weeks went by. He gave me that 'you miserable cockroach' treatment scientists often use to crush mere mortals like ourselves, and pointed out forcefully that fish are not capable of learning anything and have absolutely no memory at all.

Since that time, some American research has proven what I and many other anglers knew all along, which is that fish can learn about lures, not by being

You never know what a fish will decide to take on. This is a case of ridiculous ambition on the part of a longtom.

hooked themselves, but by seeing other fish taken on lures. The same research showed that the fish retained this memory for up to six months.

Apparently some fish, like some people, are smarter than others, and we've all seen evidence of this. Casting to schooling fish, a whole group of fish will follow the lure, but just one will finally succumb to temptation and take it. After this episode you will need to be one smart angler to get any of those other fish to take a lure.

Don't confuse this situation with one where a school of fish is on the rampage and lures are struck the moment they hit the water. It will take much longer for the message to get through in such a situation, for the fish will be busy and not taking much notice of the individual elements in the action.

On a reef where fish populations tend to be static over a reasonable period of time, with top-up and loss of population brought about by a percentage of the schools coming and going, you could blitz the fish community for a day with a brand-new jig, but every fish you took out would leave behind a higher percentage of smart fish and a reduced percentage of susceptible fish. The second day out you would be working on a smaller number of susceptible fish, and at the end of the day you would leave behind more educated fish. No wonder the most oft heard angler's remark is, 'You should have been here yesterday!'

So why do some lures go on working while others lose their effectiveness? I think this has to do with the fundamental nature of the lure itself, and with the way anglers use the lure.

The classic long-life lure style has to be the minnow, which is also a prime example of a lure that can imitate particular baits so well that it gets hit because the predator really thinks it is another fish. Some of the most popular minnow colours, such as the blue and silver combinations with dark mackerel stripes, show up in the surface layers of rough water as so close to the real thing that a predator would have to lose its taste for fish altogether if it were to completely protect itself from them.

Other lures that keep on keeping on are those where the noise the lure makes, rather than the lure itself, is the target. When you have a good popper session going you will get missed strike after missed strike, sometimes with the predator flying high out of the water as it comes up from below like a missile. Kingfish will slash and boil over the lure time and time again without connecting, and when does a kingfish ever miss any other kind of lure? Never! The answer has to be that these fish have no idea what a popper looks like – all they ever see is a surface disturbance that is exactly the same as that made by a bait being hit, with an exciting noise to match.

Fish find it a good deal harder to recognise baits as traps, for much of the bait they are offered is the same as the natural food they eat every day. They can, however, learn to identify fishing lines, sinkers and bulky swivels and leads in a heavily fished area. In wilderness fishing you can get away with the crudest tackle imaginable, but around the metropolitan centres, fine terminal tackle pays dividends in a big way.

Some years back I fished regularly with bread bait and berley for black drummer and bream, and the technique was unbelievably successful. But as time went by, and more and more people discovered the bread berley system, the method virtually became a waste of time.

In those days, however, I noticed that even in the hottest new spots, the catch would fall off by more than 50 per cent from day one to day two, and then just plummet after that. A break of a week or two would liven things up a little, probably because new, uneducated fish had moved onto the reef, but never once in later visits did I turn up fishing that measured up to the first day on the spot. The spot needed a long rest to come good again.

The bread scenario probably offers the best evidence you could find to support the theory that fish learn very quickly. Imagine a big school of drummer swimming about in a nice hole, then suddenly the water is filled with white particles drifting down, white particles that smell and taste delicious. The problem with this gourmet food from heaven is that it is in such tiny pieces, much of it not much more than a milky trail in the water, that

it does little more than drive you wild for a really decent mouthful of the stuff. Then one big chunk comes drifting down on a slender white thread. Dan the Drummer grabs it and suddenly is in a blind panic, swimming in circles to a point of total exhaustion, after which he's dragged clear up into the sky!

Now because this hole is of a reasonable size, that scenario can probably be repeated a number of times with completely gullible fish, but sooner or later, most of the surviving fish in that hole will have seen somebody eat a piece of that highly identifiable alien food. The clear lesson learned is that the stuff may taste good, but it is lethal. Stay away from it! The same fish has no hope of distinguishing between a safe prawn and a lethal prawn unless your offering can be clearly identified as being different from safe food. Bulky, clearly visible line, hooks that are too large and badly placed in the bait, heavy sinkers and bulky swivels will all contribute to your bait looking different from safe food.

If we allow that fish are learning this way, we must also accept the fact that the bigger a fish gets, the smarter it will have become. This is the way nature intends things to work, with the mentally and physically unfit being weeded out, leaving only the strongest to reach adulthood, procreate and thus refine the strain. The fish you most want to catch, then, the big trophy fish, is probably well schooled in survival skills and will test your own skills to the limit. It will also be a very important individual in terms of maintaining both the numbers and the quality of successive generations of fish. Having had the satisfaction of outsmarting this particular fish, the most mature thing you could then do is to release it, unharmed, as quickly as possible. Take home a bag of small, silly fish that are probably living on borrowed time anyway, and do your bit for the fishery by sending the big one back as an even smarter long-term survivor. You will be surprised how good it can make you feel to let a big fish go.

Chapter Three

Fish-finding techniques

Where fish live

An angler's success – knowing where to find the fish and how to catch them – depends largely on how specific their fishing knowledge is. A generalised approach is simply not effective.

An example of a generalised approach would be knowing where there is a good snapper reef and being able to find it. The specific approach would be knowing that the fish will always be located on the up-current side of this reef, and then making a point of always checking the current before dropping anchor.

We know all the general environments that fish inhabit – estuaries, creeks, lakes, open sea, beaches, rocky shores, streams and impoundments. Each of

these words describes an environmental entity made up of a complex mix of sub-environments; to put it more simply, they are all worlds within worlds. Knowing where the main world is will enable you to reach it in the car, but finding fish is more a matter of knowing about the little individual worlds.

ESTUARY

If you take a small coastal estuary as an example, near the mouth the little stream will have some sort of interaction with the beach or rocks where it feeds to and from the sea. A little way in from the mouth you may be looking at a clean sand bottom with flats and deep channels configured by strong tidal runs. As you move further upstream, weed beds will begin to develop, mangrove stands will sculpt the bank, and very often there will be mud banks and flats. Anywhere between the mouth and the uppermost reaches and rock bars may be an important feature. As you move towards the uppermost reaches, the influence of the tide will begin to wane and rainfall may determine the suitability of the environment for the true saltwater species.

The entire length of this waterway may be covered by the name Joe's Creek, or whatever, but for the creatures that inhabit this world, each of these various elements is a total environment with its own particular rules governing the way it works. For the sake of this example, let's look at a mid-east coast estuary with the usual temperate mix of species.

The mouth of the creek will be a superhighway, carrying plenty of heavy traffic in the form of those fish that come and go with every tide change, and fish that migrate at some particular time of the year. Obviously, highwaymen prefer busy thoroughfares to sleepy back lanes, so you can expect some of the larger predators to always be present here as the tide moves back and forth. Big trevally, jewfish, tailor, flathead and small sharks love these areas and the beach or rocks immediately adjacent to the mouth of the estuary.

Only garfish and dusky flathead actually spawn in the estuary, although an extraordinary range of fish use the estuary and its mangroves as nurseries. Some fish that live in the estuary will go outside to spawn, and other fish, such as the snapper, will come inshore to spawn near the estuary mouth. In both cases, the young will head into the safe backwaters of the estuary

There are probably dozens of good fishing spots out there where the water all looks just the same. But you can be sure that fish will move along the edges of this dam.

Don't know where to start? That outer rock ledge would always have fish of some kind in attendance.

at the first opportunity, finding food and shelter in the mangroves in the early stages of their development. Both adult spawning fish and young fish run the gauntlet as they come and go, with predators making the most of their exposed position.

If our stream has a deep cut near the mouth and an attendant rock bar, the odds are that bream and blackfish will be present; the bream attracted by the crabs and shellfish associated with the rocks, and also by the tiny baitfish that shelter in the eddies, and the blackfish working the weed on the rocks. These fish will be able to survive comfortably in even the most ferocious tidal runs, because they will be working inside pressure waves formed as the current 'bulges' around protruding rocks, and will usually find some form of backflow right alongside the rocks.

The channels and sand flats usually play host to a wide variety of fish when the tides are right, but they offer little in the way of permanent residence. The state of the tide will very much govern the movements of the whiting, bream, trevally and mullet that make the most of the sand flats' abundance of food, and of the flathead, tailor and other bigger fish that make the most of the deep cover adjacent to the flats to ambush fish as the tide spills them back into the deep water.

Further into the system the weed beds start to offer a more permanent home for all sorts of fish. Most of the weed beds are located at and below the low-tide mark, so there is nearly always enough water available for residents to remain in their chosen environment. The weeds provide a food source and shelter for a vast array of small, and juvenile, life forms, including shrimp, prawns, small squid, garfish and so on, and where you have a resident supply of bait, you also have a resident supply of fish trying to eat the bait. Flathead, tailor and trevally will be working the edges again, but there will be many fish living right in and over the weed, including blackfish, leatherjacket, bream, big whiting, cuttlefish and squid. The feed holds them there, as does the shelter from the force of the tidal run provided by the bulk of the weed. This shelter reduces the energy output required to stay where the food is, which makes it a particularly attractive environment for the less powerful swimmers.

As the stream breaks clear of the silted flats and channels of the mouth it will usually slow into deeper runs and holes. This is local-knowledge country to some degree, as the nature of the hole and the presence of deep rock bars and old downed timber will determine how many fish choose to stay there. Bream can always be counted on to be associated with deep channels along the shore, as can blackfish when deep weed banks are present. Whenever water is funnelled in any way, you can be sure a flathead or two will take advantage of the opportunity for ambush offered by the way this will concentrate the path of travelling fish. If the holes and deep reef are big enough, even large jewfish may find the environment attractive.

Stands of mangroves will always play host to a huge array of miniature life forms; and, with luck, to a population of mud crabs. The mangroves are often the key to an entire estuary system, and their presence sometimes determines the fish population of the whole waterway. The channels and holes immediately adjacent to the mangroves become holding ponds on the ebb tide, when the mangroves dry out, and as the tide rises there will often be a concentration of fish along the fringe as they eagerly push to the head of the queue to get back into the security and abundance of feeding opportunities offered by the dense root systems.

In between these fish-attracting zones there could be quite considerable areas of water with no particular features to attract and hold fish. Some of these areas could still be worth fishing, in that they form part of the highway fish will use to travel from one part of the system to another. This highway is nearly always the section of the stream where the main tidal run occurs, although feeder channels connecting flats and major and minor channels also work the same way when the tide is running. A considerable amount of water will still fall outside all these categories, and there will really be no reason at all for fish to be in such areas.

CREEK

A small coastal creek may be a miniature version of the estuary outlined above, but creeks should never be judged on size alone. Seemingly insignificant little stretches of mangrove-lined water often turn out to be marine wonderlands. This is never truer than in tropical areas, where creeks that run dry on the ebb tide explode with life as the tide rushes back in.

Nearly all the truly dynamic examples I have witnessed of the sheer vital energy of the sea at work have been provided by quite small creeks. At Watumba Creek, on the inside of Fraser Island, Queensland, hordes of big black stingrays, bream, small sharks, whiting and flathead storm into the creek on the front of the tide, charging way up towards the backwater mangroves that dry off completely on the ebb.

On one occasion in the Kimberley region we were stranded on the bottom of the tide, stuck in a hole so deeply drained that we were looking up 3 m at the grass on a bank we'd been looking down on when we arrived. When the tide came in it arrived in a boiling wall of foaming muddy water, solid with mullet and chopping barramundi, a big saw shark lashing and hacking its way through the feast.

Outside a tiny creek, well wide of Darwin, we got stuck on a mud bank on a falling tide and had to get out of the punt and push. Here and there the water began to heave and boil around us as big fish attacked the mullet being pushed out of the creek, and we grabbed our rods, thinking these were barramundi. We hardly got a cast away before the first of the dorsals showed above the surface; we were standing knee-deep in water crawling with sharks! So frantic were these black-tip whalers that they were stranding on mud banks and wriggling their way for metres, with half their bodies out of the water, before finding their depth again! This sort of madness is the direct result of tidal movement in and out of a tiny creek.

These creeks all have slightly different natures, and the action at the mouth is determined by the physical shape of the creek. Some tropical creeks have no well-defined mouth, simply opening up onto a mess of sandbars with shallow feeder channels all over the place. The fish coming and going in a creek like this are spread over such a wide area that it simply does not pay predators to try to work such a large expanse of water, so they concentrate their efforts further in, where the stream narrows and the bait is more concentrated. Having said that, any structure at all in a hole near that creek entrance would be a priority target.

Another creek might cut straight through a beach in a narrow, deep gutter, giving and taking a great volume of water through this funnel neck. In such a case the neck would provide predators with a dream opportunity to swim shoulder to shoulder with the hapless mullet trying to get into the creek, simply moving along with them and feeding comfortably with short bursts from side to side. This is the sort of high-yield feeding situation fish love.

Since most of the angling interest in tropical waters centres around species that are active predators, and these fish are nearly always working tidal runs, ambush locations are high-priority stations for the fish. Mullet, which are the prime bait species in

tropical creeks, will be doing their very best to get as far up into the shallows as they can for shelter, and all tributaries off the main creek will attract fish like a magnet. If there is any form of cover close to the mouth of the creek, predators will be using it. A big snag will break up light and create just the sort of confused pattern that makes predators difficult for the bait to see from the side, and at the same time will offer the big fish a shield from attack from above and behind by large birds, crocodiles or sharks. They may have outgrown the threat offered by birds, but it takes a long time to forget any of the lessons of survival.

Isolated snags along the main bank-side will have less appeal, but they will hold some fish, and the number they attract will vary according to the total number of fish using the creek. Fish will always use the best cover they can find, and will only fall back to second-best choices when the best cover is already occupied.

This is a junction where a feeder creek meets the main stream. When this photo was taken the barra were solid at the entrance.

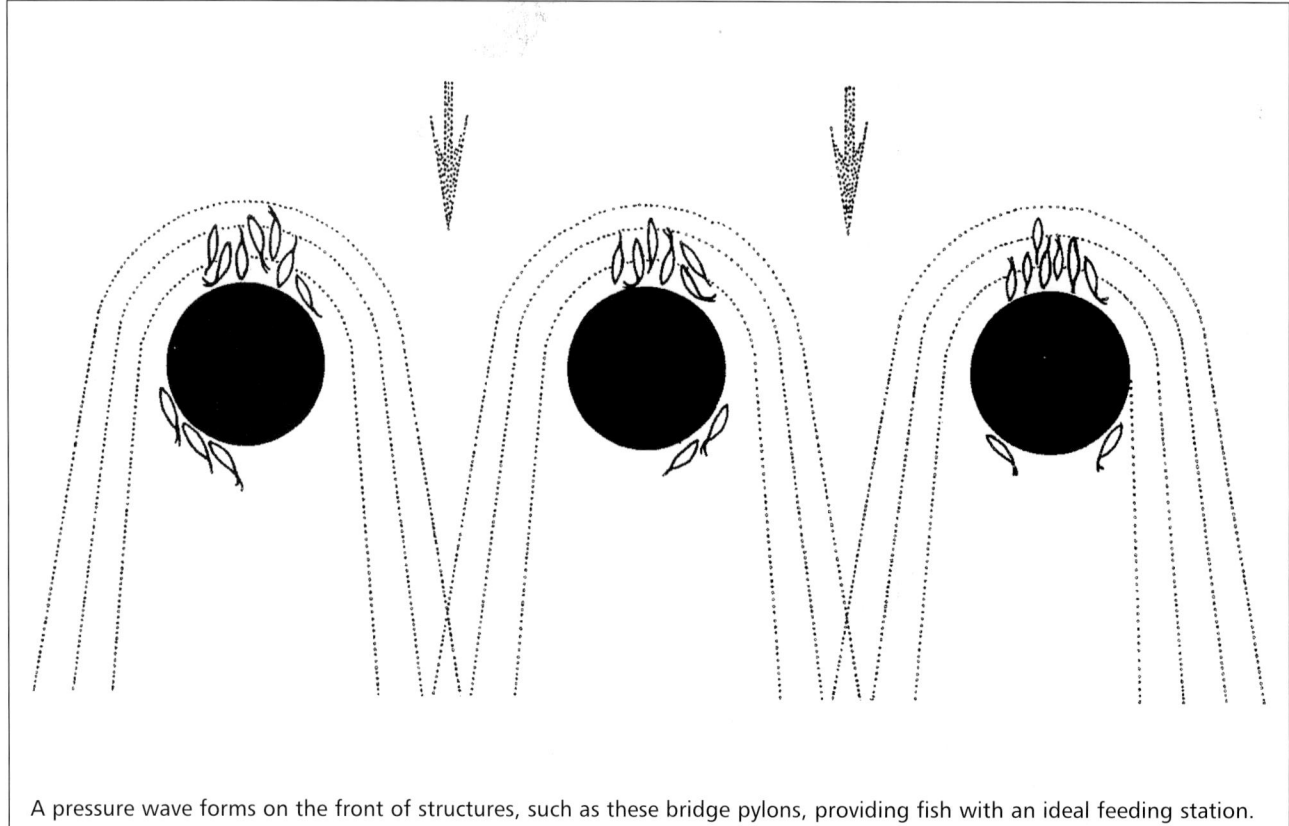

Fish are attracted to the up-current side of structure by current being forced to the surface and concentrated hard up against the structure where predators can shelter in comfort, and the same thing is found again immediately behind the canyon rim.

A pressure wave forms on the front of structures, such as these bridge pylons, providing fish with an ideal feeding station.

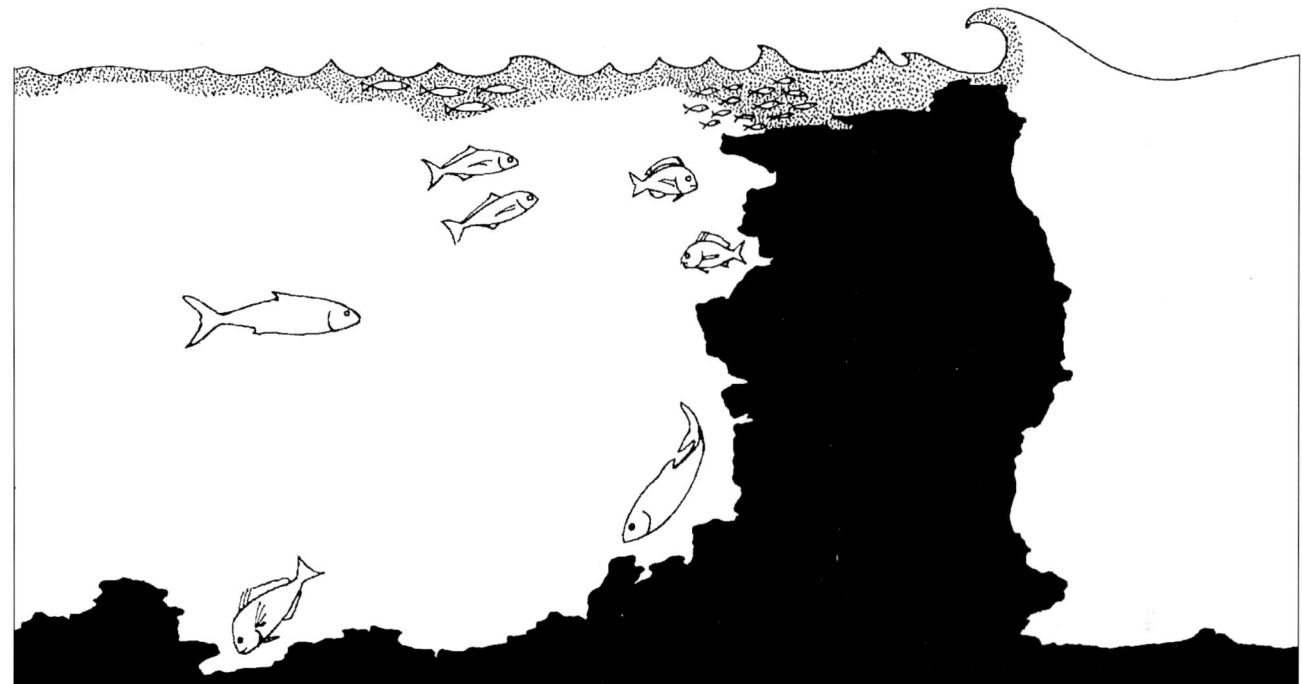

A situation where fish are concentrated behind structure happens when seas breaking on the reef carry food into the hole behind it.

Big snags in midstream can't be overlooked, nor can rock bars, weed beds, narrow runs or any major overhangs. Discoloured water discharging from a mud creek, or perhaps under a small waterfall, will attract its share of bait and those who hunt bait.

As is the case in almost every other marine environment, holes in the creek bed will have great appeal for predators. Lying just in behind the lip of a hole they can take a rest out of the force of the current, and when bait comes along it will be silhouetted overhead, so that the fish can be clearly defined as individual targets.

Creeks are often loaded with cover, and with bottom and bank-side features, and this attracts fish and anglers alike.

OPEN SEA

The open sea is the most difficult environment of all for anglers to comprehend, as there are few visual clues available as to what is going on below. However, the motivating forces governing the behaviour of fish remain much the same in the open sea as they do anywhere else. The overwhelming consideration is to obtain the maximum amount of food while expending the minimum amount of energy, and to do so without being eaten oneself.

Perhaps the greatest variables in the open sea are the currents and the water temperature, elements that are usually closely linked. Fish are extremely temperature sensitive, and when two vast bodies of water with a temperature variation of 1°C or 2°C (or even less) come together, fish will either move with the body of water representing their comfort zone, or largely cease activity until the temperature changes back to the level they prefer.

A temperature zone, in the form of a current, may provide a living environment for oceanic species, the fish going wherever the current takes them. Some oceanic currents are influenced by a combination of bottom contours and prevailing winds, tending to be fairly constant in the direction of flow, with just the rate of flow varying. Other currents are simply the local effect of huge eddies in the sea. It is now thought that what has long been known as the East Australian Current may be nothing more than a series of independent eddies that come and go along the coast.

Our knowledge of the movements of pelagic fish along our coastline is still imperfect, but some interesting facts have emerged in recent years. Many Australians still firmly believe that all major fish movement takes place along the north–south axis, but Japanese fisheries people published a paper over 20 years ago showing that the major movements of fish are east–west within quite a limited north–south range; and that generations of fish tend to stay in their own defined north–south zone. So you could have a generation of striped tuna with north–south movement limited to a couple of hundred kilometres, but with east–west movement of up to thousands of kilometres.

Obviously, there must be some spillovers and breakouts from time to time, and those spinning eddies must play a part in the scheme of things, but generally speaking the theory seems to hold together fairly well. It could be that the tuna, like the salmon migrating halfway around the world and then coming right back to the stream they were spawned in, are able to follow a current or eddy rich in food for as long as it suits them, then head right back to their home zone when driven by the breeding prerogative.

Fish like the billfish and some of the tunas are more like true oceanic nomads, wandering the sea seemingly at will; other bluewater fish seem more inclined to travel between fixed markers in the sea, such as reefs, islands, points of land and so on. But even the nomads of the open oceans seem to work defined beats, although their beats may cover many thousands of kilometres.

Water is not just water to these creatures. Where we see only surface water stretching to the horizon, the fish sees currents, temperature zones and upsurges of water created by the contours of the ocean floor. It even concerns itself with temperature strata between the surface and the bottom.

Although by far the greatest part of the seabed is a featureless desert devoid of life, there is still a great deal of richly sculptured terrain down there, especially close to landmasses. Great mountain ranges run for thousands of kilometres under the sea, appearing above the surface here and there in the form of islands or rocks. These ranges are virtual highways in the sea, attracting unimaginably vast quantities of the lower orders of sea life, which in turn provide food for the nomadic pelagics.

Structures of any kind in the sea are a focal point for life, and structures come in a remarkable variety of shapes and sizes. A structure does not have to be big to be significant – the wrecks lying around our coastline offer good examples of this. Some of these wrecks were quite small ships to begin with, and after many years on the bottom of the sea they have broken up into even smaller parts.

In a vast barren area of sand this small amount of hard structure will attract vegetation and shell growth, then the tiny fish that accompany these basic building blocks. Eventually larger fish will move in, and in no time at all a rich oasis will exist where there was nothing but desert before. It is a remarkable experience for an angler to register a wreck on an echo sounder, a wreck so insignificant that it barely shows up at all on the chart, and yet find a solid column of

Billfish of all kinds are nomadic by nature, but there are still plenty of clues available to help you locate them.

A single piece of floating debris like this could attract a host of fish, particularly dolphinfish and kingfish.

fish stacked up over the wreck, all the way from the bottom, way down deep, to the surface.

It is significant to note that some of the fish associated with such a structure – a wreck or deep reef – may stay in its vicinity for quite some time without ever closing in on the structure itself. The structure becomes a pivotal point, the hub of a wheel of life that may describe quite a large circle. An example of fish in the vicinity might be yellowfin tuna working the surface layers over reef lying 100 metres below, or kingfish suspended over the same wreck midway between the bottom and the surface.

You will often hear bluewater anglers complaining about a lack of current producing poor fishing, and sometimes you will hear them moaning that 'the fish are out there, but the current's too strong to get at them!' Not only is the current important to the fishery because of the way it moves fish around and switches them on and off as it meets, or fails to meet, their comfort requirement; it is also critically important in the way it moves food about between the top and the bottom.

In addition to the feeding chain set up by a hard structure, such as a reef or a wreck, there is another even more complex chain reaction set in motion by major underwater features such as undersea mountains, canyons, escarpments – virtually any kind of formation that presents a sudden change in bottom shape.

When a current moving along through deep water strikes some kind of formation, the current is deflected upwards, carrying nutrients and small life forms with it. This concentrates food towards the surface, and the normal feeding chain reaction sets in.

Fish working these areas are nowhere near as handicapped by a powerful current as is the angler whose lines are affected by the full force of the moving water. When a surge moves against a solid object like a reef it sets up a pressure wave, and this pressure wave creates a kind of neutral zone in which fish can operate quite comfortably.

You can understand this better if you look down from a bridge on a tide running against pylons. Right on the front of the pylon, where the full force of the current is being taken, you will clearly see a bulge in the water where this pressure wave is operating, and as often as not you will see some fish simply sitting stationary in that wave, expending very little effort. These fish are in the box seat in relation to any food being swept down in that current. Behind the pylon there will be an eddy and another feeding opportunity, but the fish on the front of the pylon will be getting the best of it. Anglers often guess this one wrong, moving into the lee of a structure, expecting fish to be sheltering there from the full force of a strong current. They are sheltering, but on the up-current side, where most of the food is.

The effect of pressure on deep structure is to force the current and all it contains towards the surface on the leading face of the structure. Once the structure breaks the surface new rules apply. Now we have wave action against rock and reef to contend with, and although the leading-edge effect remains in force, the cover provided by wave action and the feeding opportunities in the break have to be considered as well. Eddies trailing off the sides of structure can attract baitfish, and therefore also predators. In fact, the first eddies off the side of the main area of wave action can be real hot spots.

Given an area where there is a lot of reef, fish will always be attracted to particular features. Any high spot is worth checking out, as is a drop-off of any kind. Gutters are also high-priority areas, and are often favoured by large predators such as mulloway and cod. Changes in the nature of the bottom, such as a bed of gravel, or an area of hard bottom of any kind, will attract certain species of fish.

The rule with regard to fishing the open sea is clear: wherever you find change in the form of the bottom, the movement of the water, or the temperature of the water, you have an environment that is likely to be of interest to fish.

BEACH

The beach environment can be a particularly difficult one to understand, as individual beaches work in quite different ways, but there are certain ground rules that hold true anywhere, so we will concentrate on these.

A good body surfer does very little swimming, and people can sometimes be excellent body surfers but quite poor swimmers. The secret is that these people have learned to use water movement to their advantage. They go out in channels where water displaced by waves coming in across the shallows is returning to the deeper levels away from the beach, and

they come in with the white water which is pushing towards the beach. When they are threatened by large breaking waves, they simply dive to the bottom and allow the power and turbulence of the wave to pass over the top of them. By grasping this, you are well on your way to understanding how fish work in the surf.

The strength of the surf and the nature of the bottom largely determine where the fish will be. The broad overview is that the fish will generally work close to the break in quiet seas, and be forced back from it in heavy seas.

Wave surge does two important things in the beach environment – it stirs the bottom up to reveal food, and it creates foam, which affords protection for the smaller fish. If you consider light surf breaking over a long shelving sandbar, with just a metre of water over it, you could expect fish like whiting, bream and tailor to be right up there where the waves are breaking, trying to get to the head of the queue for the available

A deep hole on the shore of a beach is always worth investigating, especially at night.

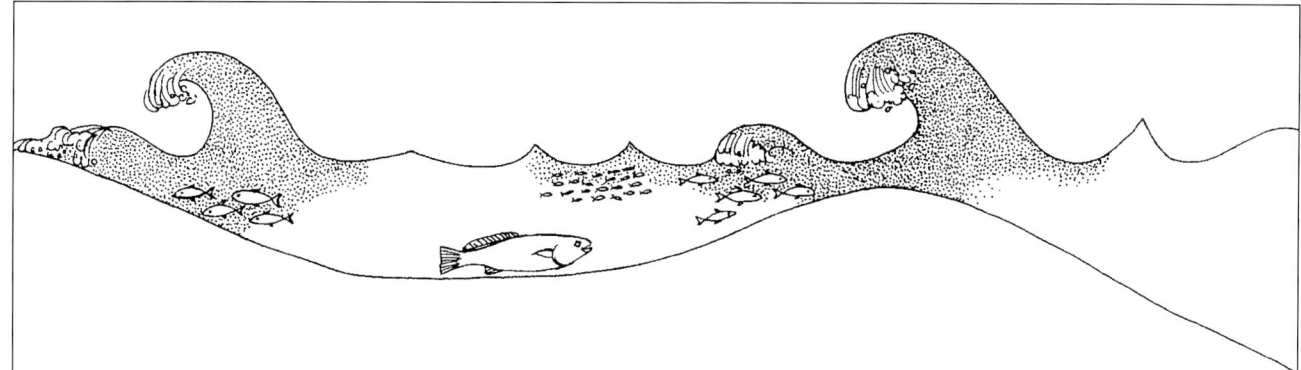

A side view of a gutter running along a beach shows fish feeding behind the outside break and also behind the shore break. If there were some wave action across the hole, or a lot of bait in the area, the fish might be scattered over the whole gutter. Note the way a large predator can always use the depth of the hole to move in on fish preoccupied with feeding.

food. They would have no real problems with energy loss working this gentle surf, and they would have plenty of foam cover to allow them to feel comfortable up in the shallows.

As the surf increases in size, water turbulence and an increasing volume of sand suspended in the water start to present problems for the fish. They will be burning up a lot of energy working in that powerful surge, and the sand will be having much the same effect on their breathing as a dust storm does on human lungs. Up to a point they will simply retreat further and further inshore, away from the direct power of the break, knowing full well that the surge will be pushing plenty of food in towards them. But in the biggest seas they may be forced to move outside the break until things quieten down.

It does, however, take extreme conditions to force fish off a beach, and so far our view of the beach has only considered a shelving sandbar formation where fish have little in the way of protection. Much more common along our beaches are bar-and-gutter combinations, and these suit fish very well. In such a situation the waves break well out off the beach on a shallow sandbar, then roll across that bar into a deep gutter running parallel to the shore. The big waves smash down on the bar, losing much of their power in the initial break, then the surge carries everything before it into the gutter, where the white water gradually dissolves. In such a case all the small scavenging species and the baitfish will be sitting as close in to the back of that sandbar as they can get, or possibly right up on the back edge of it, feeding in the last of the powerful surge and making the most of the cover before it dissolves in the deep water of the gutter.

In a really powerful swell the fish will be in the gutter close to the bar, allowing the force of the waves to pass right over them. The larger predators also love this situation, as they can come cruising up out of the cover of the depths and attack fish that are lined up in a fairly predictable way. Understanding that the small fish will be as high up on the sandbar as they can get on the top of the tide, when the maximum depth is available there, the predators also know that those same fish will be forced back into the gutter as the tide falls. Logically, then, if there are plenty of whiting on the sandbank on the high tide, the gutter should be well worth a try for any of the predators, from flathead through to mulloway, as the tide falls.

Before looking at other beach formations, we need to understand the great variable in beach fishing – the depth of the water and the nature of the waves. Usually, but not always, the depth of the water determines the nature of the waves. We will take a moment here to look at waves and how they work, because understanding waves is fundamental to understanding how fish relate to beaches and to rocks.

A wave is a band of pressure moving through the water without actually moving any water along with it. On the open sea, as a wave comes along it causes water to rise and fall as it passes, and that's all there is to it. Think of the wave as one of those long sausage balloons moving along just under the surface and you

The two basic wave forms are the dumper (**RIGHT**), a top-to-bottom break, and the combing wave (**LEFT**) that breaks down onto its own face. The dumper will scour the bottom right where it breaks and fish will be immediately inside that break. The comber will create mild turbulence and provide cover over a wider area, with the strong possibility of a heavy shore break being present.

will have the general idea. It is a band of energy in motion. As that band of solid energy moves inshore it runs out of depth and is forced upwards and distorted. At this point it does start to move water as it rears upwards, virtually trips over its own feet and then pitches forward. As it pitches forward it takes all the water with it that had been moulded by the energy band, and it is this displaced water that causes all the commotion down below.

The actual point where the pressure wave first distorts determines what type of break it will produce, and the effect the resulting chain reaction will have on fish. If the wave rolls out of deep water and suddenly encounters a shallow sandbar, it will rear up high to produce a relatively thin wall that becomes concave and breaks in an immediate and violent fashion, with the crest falling ahead of the base. In other words, the surfer's classic dumper. This type of wave scours the bottom, but tends to lose its force very rapidly, as most of the energy is directed straight into the sandbar.

The second classic wave form is the full wave, where the energy encounters a gradually sloping bottom, or a bottom just deep enough to cause a break. When this happens the wave remains quite full at the bottom, with a high peak breaking onto its own base. In this case the energy of the break is directed into the base of the wave rather than the sand bottom, and much of the wave's original energy is retained in that base to carry

on towards the beach. This often produces a violent shore break with considerable surge right at the edge, in which case fish will usually be found facing the beach and working immediately behind the shore break, sometimes within a few metres of the edge.

Naturally, between these two extremes you find subtle degrees of variation. Usually the low tide will produce the extreme of the dumper, while the high tide will produce the other extreme in the shape of the full-cresting style of wave, all over the same bottom formation. The nature of the break tells the angler how much water there is under the wave, and where that break is likely to have the fish positioned.

Holes, gutters and channels are all important to fish as ways to approach the food-bearing shallows in safety, and with some protection from the raw energy of the primary surge. They can be identified as places where broken waves tend to fill up again and where dark water can be discerned beneath the foam. You will often see waves peak over the shallows, then lose their form as they encounter deeper water.

Gutters and holes are also very important to the larger fish, particularly those that need to have some depth of water to carry their bulk. Generally speaking, the mulloway and sharks are the only ones that need be concerned about being grounded, but no fish likes to be in water so shallow that the fish becomes visible from above.

Good holes and gutters are associated with working white water, and usually carry some breaking waves across the surface. The big deep holes that sit between sandbars and produce relatively quiet water have a great appeal to anglers, but much less appeal to fish. Novice anglers like them because there is not much movement or sideways rip through them, which means that it is simple to keep a bait in place and the line remains easy to control. It is the placid nature of this water, however, that makes it unpalatable to fish, who prefer working water and cover.

The state and size of the tide is a major factor in beach fishing, where there is never a great deal of depth in the water, even in the deepest holes. On a beach a deep hole may mean 2 to 3 m of water, whereas a rock angler could be looking at 20 m of water in a good deep hole. A 2 m tide means nothing to that rock angler, but on the beach it could mean the difference between a hole and dry sand. Experienced beach anglers often drive (or walk) along beaches on the low tide to actually look for indentations in the sand that will be holes and channels when the tide is up. Sometimes these features can be quite difficult to spot on the full tide, with surf rolling across them, so they will mark their locations with branches stuck upright in the sand. This is an especially helpful strategy when you plan to fish at night, when holes are particularly difficult to pick from the rest of the surf.

Depending on the formation being worked, a rising tide might let big fish get to bait protected by the shallowness of the water, while a falling tide may force fish off a shallow sandbar into the hole or gutter where the big fish are waiting. It can work both ways. The smaller fish will generally stick with the shallowest water that will produce feed for them, which may mean staying on top of a sandbar until forced off it, when they will bolt into a shallow gutter that holds just enough water to cover them on the low tide.

Unfortunately, a hole does not automatically guarantee fish. A flight into a north coast town some years back provided me with a very sobering lesson in beach fishing. This particular airstrip was located just a few hundred metres in from the beach, which resulted in the aircraft doing a slow, low-altitude banking turn just as it came in. I looked down to see one of the best beach formations I have ever seen, with a dozen or so good deep holes. The position of the aircraft and the fact that it tracked roughly parallel to the beach allowed me to check those holes out very well through the polaroids, and every one of those holes was bare except for one, which housed around 20 big mulloway. It occurred to me, looking down on that scene, that 11 groups of anglers could fish great holes on that beach and possibly come away without a single scale, while someone on the right hole had the potential to land 20 mulloway. Those horrible odds have always struck me as being fairly typical of beach fishing, although regulars seem to develop something of a sixth sense about which holes will actually have the fish in them.

Anything in the way of structure on a beach usually becomes a focal point for fish, and wherever a reef exists close in to a beach, holes and gutters immediately adjoining that reef could be mulloway hot spots. The rocks and headlands adjacent to beaches are also worth attention when deep gutters come off the beach to curve along the rock base, or form holes just off the beach. A creek breaking through a beach always attracts flathead and mulloway near the mouth; this is particularly true when a land-locked creek or lake breaks through a beach in times of heavy seas and rain. Things can really hot up then, as mullet make the most of the chance to run to the open sea.

When beaches are not subjected to the direct and constant pounding of the open sea swell, the force that sculpts the sand to produce all the fish-attracting formations discussed here, you often find that there is a constant contour all the way along the beach, producing a uniform break. Fish could be anywhere on a beach like this, but it is always a safe bet that there will be fish travelling straight along the back of the break, close to cover but not in it.

Always keep in mind that what seems to be awfully rough water to you is often ideal conditions for a fish. They don't like the calm, still water that many anglers choose to fish in. They like the water to be moving about in a vigorous manner. A good rule of thumb is this: if you can get near enough to a hole or gutter to get a cast into it, the surf conditions will probably be just fine for fish.

This rocky gutter is a very interesting proposition, with the prospect of luderick and rock blackfish during the day, and bream and perhaps a big mulloway at night. At left you can see how the bottom can easily be read by the way in which the waves are breaking.

ROCKS

Once again, we find the fish where the food is, and where the conditions offer them the shelter they need to pursue that food with an acceptable measure of comfort and safety.

Rock environments can be roughly divided in two: those areas where the attraction is associated with the shoreline itself, and those areas where the bottom out from the shore has a feature that attracts fish. A good example of the first situation would be a shoreline covered in rich green weed that is broken free by wave action and taken to the fish as each wave recedes. An example of the latter situation would be the very edge of the reef some distance out from the shore, where rock gives way to featureless sand – a natural beat for larger fish to patrol.

The shoreline environment is a good one for fish. Rocks rich in vegetation pounded by a strong wave surge provide food, and deep white foam provides shelter from above. The fish can feed right up close to the rock face, limiting a predator's options to an approach from three sides instead of four. In shallow water, which this normally is, there is little opportunity for attack from below.

Fish will congregate anywhere water funnels back into the sea from the rocks, and spots where the return flow is concentrated will prove particularly appealing to them. For example, suppose you had a big, flat, exposed rock platform where waves were sweeping up over the top. The water will not return from this platform in an even sheet, but will drain into the lowest sections of the platform, then drain back into the sea. Those areas where the return is concentrated will be hot spots. If most of that water funnels back into one gutter and then drops back into the sea in a concentrated torrent, that would be the spot where the fish were.

Dense foam alone is a factor that always needs to be looked at, as it offers baitfish a natural shelter, even if there is nothing available in the way of feeding opportunity for them. A rock formation that consistently produces a heavy wash in deep water could be a prime target for large predatory species. This would be a natural resting or holding point for bait moving along the shoreline, and no big predator would swim by without checking it.

Any point off the shore that is subjected to breaking waves is a focal point, and fish attracted to such a feature will normally congregate in the wash either in front of or behind the structure, depending on the nature of the break. As long as the waves break on top of, or roll over the rock or reef, the fish will be in the white water immediately behind the break. The wave action breaks food away from the rock and the fish will be anxious to get to it.

Any hole or gutter cutting into a shallow reef is a natural haven or path for all kinds of fish. Small fish know that there is safety of sorts in shallow water, and big fish will make the most of any opportunity to raid shallow water. Undercuts along the edges of gutters also provide protection for a wide variety of fish.

Oceanic currents can, at times, have a good deal to do with the presence of some species of fish inshore. Some areas of the coast are more subject to the influence of currents than others: these are usually places where a deepwater contour swings inshore, or where the landmass projects right out from the main line of the coast into currents that would normally be well offshore.

In many areas, fishing from the rocks is much the same thing as fishing from the beach. The rocky element is confined to the nature of the shoreline, and the bottom immediately out from the rocks is featureless sand. In this situation you should look for the kinds of holes and outside bars that work on a beach, and generally think like a beach angler.

Whenever waves work against rock over a sand bottom, good deep holes will be produced close in to the rocks; these can provide excellent fishing at night. It is also worthwhile to do some hard prospecting for patches of reef, as they are sure to hold fish in a generally barren environment like this.

The depth of water near the shore can have a major effect on the range of species likely to be found in the area. Around the rocks adjacent to Jervis Bay, where depths of almost 20 m occur within a stone's throw of the rocks, big tuna and even marlin are regularly encountered by rock anglers. Large snapper can also be taken in quite calm conditions on a regular basis. The rocks immediately to the south of Sydney are quite different, with a shallow apron of reef extending well out from the shoreline throughout most of the region. Snapper will come in close in this area, but only in times of heavy seas. Other small species, however, proliferate in this shallow water, because it is better suited to them than to the larger predators.

Deepwater areas may attract fish in calm weather but in the shallower sections of the coast the state of the weather and the sea can be critically important, and there is a considerable amount of fish movement from place to place as they take advantage of the best conditions. We found, for example, that in one area we fished, spots backed by high cliffs were the first ones to produce fish in the afternoon. Fish normally start to feed actively just on dusk, into the early part of the night, and there is some possibility that these fish may have been fooled into an early bite by the failing light as the cliffs shielded the water from the direct light of the setting sun. It is equally possible that fish in this area made the transition to night sight before fish in the more exposed areas. Another alternative is that the low light just made them feel more comfortable moving about actively in that particular spot. Perhaps it was a little of all three factors.

In the daylight hours, most fish are light sensitive in the extreme, and they will take advantage of deep foam and rock ledges that cut out the penetration of light from above. At night, the same fish take advantage of the dark to get up into water that barely covers their backs. Fish will also stay close to the shore and feed longer into the daylight hours in overcast and rainy weather, simply because light levels are dramatically reduced. They will tend to do much the same thing

Dawn and dusk are normally good times to fish, especially those hours of light before the sun rises and after it sets.

when big seas are producing unusually dense foam cover at the surface. In any environment, the behaviour of fish is always dictated by a need to maintain a delicate balance between the harvesting of food and the constant covering of themselves against attack. Around the rocks the balance seems to swing a little further in favour of maintaining cover than in other environments – this is worth keeping in mind when weighing up potential spots along a new stretch of coastline.

Visual signs

There are all sorts of ways to find fish, including buying a good many beers for the locals at the pub. When employing this method, always take care to impress upon them that you are a complete mug and desperate to catch just one fish to save face with the

family. This gives you some chance of being pointed in the right direction. If they think you are good enough to make serious inroads into the local fish population you won't find out much at all.

If you are an angler who believes (as I do) that half the pleasure of fishing lies in being able to find fish without help, brushing up your powers of observation can pay big dividends. Unfortunately, we live in an age with little regard for subtlety, and spend a good deal of our time observing a cathode ray tube pushing out advertising messages that have about as much finesse as a scientist lighting his cigar with an atom bomb. Few of us are therefore skilled at observing natural events which tend to blend into the overall scheme of things.

A good angler with well-trained eyes will see the one fleeting dark patch in a choppy ocean that gives away the presence of a hunting fish, and on sand flats will see the shadows of fish or a patch of fin colour the size of a 5-cent piece long before the actual form of the fish can be defined.

The art of observation is to get into the habit of looking through the surface, not at it, and scanning for the single element that moves at odds with the water flow around it, or that perhaps is not the usual colour, and so on. As you practise this, you will be amazed at the way apparently dead water can suddenly become filled with life – life that was there all along, but you just didn't know how to spot it.

One little trick that sometimes works very well is to look slightly away from the specific point you are searching. In other words, you look at the area out of the corner of your eye. When you do this, your vision seems better able to select that single element that is at odds with the background. This works particularly well at night.

BIRDS

All saltwater anglers take a great interest in seabirds, watching some birds more closely than others. Even the seagulls, generally thought to be among the most useless birds God ever fitted out with wings, can point to the odd fish at times – although more often than not a gathering of seagulls simply indicates the presence of a sewage outfall.

The key birds vary somewhat from place to place, and from season to season. You would do well to pay particular attention to the birds in your local water to determine which are the ones you should be watching closely.

On the open sea the gannets and shearwaters, or mutton-birds, are obvious signposts. When the mutton-birds are down on the water in dense brown clusters, or the gannets are doing their amazing power dives into the sea, you know that the bait is there and that it has probably been driven to the surface by big fish.

Less obvious, but even more reliable, are the terns. Terns occur right around Australia, and although some appear to be very much sharper than others, they are generally considered to be the most reliable birds of the lot when it comes to giving away the presence of fish. Terns never waste their time. Other birds seem to be prepared to just stooge around all day waiting for something to happen, but if you see terns hanging about, it's a safe bet that something is going on nearby.

You will often see a tern, or a group of terns, hovering above a spot at a set height, peering intently into the water. They may start to swoop then back off and return to that same set height. What they are doing is watching bait, and their height above the water is a good indication of the depth of the bait. They can also see fish that will attack that bait. Where fish are deep and moving, the terns stay high, but as the fish move towards the surface the terns lose height and close in on their targets. As often as not, the terns will hit the surface at pretty much the same time as the bait explodes out to escape attack from below.

When there is a lot of bait about and schools of fish are breaking the surface here, there and everywhere, the birds may race from one spot to another as one school subsides and another one surfaces. Some anglers tear around the ocean after the birds, and in time spook all the bait and all the predators, to the point where the whole bite shuts down. It is often the case that several schools of bait are simply sounding and surfacing in much the same area, but the birds can't afford to hang around waiting for one school to come up again when the next working school is just a few wing flaps away. The angler is advised to cut the motor upwind of the working school, drift down into it, then stay put even when the school sounds. The school may well come up close to the boat again, and if the boat is quiet enough

Not all seabirds are created equal. Some are much smarter than others, and it pays to study your local bird population to work out which ones are most worth watching.

there's a reasonable chance that the bait will come in under the shelter of the boat, which is an ideal situation for the angler.

Some birds, especially the shearwaters, can also indicate that there are no fish in an area. In quiet times these birds will spread out all over the sea, and you will see them circling downwind, rising and falling close to the surface. With this sort of observation network in place and not turning up fish, nearby anglers should take the hint – there are no bait schools around to concentrate surface activity, and you may be wasting your time fishing the surface. If there are fish around they are probably going to be deep.

Sometimes the flight paths of birds can be a good indicator as to where the fish are. When birds are searching for fish they will usually work high and employ circling patterns, or move about in a fairly casual, sometimes erratic manner. If they are flying in a straight line in a particular direction, with birds from various points appearing to be aimed at a common convergence point, then perhaps you should follow suit.

You can't define all the behaviour patterns of birds, as they vary from time to time and from species to species. And while birds can show you that there is bait near the surface, that does not necessarily mean there are bigger fish around. You develop an instinct about bird behaviour after a while. Sometimes they can work themselves up into a fit of industry over nothing very much, and at other times the presence of one tiny hovering tern may be the key to some of the hottest fishing you've ever experienced.

WATER SURFACE PATTERNS

The surface of the water can be an excellent indicator as to what is going on below, even if you can't actually see even a centimetre below the surface.

A current line will often appear as an oily slick differing from the water around it; this is particularly true of the water at the edge of a current.

You can often detect the presence of deep reef or underwater structure by surface patterns. When a strong current is running, an underwater object will cause pressure waves to hump at the surface where the flow of water is deflected upwards over the object. This will occur whether the object is a rock bar in a river or a deep canyon wall hundreds of metres long in the open sea. The end result will be to produce local wave conditions that are much rougher than those produced by the prevailing wind or swell.

Another surface sign of deep structure is eddies. Whirlpools boiling to the surface, or sometimes just big pools of oily-looking water, are good indicators of irregularities at the bottom, and these are of great interest to the angler.

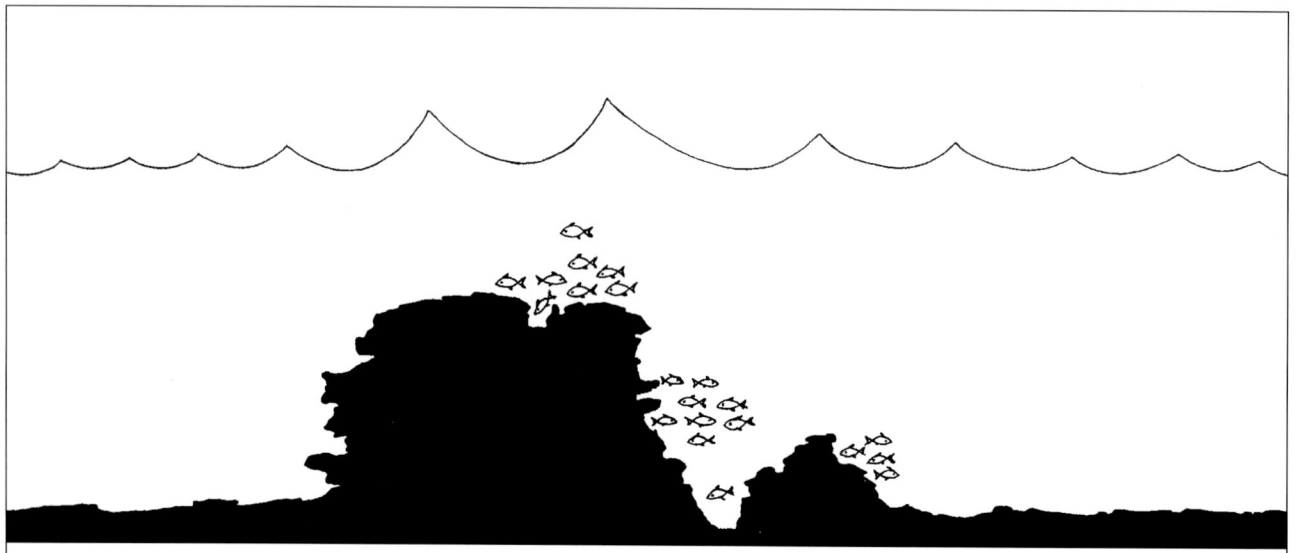

You don't have to see reef to know it's there. Any high points on the bottom will cause waves to stand up higher than those moving over the deep spots. If you can read waves inshore, you can read the bottom.

Eddies are also produced when a prevailing sea condition, current or tidal run encounters structure and is forced to change direction. A rock bar protruding into a river would be a good example, as would a long headland intersecting an ocean current. In such cases the eddy would be a pool of water rotating in much the same spot, providing a haven and shelter from the main flow of water. It would be a natural ambush point.

Waves are a prime indicator for rock and beach anglers, and a good understanding of waves may also stand the bluewater operator in good stead. Waves are a mirror of bottom conditions, standing up over shallows, and filling in and flattening off in deep water. A rock angler watching an ocean swell approaching the shore can pick where the reefs, holes and gutters are, and can even gauge depth with reasonable accuracy by the way the wave shape varies as it moves along.

If you have had no surfing background to make you familiar with the way waves work, spend a bit of time on the cliff tops on a sunny day. Wear polaroid glasses, as they will help you to see through the water to the bottom, and see how the incoming waves react to the bottom shapes. You will soon learn how surface water looks over a hole, a reef and so on, and you will then be able to read the bottom like a book, even when you can't see it.

In a tidal flow, water will run fast through shallows, and slow down in the deep sections. The shallows will often produce rough surface conditions, while the deep spots will be calm. You get a perfect, extreme example of this when you look at rapids. All that surface activity is caused by the bottom, which is inducing water pressure to be deflected to the surface as water moving at speed is forced to deviate around and over boulders. Pottering along in your boat on a strange body of water, a patch of rough surface ahead, or a whirlpool, may well indicate a submerged rock that is about to wipe your propeller out. It could also be the home of a few fish.

BAIT BEHAVIOUR

Large bait shoals will eventually attract predators, so you want to be able to stay with them, but many anglers don't see bait until it breaks through the surface. Big schools of bait are sometimes called 'ripplers', for the simple reason that they ripple the surface as they move along. Sometimes this pattern will be obvious; at other times you will see no more than the slightest shimmer. Remember the rule of observation – you are always looking for something, even the slightest thing, that is at odds with the prevailing scene. Anything abnormal is of interest. Sometimes large schools of bait will appear at the surface, moving along in plain view. You don't see this very often, but when you do it suggests that the bait feels relatively secure. I have noted that where I live and fish, this often coincides with low water temperatures. The bait may be sticking to the surface layer to find a comfort zone, secure in the knowledge that the cold has the predators quietened down for the time being. That is only a guess, but it feels right.

An attack on bait is usually obvious, with fish exploding from the water and the hunters throwing a lot of spray around as they chase the bait on the surface. In the most exciting situations you might see something like a 20 kg mackerel sail 3 or 4 m straight up into the air with a bait clamped between its jaws.

Not all bait schools react the same way to attack, though, and you need to be aware of the more subtle signs. Some bait schools may simply ball up tightly as a reaction to attack, while others may betray an attack with little more than a shimmer running through the whole school. It depends how they are being attacked, and by how many fish.

When you have quantities of bait and just a few predators, the hunters will not crash into the school and break it up. They will move around it, picking stragglers off the edge, and the school is likely to react by shrinking into a tighter ball, with every bait trying to find its way into the middle. When big fish are attacking a school that is spread across the surface rather than balled up, the attack will often come from below, and then the surface signs are obvious.

SHORELINE FEATURES

The shape of the shoreline can often provide clues as to the whereabouts of fish. Rocky points, for example, often extend beyond the shoreline under the surface of the water.

As often as not, the contour you can see will continue, so if the face of the outcrop descends into the water at a steep angle, odds are that it will continue down into the water at much the same angle and not extend out very far from shore. A tapering rock

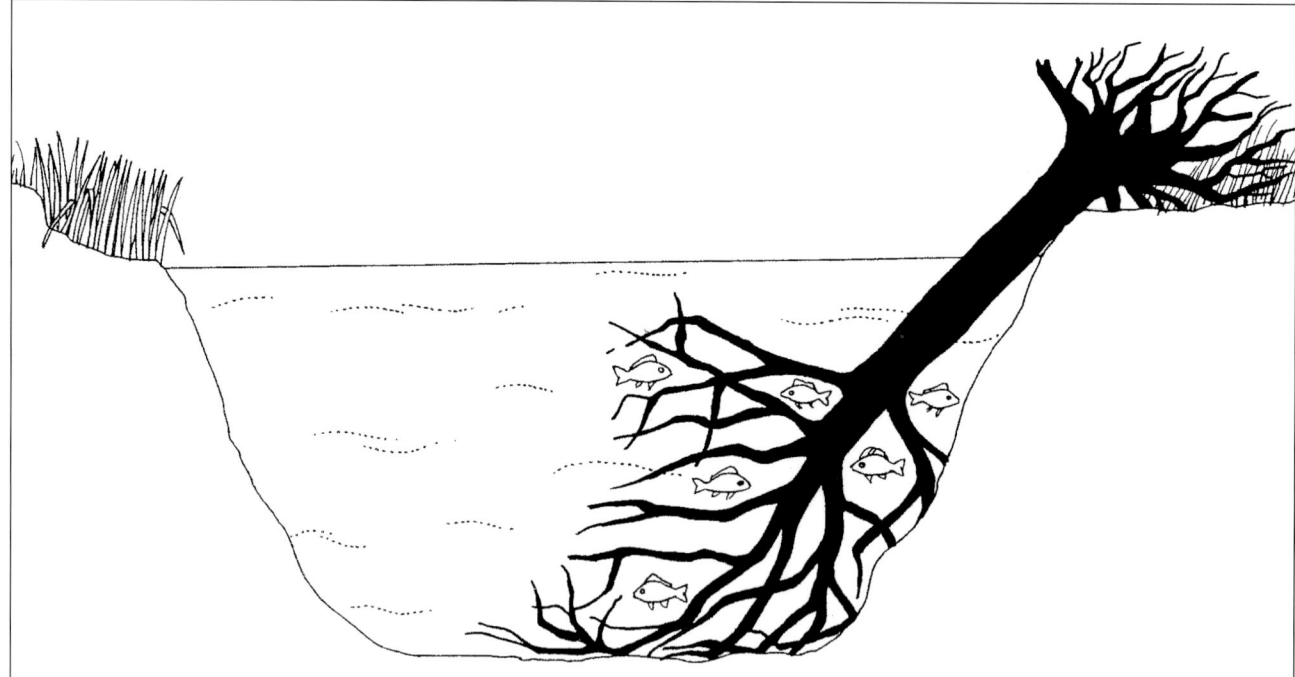

The trunk of this downed tree is visible and obvious, but it is a guide to the less obvious hot spot below the water where the branches form a perfect habitat for fish.

outcrop, on the other hand, might extend well out from the shore to become an underwater reef.

The shading effect of a shoreline can be very important, keeping in mind that fish prefer low light situations. Given three or four similar situations along a coastal shoreline, with just one of these backed by a cliff, the area under the cliff will be the first to lose light as the sun sets behind that cliff (on the east coast), and will therefore be the area in which fish can get an early start on night vision conversion, and thus an early start on the evening feeding session.

A big tree trunk leading down into a stream probably means that all the branches and the cover that goes with them will be out in the deep water, providing a natural haven for fish. A tough place to fish, but you could run a few shallow running lures over it, or hang back on an anchor and fish vertically with baits, small jigs or sonic lures.

POLAROIDING

Discovering the value of polarising glasses is a little like turning the light on in a dark room – all of a sudden you can see.

Polaroid glasses eliminate the glare reflected off the surface, which allows you to see down into the water. Sometimes this actually allows you to see fish, but more often it allows you to see cover and bottom contours clearly, which is almost as good as seeing the fish themselves.

You have to be careful about selecting sunglasses with polarising lenses, as not all have been created equal. Some appear to have precious little polarising effect, in spite of labels claiming that they are polarised. The rule of thumb is to stay away from the fashion brands and buy glasses sold by tackle stores (even though the prices will often be ridiculously high), or go for Polaroid brand glasses. Polaroid brand glasses always offer superb polarising, but the shape of the glasses tends to be dictated by the current season's fashion.

If you have light blasting in onto the back of the lens you will negate much of the value of the polarising effect. Similarly, if plenty of sunlight is reflecting off your face immediately behind the glasses, this will also be reflected onto the back of the lens. (Face paint to blacken your cheeks solves this problem.) You need frames that fit pretty well across the brow, then wrap back along the sides of your eyes to block light from that angle. It helps if you can get a fit down onto your cheeks, too.

The best fishing glasses are those with some sort of light-blocking shape to the arms. Sometimes glasses with lots of light blocking shaped around the actual lenses do not allow sufficient circulation of air behind the frames, and so tend to fog up. Make sure such glasses are well ventilated, or see if you can make some air holes without messing up the hooding effect.

Once you have the glasses, you have to get used to the idea of looking *through* the water, not *at* the water. This means you have to focus beyond the thing you can clearly see. Although your eyes won't have any problem with this, your mind will. So you will have to train it.

One slightly more eccentric point: when you are looking into the water with polaroids and actually trying to see individual fish, no matter what the actual colouring of the fish is, it will appear to be a shade of grey–brown, through from olive tones to quite dark browns, with the colour muted by a grey cast. Only fish seen right in the surface layer will reveal their true colours. Remember, the bright colours you see when the fish is out of the water are never intended to be seen under such conditions. The range of subtle shades and bright colours you see are designed to reflect, absorb and react to light in an assortment of ways to make the fish *difficult* to see over a wide variety of light and background conditions. You need to become an expert on seeing, and interpreting, shadows, which is about as much as you can often expect to see.

OBVIOUS STRUCTURE

Any structure, any structure at all, will be of interest to fish: bridges, wharves, reefs, islands, downed trees, large rocks, wrecks and so on. Anything that is not just flat sand is a structure, and will attract life of some kind.

Fish love structure like this – no angler worth their salt would pass up such a snag.

Obvious structure is often a key to less obvious structure. You only see the smooth pylons of the bridge, but in building that bridge all sorts of rubble may have been left on the bottom, forming an artificial reef. The single rock sticking up out of the sea is rarely an isolated rock: it is usually just the highest part of a reef system of some kind.

The boom that has occurred in impoundment fishing, with many thousands of anglers taking to the fresh water for the first time, has called for a new attitude towards fish-holding features. There are many new environments to consider, such as thermoclines, weed beds, drowned trees and even ancient river beds.

For some strange reason, when a dam is created, even though there might be 50 m of water over the original river, fish will still be attracted to the river bed. It is quite common to find them along what used to be the drop-off from the bank to the river.

Weed beds can be hot spots for bass, with the fish working in, through and above the bed.

A saltwater angler coming to the fresh needs to re-order his priorities, and become skilled in the specialised techniques used to exploit these environments. Saltwater anglers have traditionally classified their fish as either reef or surface fish. They have cast to, or trolled for, surface-feeding pelagic species, or they have used jigs or weighted baits to fish species that feed on or near the bottom. Freshwater fishing is not like that at all. Many of the prime species feed anywhere from the surface to the bottom, and many highly specialised fishing techniques are used to exploit various depths.

Trolling is often done with downriggers, devices that allow a trolled lure to be presented at any level between the surface and the bottom, even in very deep water.

In this environment a good echo sounder is not just essential to finding fish; it also alerts the angler to the need for a specialised approach and set of tools to exploit the situation. Electronics have become fundamental to the new age of freshwater fishing.

Using charts and maps

Marine charts and maps of all sorts can be a great aid in finding fish. Government departments produce detailed maps covering every centimetre of this country, and freshwater and estuary anglers can find many new spots

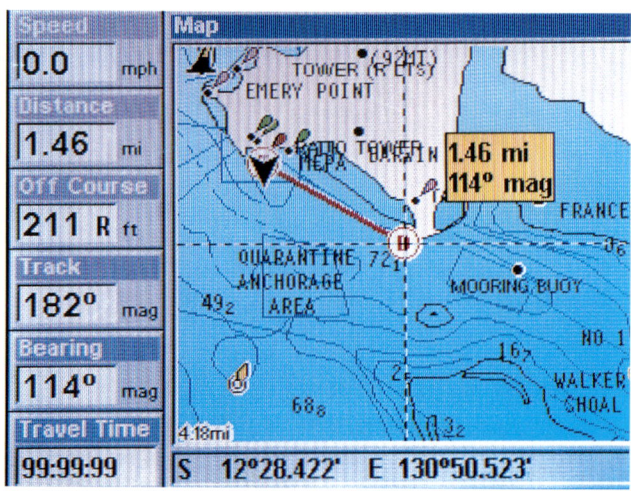

Anglers have always used paper charts to locate prospective fishing grounds. Now that we have the global positioning system (GPS) in the sky, electronic mapping has become the order of the day. By placing a cursor over a spot on the map the GPS system will guide you where you want to go.

simply by visiting the local Lands Department office and buying maps covering areas of interest.

Ocean anglers are better served by the marine charts used by boat operators, as these show the features of some areas in great detail. These charts provide a wealth of vital information, such as constant depth contours, prevailing currents, areas where overfalls occur (rough water created when wind and currents oppose, or where there is an upsurge of current over deep structure), various bottom features, such as gravel or rock patches, areas of reef and so on.

Charts can be quite difficult to decipher, and it pays to buy a publication that explains what all the symbols mean. There are plenty of handbooks on coastal navigation available, and most of these go into some detail on the use of charts.

If a chart tells you that something is there, it is usually right, but take care not to assume that the chart shows *everything* that is in the area. Remember, these charts were put together as an aid to shipping, not to anglers, so there are plenty of features of great interest to anglers that never make it onto the charts.

Travelling rock anglers can also learn much from marine charts, particularly about bottom depth contours. Random depth samplings are scattered all over these charts, but lines are traced along points where a set depth occurs to give a picture of the bottom contour. Thus you might look at a section of the coast and see the 20-fathom line (36.5 m) snaking along some 10 to 12 km offshore. You might also see a section of the coast where that line curves sharply in towards the shore, with all the corresponding depth contours inside that curving in also. If, for instance, you had an interest in catching a deepwater species such as snapper from the rocks, it would pay you to go into such an area and have a good look at the shoreline for potential fishing spots. When strong southerly conditions bring snapper inshore along the coast, such an area would be a better bet than most.

More and more books with maps showing the best fishing spots for various areas are coming onto the market these days. Some are useful, but others are not worth the cost of the paper they are printed on. For them to be of any use they need to give a good description of the spot (is it a hole, a reef, a channel or what?) and a detailed description of the marks (or GPS positions) you should use to position yourself on that spot. Telling people to get the white house over the pine tree when you are looking for a mark off Sydney's Eastern Suburbs is like giving directions in the desert by lining up various grains of sand. It's hopeless.

The best books give a picture of the land with the reference points clearly marked: you need at least two good sets of land marks to give you intersecting lines, and you need intersecting lines in order to get a reasonable position fix.

Don't forget, this approach only puts you on, or near, a spot. It does not find you fish. The fish may be in just one small part of the area, so the way you position yourself once you find the spot will determine whether you come in contact with them or not.

Locating fish from a boat has been greatly simplified in recent years by the widespread use of the Global Positioning System (GPS). Mad old Ronald Reagan got this project underway as part of his plan to have laser gun ships orbiting in space ready to demolish anything on the face of the Earth that threatened America. Happily for children who like to fire off skyrockets on cracker night, and fishermen with no interest in star wars at all, the targeting system made it into space without the laser gun ships.

A gross oversimplification of the GPS system is that it involves something like 23 high-altitude satellites orbiting the Earth in positions that allow several to be in sight at all times, no matter where you are on the face of the Earth. Each of these satellites has a number, and each constantly broadcasts information on its precise position and the precise time at which this information is broadcast.

On Earth, day or night, fine or foul, a handheld GPS receiver costing only a few hundred dollars can pick up these broadcasts, and by knowing precisely where those satellites are, figure out where it is, to within 20 metres. On a good day it can place itself within a few metres of dead centre of its precise position.

A GPS system recognises and displays its position in degrees, minutes and seconds of latitude and longitude. Thus your hot bream spot might become 27° 53'092" south by 153° 20'058" east. (Don't try to find the spot – I just made that up as an example. It could be the edge of a cliff in Lower Slobovia for all I know!)

GPS now works hand in hand with charts, and many fishermen who have GPS have never looked at a paper chart in their lives and probably never will.

Using fish finders

As important as sounders are in locating fish and giving the angler a clear picture of the way in which the spot should be fished, they also play a key role in showing that there are no fish in an area, even if all other signs tell you that it could be a good location. Instead of wasting time with exploratory techniques, the angler can focus time and effort on those areas where the fish finder has shown that there are fish to be caught.

There are many makes and models of sounders available these days, so if you want to buy smart you need to know how they work, and then figure out how much power and quality is right for you.

Echo sounders basically consist of a computer, a display and a keyboard in what is called the head unit. This connects to a power source and a transmitter (the transducer) which is usually mounted on the transom of the boat. Transducers can also be set up inside the hull to shoot the signal through the bottom of the boat, or they can actually go through the hull in what is called a 'bolt-thru' configuration. You will normally only find a bolt-thru set-up in a fairly large boat.

The transducer fires a pulse at the bottom. The time it takes for that pulse to bounce off the bottom and return allows the computer to calculate the depth of water beneath the boat. But that's just the easy part. The signal can also return to the computer with information about anything in the water between the

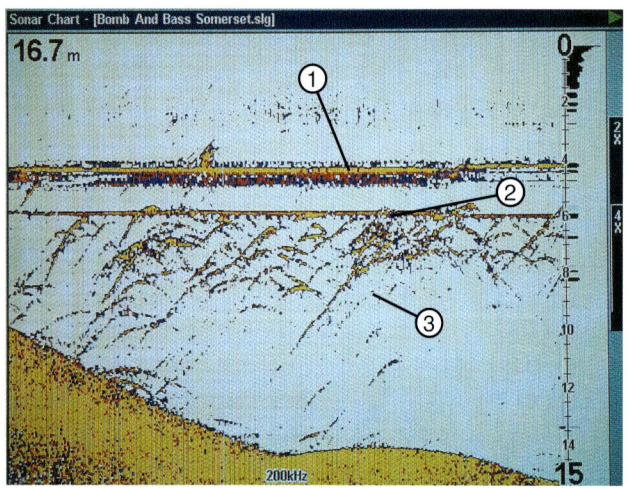

This shows a good echo sounder at work. Two downriggers are being used here with the bombs (weights) showing up as the straight lines across the screen (1 and 2). One is much thicker than the other as it is the one closest to the transducer. The arches below the bombs are good-sized bass. To the left they were between mid-water and bottom when the boat came over them, then centre and right you see them come up to the downrigger to check out the ball and trailing lure (3). Note how the bass have only risen as far as the deepest bomb, allowing anglers to adjust trolling depth to match the exact depth to meet the fish.

surface and the bottom, and this could include fish of all sizes. It can tell whether the bottom is hard or soft; it can work out that weed or downed trees are separate from the actual bottom; and it will even display a thermocline, where two temperature layers come together in the depths. Intelligence in interpreting the returning pulse is one of the most important aspects of sounder performance, and unfortunately for the buyer, intelligence can't be described in the specifications. I have known of plenty of sounders that have been sold on the basis of price, some attractive gimmick, large power output or any one of a whole bunch of reasons, and they aren't worth putting in the boat when compared with an intelligent unit sold for a slightly higher price. Software development costs money, so the smartest computers are usually going to be a little more expensive.

Not all sounders are equal when it comes to interpreting the messages contained within the returning pulse. Also, a sounder operated in the manual mode by an experienced operator will reveal far more information than one operated in automatic mode by an inexperienced or lazy operator.

Once you have the intelligence of the sounder matched up with the appropriate power and frequency to give the best results in the area in which you intend to operate, you then have to consider the ability of the screen to display this information. An echo sounder screen operates by turning single pixels on or off. The more pixels it has available, the finer and more detailed the image it can create. Because the vertical pixel count relates to the depth scale, the pixel count is normally considered in terms of the number of vertical pixels on the screen rather than the number horizontally.

An easier way of picturing this is to consider an extreme example. Suppose you are in 10 m of water using a screen that has 100 vertical pixels. At that rate you have 10 pixels per metre of water. Because your set will place the bottom somewhere between the middle and two-thirds from the top of the screen, you will actually be working with just 60 pixels in the water area, which means that you now only have six pixels per metre of water, or two pixels with which to display quite a decent sized fish. You won't have enough pixels to show any sort of detail and most fish will simply display as a blob.

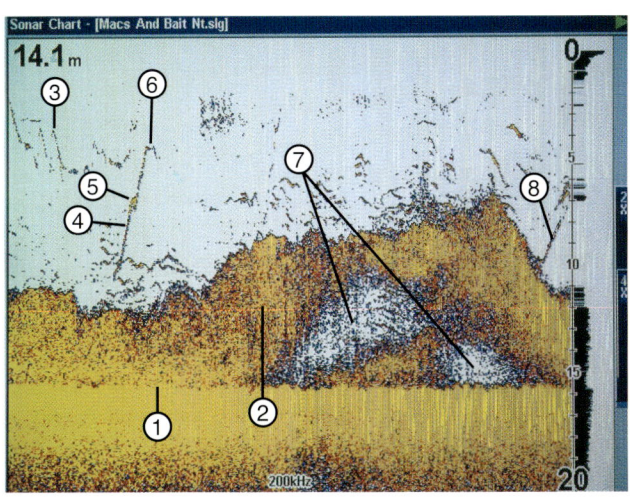

How much can a sounder show you? This screen is a great example of just how powerful a sounder can be. (1) Even with a massive bait school pressed close to the bottom, the clear yellow band across the screen separates the bait from the bottom. (2) The dense speckled area is the bait school, in this case frogmouth pilchards. (3) A Halco Twisty is jigged vertically above the school, creating the zigzag line. (4) A mackerel leaves the other fish in the school (arches and wavy lines), and rises to investigate the lure. (5) The fish hesitates for a moment, causing a heavier signal to register. (6) Hook-up! The fish takes the lure and bolts, disappearing from the screen as it leaves the cone of the transducer signal. (7) As line is gained the fish again enters the transducer beam and takes off for the bottom. The presence of a rampaging mackerel causes the bait school to scatter. (8) The mackerel on the way to the surface to be boated.

In front of me as I write this I have specifications for new models from a major manufacturer. Their bargain-basement entry-level model will have 168 vertical pixels and power output of 800 watts. So if you are fishing dams, rivers or bays you could expect a basic set like this to work quite well. The sets most serious anglers will buy over the next few years will have vertical pixel counts of 320 or more, and at least 3000 watts in output. Top-of-the-line models will offer 480 pixels with 4000 watts output at 200 kHz, and 8000 at 50 kHz, using specially designed dual-frequency multi-element array transducers capable of operating to 1500 m.

If you now understand the way the vertical pixel count works to deliver detail on your screen, you will be happy to know that some sounders offer a way to enhance that pixel count by setting the screen up so that you are using a lot more pixels in the area where the fish are. If you turn the sounder off 'auto' and go into 'manual operation', you can search through the menus that pop up and find one that says 'set upper & lower limits'. This simply means that you can tell the machine to expand one particular area of the screen, and in this case let's just look at an area 3 m above the bottom. If you set the lower limit at 12 m and the upper limit at 7 m, the entire display area is now focused on just the critical 5 m you are most interested in, and you now have 20 vertical pixels available to show the fish. It is not unusual for what appears to be a barren bottom to come alive suddenly after setting the upper and lower limits.

If you increase sensitivity in manual mode, you will see all sorts of background rubbish appear on the screen until it becomes a real mess. By reducing the sensitivity setting gradually until you just have a small amount of clutter in the background, you will be operating at near peak performance.

When you are searching for structure or other potential fish-holding ground it is much easier to leave the sounder running on 'auto', where it will adjust depth settings to cater to constantly changing bottom depths. But once you are over an interesting bottom feature, especially in deeper water, it is always worth going to 'manual' and having a good look around at maximum power before moving on.

I urge all sounder users to experiment. You can't hurt the machine, but you may find that it has been operating in half-asleep mode and is capable of delivering a great deal more information than you have been receiving in the past.

Exploratory fishing techniques

Getting yourself into the vicinity of fish is not always the end of the search. You may be up- or down-current of the fish, they could be on the top or the bottom, or they may be suspended in mid-water. They could be out in the open or hard up against cover. You could be sitting right on top of a huge school of fish and miss

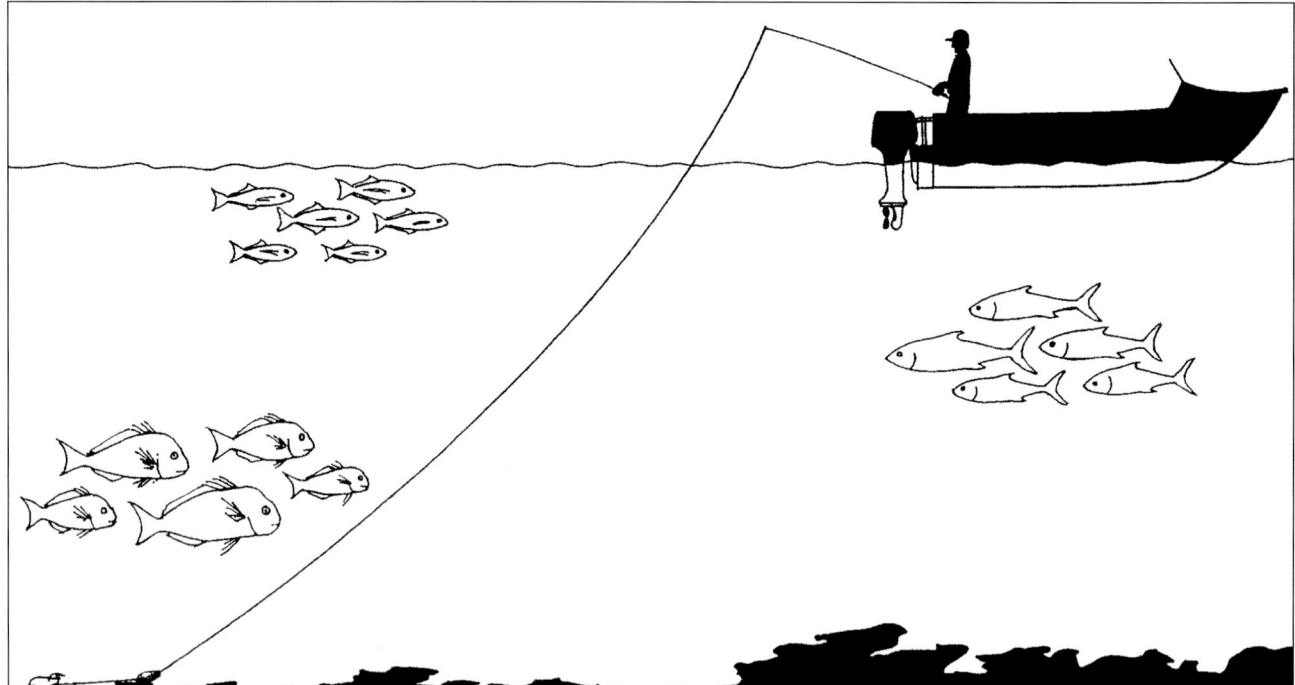

Getting to where the fish are is just the first part. Whether fishing from a boat or the shore, you also need to have a fishing system that will locate fish at any depth.

out completely by simply fishing at the wrong level. Here are a couple of examples that underline the nature of the problem.

Fishing for barramundi one day, we worked all the obvious bank-side snags with lures without getting a single look at a fish. At this stage my companion suggested trolling right up the middle of the stream with deep-running lures. We did this, and took a double strike in one particular unremarkable stretch of the stream. Then we went over the same spot again and again, taking a dozen more strikes off exactly the same mid-stream spot. It seemed that every fish in that long section of stream had taken to a single deep snag.

Snapper are fish that can be anywhere between the bottom and the top. Sometimes running out a berley trail will bring snapper right to the surface and close to the boat. If you fish with any lead at all you may simply be taking the bait down right past them. At other times they will stubbornly remain glued to the bottom, and if you want to catch snapper you have to get a bait all the way down there, even though the fish are feeding very aggressively. There

are also times when the fish will be scattered from top to bottom – in that case you need to use techniques that allow your baits to work effectively throughout the depth range.

BAIT AND LURE PLACEMENT

Freshwater anglers working with lures are adept at covering water from top to bottom, and choose lures to cover a particular depth. They might use a shallow running pattern to fish right across the top of cover, then a deep diver to work down across a rock face or sunken log. Even greater depths can be worked over with patterns that are allowed to sink at the end of the cast to a desired depth, then are slowly retrieved at that level for most of the length of the cast.

Recent interest in sonic patterns has opened the doors on vertical fishing techniques that allow anglers to probe right into the middle of cover. Most of this interest has centred around lures with some form of rattle inside the body, but the term 'sonic' applies to a much broader range of lures, many much more subtle than the rattles.

Anything with spinning blades makes a sonic pattern, as do jigs with a single blade attached to the body. These lures need to be worked quietly up and down in the one place, giving fish time to hear them and home in on the source of the sound. Big jigs with a strip of squid attached to the hooks can be very effective when bounced hard on the bottom over and over again. Old-time flathead anglers knew all about this when they fished live baits off a long trace, yo-yoing their leads all the while to make some noise on the bottom and attract the flathead.

Live baits have a combination of sonic attraction and smell going for them. (If you have trouble comprehending this, go back to the section on the senses of the fish, and read the part about hearing again.)

Using sonic effects is one approach to finding fish, in that you operate close to what you believe to be the right place and try to attract the fish to your offering. The other approach is to use techniques that actively seek out fish, and the floating bait is about as good an example of this as you can get. The term 'floating bait' is a little erroneous. 'Slow-sinking bait' would be a much more accurate description. When floating baits first came into vogue, the popular alternative was to anchor the bait to the bottom with a large lump of lead that stopped movement altogether, so I suppose anything that was not 'nailed' to the bottom in this way was considered positively buoyant.

A garfish mounted on a four-hook rig was the original floating bait, but the garfish soon gave way to the blue pilchard, which was a cheaper bait to buy, a better average size of bait, and an excellent weight for casting. The flight of three or four hooks has been generally accepted as being the right way to go with floating baits, and the style of hook has been dictated by the ease with which the hooks can be linked, which may actually be a drawback in some cases. Floating baits were originally designed to be fished in the surf, where the greater weight caused by linking the hooks was largely negated by vigorous water movement. However, when floaters are fished in less vigorous water, it may pay to look again at hook weight and the whole hooking arrangement, as the rate of sink determines overall effectiveness.

When cast from the shore, floaters are normally fished with a draw-and-sink method. The bait is allowed to sink just so far at the end of the cast, then it is drawn back towards the shore with the rod tip, which usually brings it back towards the surface. The sink phase can be varied to work the bait through quite a narrow range of depth, or to have it come back in a series of big loops. A very narrow range might be used to search below a spread of deep foam cover; a deep drop could be used when a variety of fish might be expected to be anywhere between the top and the bottom.

When fishing cut baits as floaters, especially when working a berley trail, the rate of sink is crucial to success. In a strong current it might be necessary to add quite a lot of lead to a floater to overcome water pressure on the line and get the bait to sink at the same rate as the berley. Getting this right is quite an art. The more common problem is that the bait sinks faster than the berley and is out of the berley trail before it gets far enough away from the boat to encounter fish. Hook size and weight, and line diameter are the crucial factors here. Reduce both, and if the fish are big, go to a smaller size but a stronger pattern in your hooks. A very small hook's reduced holding power can be overcome by allowing the fish a little longer to swallow the bait – which it is more likely to do when a small hook is used. But you need to remain mindful of the hook size when you are fighting the fish.

An unweighted bait will seek fish out at every level as it slowly sinks to the bottom. Watch the hook size, though – too big a hook will act as a sinker.

Wherever it is practical to do so, use rigs that move about to seek fish out. An anchored bait fishes only one spot and a fish has to get directly downstream of it to pick up the scent. A moving bait wanders about looking for fish, and will spread its scent over a wider area.

When you are fishing a beach it is advisable to fish a lead that will facilitate the length of cast you need without then anchoring the bait in one spot on the bottom – unless of course you want a bait to stay in one particular place. As the waves move your bait inshore, simply keep picking up the slack and let the bait wash back in towards you. This is a perfectly natural presentation of a bait, as it is moving in exactly the same direction as any other food would be out there, and the fish will be positioned somewhere along or across this path of travel.

If you need extra weight to cast a particularly long distance, and this weight then anchors your bait, simply let the bait sit for a time, then move it inshore a couple of metres. Repeat this process all the way back to the shore. You have to remember that it is completely unnatural for anything to be anchored to the bottom out there in all that moving water, and a moving bait is more likely to attract than frighten fish.

If you are fishing from a boat in an estuary tidal run it is always a good idea to cast lightly weighted baits ahead and to the side of the boat, allowing the current to carry the bait back around the boat in a wide arc. This is a nice way to fish a sandbar when a tide is rising over it.

In a rock, boat or river situation, when you are fishing near any sort of structure or cover, casts should be fanned out to cover as much water as possible, then systems should be used that probe all depths of water. Cast floaters are great, because they can be placed anywhere and worked to any depth. They may not ultimately prove to be the ideal way to go on fishing, but they are the most suitable way to make contact with just about anything in the area. For example, mauled pilchards that fail to get a hookup are often the first stage of an excellent breaming session.

No matter where, or how, you are fishing, live baits never go astray, and if your fishing involves you being stationed in the one place for any length of time, never pass up the opportunity to put out a live bait. Those people who have the most photos of huge fish to show off are almost certain to be devotees of live bait. It will pull big fish out of the proverbial bathtub.

Live bait does not have to be the conventionally approved bait species, either. Anything that is alive is a live bait. I recall catching a beautiful bream of around a kilo once when fishing hard up against a little offshore rock island. As soon as my back was turned, a 'mate' had my bream back over the side on a large hook, and in no time at all he took a strike from a fish that completely spooled his 4/0 Penn Senator before we could get the anchor up and the boat going after the fish.

I have seen anglers spending hours throwing sweep after sweep back into the water and cursing them for beating the yellowtail they are trying to catch to the

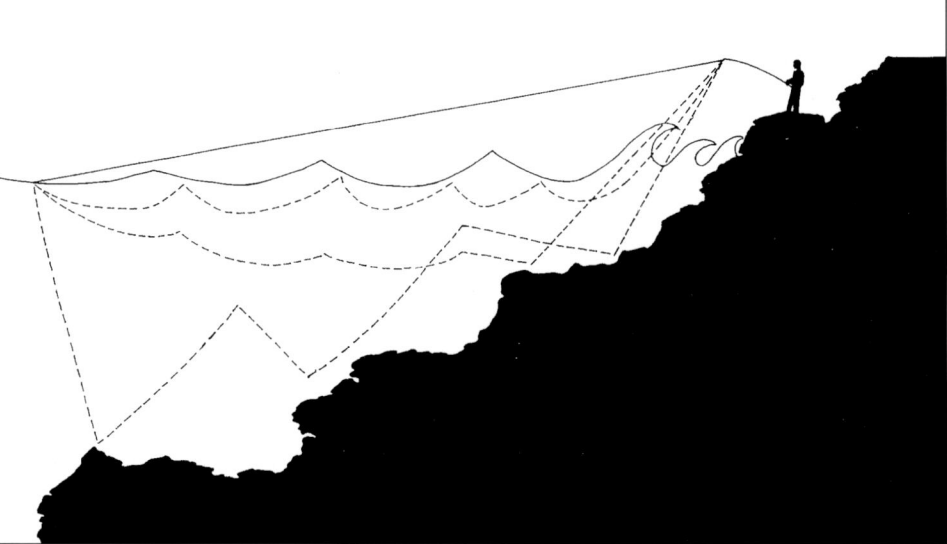

Unweighted baits are great fish finders, as they can be used for a top-to-bottom search. Sometimes a large floater like a pilchard or garfish may be used to locate fish too small to be hooked on this rig, but once the fish are located you can go over to another rig to exploit the fish at any depth they are holding.

hook. Those same sweep are eagerly sought elsewhere by jewfish anglers, and will catch just as many game fish as anything else. Luderick are another fish few people consider when looking for a live bait, but jewfish rather fancy them, too.

The good thing about a live bait is that it will draw fish from far and wide and can be left to its own devices to find its own fish. This means that an angler has a far better chance of catching something if fishing a set live bait while casting lures or floaters off another line.

Floats can be used to get a bait in over the top of impossibly hostile territory. A heavy float is also a useful way to get a long cast out with a bait that you need to keep suspended near the top.

Going the other way, you might want to fish just off the bottom. This can be done by using a needle to run your trace line through a small piece of cork. This is a handy rig to know about when sand crabs are tearing baits to pieces off the beach. Sure, they can swim up off the bottom, but they can't feed anywhere near as effectively when swimming as they can on the bottom. The rig is also handy for fishing a kelp bed, where the sinker can safely be allowed to sink into the weed but the hook needs to be kept up out of it. Use a soft bait with the point inside the bait.

The underlying principle here is this: fish will always feed in the manner involving the least expenditure of energy, and they will always make maximum use of water movement to bring food to them. Get your offering into that water movement and let it go with the flow to become a natural part of the cycle. Also, in any given body of water, fish are sure to have a preference for just one part of it. Seek them out by varying your presentations and the placement of your bait or lure. Patience is a virtue in fishing, but it is no substitute for an energetic and aggressive approach to the art.

TROLLING

If the target fish are lure eaters, trolling may well be the best exploratory technique to use. Trolling is not always the best way to keep working a group of fish, as the continuous noise factor may eventually have an adverse effect, but it is a great way to locate them in a large body of water such as a big river, a dam, a lake, or the open sea.

Trolling allows a continuous presentation to be made at a fixed depth. For example, if you cast a deep-diving lure, the lure will take a little time to hit its maximum depth, work there for a few metres, then start planing up again. This means that only a portion of each cast is working down where you want it. When you troll a lure capable of diving 2 or 3 m, it stays at that depth.

You also need to consider that with a spread of lures working various depths as you move along, you are actually making a presentation over quite a considerable volume of water, and that is the name of the game when you are sorting out new water or are having trouble finding fish on home ground.

USING BERLEY

Remember how extraordinarily well developed a fish's sense of smell is? Once you know also that the movement of scent is virtually unlimited in water, you will understand why the use of berley is fundamental to success in the great majority of fishing situations. It is almost impossible to dilute berley to a point where fish within striking range of the angler will not pick it up and home in on it. This means that the angler, physically limited in range by the position of the boat and the length of the cast, can virtually cover kilometres of fishing water through its prudent use.

Half the power of berley lies in its ability to reach, and then concentrate, widely scattered fish. The other half lies in its ability to switch fish on and get them feeding aggressively outside normal feeding cycles.

Just think back to the number of times you have been out and about, not thinking of food and not ready for a meal, and then have walked past a house where a baked dinner or bacon and eggs are being cooked, or perhaps the odour of frying onions and steak on a barbecue has come your way. Your mouth starts to water and you suddenly find that you have more than a passing interest in getting hold of a big plate of whatever it is that has just turned you on.

The same thing happens to fish, but for a fish tracking down that scent, the urgency is greater. By the time that fish is well and truly switched on, there's a good chance that a whole bunch of other fish in that same trail will also be switched on, and who knows if

When you have no idea where fish are and no echo sounder to locate them, trolling can be a good option.

there will be enough food at the end of the trail for everybody? Completely out of control feeding sprees can be the result, with fish abandoning all caution to compete fiercely for the available food. Having said that, be cautioned that this is the ideal, extreme example, and not at all the way things will always be. The one thing you can absolutely rely on, though, is that the fishing will always be better with berley than without it.

Berley can be laid down in a great many ways. Choose the way you operate according to how sensitive to sound you expect your target fish to be, and how you wish to get the berley to them. If your berley operation involves a lot of banging and clanging working a metal ram into a metal berley pot, you should present your baits well down the berley trail, not right up close to the boat.

The ideal berley trail is one in which there is a great deal of odour and very little substance. You can take the fire out of fish by overfeeding them on berley, although berley often seems to get fish feeding to the

point where they will keep biting even when they are full to bursting point. My attitude is that you can't go wrong by always assuming that you are dealing with difficult fish. You will then still get a result when they are being fussy, and it won't make any difference when they're not.

You can use almost anything for berley, starting with the cast-offs from the bait you are using. Very little berley can be made to go a long way by mixing the base with sand or water. Estuary luderick experts have long used the technique of cutting up green weed very finely and mixing it in with a large amount of wet sand. They fashion bombs out of this mixture and the bombs dissolve on the way to the bottom, taking the scraps of weed down to mid levels as the bomb comes apart. Every grain of that sand is also effective as berley, because it too carries the scent of the weed. Likewise, only a small number of pilchards or sardines need to be crushed and mixed through sand to produce a large amount of effective berley.

Another little trick is to take something like prawn heads and shells and freeze them in water in an ice-cream container. The resulting ice block will be prawn flavoured. If you pop this in a mesh bag along with half a house brick, you can have a slow-release berley system hanging from the side of your boat.

Another nice system for estuary fishing is to mix the berley with wet sand, and then pack the sand into an open tin which has a couple of holes punched in the bottom and a suitable length of line attached to it through the holes. The tin is gently lowered to the bottom then, with a few sharp pulls on the line, the berley is dumped out.

Bread can be soaked in a garbage bin full of water until it is a milky mix with very few solids left. Chook laying pellets, wheat and all sorts of other produce items are excellent fish attractors; the wheat and pellets have two great assets – they do not present storage problems and they are the easiest berleys of all to dispense. Even the carcass of a large fish, such as a tuna, roughed up a little with a scaler or a serrated knife, suspended on a rope and allowed to be dragged about over the rocks by the wave surge, will stir up interest.

Freshwater anglers sometimes use a natural berley dispenser – hanging a dead animal in a tree branch over a likely-looking hole in the river. They leave it there until it is well and truly flyblown, with a steady stream of maggots dropping into the water below, then they fish the spot. You need a strong stomach for this one.

Whether you have the standard berley bucket and metal ram at the top or bottom of your berley dispenser list depends on how you feel about sound. Some anglers will go to extraordinary lengths to mince and freeze berley in ice blocks so that it can be dispensed in absolute silence, while others smash away at their metal pots with plenty of vigour and hope for the best. A high-impact plastic berley pot is better than a metal one, but whichever you are using you should exercise some restraint, grinding rather than belting the berley into submission.

However you choose to dispense your berley, the golden rule is to keep it going in an unbroken trail. If you put a steady trail down for 30 minutes, you

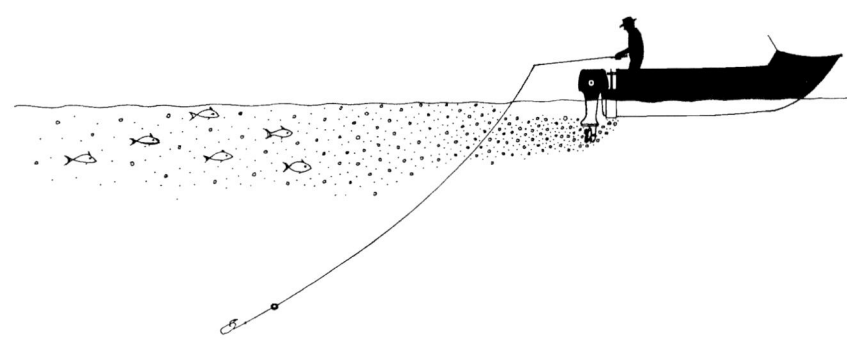

Berley pulls all the fish in the area into the trail, so you need to be sure that your bait stays in it too. Be very careful about the size of sinker you use, and even give consideration to the weight of the hook. A thick line will also sink much more slowly than a fine line in moving water.

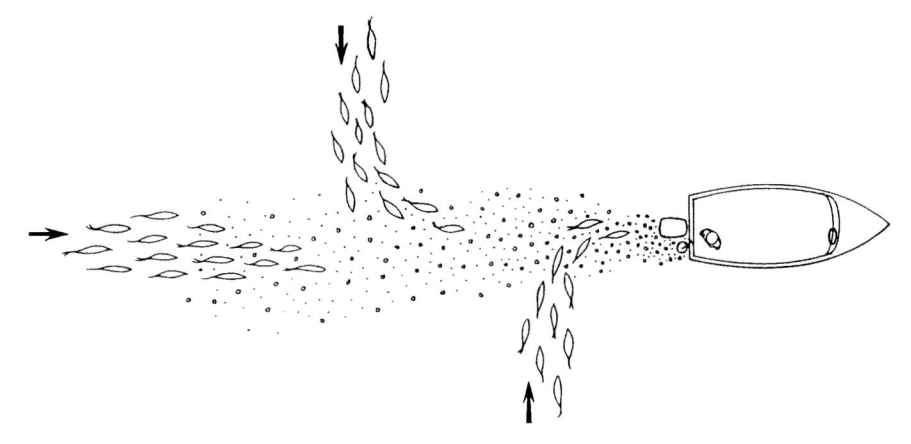

A good berley trail will collect all of the fish directly in the stream, along with those that cross it for a considerable distance downstream of the source.

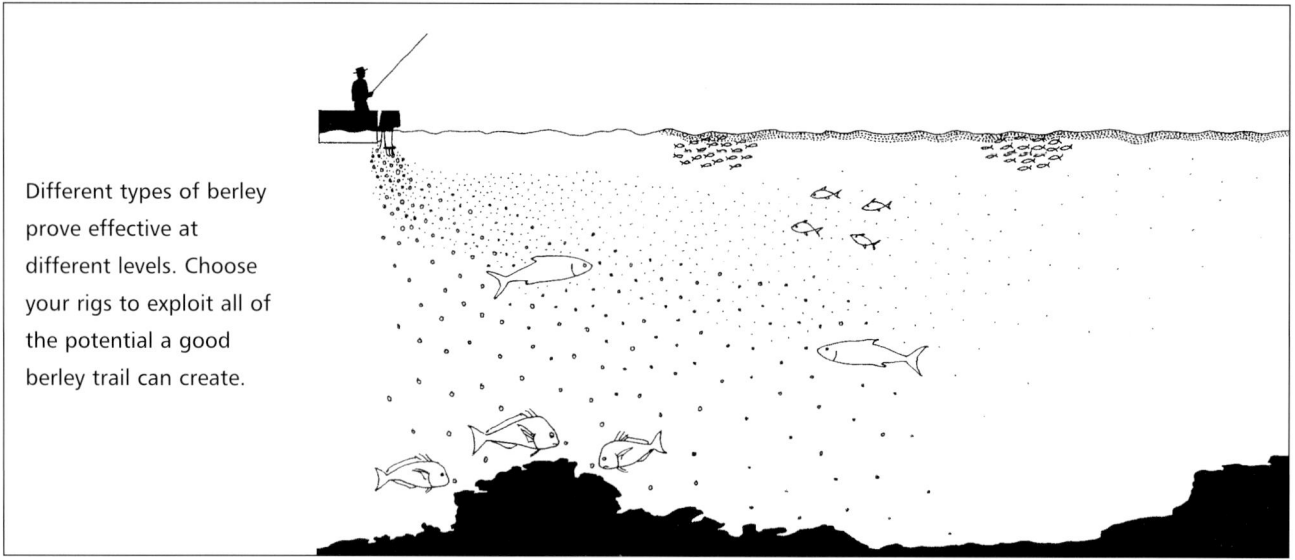

Different types of berley prove effective at different levels. Choose your rigs to exploit all of the potential a good berley trail can create.

might have just reached a large school of fish moving across your position, and they will have turned and locked into the scent, moving up the trail. If you then stop for a 15-minute drink break, or have your attention diverted by a fish you have hooked, and forget the berley, your efforts will have been wasted. When those fish moving up the trail get to the end of it, they will turn back and stay in the scent trail, moving away with it. Even worse, the scent trail will continue to collect fish as it goes downstream, taking them with it.

To keep a berley trail going, you must give some thought to how you are going to work it. If you are by yourself, you need to have a system that you can keep going once you start to catch fish, such as a suspended bag of berley laying down an unbroken scent trail. If you are using chook pellets, the problem is not great, because you are essentially using a ground bait that will hit bottom and not spread all that far. If you are working fish frames in a berley pot, especially in a good current, you need to keep things going, because there will be no residue building up on the bottom to hold fish. With two people in a boat there should be no real problem whatever system you're using.

The critical element is the flow of the water you are fishing. If it's fairly still, you don't have much of a problem, because you are essentially laying down a bottom berley in a limited area. But when you are working a good current or tidal run, which is particularly effective because it gets your message over

a wide area, it is absolutely essential that the flow be maintained, and that calls for discipline.

An effective method of berleying bigger fish is to use cubes from a large fish, or to drop individual pilchards or whitebait over the side one at a time. The approved dispensing rate is to have the next piece of berley coming into sight just as the current one is being eaten by a fish moving up the trail. Again, discipline is called for.

Herring (or ruff) are often fished for from the shore with a berley bomb float. To get the berley out that little extra distance to where the fish are, the angler uses a quite heavy, hollow float (called a blob) which is packed with berley. When the float hits the water at the end of the cast, the berley breaks out and disperses down towards the hook and bait. This system is used a great deal in Europe, but seems only to have found favour here with people fishing for herring.

You also need to give some thought to where the fish you are after are likely to be. Do you need a surface berley, a bottom berley or a slow-sink system that will search all levels for you? Fish frames and heads ground out of a berley pot usually look after the surface and slow-sink needs, as they tend to produce a range of particle sizes, some sinking faster than others, and a lot of oil is released as the berley is broken up. If you are interested in the bottom close to the boat you might have to use another berley, such as pellets, a sand mix or a bomb such as the tin idea.

In one spot I fish I always get some bran, or finely ground Sao biscuit, out on the surface to bring the garfish in, then use crab shells mashed into sand for a bottom brew. Sometimes I put fish through the pot. On a few occasions the garfish have schooled up near the boat, and in turn have attracted kingfish and tailor. This secondary effect of berley should not be overlooked. I have taken some excellent hauls of tailor after berleying with bread for drummer, the tailor coming in after mullet were attracted to the bread.

One of the Hawkesbury River's best mulloway anglers used to berley eddies with bread to concentrate the bait, some of which he caught for his own live bait. Even when he had his bait, though, he continued to berley the baitfish, knowing that a concentration of these fish would call the big fellows in like a dinner bell. Because of the berley, that bait would no longer be swimming calmly and quietly through the water, but would be active and excited, giving off vibrations that travel well underwater.

No matter how you put the berley out, fish will be extremely boat shy at times, and it pays to think about how you fish your berley trail. Working from a boat, lines should go down where the berley first makes contact with the bottom, then light lines should be fed down the trail to explore all levels. A case can be made for very long traces, or leads dropped over the side after a long length of line has been fed out – rigs like these search a good area of water clear of the bottom.

There is a strong likelihood that large fish, being more cautious than small fish, will hang back further in the trail, which could mean that the small fish get all your baits. It would therefore be a good idea to make a long cast down the trail to get baits right back to where the big fish may be holding. Slow-sinking baits can also do a good job in such a situation.

A friend of mine used to fish a reef for snapper, and noted that the fish did not mind coming to the surface, but they were very boat shy. He came up with the idea of using frozen berley blocks, placed in a mesh bag then floated back close to the shallow waters of the reef. The snapper were happy to attack this bag, and he simply had to cast back to his berley to get into the action.

There are particular instances when anglers tend to misjudge where the fish will be. Around the rocks, fish will sometimes come all the way up to the source of the berley. Earlier I mentioned the common situation where water coming up over a shelf funnels back into the lowest section of the shelf as it returns to the sea. In such a case, the fish will be *directly under the return flow*, and any sort of cast at all will put the bait out past them. Remember this when using berley on the rocks.

People catching worms often amuse me. They will work a section of beach for quite a long period, with their berley bag in the wash attracting worms, and then go off and fish somewhere else. Doesn't it seem logical that the same 'flavoured' backwash that brought the worms up would also have concentrated fish in the shore break? Also, why put the stink bag away after worming? Why not stake it out in the wash so that it keeps working? Berleying a beach appears to be a lost art, or one that has never been established, but why should berley be any less effective on a beach than anywhere else?

The more things you try out, the more problems you solve, so give just about any berley system that comes to mind a go. Berley freaks – and most good anglers are berley freaks – never throw anything away, either. Chop bones, prawn heads, stale bread and green peas are all grist for the mill, and a thumping great off-colour ham bone is a genuine collector's item. The garbage bins outside an RSL the morning after a beer and prawn night are like a major lotto win to a dedicated angler. For these people, cleaning fish will only mean separating parts of the fish – some are eaten, others go into the freezer to be recycled next fishing session. The freezer does not hold food for human consumption; it looks more like the refrigeration unit on the island of Doctor Moreau.

Interestingly enough, at this point, amusing though these characters may be to friends and neighbours, they have blended almost perfectly into the marine life cycle, taking an absolute minimum from the sea and returning everything that has not been eaten for another generation of fish. Their berley will often put nearly as much protein back into the sea as it takes out, and if they have a few quiet days, the fish could actually end up in front, although berley freaks tend not to have too many quiet days.

Without berley you are a little like Ali Baba standing outside the cave without the password.

Chapter Four

Natural bait

The bait you use, and the care you take of it, can be crucial to your fishing success. The best way to get on the right track about bait is to assume that the fish feels exactly the same way about food as you do. If you won't eat a ham sandwich that's been left lying in the sun until the bread is stiff as a board and the ham is a nice shade of green, why assume that a fish will eat a prawn that's been given the same treatment? After all, most fish eat food that is much fresher than anything you ever get to eat, because the fish eats most of its food while the food is still alive.

There have been times when I have caught fish on bait that is so off I have had to take a couple of deep breaths before handling it. But there have been many more times when the freshness of the bait in use has been the key to success.

I recall an occasion when a friend and I fished a shallow reef off Kurnell, in southern Sydney. Between us we had six or seven different kinds of bait, all fresh, and all baits that a snapper will normally eat. I had some Sydney Harbour prawns and I started fishing with these, throwing the heads and shells over the side as I baited up with just the meat of the prawn. Fishing with only a very light lead on the line, I started to get fish just off the bottom, but as we fished on and I used more bait and threw more shells over the side, the fish came closer and closer to the top. All this time my friend, using everything but prawn as bait, did not get one snapper bite, although he did get the odd rubbish fish off the bottom. He even tried fresh squid and failed to get a touch at first. Then, just before dusk, a southerly front approached, and the barometric pressure plummeted. The snapper came to the top in an incredibly hot bite that saw them ready to eat anything in that brief period before the southerly slammed through, bringing proceedings to an abrupt halt.

That is just an extreme example of the way fish can have an obsession with one particular bait and then, under different circumstances, be prepared almost to eat the label off a can of sardines. Since you never know what sort of mood the fish are likely to be in when you go fishing, the safest approach is to make sure that you have on hand the bait that you know they are *most likely to accept.*

Using local bait

You should never underestimate the potential value of using bait collected from the area in which you plan to fish. Fresh or live prawns are usually among the better baits available, as are yabbies and any kind of worms. If a bait shop has packaged prawns available along with a tray of fresh, locally caught prawns, the fresh prawns would usually be the best bet, even at twice the price of the packaged item. There are variations to this rule, and the packaged Hawkesbury prawns are an exception where I fish. They work beautifully, while other packaged prawns prove to be a most economical bait to buy, because the fish rarely touch them!

You have to experiment a bit with the packaged and fresh prawns available in your area. A lot of the packaged prawns supplied by big bait companies are treated with chemicals, and these make very poor bait. In other parts of the country professional fishermen bag and freeze local prawns for sale; these can be the best bait of all.

I was reminded of the sheer contrariness of fish the other day when a colleague was making the point that on the surf beach where he fishes, blood worms taken from a distant area are far more effective on whiting than the beach worms caught right on the spot. It made me think of the days when I used to fish for bream from Brighton Beach in Botany Bay. Most of the keen anglers there went to a lot of trouble to dig blood worms found in one part of the bay, but I used to get beach worms from a distant surf beach. Those beach worms would out-fish the local blood worms three and four to one. The lesson there is never to take anything for granted in fishing. Always be prepared to try something new.

Catching beach worms is something of an art, but it is a skill well worth acquiring if you are serious about beach fishing. The idea is to attach some sort of berley to a string. You can also use pantyhose with small chunks of berley stuffed down into the foot section. You work along towards the top of the wash on the beach, swishing the berley back and forth as you go.

The smell of the berley is carried down into the surf with the backwash, and the worms will start rising to the surface looking for the food, poking their heads up out of the sand to taste the receding water. When a worm does this, the retreating water creates a 'V' as it flows around the worm's head. The mark indicates where the worm is.

Experienced wormers have their own special likes and dislikes with regard to berley. Some prefer fresh ingredients, while others believe that the longer berley is dead, the better it is. My personal preference is for smoked kippers. Once again, my advice is to experiment.

Worms are best berleyed from towards the top of the wash on a relatively flat stretch of sand. Work too far down the beach and you will find the retreating wash too deep to see the worms; on a steep bank, water will be coming back too hard and creating too much disturbance for you to get at the worms. Don't give up and move on if you find all the worms well down the wash towards deeper water. They move quite quickly and will work their way up the beach if you keep the berley going.

You need a bait – preferably something tough that the worm can't tear bits off. Hold this down on the

Beach worms are a red-hot bait for a wide variety of fish.

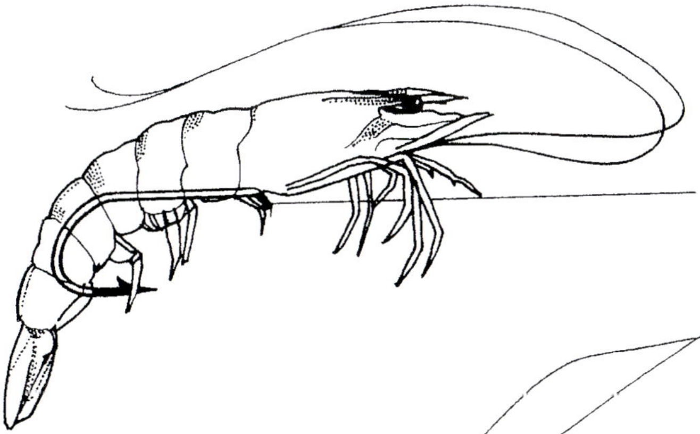

This is a fairly standard method of hooking a dead prawn or yabby. An alternative is to reverse the procedure with the hook entering the bait under the tail then coming out behind the head. In the latter case, a half hitch over the tail will make the bait more secure for casting.

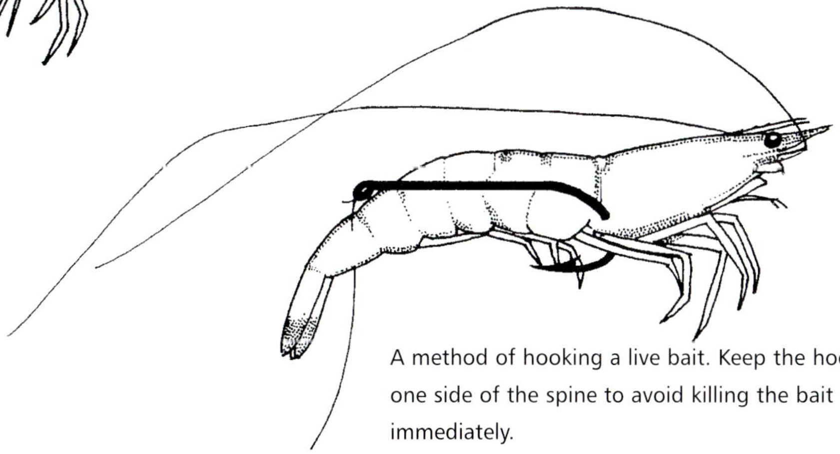

A method of hooking a live bait. Keep the hook to one side of the spine to avoid killing the bait immediately.

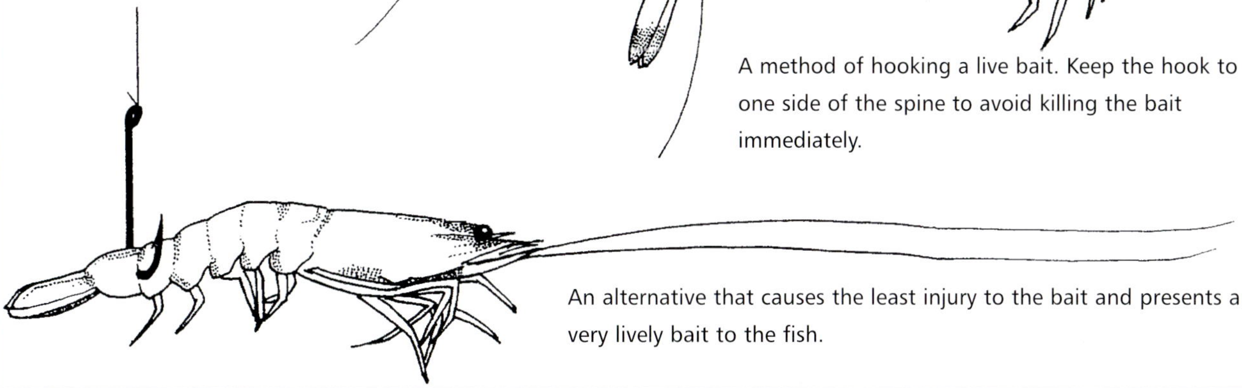

An alternative that causes the least injury to the bait and presents a very lively bait to the fish.

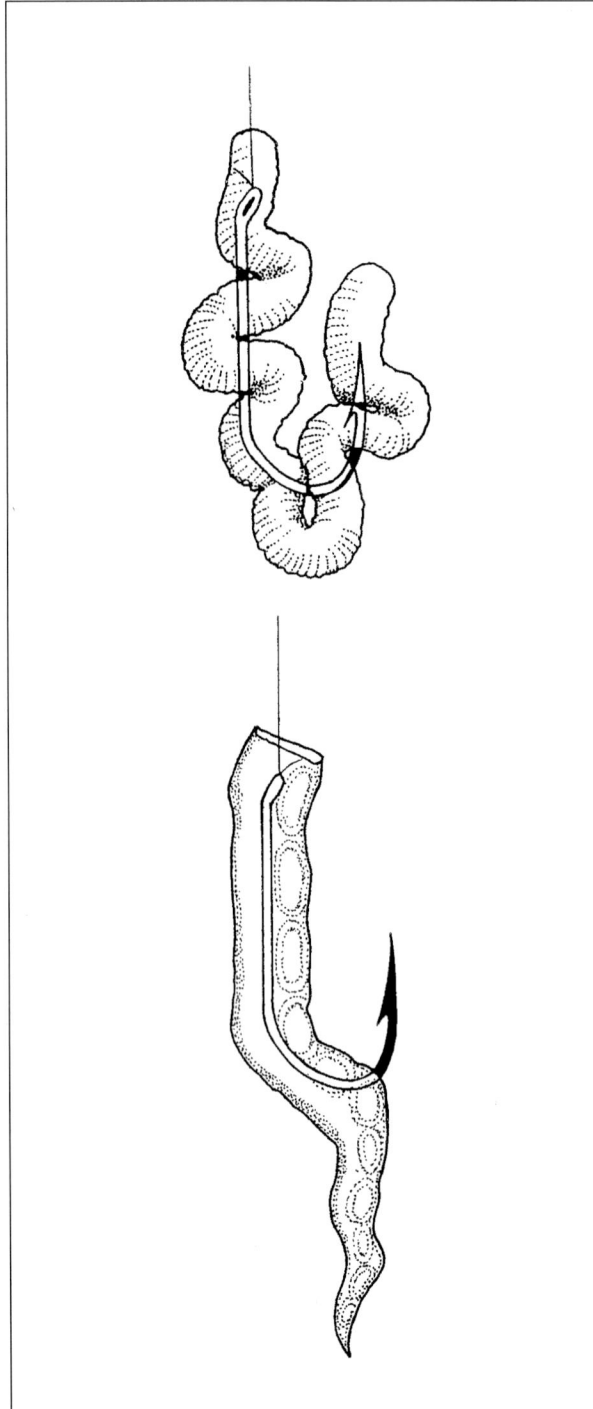

Long baits come in for different treatments. Worms are the only bait you should ever bunch up on a hook like this. Any bait with more substance than a worm may cover the point of the hook and you will fail to hook up. Make sure you get the eye of the hook down inside the worm if that's possible. The squid or octopus tentacle is laid out straight on the hook as shown, and can be secured with a half hitch.

sand just in front of the worm's head. It will come forward, grab the bait, and then arch quite high before snapping back, trying to tear off a piece of the bait. Just as it arches, slide the first finger and thumb of your free hand into the sand either side of its head, then smoothly apply pressure to the neck at the base of the head, with sand between your fingers and the worm. If you get it right you will find that you have some worm between finger and thumb. Wait until the worm relaxes, then pull it out in one smooth movement.

All this is much easier said than done, and timing is everything. Even a small worm can achieve an astonishing amount of purchase on the sand around it throughout the length of its body. If you don't get the worm the first time you feel that grip loosen, the next contraction will almost certainly see the worm rip free of your fingers, often leaving the head behind.

An easier way for the novice to catch worms is with worming pliers, but there's a knack here, too. You have to hold one leg of the pliers firmly between thumb and forefinger, and the other leg swings free inside the other three fingers. This remaining leg must be the only leg to move when you go for the worm – you slam it closed with those free fingers.

Don't try to close the pliers as you would normally: this will result in a 100 per cent missed-worm score. When you have the worm's head in the pliers, dig down beside the body a little way with your free hand, take a second grip with sand between your fingers and thumb and the worm, then slip the worm out as you feel its muscles ease off. Make sure you have sand between your fingers and the worm, or you won't hold him.

The other bait you can catch on the beach is the pipi. Once again, you can sometimes find them by looking for the giveaway 'V' made where the retreating water runs back over the pipi feeding at the top of the sand. If you stand midway down the wash and start doing the twist, your feet will gradually begin to sink in, and your gyrations will break the pipis free from the sand. You will also feel ones with your feet that you can stoop down and pick up as you go. Even when you can't actually see pipis, you will often turn them up towards the bottom of the wash. Pipis make excellent fresh bait, and they keep pretty well in the shell if wrapped in a few sheets of newspaper and stored in the fridge. You can also pickle them: one of our best fishing writers, Ted Clayton, suggests using a screw-top jar and putting one-third of a teaspoon of salt, and a little less sugar, in between the layers of pipis. Keep your bulk supply in the fridge and just take out what you need to fish each day.

We all have to learn to take only as much bait as we actually need. Try to release any live leftovers back where you got them in the first place, or in some other location where they stand a good chance of survival. Even in this relatively enlightened age, there are still far too many anglers who are motivated by greed.

Although good bait pumps are expensive these days, they can be worth their weight in gold where an estuary has extensive sand flats containing beds of yabbies. Half an hour of pumping on the mid tide will usually turn up all the bait you need. If you want to be able to pump them on all tides, simply fix an inner tube or some other form of flotation to the edge of a plastic garden sieve and pump into that as you go. Commercial pipi sieves are also available, and they are just the right size to fit inside a cycle tyre.

Yabby banks are easy enough to find: they are tidal sandbanks riddled with holes that are roughly the diameter of a little finger. Soldier crabs make holes much the same size, but you can usually identify these by the little mound of sand around the entrance where the crab has been doing its house cleaning. There is a knack in pumping yabbies, and you will pick it up soon enough. It revolves around using just a slight downwards pressure on the handle of the pump, allowing the pump's own suction to actually pull the barrel down into the sand. When you work this way, the pump pulls the bait out of the sand to either side of the nozzle; if you push down hard to drive the pump in, you tend to get only those baits that are directly under the pump.

In hot weather, change the water in your bait bucket often as you collect the bait to keep the water temperature as stable as possible and get rid of any dead baits in the bucket. Yabbies can be kept alive for quite some time if you put them into something like a fish box where there is a good surface area on the water – surface area and water temperature are the important elements. Running a bait pump on the container to aerate the water will also help.

In some areas you can also pump red squirt worms, or sand worms, an excellent bait much loved by bream, whiting and luderick. Squirt worm holes are

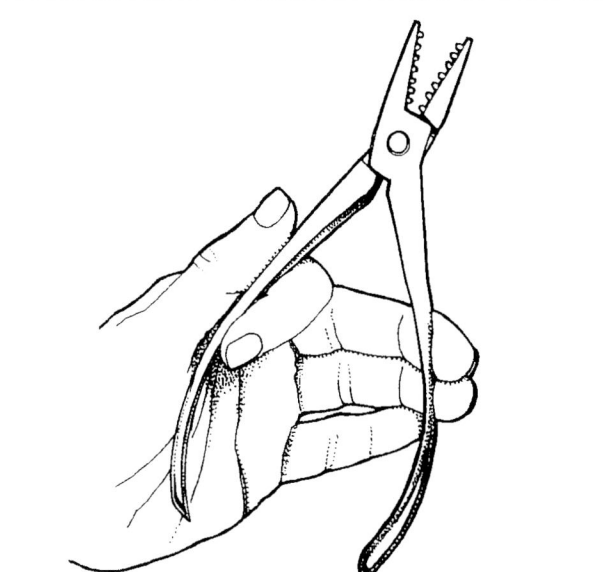

The correct way to use worming pliers is shown here, with one leg of the tool grasped firmly between thumb and forefinger, and the other leg swinging free inside the remaining fingers. These fingers are used to slam the free leg shut against the fixed leg once the worm's head is between the jaws of the pliers.

tiny and so close together that you would probably be looking at a thousand holes in a square metre of sand in a place with a healthy population. The worms seem to prefer dark sand that has some mud content, but you won't get them where there's more mud than sand. Squirt worms are difficult to care for, and if you just pump them and put them in a bucket they will wind themselves up into a tightly knit ball, falling apart when you try to sort them out later. One of the best systems I have seen for handling these worms involves the use of a wooden frame with a relatively fine wire mesh stretched across it. This is placed on a wet hessian bag, wire side up. As the worms are pumped, they are dumped onto the sieve, and for some reason known only to the worms, they crawl through the mesh of the sieve. This sorts them out, and once they are on the bag they seem content to crawl about instead of balling up. When you finish pumping, turn your box frame over and place the wet bag covered in worms inside it, then pop a second wet bag on top of the first to keep the worms fresh and cool.

Crabs are another outstanding bait that is readily available around much of our coastline. Estuary

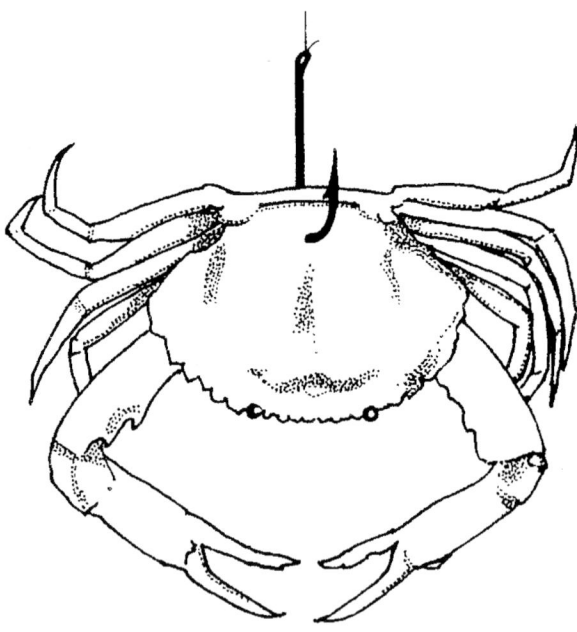

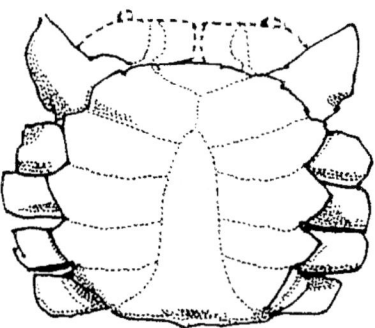

A live whole crab can make a very hot bait for a wide range of species, and this is the ideal way to hook the crab.

To fish crab sections, turn the crab over and remove the back shell by lifting the vee flap on the underside, then levering the whole back shell free. The crab's body is made up of two halves which in turn are formed from a series of sections terminating in the leg and claw sockets. You can bait up with either a half a crab or any number of sections individually threaded onto the hook. The latter is a great method when pickers are a nuisance, as it will take them a lot longer to take all the bait off the hook and this gives a bigger fish a chance to take it.

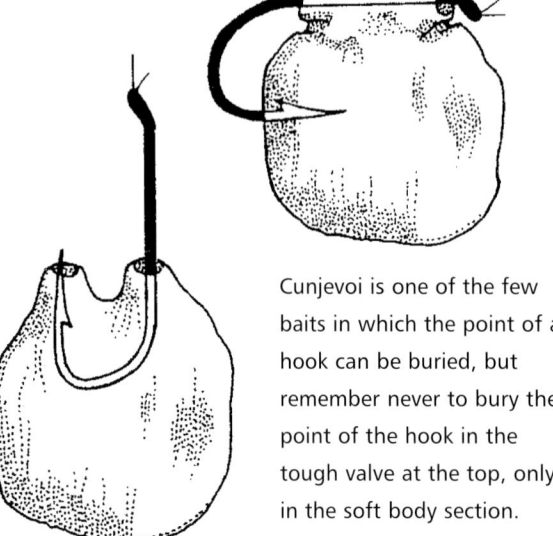

Cunjevoi is one of the few baits in which the point of a hook can be buried, but remember never to bury the point of the hook in the tough valve at the top, only in the soft body section.

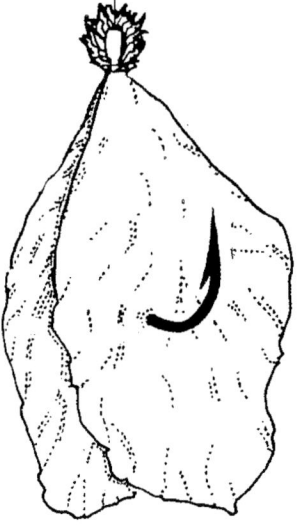

Luderick specialists have their individual quirks when it comes to baiting up with a leaf of cabbage, but this is the basic approach. An alternative would be to thread the leaf over the hook point once more. Note that the stem of the leaf is secured with a couple of half hitches of line below the eye of the hook.

anglers after the biggest whiting will often resort to tiny soldier crabs; the bigger crabs make great bream and snapper bait. Soldier crabs are easily caught on sandbanks at low tide as they come out of their holes to forage about for food.

Many different kinds of crabs are found around ocean rocks, and they all make good bait. East coast rock hoppers favour the red crabs that are always in the water during daylight hours but are rarely seen. They catch them by groping around blind in rock crevices until they feel one with their hand. Not everyone has the stomach for this, with green eels and blue-ringed octopuses also living in those same crevices. The alternative, and by far the easiest method of catching all the crabs found around the rocks, is to go out at night with a flashlight and a bucket. The crabs come right out onto the flat, weedy rocks in the dark. They usually just sit there once you turn the light on them, and are therefore easily captured. The best tide for this varies according to the terrain you are working, but I like a falling tide towards the middle of the run. Very few rock fish will pass up a live crab, or at least one that's fresh.

Cunjevoi is another great rock hopper standby. You will find cunjevoi growing in clumps at the low-tide mark around the rocks, and you will also often find it on pylons and the like. Inside the leathery pod you find a soft red body, attached by two tough valves to what looks like a circular lid on top of the pod. These valves and the meat immediately below them are the tough section you use for bait.

You need an old, heavy-bladed knife for collecting cunje: this is about the only time you will find one of those Rambo specials useful for anything. The simplest method is to drive the point of the knife into the centre of the cunje, midway between the top and bottom, then rotate the blade around until you virtually take off the head. Feel in the top section with your fingers and you will find those two tough valves, which you can then prise free of the lid of the tube. This is your bait, but there is still a lot of soft meat in the lower half of the shell attached to the rock. Pop this in a separate container, chop it up finely and use it for berley.

Small live fish of all kinds make great bait, and there is a great variety of baitfish available throughout the country. Where cast nets are legal, small mullet of all kinds are usually the preferred bait. Where the cast nets are not available, anglers catch their mullet in a variety of traps and bottles. Old fluorescent light tubes make great poddy mullet traps, as do large plastic fruit juice bottles with a small door cut in the side. Bait these with bread, and the poddy mullet will find the entrance sooner or later. Some days they can be incredibly frustrating about this, swimming around and around the bottle, apparently unable to locate the entrance: other days they will storm on in as if this were what they were born to do.

For other kinds of baitfish, such as yellowtail, slimy mackerel, herring and the like, bait jig strings are the way to go. These are normally sold with too many jigs on the string, and they soon find their way into a fine old tangle that will defy your best efforts to sort out. Most people cut them in half and use half the number of hooks – this results in more fish, as you then rarely have a tangle to waste time on.

The bait-collecting exercise can sometimes be more than half the fun of the game for the fishing family, and the smart fishing parent can do very well by associating the supply of pocket money with a supply of fresh bait from the kids.

Cunjevoi is a great bait for many of the rock species, but, unfortunately, hordes of rubbish fish are also very keen on it.

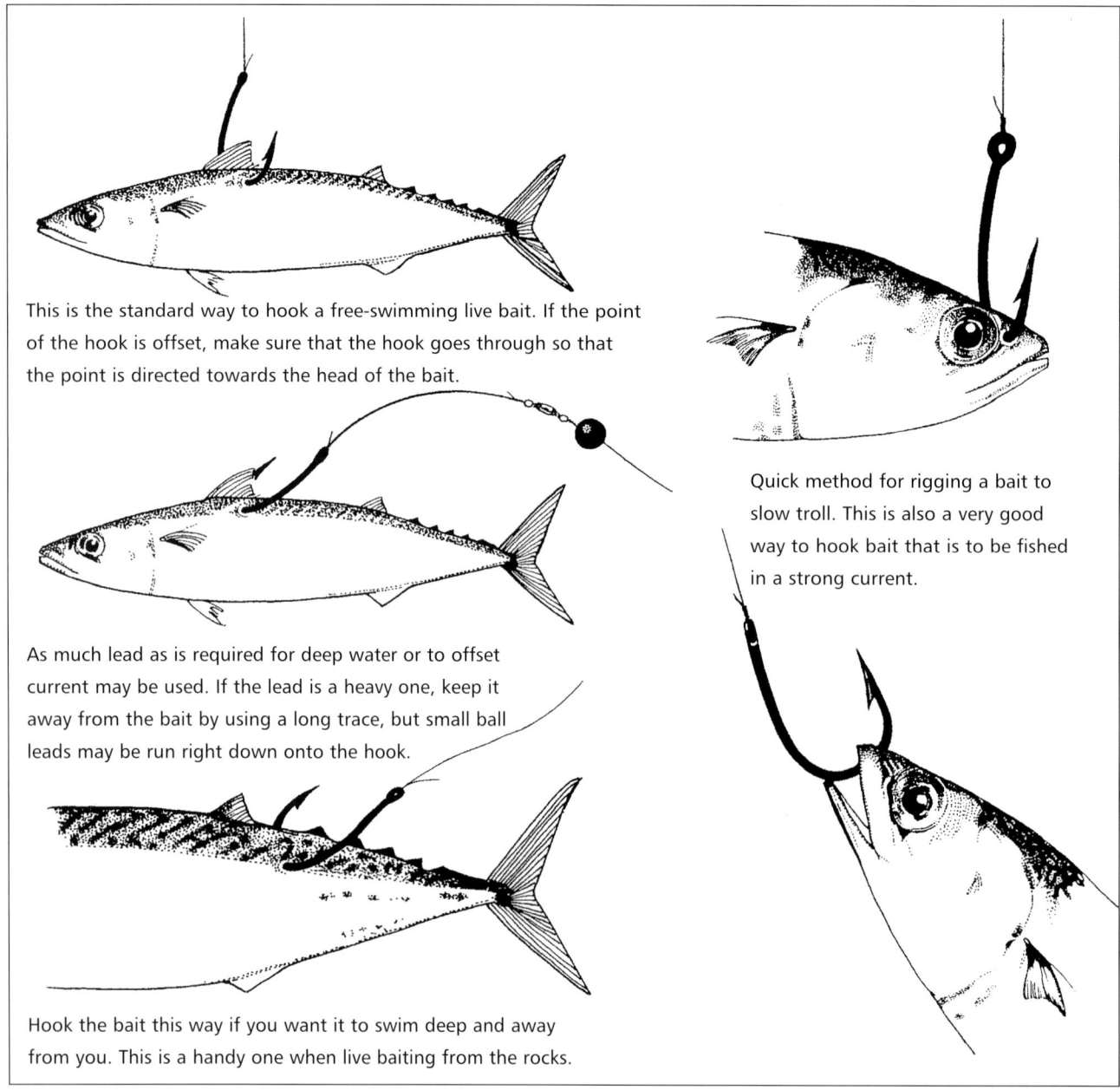

This is the standard way to hook a free-swimming live bait. If the point of the hook is offset, make sure that the hook goes through so that the point is directed towards the head of the bait.

As much lead as is required for deep water or to offset current may be used. If the lead is a heavy one, keep it away from the bait by using a long trace, but small ball leads may be run right down onto the hook.

Hook the bait this way if you want it to swim deep and away from you. This is a handy one when live baiting from the rocks.

Quick method for rigging a bait to slow troll. This is also a very good way to hook bait that is to be fished in a strong current.

Universal baits

Having said so much about using local bait in preference to anything else, there are a number of baits that are truly universal in their appeal. One of the best universal baits available on the east coast of Australia is the West Australian pilchard. Sydney Harbour prawns will also hold their own anywhere around the country. At Lord Howe Island the boats often use imported Californian squid for bait.

Most of the baitfish come under the heading of universal baits, as the majority of them can be caught right around the country. Octopus and squid come into the same category, as do the blue pilchard and most, but not all, of the garfish family. Garfish mounted on four- and five-hook rigs were once the hottest bait you could use right along the east coast of Australia. Fillets of garfish are also a superb bait for just about anything that eats other fish.

Now unless you catch them yourself, garfish are prohibitively expensive to use as bait, and their place has been taken by the pilchard. Pilchards are one of the ocean's great baitfish, and are a vital link in the food chain. They can be fished whole or ganged on a

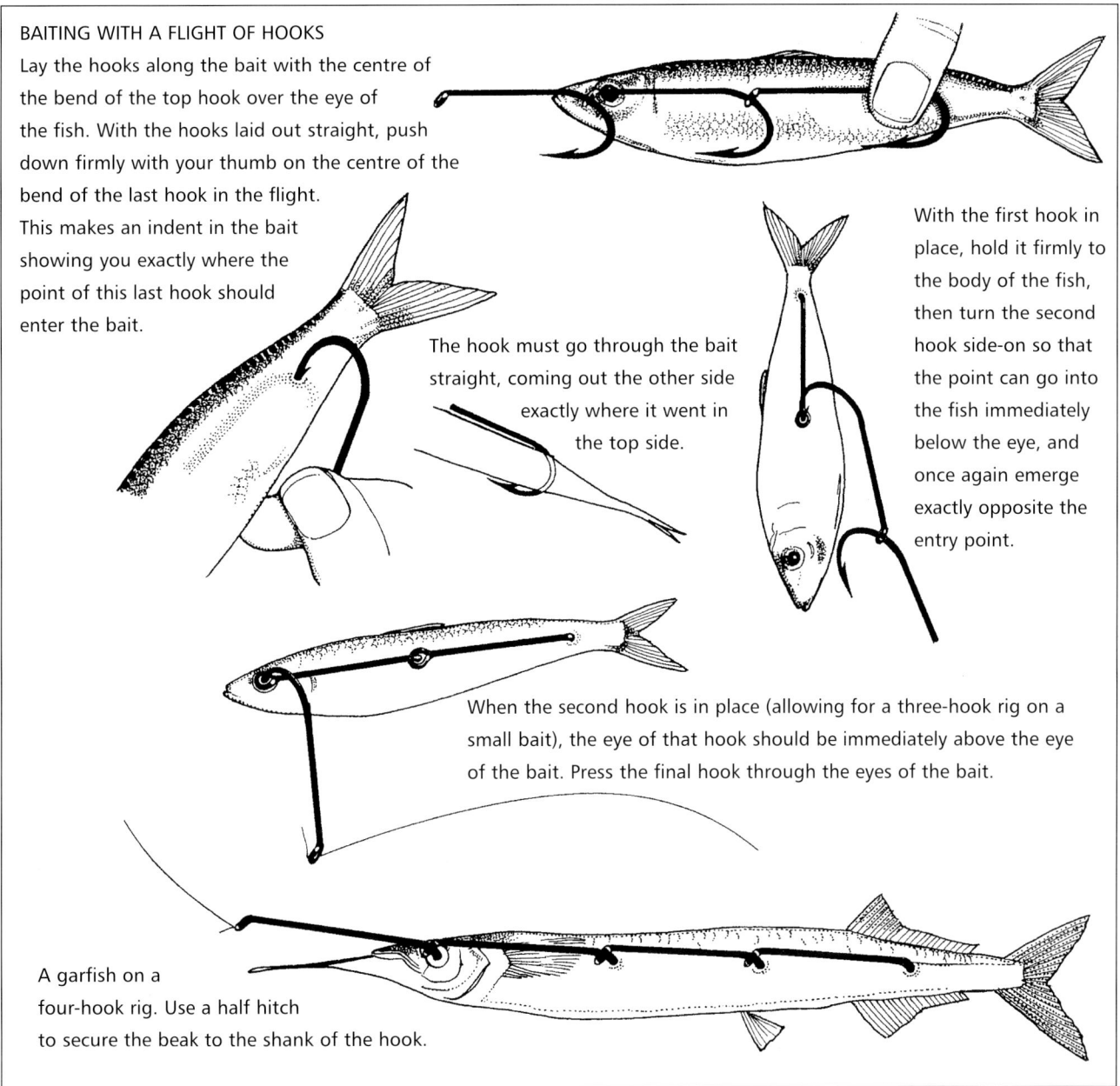

BAITING WITH A FLIGHT OF HOOKS
Lay the hooks along the bait with the centre of the bend of the top hook over the eye of the fish. With the hooks laid out straight, push down firmly with your thumb on the centre of the bend of the last hook in the flight. This makes an indent in the bait showing you exactly where the point of this last hook should enter the bait.

The hook must go through the bait straight, coming out the other side exactly where it went in the top side.

With the first hook in place, hold it firmly to the body of the fish, then turn the second hook side-on so that the point can go into the fish immediately below the eye, and once again emerge exactly opposite the entry point.

When the second hook is in place (allowing for a three-hook rig on a small bait), the eye of that hook should be immediately above the eye of the bait. Press the final hook through the eyes of the bait.

A garfish on a four-hook rig. Use a half hitch to secure the beak to the shank of the hook.

large single hook for any of the larger food fish, and when they are chunked or filleted they will account for anything that eats another fish. Lightly salted to firm them up a little, fine strips of pilchard can be mounted on extra-small linked hooks to take the smallest of predatory fish, such as whiting.

The whitebait is another of the truly universal baits, although it has never gained the acceptance with anglers that pilchards have achieved. Frozen packets of these little fish are available anywhere. They, too, account for just about anything that eats other fish. They can be fished on either a single large hook or a flight of tiny hooks, ganged as you would for a pilchard bait.

Mullet are one of the very best of all the fish baits, either fished live or as a strip bait. They do not keep very well, though, so you are better off using ones you catch yourself than anything out of a fish shop. Certainly never buy mullet from a bait shop unless you know the operator is getting fresh stock that is in good shape. Mullet don't freeze well at all.

Almost any of the fish with a high blood content make excellent strip baits. This group includes tailor, slimy mackerel and most of the tunas. If you don't use them fresh they are best salted before freezing.

If you are fishing regularly, it is sometimes a good idea to keep a brine bin going, especially if you are going to be reef fishing from a boat. A nappy bucket with a sealing lid is good for this. You simply take the fillets off any baitfish you troll up as you go along, and toss in a handful of salt with each lot of fillets, making sure you get plenty of salt all over the first fillets that go in. The salt leaches the blood and moisture out of the fish flesh and this mixture soon turns into a very salty brine which preserves the fish and makes the flesh rather tough.

When you have a good supply of any kind of bait on hand it is a good idea to package it in small quantities before you try to freeze or store it. It is better to have to take two or three small packages out with you than to have to defrost a large amount of bait when you only need a small quantity. Trial and error will show you which baits can be frozen successfully, but all bait will handle freezing better if you freeze it in a saltwater solution. Plastic ice-cream containers are ideal for this. Make a powerful salt and water mix in the container, then add your bait. If you are taking an Esky out with you, the bait blocks can provide some of your ice for the trip.

Rock anglers need to keep the weight of their gear down and will not want to be carrying blocks of ice around. In their case the bait should be salted for a couple of hours before freezing. The bait lasts a lot longer after defrosting if you do.

HOMEMADE BAIT

Bream anglers are great innovators, and many of them use strange home-brewed concoctions to catch their fish. Plain flour dough is usually the basic binding ingredient, and such exotic elements as garlic sausage

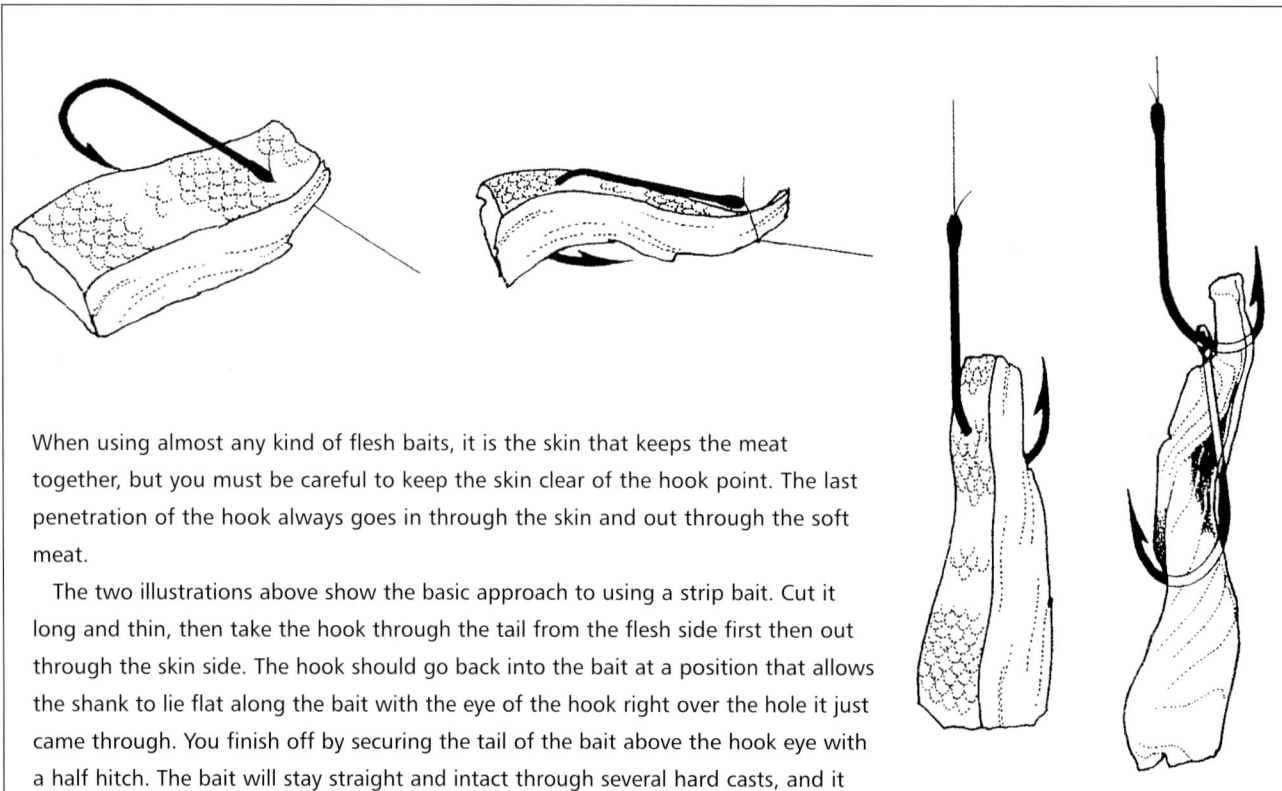

When using almost any kind of flesh baits, it is the skin that keeps the meat together, but you must be careful to keep the skin clear of the hook point. The last penetration of the hook always goes in through the skin and out through the soft meat.

The two illustrations above show the basic approach to using a strip bait. Cut it long and thin, then take the hook through the tail from the flesh side first then out through the skin side. The hook should go back into the bait at a position that allows the shank to lie flat along the bait with the eye of the hook right over the hole it just came through. You finish off by securing the tail of the bait above the hook eye with a half hitch. The bait will stay straight and intact through several hard casts, and it will also stay away from the point of the hook if small fish pick at it. **RIGHT** This is a good way to present a snapper bait – especially a floating bait. The illustration shows a large hook in use, but don't hesitate to go down to small, strong hooks for sensitive fish. A fish will virtually inhale a nice slim bait like this, so the hook only needs to be through a solid piece of skin right at the tail of the bait to do its job. **FAR RIGHT** The back-to-back rig is a popular way of presenting a big strip bait for mulloway.

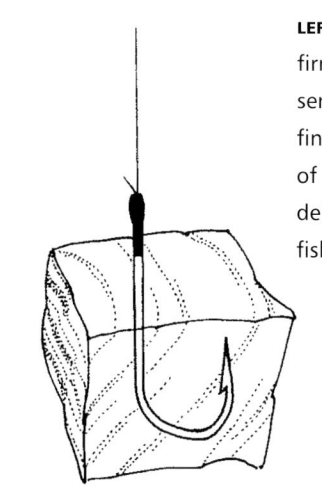

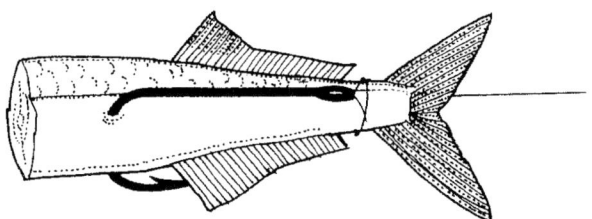

LEFT Cubes like this are most often used when fishing for yellowfin, but if you have some nice firm baits available, such as large slabs of tuna, it can be another effective way to bait for sensitive fish. Keep the hook size up in relation to the size of the cube, as a tiny hook may not find its way through the meat to make contact with the fish. **BELOW** This is one of a number of methods of baiting with sections of small fish. If garfish are being used, the soft flesh and delicate skin allows the point of the hook to be buried just under the skin, and this bait can be fished right into kelp beds and other places where an exposed hook would be a nuisance.

and cheddar cheese find their way into the mix. White loaf bread is a popular item on the menu with bream, trevally, garfish, rock blackfish and a number of other species. Chook gut goes through periods of popularity, as does chopped liver.

BERLEY

Berley has been covered in detail in Chapter 3, 'Fish-finding techniques', but I will touch on it here because the use of berley sometimes has a good deal to do with how well your bait works. Contrary to what most anglers would like to believe, fish are not always hungry. This leaves you with two options. Either you can go to the trouble of working out just when fish will be actively feeding and only fish at those times, or you can come up with a system to make fish feed when they are not hungry. In the latter case, berley is the answer.

A few fish darting around snapping up berley scraps will prod other fish into action. Once they are all on the job and starting to compete, much of the selectivity will go out of their attitude towards food.

The relationship of berley to bait varies greatly from fish to fish. You can berley bream on wheat and catch them on prawns, but if you are berleying yellowfin with pilchard chunks you may need a pilchard on the hook to get a strike. Sensitivity in fish varies a great deal from species to species, and any given species may vary greatly in behaviour from place to place. Whatever the situation, your bait will work best for you if the fish are stimulated by the presence of berley of some kind.

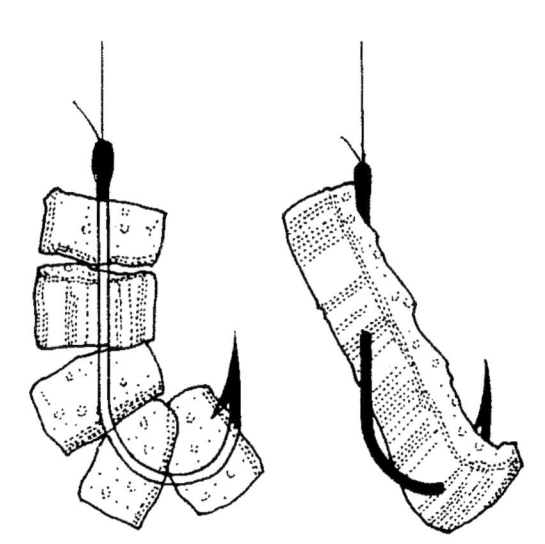

ABOVE LEFT This is a system of baiting with bread crust, but you can use it with other baits when small fish are tearing baits off the hook before bigger fish can get a look-in. The idea with bread is that some of the baits may soak off but the toughest will remain on the hook longer.

ABOVE RIGHT An alternative method of baiting with crust. The best bread baits come off the rubbery top crust of a regular sandwich milk loaf. You should remove these from the bread before fishing and keep them in a cool spot to avoid the bread drying out and going brittle.

Chapter Five

The basic rigs

Knots and connections

We need to get a little ahead of ourselves here. In the next chapter, on 'Fishing Tackle', we will get into the subject of fishing lines in depth, but we need to deal with lines in brief at this point as the development of new types of fishing line has changed some of the basics in the knot-tying department.

New lines based on new technology are appearing on an almost weekly basis, but for our immediate purpose, discussing knots and rigs, we need to know just a little about braided and fused gelspun (GSP) lines and copolymer (advanced monofilament) lines. The gelspuns are of most interest, because they don't look, feel or act like any fishing line that has gone before. Most importantly, they have diameters of around one-third to one-half of that required to achieve any given breaking strain in monofilament lines.

The early gelspuns would simply not work with many of the knots fishermen have used over the years, and some of the knots developed for these new lines have been as hard to figure out as advanced Chinese puzzles. In the lower breaking strains they are so fine as to become a real pain in the neck to knot in a bit of wind and low light.

Most manufacturers supply instructions in each package of line as to what knot they prefer to be used, and these seem to vary from brand to brand. I suggest that you try the knots they recommend and see if they work for you. In the meantime, those knots suited to gelspun lines are noted here.

Having said all that, as this is being written new gelspun braids are appearing that seem to accept the knots used on mono and copolymer lines.

The line-to-line connections shown here are very important, as the gelspuns are normally used with a length of either monofilament or special-purpose leader materials. Unless you are using a very high breaking strain gelspun line, there could be considerable discrepancy between the diameter of the line and the trace, which means that you should double the tying end of the gelspun when doing the knots. Many fishermen use superglue on the finished knot to ensure that everything holds together, but this is not always effective, as some gelspun surfaces do not bond with the glue – or anything else, for that matter.

Keep in mind that your tackle will only be as strong as the weakest link in the system, and that is nearly always the point at which you make connections with your line. All knots reduce the breaking strain of the line to some degree, and badly tied knots will weaken things even further.

Many very good knots are ruined when they are snugged down tight. Don't just yank on a knot until it won't go any further. Put your knot together loosely, then begin to snug it down, usually by pulling standing and tag ends alternately, depending on the knot. When the knot is ready to tighten, wet it with plenty of saliva to avoid damage from the considerable friction that can be generated as monofilament is placed under pressure.

There are literally hundreds of knots and connections available to anglers, many of them highly specialised. Knots and connections also tend to evolve as technology produces different types of lines and traces. The knots we present here are the basics, but they cover over 90 per cent of the fishing done in this country and are relatively simple knots to tie. If you wish to go into this further, there are many excellent books available on the subject.

ALBRIGHT KNOT
The Albright knot is used to connect two pieces of line with greatly varying diameters. It is most commonly used to connect very heavy mono trace to a main line or double. Note that it is the heavy line that forms the receiving loop and the light line must exit the same side of the loop from which it originally entered. Wet the knot thoroughly and then snug it down with some care. Test the knot with plenty of pressure before using.

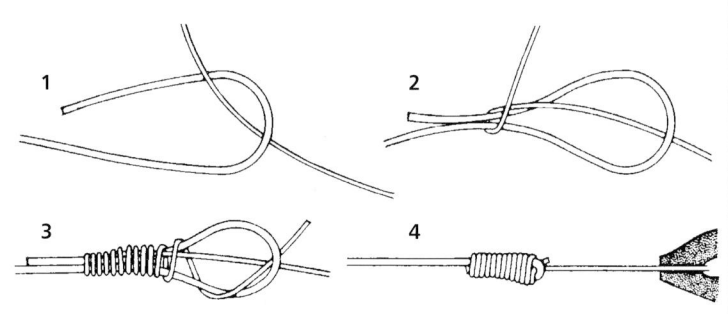

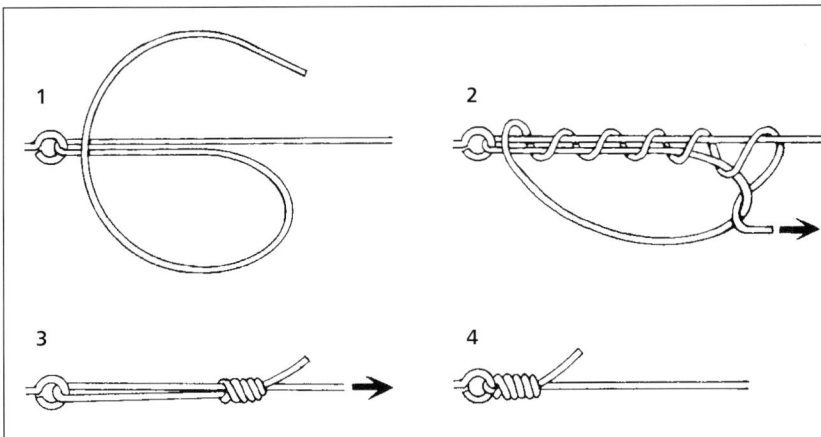

THE UNI KNOT

The Uni knot is a particularly useful knot for connecting hooks, swivels and rings, and can even be used as a sliding loop to attach line to a reel spool.

Instead of turning through the eye of the hook to tie the knot along the standing part of the line as shown here, you can take the tag end right through and reverse the loop to tie the knot along the shank of the hook, thus effectively snelling the hook.

You can also use this knot in very heavy line by reducing the number of turns through the loop to three instead of five.

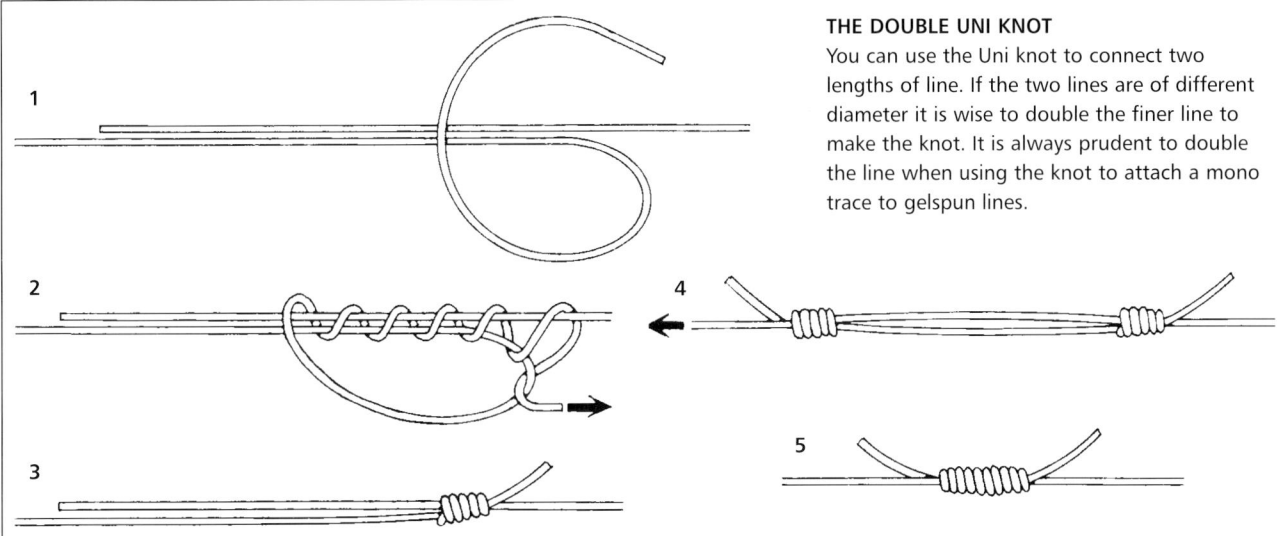

THE DOUBLE UNI KNOT

You can use the Uni knot to connect two lengths of line. If the two lines are of different diameter it is wise to double the finer line to make the knot. It is always prudent to double the line when using the knot to attach a mono trace to gelspun lines.

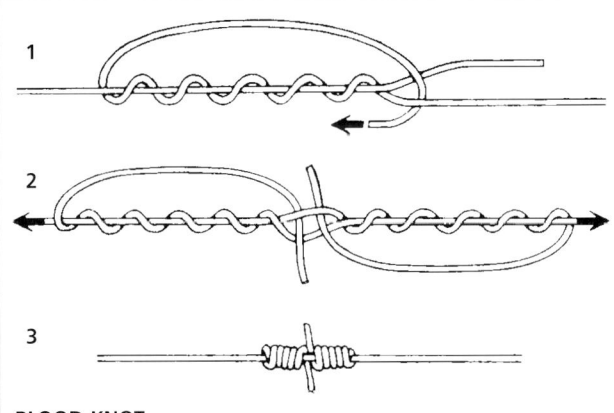

BLOOD KNOT

The blood knot is the standard method for tying two lengths of line together. Properly tied it can be snugged down into a very compact knot that will travel well through the rod guides. This makes it useful for attaching casting shock traces. You can also use this knot to connect a new length of line to old to top up a reel. This knot is also useful with some of the newer GSP lines.

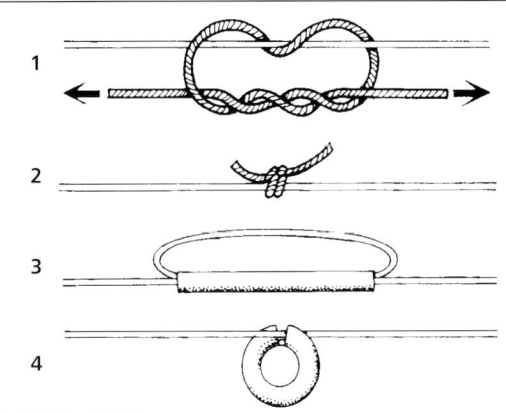

STOPPER KNOT

A stopper knot is a handy way of setting depth for a running float or bobby cork. The knot is usually tied with wool, which bulks up well, but if you get into the habit of placing a bead with a small internal diameter on the line above the float, even the limited bulk of a knot tied with mono will do the job.

The stopper made up from a small piece of soft plastic or valve tubing is very good because it is easily adjustable.

BIMINI TWIST

This is the preferred method of forming a double. It can be fairly easily tied by one person with a bit of practice, but it is easier for two people to tie, especially when a long double is required.

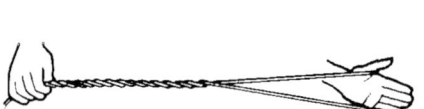

1: Measure a little more than twice the footage for the double line. Bring the end back to the standing line, then rotate the loop end 20 times in mono or 30-50 times if using gelspun lines.

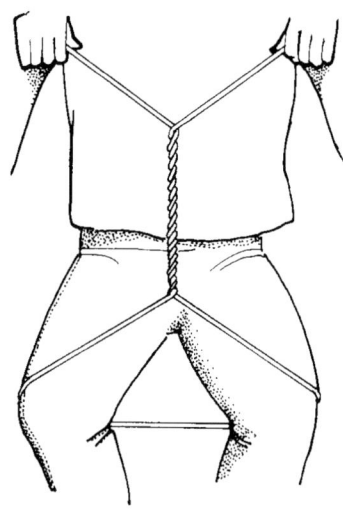

2: Spread the loop which forces together the twists to about 25 to 30 cm below the tag end. Step both feet through the loop and bring it together around the knees so pressure can be placed on the column of twists by spreading knees apart.

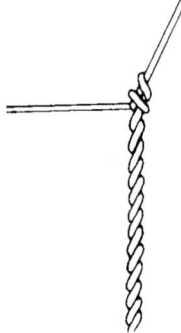

3: With twists forced tightly together, hold the standing line in one hand with tension just slightly off the vertical position. With your other hand move the standing end to a position at right angles to the twists. Keeping tension on the loop with your knees, gradually ease the tension off the tag end so it will roll back over the column of twists, beginning just below the upper twist.

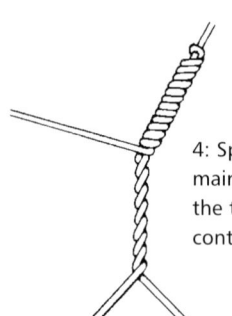

4: Spread your legs slowly apart to maintain pressure on the loop. Steer the tag end into a tight spiral coil as it continues to roll over the twist.

5: When the spiral end of the tag has rolled over the column of twists, continue keeping knee pressure on the loop and move the hand which has held the standing line down to grasp the knot. Place a finger in the crotch of line where the loop joins the knot, to prevent slippage of the last turn. Take a half hitch with the tag end around the nearest leg of loop and pull it up tight.

6: You can finish this off with another half hitch around the other leg, then a series of hitches around both legs to lock the knot. A preferred alternative is the one illustrated here where you take a loose hitch over both legs after the first leg has been locked, but you leave it slack. Then take two more turns – not hitches – around both legs of the loop, winding inside the bend of line formed by the loose half hitch and towards the main knot.

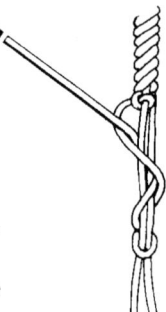

7: Pull on the tag end slowly to force the three loops to gather neatly into a spiral.

IMPROVED CLINCH KNOT

The improved clinch knot is a standard that many anglers use for connecting their hooks, swivels and rings. It is simple to tie and very reliable.

1

2

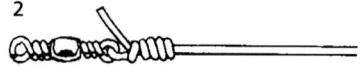

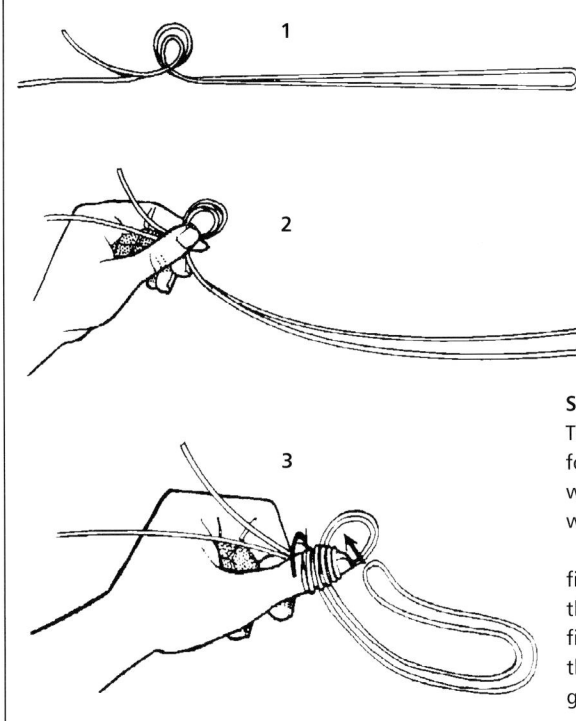

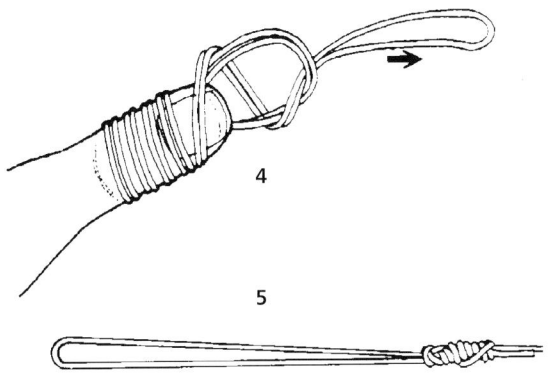

SPIDER HITCH

The spider hitch lacks the strength of the Bimini twist, but it is adequate for sportfishing situations with line to 15 kg. It is quick and easy to tie which makes it an attractive way to form a double for some situations where line is not being pushed to critical limits.

You form a loop in the doubled line then hold this between thumb and first finger. Take five turns of the doubled line over the thumb and loop, then pass the end of the double out through the loop held between finger and thumb. Keeping a light pressure on the loop, steadily pull on the end of the double, lifting the turns off the thumb one at a time and gently drawing them down tight. A little practice will get it right.

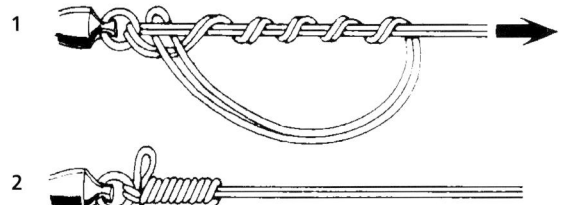

QUICK-CHANGE DOUBLE KNOT

This is a simple way of tying a double directly to a swivel or ring. Only use this when you want to keep changing the terminal tackle to which the double is attached without having to cut the double. By plucking at the knot you can draw it back up the double enough to undo the knot the same way it was made.

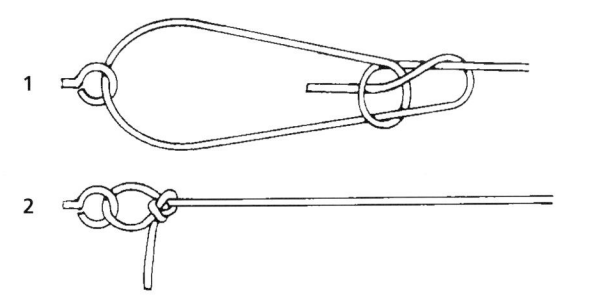

LURE QUICK CHANGE

A handy one when fishing with heavy mono trace, the bowline is easy to tie and provides a good loop for lure connections.

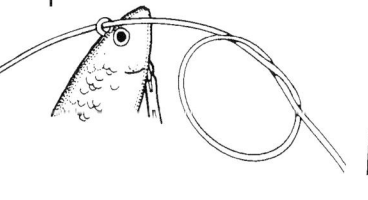

HOMER RHODE LOOP

A more traditional method of forming a loop to a lure eye, this one works well with plastic-coated wire and heavy monofilament. When you close that first overhead knot, make sure you have the lure in one hand and both the tag and standing parts of the line together in the other hand. Take care where you form the second overhead knot, for that is where the finished knot will form, thus determining the size of loop you end up with. Pull the second knot tight, then with the lure in one hand and the standing line in the other, draw them apart and the first knot will slide up to lock on the second to form the loop.

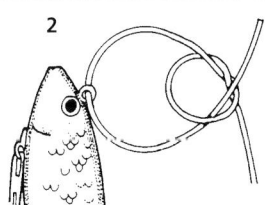

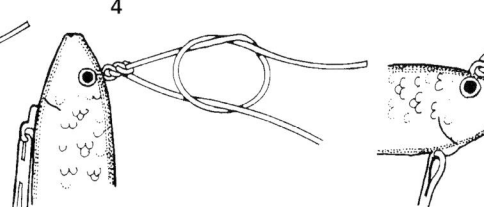

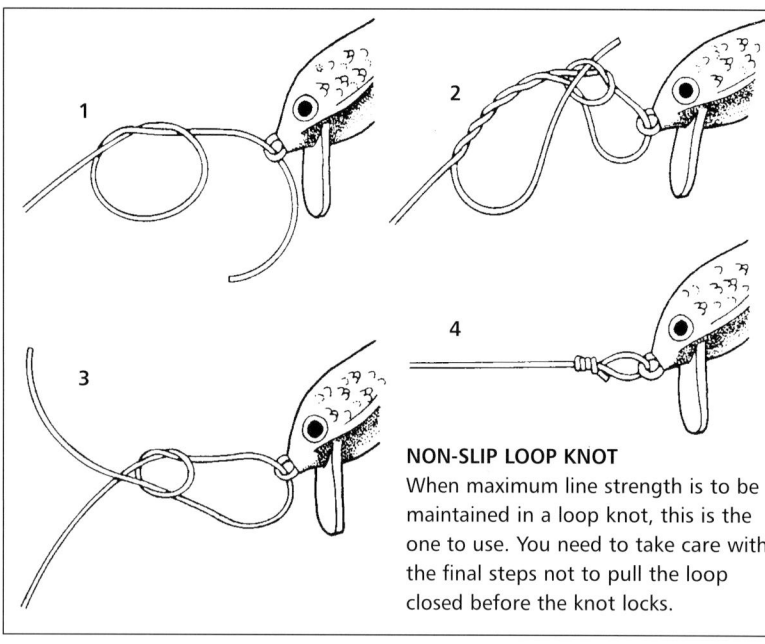

NON-SLIP LOOP KNOT

When maximum line strength is to be maintained in a loop knot, this is the one to use. You need to take care with the final steps not to pull the loop closed before the knot locks.

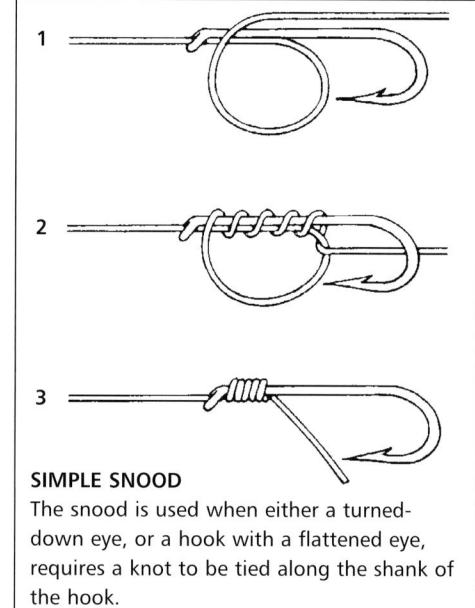

SIMPLE SNOOD

The snood is used when either a turned-down eye, or a hook with a flattened eye, requires a knot to be tied along the shank of the hook.

CABLE CONNECTIONS

To make connections with multi-strand wire or cable, you need to have a crimping tool and the right sized sleeves for the wire in use. Further care needs to be taken that the right part of the crimping tool is selected to lock the sleeves on the wire.

You have to remember to slide the sleeves on the wire before it goes through the eye of the hook or swivel, and to keep the sleeves at least 3 cm apart when locked.

Another similar loop can be formed in the other end of the leader which can connect to the double with a snap.

In waters where mackerel and wahoo are about, it is worth locking on a crimp some half a metre or so before the end of the cable. This stops the lure sliding all the way up the trace to the mono connection when fighting a fish, and reduces the chance of a wahoo trying to hit the lure and biting through the mono at the same time.

It pays to keep an eye on terminal tackle developments as there are all sorts of small extras coming onto the market that can streamline and improve terminal rigs, such as plastic sleeves you can slide over the cable loops to eliminate abrasion.

HEAVY MONO CONNECTIONS

When trolling heads are to be rigged without wire, the same method of rigging is used with special heavy-duty mono materials. This is usually a very hard skinned line designed to offer maximum abrasion resistance and to handle crimping without losing too much strength.

Many anglers these days prefer to buy their skirted trolling heads already pre-rigged by professionals.

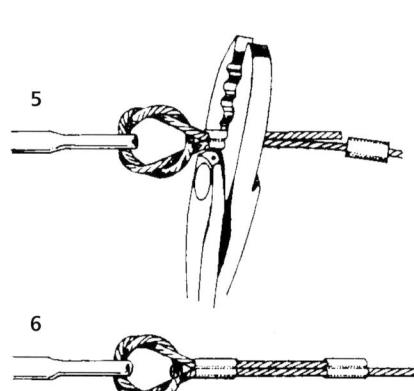

THE HAYWIRE TWIST

Good wire men get every haywire twist as neat as the one shown in the illustration, but that takes a bit of practice. The haywire is used with single-strand wire, and the last step where you form a little crank to break off the tag end is quite important. If you just clip the end of the wire with pliers, a small stub is left standing out from the tie, and this can cause some nasty cuts to the hands. The crank causes the wire to snap off flush to the turns without any protrusions.

Nylon-coated wire used with light tackle can be fixed by taking several turns of the tag end over the standing part, then melting the plastic with a match or lighter flame. Both parts fuse together when the melted plastic cools.

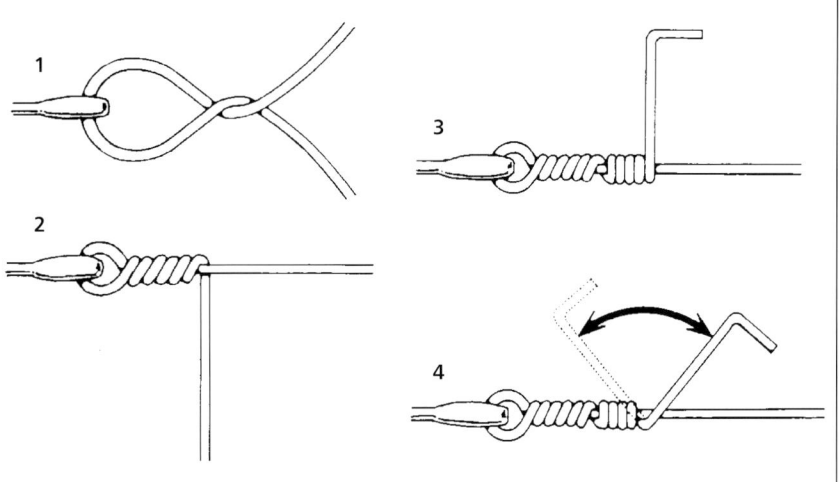

PALOMAR KNOT

One of the strongest, most durable and simplest knots to tie, the Palomar is recommended for almost any situation short of extremely heavy trace or leader line. It is an excellent knot for braided line as well.
1: Double about 15 cm of line and pass it through the eye of the hook.
2: Form an overhand knot.
3: Pass the hook, lure or swivel through the loop.
4: Tighten the knot and trim the tag end. Make sure the two lines in the eye are parallel. If they are crossed, cut the knot and re-tie.

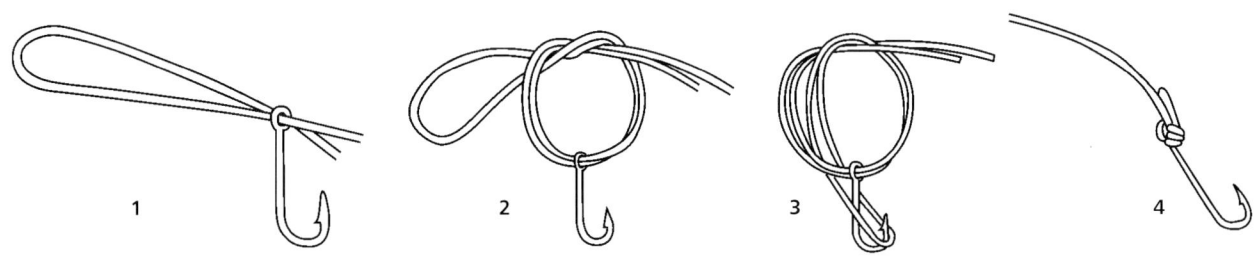

SURGEON'S KNOT

Yet another relatively simple way to join lengths of line of different diameter

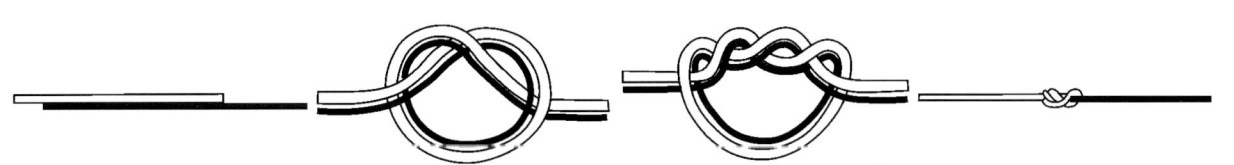

DOUBLE IMPROVED CLINCH KNOT

A knot of greater strength that is useful when tackle is to be pushed to the max.

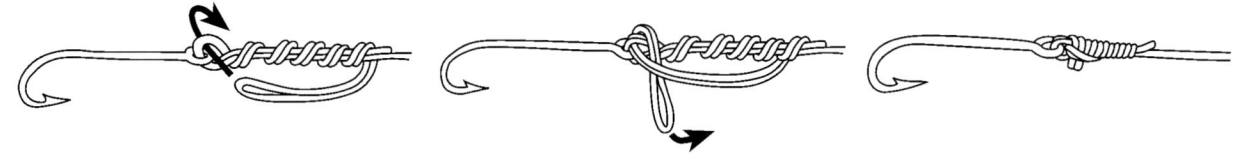

Basic rigs

The perfect rig is an unweighted line running straight through to a sharp hook: there's an absolute minimum of bulk to arouse the suspicions of a sharp-eyed fish, and nothing more than the drag of water on line to give away the fact that the bait is anything other than a completely natural offering.

In its purest sense, the line would be so fine that it could not be seen, it would create no friction drag through the water, and the hook would be so small that it barely altered the natural sink rate of the bait. It would be hard to imagine anything more that one could do to make an offering more natural.

It is also, unfortunately, quite difficult to imagine a fishing situation in which such a perfect rig would be a practical item of tackle. Larger hooks would be required, and almost any line that would be practical in salt water would have enough diameter to be affected to some degree by wind and water movement. So we have already begun the process of degrading our perfect rig by making it vulnerable to friction, easier to see and adding weight in the form of a heavy hook.

The weight of a hook can make a big difference when you are trying to make a floating bait look just like a free-drifting chunk in a berley stream, and it can also count for a lot when you are casting unweighted baits into a wash. The less weight in the hook(s), the longer that bait will be washing about between surface and bottom seeking out fish.

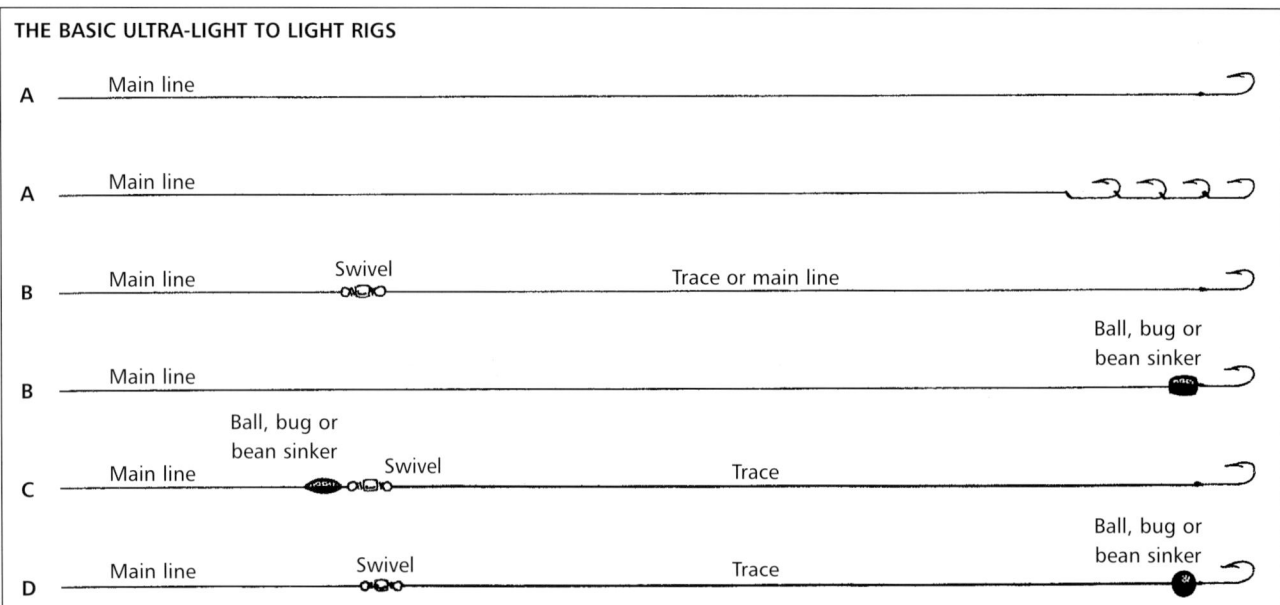

THE BASIC ULTRA-LIGHT TO LIGHT RIGS

A — Main line

A — Main line

B — Main line — Swivel — Trace or main line

B — Main line — Ball, bug or bean sinker

C — Main line — Ball, bug or bean sinker — Swivel — Trace

D — Main line — Swivel — Trace — Ball, bug or bean sinker

Rig A is our perfect rig. The hook, razor sharp and the smallest that will do the job, and the line as fine as the situation will allow. It is, in fact, the perfect floating bait rig. An alternative would be the multi-hook approach when a whole fish of some kind is being presented.

Rig B has a swivel added to the rig to keep twist out of a line being used with a sidecast or perhaps a threadline reel. A lead running right down onto the hook is used to control sink rate in turbulent water or air conditions, and this lead will be the absolute minimum that will do the job. If you want the bait to move on the bottom, use a ball that can roll, and if you want it to stay still, use a flat-sided bug.

Rig C has the swivel being used as a stopper to keep the lead away from the hook. You might do this because the lead is too big and you think it is creating a visual problem there. You might also take the lead away from the hook because you want to use lead to cast, or to keep your bait in a general area, without the bait anchoring to the bottom. So far, we have compensated the handicap of the lead to some degree by using a running sinker that the line can flow through. Take care that you don't have a situation where a small swivel can jam and lock in the hole in the sinker. Also, if you are using a sidecast reel, you will need to have another swivel above the lead.

Rig D is for a situation where the swivel is required to control twist and a small lead is used right on the hook to control sink rate. The lead on the hook is also useful when fishing a rough bottom, and in turbulent water where fish have to grab a bait on the run. If you rig this way, a hook snagged on a rocky bottom can often be freed by bouncing the lead against the hook with a series of flicks of the rod tip. A bean is the most commonly used lead in this situation as it rolls about less than a ball.

DEALING WITH WEIGHT AND ROUGH WATER

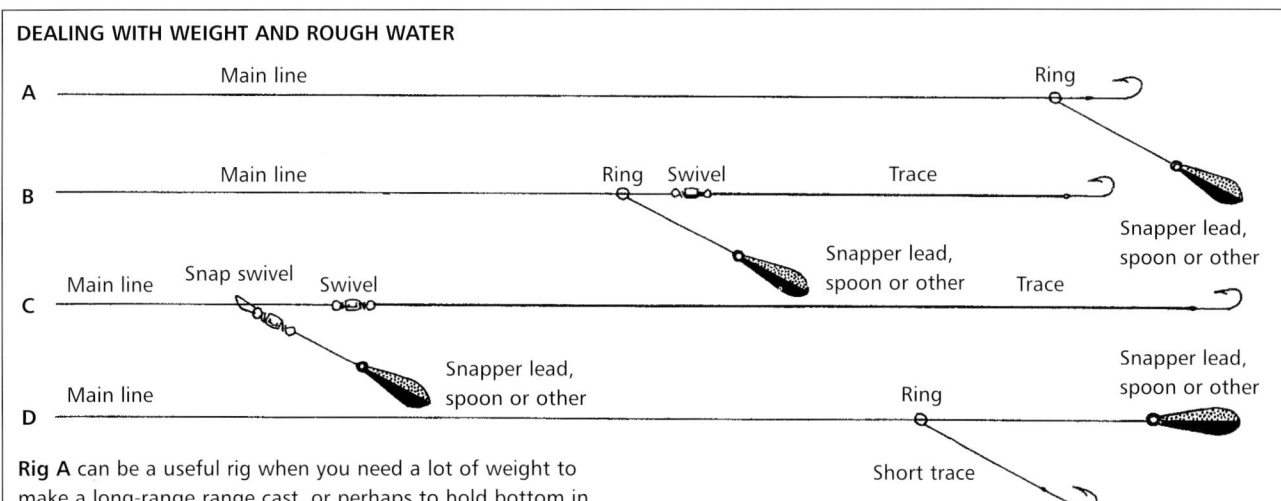

Rig A can be a useful rig when you need a lot of weight to make a long-range range cast, or perhaps to hold bottom in very rough water off a beach, and you are dealing with weight-shy fish that will drop the bait if they feel resistance. The ring slides right to the eye of the hook allowing the weight to lead the bait and minimise the potential for a tangled trace. You need to take care that the ring is too small to go over the eye of the hook, and may even want to slip a small bead on the line between hook and ring to make sure of this. Sidecast users need to have a swivel well up above the hook.

Rig B is another version of the same thing but allows for the use of a trace finer than the main line. You might use this when a heavy line is required for hard casting with a heavy weight, but you still want a fine trace for bait presentation to sensitive fish. Obviously, you need to keep that light trace in mind when hooking and fighting fish.

Rig C is yet another variation on the theme, but this time a clip swivel is used to enable a quick weight change. The idea is that you set up a series of weights with short traces to a clip swivel, and simply clip on the weight you want. This is an ideal way to

go if you find yourself fishing a tidal run that may vary in intensity during the fishing session. You never want to have more lead on than you need, so whenever you find your lead failing to keep up with the run of the tide, you change up to a heavier lead – it takes seconds instead of the minutes involved in tying knots.

Rig D is unusual but handy. It is called the slider and is used by some smart live bait anglers, especially when fishing from a height. The lead is cast, pretty much leaving the bait behind as the line runs through the ring, then the bait comes down on the surface and slowly sinks, much the same as the 'floaters' used by boat anglers. An even better option is to have the bait on a clip swivel, cast without it on the line, then clip it on and let it slide down to the water. The rig is also used over a bad bottom: a ring is tied to the end of a heavy line, then a slightly lighter trace is used down to the sinker which can be broken away when a fish takes the bait.

The drag created by water friction on fishing line can be enough to make a shy fish reject a bait. The more we add to our perfect rig, the smarter we are going to have to be to neutralise the adverse effects of these additions. Getting back as close as we can to that perfect rig is what smart rigging is all about.

It is standard practice in fishing books to give all sorts of measurements for traces, but I can't see much logic in that. I don't think I've ever tied two traces the same length in my life, and I tend to do everything according to the way I feel about the conditions at the time. In still, clear water, I might use a very long, light trace away from the lead, then the next day chasing the same fish I might fish the main line straight through and run the lead right down to the hook. You have to learn to think about the situation in front of you, consider what you think you want to do about it, then

take one of the rigs you see here and modify it to suit your needs.

Lead size and shape is determined by the conditions from hour to hour, and I find I use all sorts of hooks according to the type of bait I am presenting, where I am presenting it, and the mood of the fish on the day. If fish are rejecting your baits, or fiddling with them, try going down to what may seem a ridiculously small hook and get as much of that hook as you can inside the bait with just the point standing free. This may or may not fix the problem, but it is an option well worth trying. In heavily fished parts of California they sometimes go down to No. 4 hooks for quite large fish such as tuna and yellowtail kingfish, and it takes the combination of such a tiny hook and the liveliest live bait to get a bite. Things aren't that bad here yet, but it does show that subtlety can pay

LIVE BAIT RIGS

A — Free swimming rig

B — Bubble float — Balloon — Small lead

Light trace — Ring — Ball trace

C

Stopper knot — Bead — Bobby cork

D

Boat anglers can return to the perfect rig (**Rig A**) to fish a live bait. Heavy traces are often used when fishing for big fish, such as yellowfin, but on quiet days with clear water, it may be better to fish 15 kg line straight through to the hook.

Rig B is a good way to use a tidal run to work a small live bait, especially for flathead. You use just enough lead to get the bait down to the bottom, and the float can be anything that is easily adjustable. Adjust the float so that the bait is just off the bottom, then allow the float to drag the bait along with the tide as you walk the bank beside it. It won't matter if the bottom varies and your bait is well off the bottom at times, as a flathead will hear it long before he sees it and come up looking for the meal. Give the fish plenty of time to swallow the bait. Balloons are used a lot when live baiting from the rocks (**Rig C**), and they can also be used to suspend a bait at a fixed depth

when fishing from a boat. A balloon can be tied to a ring or straight onto the main line, and offers the advantage that it will burst when a big fish dives, thus leaving the line unencumbered. Some of the game fish create so much drag on a conventional float it can contribute to tearing a hook loose.

Rig D is the alternative bobby cork rig, often favoured when a bait needs to be cast. A big float is capable of suspending quite a heavy lead, and so the angler can enjoy the benefit of a heavy casting weight and a floating bait in the same rig. Always try to ballast a cork with the maximum amount of lead it will carry and still float, as this reduces resistance when a fish takes the bait. Use a small bead above the cork to ensure that the stopper knot does not slide down into the eye of the cork, or use a short piece of inner tube with the line passed through twice as a more bulky stopper.

off. Fish are nowhere near as dumb as it might suit us to think they are.

Keep in mind that the only real bream rig worth knowing about is the one that is working for you right now, and if nobody has ever fished for bream that way before, congratulations! You have just become a thinking angler, and that makes you a good angler.

MULTIPLE HOOKS

Multiple-hook rigs came into vogue with sidecast users, who ran up flights of four and five connected hooks on which they mounted quite large, whole garfish baits. Later pilchards became the common casting bait using three-hook flights and smaller hook sizes.

Perhaps because the whole system came into being to deliver what were virtually unweighted baits, where the bait itself needed to be large enough to be cast, a

lot of anglers have not explored the great possibilities associated with multiple-hook rigs of all sizes.

If we turn the system around and say that the bait no longer has to be the casting weight, we can start using tiny whole fish baits and strips on three- and four-hook rigs, and we can also go down on hook size and use six hooks if we want to and put a whole lot of tiny points in a reasonable sized bait. Why do it? The answer is that these baits have the wonderful advantage of being able to hook and hold everything from a whiting through to a big flathead or tailor. That can be a great benefit when fishing a spot where a real mixture of species has you scratching your head as to just how you should rig.

People have all sorts of ways of making up multiple-hook rigs, and there are hooks such as the Mustad 4202 'open eyes' made for just this purpose. Alternatively you might go for Mustad 8260s. The hooks need to be straight, not kirbed or reversed, and the eye of the hook needs to be bent down with pliers to an angle of 45°.

FLOAT RIGS

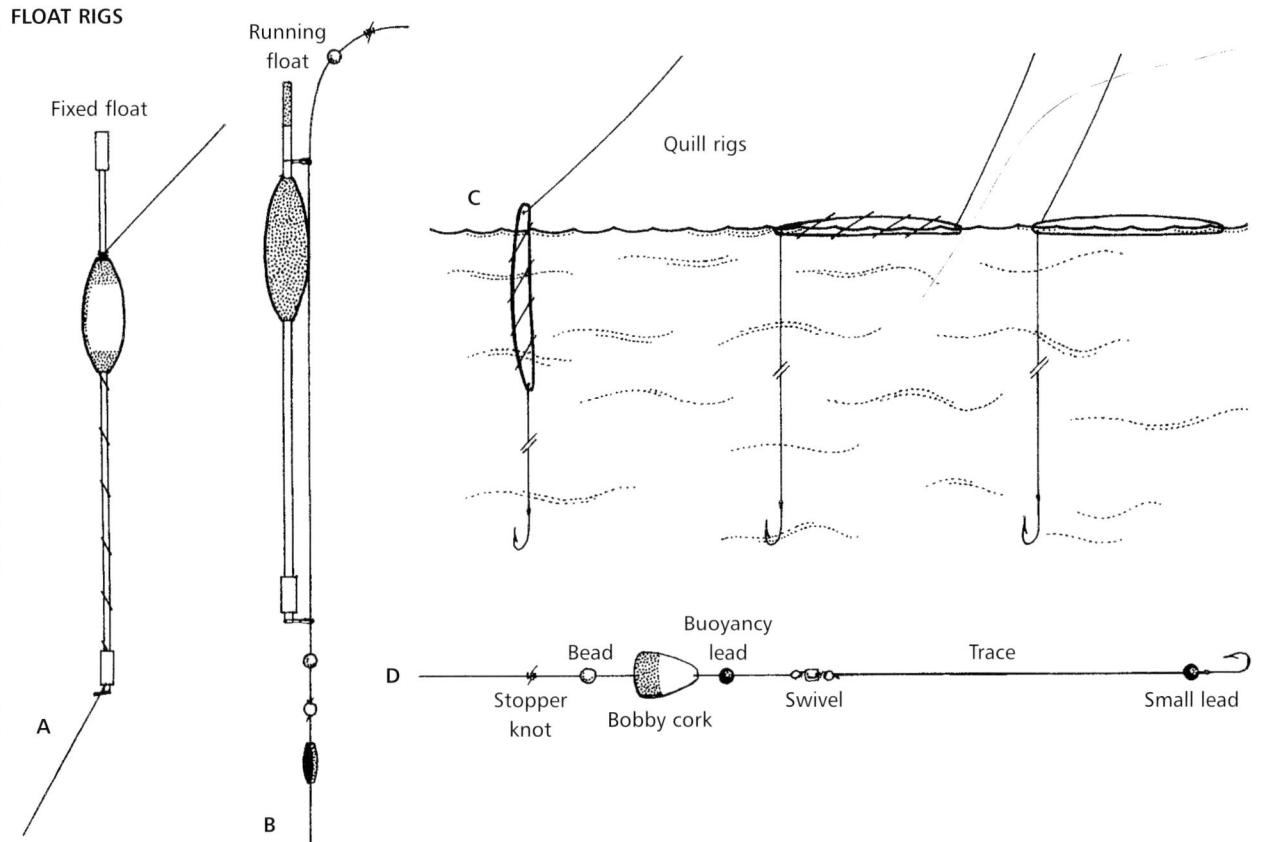

Stemmed floats like the one illustrated here (**Rig A**) are usually associated with blackfish, but it's not a bad idea to keep them in your bag of tricks for those times when you need to use a float for presentation to fussy fish. A stemmed float can be precisely weighted so that it is only just floating, and that's all; the slightest pressure is enough to take it below the surface without resistance.

It is possible to get into a lot of detail about the way split shot is to be distributed along the line to weight a stemmed float, but, much of the time, a single piece of sheet lead wrapped on the line above the swivel will do the job as well. Distribution of split shot along the line is mainly used for keeping the line between the float and the hook straight.

Generally speaking, it is much easier to rig and fish with a fixed float than with a running float, especially if you want to distribute split shot along the line. The limiting factor with a fixed float is the length of the rod in use, as the distance between the float and the hook must be shorter than the length of the rod otherwise it will be difficult to lift the bait or a fish from the water once the float reaches the rod tip.

You need to think about whether you want to weight the trace or leave it weight free. Depending on the strength of the current, this will have some effect on the depth at which the bait is being presented, and very precise depth can at times be critical when float fishing.

With this running float rig (**Rig B**) the angler can fish at any depth, as only the length of trace needs to be considered when the rig is handled on shore. Running floats are also easier to

cast than fixed floats. The stopper can be a knotted piece of wool or a short length of valve tubing.

Quill or pencil floats (**Rig C**) are handy for calm water and small fish. They can be rigged in a similar manner to the fixed stem float, or simply attached at one end so that the float stands upright to register a bite. Any small length of wood can be used this way at a pinch, and there is no need to use any weight at all on the line as the float itself is the casting weight. This is a good system for garfish.

The versatile bobby cork is a classic rock hopper's tool (**Rig D**). It can be used as a casting aid, a way of floating a bait a long way out in a rip, or in the more conventional role of a float, keeping a bait at a set depth. Bobby corks can be any size, from tiny thumbnail-size through to great bulky foam balls that can hold up quite a lot of lead.

Never forget that you reverse the rule when using a float and pack on all the lead the float will carry. To minimise drag on any other rig you take lead off, but to minimise drag on a float you put lead on to negate the buoyancy of the float. A float that is only just floating is well rigged.

I have found that when fishing rough water, a small additional lead allowed to run right down onto the hook will often increase the number of bites. I have no idea why this is so, but others using the system report the same result.

Don't handicap yourself by thinking in terms of relatively shallow water when fishing running floats. You can use a large, free-running float off some deepwater rock platforms where you may set the depth at 10 m or more.

RIGGING LURES

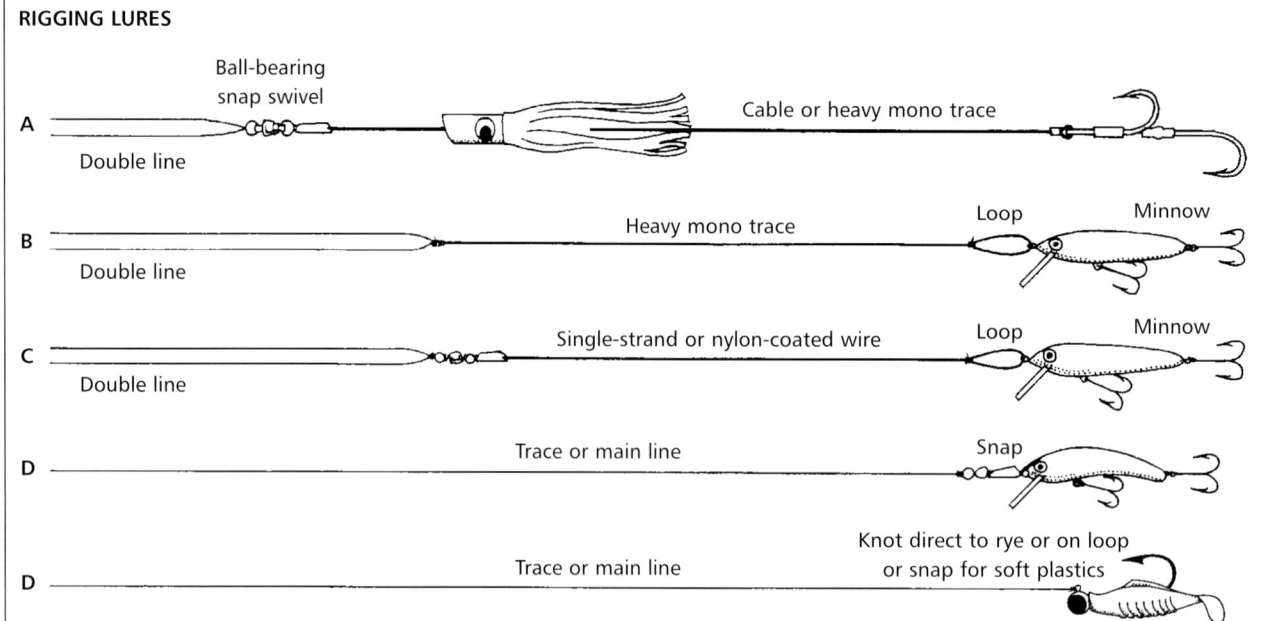

Snap swivels are commonly used to connect leaders to lures, and leaders to main lines, and they can be very convenient things at times. However, unless you are using top-quality swivels and snaps designed for heavy-duty bluewater use, regard all snaps with suspicion and work with knots and direct ties wherever possible.

In fishing situations where the fish are smaller and the tackle lighter, good-quality snaps with a rounded connection are popular, especially when frequent lure changes are being made. I still have preference for a good loop myself.

Rig A is the basic offshore trolling rig with a single or double hook set-up, depending on the size of lure in use. A cable or heavy mono trace goes to a snap, or a loop in the end of the trace can be tied straight to the double.

You can have a problem when a fish is hooked and the pressure of water forces the lure to run back up the line to the swivel, where it is sometimes attacked by a second fish, usually a razor-toothed wahoo, who then bites the line off at the swivel. Some anglers try to 'wahoo-proof' their rigs by crimping a sleeve halfway along the trace so that the lure stops there, well away from the swivel.

If you are making these rigs up for the first time, go to a good tackle store and buy all the components at the same time and ask the attendant to explain the method of rigging to you. It really is very important to have the right crimps for the trace

you use, and there are some tricks in putting these rigs together. It won't matter so much on the average fish, but you can be sure that the fish you most want will find every little flaw in a rig that is less than perfect.

Large minnow lures and a number of other patterns are commonly used to troll for light game (**Rig B**), and this is the standard rig with a double connected to a heavy trace with an Albright knot. It is most common to connect the lure to the trace with a loop, but if the connection point is a free-moving ring attached to a fixed eye, then a knot straight to the ring may be used.

Rigs C and **D** are similar using single-strand or nylon-coated wire, and if wire is being used a lot, a number of lures can have wire traces attached, with a loop in the end of the trace that can be clipped onto a snap swivel. Think about this before you get into it, as it is more suited to light fishing with fish that run than it is to knock-down, drag-out, stump-pulling-type brawls. For the latter, do away with the snaps and connect straight to the lure and heavy-duty game swivels or use the Albright knot to connect the loop in your wire to a double. The general rule with wire is never use it unless you have to.

Any of the loop or snap connections can be used with all lures that swim and need to move around a lot at the connection. Soft plastics are generally attached with a knot direct to the eye, but you can still use a loop if you wish.

Using the right hooks and with the eyes bent down, if you take a flight of hooks and shake them about they should be able to move freely then hang straight. If they won't do this, and want to lock up at odd angles, they are going to tear out of the bait as you cast, and probably tear out of fish the same way.

People link hooks in all sorts of ways, the simplest being to use those open eyes and simply close them

with pliers after the barb of the next hook has been passed through. An alternative method is to take hooks with closed eyes and close down the hook barbs to get them through the eye. Another method is to use

OPPOSITE PAGE When you see the mess this mackerel has made of the lure, it's not hard to understand why a wire trace is always required when fishing for these fish.

8260s and open the eye with sidecutters. You simply close down with the sidecutters right where the bend of the eye comes up against the shank, and this just nudges the eye open enough to allow the barb through. It can then be closed again quite easily. The 8260s are good for rigs using hooks in sizes from 3/0 up, but for the tiny rigs try some of the straight Tarpon or VMC hooks.

Putting it together

The need to practise catching a ball or swinging a golf club is readily understood by most sportspeople, but very few anglers understand the value of practising tying knots and making up terminal rigs.

The living room or workbench is the very best place of all to become competent with knots and to understand how to put rigs together. Once the water starts to explode with feeding fish or a big fish takes your bait, the resulting adrenalin surge can cause your hands to sprout ten thumbs and your brain will instantly turn into a pumpkin. This is why your knot tying and rig assembly should be second nature – so that your hands know what they're doing even if your brain is on holiday!

Some knots, like spider hitches, Albrights and Bimini twists, require more practice than others. If you give it some thought, rigs tied in practice sessions need not be wasted. Some anglers do most, if not all, of their rigging in front of the television set at night, and always head off on a fishing trip with rigs assembled ready to be tied on. Buying in bulk snap-lock plastic bags (mostly small ones and some large bags) to hold pre-tied rigs is well worthwhile. You can then pre-tie your rigs, put each one into a separate bag and store all like rigs in one large bag. Use a marker pen to label the bags.

DEALING WITH TOUGH FISH AND HARD CASTING

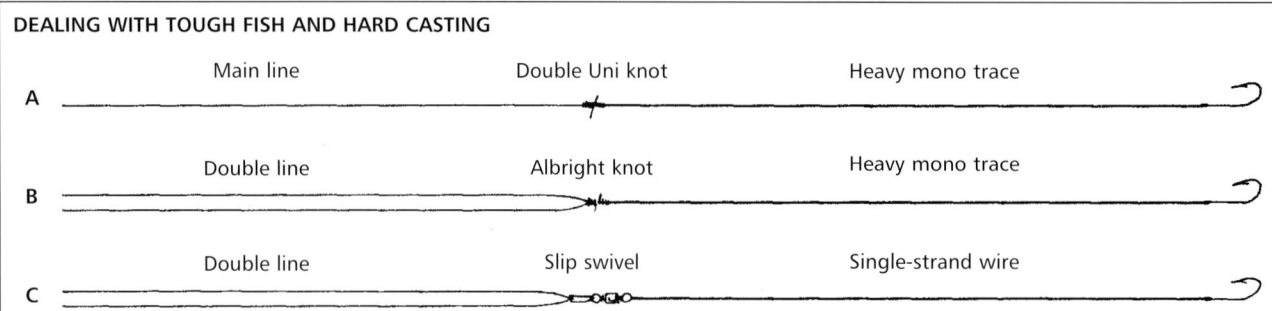

Rig A is a basic live bait rig using an Albright knot to join a heavy length of trace to the main line. It can also be the basis of a rig for when hard casts with heavy weights are to be made.

The Albright knot is nearly always used in conjunction with a double length of line when dealing with large or difficult fish, so if you are going to use it as a connection to your main line to make a shock trace, you will need to simply double a short length of the main line to make the knot. It is normal to use enough length in a shock trace to get a turn or two of the heavy line onto the reel, but the spot where the line normally breaks is right at the tip, where it is bent over the lip guide at a radical angle and worked there under extreme pressure.

The length of heavy mono trace used for difficult fish varies according to the nature of the fish. Fishing for mangrove jack and barramundi, 10 to 15 cm of 30 kg trace backed by a long double is a common approach. Some people use quite long doubles of up to 8 m of very heavy mono when live baiting yellowfin or billfish.

The heavy trace is used for two reasons: the first being to cope with the teeth of some of these fish; and the second is to deal with the wear and tear associated with the line working over the bony jaw and sharp edges of gill covers during the fight. The barramundi has some razor-sharp edges on the gill covers, and tuna all have rock-hard edges either side of the body just forward of the tail.

Rig B shows a length of the main line doubled, with the double doing two jobs. A double is a shock trace when casting, but its most important function is to allow the angler to lock up on a fish when it is alongside the boat and most in need of control. With a couple of turns of a double on the reel, you are fishing 50 per cent or more over the regular breaking strain of the main line and can afford to apply considerable pressure.

Not all anglers like to fish wire (Rig C), and do so with some reluctance. It can also be a real hassle changing lures when using wire. When fishing country where wire is often called for, make your rigs up at home and keep them in separate snap-seal plastic bags.

Using single-strand wire you have the option of wiring some hooks then putting either a ring or loop in the end of the wire to attach to a snap swivel tied to a double. When you do this, spend up and get the good game-quality swivels and snaps, as the regular wire jobs can pull apart on good fish. Also buy black snaps and swivels, not the bright ones that may attract other fish to bite at them.

The bag system is also effective because you can return rigs to their bags as they are changed then consign all of the bags of used rigs to a single large wash bag. Wash the rigs in fresh water when you get home and dry them before bagging again. Don't forget to turn the bags inside out and wash them too.

It is also a good idea to have an extra empty bag with you. This is the bag you can use for all your lengths of discarded line and old hooks. Discarded fishing line and hooks in the water do enormous harm to the fish, birds and animals that come into contact with them, so please take all of this home with you and dispose of it in a safe and thoughtful way.

Multiple-hook rigs can present a problem, especially the tiny ones. The best way to store one of these is to cut up a strip of stiff cardboard, lay the rig out straight on it, then tape it down with some sticky tape and pop it in a plastic bag. Multiple rigs using large hooks are easier to handle as you can simply fold them up and then run a piece of tape around the centre to hold them all together.

Those rigs utilising a sliding sinker are easy to customise if you pre-rig your sinker traces with snap swivels. You could tie short traces onto the sinkers with a snap connection on the other end, or simply do up traces with a snap at either end and add the appropriate sinker as required. Unless you are using ball-bearing game swivels, it is best to keep snap swivels out of the rig that links the main line to the hook unless you can be sure that you will only be dealing with small fish.

The rigs presented in this chapter are simply intended to provide you with a foundation. Never be afraid to experiment and always be prepared to modify your rig to suit a particular situation.

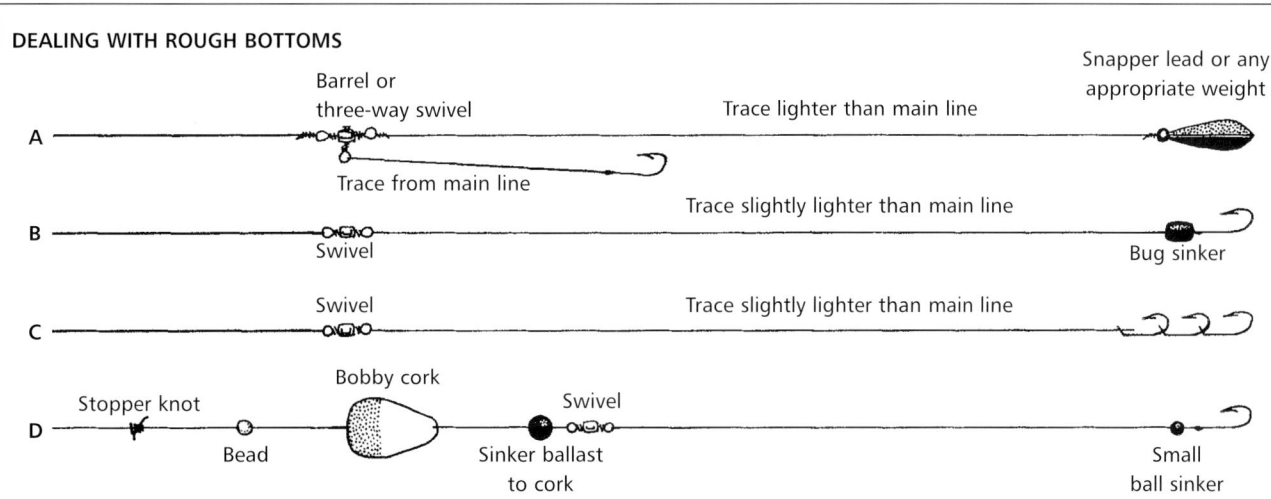

DEALING WITH ROUGH BOTTOMS

Rig A is one of the oldest rigs in the book, with the main line terminating at the swivel or ring, then a short trace of heavy line to the hook and a long trace of light line to the casting weight. Reef anglers like this rig for the obvious reason that you can foul the weight on the bottom, and break it off without losing everything. You can save money by using spark plugs or big nuts and/or bolts as weights, instead of lead. Other reef anglers working from boats prefer to use more conventional rigs with hooks sitting on the lead. They drop these to the bottom then quickly lift them off a metre or two where they are clear of the rough stuff but still within sight and smell range of the fish.

Rig B is an approach favoured by rock anglers who want to fish right into the heart of the rough stuff with a very light rig. They know the sinker is going to settle on the rocks eventually, and by using a sinker with flat sides, such as the bug, minimise the chance of it roiling about, as any ball sinker will do, until it finds its way into a crevice.

The multi-hook without weight (**Rig C**) is not just another variation on this theme, it is really a total fishing system that can be used with great skill to fish the worst reef country. The whole baits that are fished with this system, varying in size through from small whitebait on tiny hooks to big sea garfish on 4 and 5/0 size hooks, may sink at the same rate as a small sinker, but they have great planing qualities when retrieved. Skilful anglers, familiar with the layout of their reef, will cast maximum distance, allow the rig to sink until close to the bottom, then lift the rod to draw the bait towards them, rising upwards as it comes. It's a drop-and-rise retrieve system that covers a lot of water and is incredibly effective at taking fish under just about any conditions.

Finally there's that versatile bobby cork again (**Rig D**), allowing a bait to be suspended just where you want it over the rough bottom.

Chapter Six

Fishing tackle

Fundamentals of balanced tackle

If you can understand why it won't work to put a motorbike engine into a semitrailer to achieve improved operating economy, or a racing engine into the family car so you can tow a boat, then you can easily grasp what the term 'balanced tackle' is all about.

Whenever you think fishing tackle, don't start by choosing rods and reels that look nice. Start by thinking about where you are going to fish and what sort of fish you are likely to encounter in that environment. Then select the appropriate set of tools best suited to that job.

To give you an example, one person may plan to fish with bait from a small boat in a river, hoping to catch relatively small fish. The next person may be intent on catching much larger fish from ocean rocks.

The angler in the boat will only need a light 2 m rod, a light threadline reel and some quality monofilament line. None of that will cost very much at all and it will do everything the angler asks of it. There is no call for distance casting, and the tackle will not be pushed to the limit dealing with oversized fish capable of running away with hundreds of metres of line. Basic off-the-shelf gear and a few hooks, sinkers and swivels will do the job very well.

The person planning to fish from the rocks, on the other hand, has a lot of problems to deal with. The rod will require a lot of casting power, it may need to offer good reach to clear the rocks when holding a strong fish in close, and it will need to have plenty of fish-fighting power. The reel will need to cast very well and have a strong and reliable drag system to cope with the high-speed runs big fish are capable of. It will need to have good line capacity for the same reason, and the construction of the reel will need to stand up to the punishment handed out by compressed line being packed onto the spool under real pressure. The breaking strain of line will need to be matched to the power of the rod. Obviously, this gear is far more specialised and will probably be far more expensive to buy.

There are literally dozens of scenarios like this that call for a specialised kit of tackle, and not too many general-purpose outfits that will perform well in any one specialised field of fishing.

Defining your needs defines the tackle, and you will usually find that one part of the tackle defines what the rest will be.

If you want to fish for whiting and bream in an estuary, for example, the key is to fish light. The lighter the line the better your chances of catching what are often sensitive and wary fish. A good angler will always use the lightest sinker that will do the job, so we start with a light line and terminal tackle. From there a light and flexible rod is dictated, as a powerful rod would simply break the line all the time. The reel then has to fit in with the line and rod, so you have to have something that doesn't weigh much and has a pretty good drag system, in the interests of avoiding break-offs when a fish is hooked. Everything has to balance with everything else.

Fishing line is often the foundation of a fishing system. You should never fish with a line that is heavier than you actually need, and the rod and reel are matched to the line class. The majority of anglers fish with heavier tackle than is required, and that is one of the reasons why 10 per cent of the anglers catch 90 per cent of the fish.

Consider this when you think about monofilament lines. The stronger the line, the thicker it will be. The

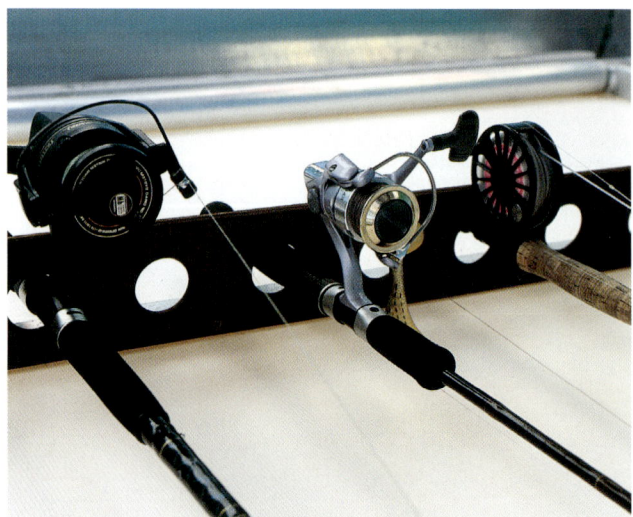

A range of tools for a range of jobs. From left, a double-handed heavy-duty threadline outfit, a single-handed light threadline, and a saltwater fly rod and reel.

thicker the line, the easier it is for a fish to see, and that's just the start of your problems. The thicker the line, the more it will be subjected to friction from wind and water, friction that will pull it around all over the place. To control that line you have to add weight in the form of lead sinkers, and the bigger the sinker the less chance there is that a fish will pick up the bait and take off with it. After all, if you picked up a sandwich that weighed half a kilo you'd be a mite suspicious, wouldn't you?

So in the great majority of cases the angler determines the particular class of line he needs to get the job done, and then builds his fishing system around that.

There are, of course, situations in which things work differently. The size of the fish might be offset by the environment in which it is found. Fish like barramundi, mangrove jack and bass are commonly found around and in snags. They can hit a lure close to cover and get back into that cover to cut the line with the speed of lightning.

The angler has a problem here: an outfit that will cast relatively light lures is called for, but the moment that fish strikes it must be stopped dead in its tracks, then muscled away from cover. It's real heart attack stuff with big fish, and tackle is frequently red-lined in the heat of battle.

In a situation like this it is common for a small overhead bait-casting reel to be matched to a relatively short single- or double-handed rod with an extremely fast taper and very fast recovery characteristics. The tip of the rod does the casting, then the powerful mid section and butt provide the 'don't argue' component. Because the casting distances are always relatively short, the line is chosen for its ability to stop the fish in its tracks. In other words, it needs to be strong, have as little stretch as possible, and have high abrasion resistance.

A far more extreme situation is represented by a big-game outfit, where the reel is massively strong and heavy, has to hold enormous lengths of line, and must be fitted with a drag system not far removed from the brakes on a racing car. The rod will be a brutal lever capable of turning the head of a massive fish sulking at great depths, and sometimes, when enough line is out there in the waves and current, it takes all that power just to recover line against water friction.

Every part of a fishing outfit is important to the end result, from the material from which a rod has been made and the friction component in guide rings, to the strength of the frames. Reels can be loose and clunky or as smooth as oiled silk. The best are built with fine tolerances and constructed from space-age metals that deliver light weight combined with great strength.

The bad news is that the best fishing tackle is very expensive these days. The blow is softened, to some degree, by the fact that we have never had anything like the quality of this tackle available before. It is simply brilliant.

The good news is that manufacturing technology has advanced so far that mid-range tackle at an attractive price is incredibly good value for money. It works so well you would need to be quite an expert angler to appreciate why it should be cheaper than some of the other tackle available.

Naturally, there are bargain-basement offerings in abundance, but you can't really afford to have suspect tackle when you fish. If it lets you hookup on a great fish some day, it will probably put the odds very firmly in the favour of the fish. Buy from the middle to the top of the range. If the budget is a problem, buying less tackle of higher quality is the way to go.

Fishing lines

When I wrote the first edition of this book it seemed to be a big deal to discuss the number of fishing lines on offer in the modern tackle store. They were, of course, all monofilaments, but they still managed to offer a range of characteristics and finishes that could make selecting the right product a thought-provoking task.

Some were finer than others for the breaking strain of the line, some were stiff, some were supple, and between them they offered a veritable rainbow of colours from which to choose.

Sadly, the marketing blurb for fishing lines leaves a great deal to be desired. You will constantly see claims that this line or that line is 'stronger' than other lines. That is sheer nonsense. You can't have a 6 kg breaking strain line that is stronger than another 6 kg breaking strain line. A 6 kg line is a line that is supposed to break at 6 kg. If it breaks at 10 kg, then it's a 10 kg line, not a 6 kg line.

Just a tiny sample of the range of fishing lines on the market today.

Like most things in modern life, the pace of technology has had its effect on fishing line, and this has had such a profound effect on fishing that I feel I need to deal with fishing line before getting into rods and reels. So fishing line has gone from third place to first in our discussion of fishing tackle.

In recent years a whole new breed of fishing line has appeared on the market, and the characteristics of these lines are so dramatically different from everything that has gone before that they really have turned modern fishing on its ear. It's a whole new world out there, but before we get into that, you need to understand the fundamentals of fishing line.

BREAKING STRAINS AND DIAMETERS

Most anglers buy their fishing line by breaking strain, and most buy line far stronger than they need. What you should be doing is buying the lowest possible *practical* breaking strain for what you want to do. Going too light can create as many problems as going too heavy.

Nearly all fishing rods will have a range of breaking strains printed on them just above the foregrip. These are usually a bit on the high side: what manufacturers classify as a rod capable of using 6–10 kg line would

probably be rated as around 6–8 kg by an experienced angler.

There is a direct relationship between breaking strain and line diameter that has a ripple effect when putting an outfit together. When you go for a stronger line you usually get a thicker line, so you won't be able to get as much line on the reel. Thicker lines also tend to 'remember' the coils from the reel spool, so if you are using a threadline reel where the line comes away from the reel in coils when you're casting, the stiffer line will generate more friction as it goes through the guides, which reduces casting distance considerably.

Sometimes a case can be made for thicker, more abrasion-resistant line. For example, if you are fishing for bream or drummer in the wild white water around the ocean rocks, tough, abrasion-resistant line will be the right thing to use.

Fishing line manufacturers can control the diameter of monofilament line to some degree, and many premium brands of line are notable for high breaking strain to diameter ratios. Strong, fine line is excellent for threadline reels where friction through the guides can be a real problem. High diameter to breaking strain ratios tend to be preferred for situations where line may be subjected to high levels of friction or abrasion.

All monofilament line will have a memory of the spool it comes on. In other words, it remembers its coils. If you hold a spool of line on its side and allow line to simply fall off the spool onto the floor, you will see that the line will arrange itself in the same coil shape it had on the spool. When you put it on the reel it will learn a new memory, and will 'remember' the tighter coils created by the smaller spool diameter.

Some hard lines have a very good memory, and the coils can become a darned nuisance. This is not usually a problem on an overhead reel where the line goes out through the rod guides in a straight line. It is a real nuisance on threadline and sidecast reels.

Softer lines generally have less memory; they are ideal for threadline and sidecast reels where the line comes away from the reel in a series of loops.

It is difficult to produce a length of monofilament line that has exactly the same breaking strain along its entire length, so lines guaranteed to break below the International Game Fish Association line classes are generally sold at a premium price. Near enough is close enough for most of us, but if you fish in a club or association where records are kept, it is critical that your line does not break above the line class after you have caught a potentially record-breaking fish.

The life of a monofilament line is determined by many things, including exposure to UV radiation. Some quality lines have an exceptionally long life, while cheaper lines may break down in no time. This is not always the case, but you will generally find that cheap lines are coarse, hard and have a lot of memory. They are also difficult to knot well.

Some anglers want line to last forever, but most enthusiasts will change their line often. Unless you fish in situations where big fish will regularly take out a good part of your reel's line capacity, you need only top up around the top third of the line load every now and then. At less frequent intervals dump the lot and completely re-spool the reel.

If, on the other hand, you regularly go after hard-running fish and tend to red-line your tackle in these encounters, regularly re-spool the top two-thirds of the reel or the whole darned thing.

Because fishing line has been, and still is, undergoing an unprecedented period of development, I can only speak in very general terms here. In the time I have been working on this edition of the book there have been two new lines developed that have proven to be quite revolutionary, and you can expect that kind and degree of change to continue for some time yet.

Buying fishing line is a bit of a 'suck it and see' exercise, and there is no one best line. Anglers normally get some advice from the tackle store, then try a few brands before they find one that works for them and the fishing they do.

Most anglers use heavy trace for dirty fighters like the mangrove jack or drummer from the rocks, but specialists might also look for an abrasion-resistant main line.

THE SUPERLINES

In the early 1990s a new breed of fishing line came onto the world market, and in no time at all most manufacturers were introducing their own versions of what became known as the superlines. Under that general heading you have gelspun fused lines and gelspun braid.

I know it's an oversimplification, but to keep this simple, let us just say that monofilament line is extruded from a machine pretty much as you would squeeze toothpaste out of a tube. You get a continuous stream of material of the same diameter and strength.

Both the gelspun (GSP) line styles are created in a completely different way. The machines used for these products extrude an amazingly fine fibre that is ten times stronger than steel of the same diameter.

There are two approaches to the end product. To make braided gelspun the machine very slowly braids the material to extraordinary tolerances, resulting in a line that achieves any given breaking strain at just 25 per cent of the diameter required for monofilament to achieve the same breaking strain.

The fused gelspun can be manufactured at a greater speed, as it relies on a bonding agent to fuse the fibres together rather than on what amounts to precision knitting. Because fused gelspun has added the bonding

The new GSP lines come in many shapes, forms and prices. Generally speaking, the finer the diameter the more expensive the line.

agent to its fibres, it comes at around 50 per cent of monofilament diameter for a given breaking strain.

It would not be hard to write pages and pages about the way these new lines are made and the materials involved, but that can get tedious. For the purposes of this book I am far more concerned with the way these lines have impacted on the fishing scene and the way we do things.

Both fused and braided gelspuns are more expensive than monofilament; the braids are a lot more expensive than the fused lines because they are slower and more difficult to manufacture. Both lines are more like cotton than mono in character, with virtually no memory and no stretch.

Both braided and fused gelspun lines offer the obvious advantages associated with such incredibly small diameters. If you want to, you can fit a lot more line on any reel, although most anglers partly fill the reel with mono and then top up with gelspun. Wind and water friction is minimised, so you can continue to fish high breaking strains without any of the penalties normally associated with mono lines.

One of the great advantages associated with the gelspun lines and their very fine diameters is that deep running lures – any diving lure, for that matter – will run much deeper when used with gelspun than it will rigged on the same breaking strain in mono. Any diving lure has to drag the line down with it, and the greater the friction on that line the more difficult it is for the diver to make ground. Reducing the friction increases depth to a considerable degree, with some claiming more than 30 per cent improvement in depth.

The casting problems associated with threadline reels, where loops create friction as the line goes through the guides, have virtually been eliminated. In fact these lines are so fine, limp and slippery that it is possible to increase line breaking strain by as much as 50 per cent and still cast much further than you could with any mono line. As we will see a little later, this has revolutionised the role of the threadline reel in sportfishing.

The non-stretchiness of these lines has impacted on fishing in a number of ways. Obviously, teamed up with a rod that has a high graphite content and very fast recovery, the gelspuns allow fishermen to apply far more direct pressure to a fish without the delays associated with the spring of fibreglass in rods and the stretch of mono line. These combinations are far more sensitive in terms of feedback, and advanced anglers talk about being able to feel every bump on the bottom as a jig is retrieved.

Naturally, the impact of a strike is far more immediate, and angler reaction time is reduced dramatically. Sometimes, when fishing for larger fish with lures, angler reaction is too fast, and strikes can be missed. Many big fish feed by virtually inhaling a lure along with a mouthful of water. If the angler reacts too quickly the lure is pulled straight back out of the mouth. It may be necessary to build in a slight delay to ensure that the mouth is closed before striking.

So, should we all abandon monofilament and spool up with the best braids? Well, before we do that we should consider the downside of gelspuns. There are weaknesses at the moment.

Because these lines are so thin and do not tolerate abrasion and nicks anywhere near as well as monofilament lines, most anglers use a short length of mono trace on the end of the gelspun.

Gelspun lines are so slippery that they are difficult to knot – the first lot demanded complicated new knots if they were to remain attached to anything. If you used old favourite knots, gelspun would simply reverse out of the knot like Houdini making one of his famous escapes. The totally limp nature of these fine lines also makes it more difficult to create any knot than it is with mono. This all seems to be changing as time goes by, though.

On threadline reels, where they definitely deliver the greatest benefits, these ultra-fine limp lines tend to pick up wind knots. They fold a loose loop away on the spool as you retrieve, then on the next cast that loop picks up other loops and goes out into the guides as a bird's nest tangle or tight knot, which will be extremely difficult to undo. You need to be aware of retrieving under tension at all times.

The fusion lines tend to lose their skin after a while – it looks as if the line is coming apart, with fibres sticking up everywhere when you take a close look. I have kept fishing with one line after this rather frightening deterioration started, and the line seems not to be losing any of its strength.

Finally, if you do get yourself snagged when using gelspun line of any strength, don't make the mistake of wrapping the line around your fingers and trying to bust it with brute strength. You'll end up having to count

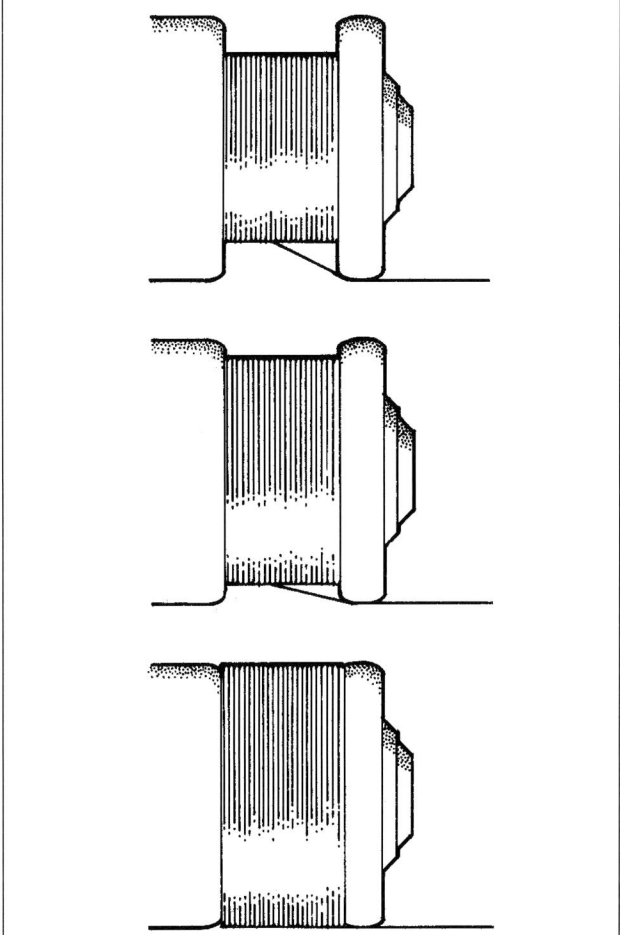

It is vitally important to have reel spools filled to the correct height, and this is especially true of sidecast and threadline reels. The top spool line load is too low, presenting line to the spool lip at an angle which creates cast-limiting friction. The bottom spool is over-filled and will probably release multiple coils of line at the same time to jam and tangle in the rod guides.

how many fingers you have left: it cuts like a knife.

The thing to keep in mind about gelspun lines is that even the best of them are still evolving. After all, this radical new technology has only been around for a few years, and the latest products bear little resemblance to the pioneering products.

When I was writing this I was given a sample of what was at the time the latest release from a new company. FINS Inc. is an American company producing a range of braids, this latest going under the impressive title of FINS PRT Braid, Spectra Superline. The line was 4.5 kg breaking strain with an equivalent diameter to 2 kg mono.

The blurb on the package told me that new polymer-reinforcing technology had solved the knotting problems associated with previous braids, and that I could use such standard knots as a Palomar, a Uni knot, a double Uni knot, a blood knot, an improved clinch knot and the surgeon's knot. I tied a rough mono to braid connection straightaway and it would not pull apart. It was for all the world like working with mono.

As if that's not enough, they also claim that this line will eliminate wind knots, and has a 500 per cent increase in abrasion resistance over traditional superlines. We can only expect this sort of progress to continue, with every new step keeping the advantages and eliminating the drawbacks associated with the previous product.

If you do decide to try these lines, give it a little time before you decide for or against, and try both the fused and braided varieties. I have to admit that it took me a little while to come to terms with the very real difference experienced when fishing with braided gelspun lines, but I am wired to it now and would find it hard to go back to even the best monofilaments, especially for any sort of lure fishing.

THE POLYMERS AND COPOLYMERS

A lot has been going on in the world of non-gelspun lines, but it has been completely overshadowed by the development of the gelspun superlines.

Polymers and copolymers are advanced products that more or less remain in the monofilament camp. Reading what can be found on dozens of brands of line, you can see that manufacturers are trying all sorts of different things to produce a mono look-alike that will have a personality and features all its own, depending on what they use in the brew. Polymers are still produced as a single extrusion, but the more advanced chemical ingredients allow more control and variation in the end product. It is even possible to include elements that will work their way to the surface after the line has been extruded and give it a slippery skin.

Copolymers, on the other hand, are formed when a central element is bonded to a separate outer skin. Some manufacturers are laying longitudinal reinforcing fibres in the core of the line and adding a tough external skin to create an exceptionally tough line. Others are looking for fine, slippery, low-memory lines that will cast exceptionally well, and so on.

The latest developments show a trend towards lines that try to emulate the best characteristics of the gelspun lines: less stretch, low memory and finer diameters. Progress has been made in both areas, but not enough to go anywhere near the superlines.

Beyond these factors there does not seem to be much consensus among manufacturers of the polymers and copolymers as to how they should proceed. One thing is for certain: these new lines are far superior to the basic mono lines that preceded them.

Having devoted most of the available space here to the superlines, it should be noted that they still only account for a fraction of the market. The great majority of anglers are still choosing basic monofilament fishing lines, on the basis of price alone.

COLOUR

Before you read this section it might pay you to go back towards the beginning of this book and re-read the section on the senses of fish and the way they see under water. A significant point made there is that fish do not see things under the water the same way we see them in daylight. At just a few metres depth, some colours, such as red, are starting to lose colour and

You can now buy mono and GSP lines in a wide range of colours. The brightest colours are usually used with a trace so the fish does not see the colour but the angler does, which helps to keep track of where the line is going.

move towards black. Others are losing their daylight colour and beginning to fade.

You must always remember that most colours are affected by filtered light under the water at various depths, and that fish are not looking at things against the same background you see them against. The scales of a silver fish will flash when you hold the fish in sunlight, but beneath the water those scales will simply reflect the light and colour around them – they will become virtually invisible.

It is interesting to spend a little time under the water, looking back up towards the surface. You will notice that many things that are hard to see when viewed from above against the dark background of deep water are very easy to see when viewed from below, against the bright background of sky and light. Logically, this would suggest that lines intended to be fished deep can be almost any colour, including red, which is the first colour to be lost from the spectrum as we go below the surface, and that lines intended to be fished near the surface should have a reflective or transparent quality of some kind.

Most anglers fishing with gelspun lines add a mono trace of low-visibility line. What 'low visibility' actually means may depend a lot on the colour and clarity of water you are working with; a pale green or brown that might be hopeless in most saltwater situations, for instance, will be the very thing in some freshwater environments.

One manufacturer offers fluorocarbon-coated line, claiming that it offers both low and high visibility at the same time because it has a refractive index very close to that of water and a built-in clear fluorescent colour that makes it highly visible in sunlight. The same manufacturer offers another version of the same line without the fluorescence in it. The only way to sort all these claims and counter-claims out is to test the line for yourself if you think it looks like fitting in with your kind of fishing.

Fishing line is not meant to stay on a reel forever, and it pays to try a few different colours that you think might be suitable and see if one gives you a better result than another.

While colour is most often thought about in terms of making our offering invisible, a case can also be made for using the brightest coloured lines imaginable – lines that are meant to be seen. I have recently joined the ranks of those with failing eyesight, and while I can see quite clearly with glasses, I find that I have a lot of trouble keeping track of a low-visibility line in poor light. Not knowing where your line is can result in lures being ripped out of the water in a dangerous fashion because you don't know how close they are to the surface. There's a strong case right there for a very bright line with a low-visibility trace at the fish's end of things.

Some anglers who do a lot of trolling with multiple lines in the water at the same time also like to see some bright colours out there so that they can distinguish one line from another, which is very handy when making a turn, for example.

It's hard to know just how important the colour of a line really is in fishing, but having observed extraordinary sensitivity in fish inhabiting heavily fished areas, and an almost total lack of sensitivity in fish found in wilderness locations, I would always lean towards lines that are hard to see when given a choice. Just keep in mind that 'hard to see' means from the fish's point of view, not yours.

FLY LINES

A fly line is not so much a fishing line as a casting weight. Because there is virtually no castable weight in the fly itself, a weighted line is cast to deliver the fly.

Fly lines come in many shapes and forms, involving a variety of tapers, with weight bias varied throughout the length of the line, and with floating and non-floating properties ranging from fully buoyant to weighted deep sinkers.

The shape of a fly line varies according to the job it has to do. A shooting head with the weight bias forward is designed to deliver maximum casting range. A tapered line reduces gradually to a fine tip, which in turn is further reduced down through a series of trace sections of steadily reducing diameter. This style of line can be cast so that the actual delivery involves the last of the line and trace unrolling to place the fly on the surface of the water with great subtlety.

The fly line has a considerable length of backing, which could be gelspun braid or Dacron. It is interesting to note that for the purpose of record keeping, the actual class of the outfit is determined not by the breaking strain of the backing, or of the fly line, but by the weakest link in the trace connecting the fly to the leader.

The most popular reels in the world today are the single-handed threadline models. The reels pictured will cost you an arm and a leg, but they are very, very good reels.

Reels: basics to blockbusters

Fishing reels are all used to store fishing line. Some do no more than that, while others are extremely sophisticated pieces of equipment.

The simplest of fishing reels is the centrepin, a basic spool mounted on an axle, rotated with one or two direct drive handles. All it does is rotate either to feed line out, or retrieve line and store it on a no-frills spool. The centrepin in its most refined form runs like oiled silk on ball bearings, and in expert hands can be used to cast surprising distances. The sidecast reel is a development on the centrepin reel in which a mechanical device allows the reel to be turned sideways to facilitate easy casting.

The next step up the ladder is gearing, sometimes even the ability to shift gears, and a slipping clutch or brake system. These are the basic requirements of all modern fishing reels.

It is a common misconception that fishing reels are machines designed to drag fish through the water to the angler. This is wrong – dead wrong! Fishing *rods* are used to drag fish through the water towards the angler. The only time the rod is not used this way is when the fish is a small one, and the application of constant pressure is enough to make it swim in the

desired direction. The majority of our small table fish, such as whiting, bream, tailor, flathead, luderick and so on, fall into this category, with the exception of the odd large specimen. People who grind away on geared reels, usually using much heavier line than the reel was designed to cope with, keep tackle repairers fat and happy. Tackle manufacturers make a major contribution to this problem by not having the gumption to nominate a realistic line breaking strain range in their skimpy little manuals and product packaging.

A few reels, such as the sidecasts and the game reels, are expected to cope with considerable direct pressure. Such reels are generally identified by the gearing. The sidecast is not geared at all and has a solid fibreglass spool, whereas the game reel commonly has gearing available of 1:1 or 1.2:1 in the heavy line classes, and over 3:1 in lighter line classes. Even these reels are not actually expected to move the fish, although they are asked to recover line under considerable pressure.

These days there is a general drift towards higher gearing speeds in many categories of reels. Skilled anglers like to get a lure or bait out of a non-productive situation with maximum speed, and have the skill to keep the stress off the reel and on the rod when moving a large fish. They also like to stay on top of the situation when a fish suddenly bolts for the boat. Nothing loses fish like slack line, and high-speed gearing gets an angler tight again – fast! You'll hear it said that you can wind a fast reel as slowly as you want, but you'll soon get sick and tired of trying to wind a slow reel fast.

It is important to understand something about gearing and line retrieve speed. Gearing is only half the answer when considering retrieve speeds. The size of the spool has just as much to do with line recovery as the gearing does. For example, a game reel with a large spool may well recover more line per crank of the handle than a smaller reel with 6:1 gearing.

Master anglers catch gigantic fish on spider web lines, simply because they never allow the fish to place a greater strain on the line than it can comfortably cope with. They do this by setting a pre-determined amount of drag, or friction, at the reel before they begin to fish. Most reels have an internal clutch called a drag system, where the ability of the spool to revolve and release line is governed by the pressure applied to a series of washers bearing directly, or sometimes indirectly, on the spool. When the pre-set pressure is exceeded the washers begin to slip, and the spool begins to turn and release line.

Since considerable friction occurs as the line travels over the guides of a loaded rod, the line is always stressed to a greater degree over a loaded rod than it is at the face of the reel. Allowing for this, the amount of drag is usually pre-set at the reel to one-third of the breaking strain of the line. In other words, if you had a reel loaded with 3 kg breaking strain line, you would have the drag set so that the spool began to turn and give line when more than 1 kg of pressure was exerted on the spool.

If you are thinking that one-third seems a bit on the conservative side, keep in mind that you don't have a full 3 kg breaking strain available from the line anyway. You will have lost at least 10 per cent, perhaps a lot more depending on how you tie your knots, in your connections. You also have to keep in mind that resistance to a steady pull increases as you go from a full spool of line, where the lever factor is in your favour, to a low line load, where leverage is diminishing rapidly.

I go into the subject of drag systems a little later, but for the moment note that good drag systems, and the ability of the angler to use them properly, are at the heart of modern sportfishing technique. Locking the drag up tight is an option, not a sensible all-purpose approach to fishing.

Tom Bethurem has been on this fish for so long that he has to take time out for a bit. Some huge fish are taken on small, high-quality reels.

THREADLINES

The threadline family of reels are the most popular fishing reels in the world today. Most of them are sold to people who just want a knock-around, general-purpose fishing tool that is cheap to buy and easy to use. At the bargain basement end of the range, that probably describes the threadline reel quite adequately. But from the medium to the top end of the price range, threadline reels are quite remarkable precision tools that have done much to change the way we fish, and they have made high-performance sportfishing available to the masses.

Designed to be mounted under the rod, they cover a practical range of fishing that encompasses ultra-light fresh water at one end and medium game fishing at the other. These days the big ones are popular tools for live-baiting sailfish and marlin.

Steve Starling with a red-hot queenfish, which was well matched to the tackle.

The design of the reel is aimed at ease of use and operation. With the spool located right at the front of the reel, the line is checked by a spring-loaded bail arm fitted with a small fixed or rotating line pickup/roller at one end. When this bail arm is flicked back into the 'off' position, line can run freely from the spool. At the completion of the cast, a turn of the handle activates an internal or external trip and the bail snaps closed, picking the line up on the roller. As the handle is turned, the bail rotates and retrieves line onto the spool, which oscillates back and forth to lay the line down evenly.

All threadlines are geared, with ratios varying from a low of 2.5:1 through to 6:1. Drag systems can be located at the front or the rear of the reel, although with only odd exceptions the front drag systems have been more successful. Drag systems also vary in design, with some using a series of basic washers and others containing very sophisticated washer materials. You can get superb drag systems in threadlines these days, and their ability to cope with quite substantial hard-running fish now allows them to play a far more serious role in the sportfishing world.

Threadline reels have benefited most from the introduction of the low-diameter GSP lines. Casting range has always been directly related to line diameter in the world of threadlines, so increasing the diameter/breaking strain of the line in use had a direct impact on casting range. You could actually hear it when somebody nearby was casting with either cheap, stiff line or a breaking strain too high for the threadline outfit. All that noise was the sound of pure friction killing the cast.

The very system that makes the threadline such an easy reel to cast is also the limiting factor when the range of line classes is considered. Because the line has to be stored on a spool with a relatively small diameter, then flow off that spool sideways in a series of tight coils as a cast is made, friction plays a dominant role in determining the viability of any threadline for a given line class.

Light lines with a small diameter allow a great many coils to leave the spool without making an appreciable difference to the profile of the line load on the spool. This is vitally important, for as the line load shrinks on the spool, the angle at which the line crosses the lip of the spool increases, leading to a dramatic increase in friction. Further friction

Most of the fish taken in this country are caught on light threadline outfits.

occurs with heavy line, as it tends to have a very good *memory* of its coils and retains them as the line enters the guides, creating further friction along the length of the rod. This all ads up to greatly reduced casting ability.

You will always get the best performance out of a threadline using a premium, limp, low-diameter line. These days an angler moving from monofilament to GSP lines can make a number of performance-enhancing choices. Fishing where fighting power is a definite asset, the same line diameter can be maintained while gaining the benefit of a considerable increase in breaking strain. Alternatively, where casting range or perhaps the desire to get lures down deeper is the main consideration, the angler can hold the breaking strain and get a dramatic decrease in diameter, which improves both casting range and lure diving performance. You get a further benefit in that

being so fine, the GSP lines can provide a long cast without diminishing the profile of the line load to any serious degree, thus minimising friction over the spool lip.

LIGHT THREADLINES

Threadline reels intended for single-handed use with rods of 1.5 to 2 m should use lines with breaking strains from 2 to 4 kg (more if using GSP line). If you go to the top end of the range of these lines now available you may have trouble finding a suitable rod, as threadlines are normally considered a light line outfit. This class of reel is ideal for spinning with light lures, and for baitfishing in rivers and creeks where very light terminal tackle can be used.

Most people wanting to fish heavier line classes with a threadline reel step up to the medium class of reel with a double-handed rod.

MEDIUM THREADLINES

The reels in this group vary quite a bit in size, with the smallest being well suited to 5 kg line and the largest with 8–10 kg and more.

All medium threadlines are married to one of the double-handed rods described in the rod section of this book, and they usually fall in the range from 2–2.5 m. The lightest outfits fall into that ubiquitous *multi-purpose* category where the tackle does a respectable job without really being the best tool for any specific job. Easy to use, forgiving of error and possessed of reasonable to good fish-fighting ability, they are the best, most cost-effective tool for anyone other than the serious angler.

They are commonly used in high-performance fishing where a range of lures and live baits are cast to quite large fish at times. In mid to top of the range models you will find reels with superb drag, capable of handling the speedsters like Spanish mackerel, the high flyers of the small billfish world, and the bullies of the water world in the form of huge trevally and barramundi. If you are setting up with the specific aim of targeting big fish, and especially if you are going to use low-stretch GSP lines, spend the extra money and buy the best reels available.

It would be remiss of me not to point out that in spite of superb engineering and the use of the best materials, the very best threadlines will fall short of an overhead reel in the brute force stakes, simply because of design limitations.

HEAVY THREADLINES

At the top of the range of threadlines you get into the mega reels with high line capacity, high-speed gearing and seriously large drag systems. They are normally matched up with double-handed rods of 4 m or more in length, and with fishing line classes anywhere from 6 to 10 kg in mono and up to 30 kg using GSP lines.

Although still a relatively easy outfit to learn to use, these large threadlines have never gained the popularity in this country that they enjoy overseas. They are cumbersome and heavy, and there is an inherent problem in the design when trying to use them with heavy casting weights. When you cast a threadline reel, you pick the line up over the first

This sequence shows a knock-down, drag-out battle with a tough longtail tuna. Hooked from the foredeck of a boat high above the water, the fish had to be dominated in order to allow the deckhand, with what must be the world's longest gaff, to get a shot at the fish.

finger and open the bail. After that the entire casting weight is checked by that single finger with the line coming over it at a hard angle. As you go through the accelerating phase of the cast, that load on the finger is dramatically increased, then when you open the finger to release the line it still goes over the ball of the finger under great pressure. After a few dozen casts you end up with a very sore finger, and if you are using braid, the wear and tear on the flesh might even be more severe.

At this end of the tackle spectrum the maxi threadline comes into direct comparison with the sidecast; it runs a poor second here in the lightweight casting department, and a poor second again when compared with overhead reels in terms of long-range casting.

If you must do everything with a threadline reel you might consider one of these, but if you are simply looking for the most effective tackle to get particular jobs done, there are far better options available.

FREE-SPOOL THREADLINES
The free-spool threadline or BaitRunner system was introduced by the Japanese Shimano tackle company, and like GSP fishing lines, the system revolutionised threadline reels, making them a far more useful tool. Leading American fishing writer Mark Sosin nominated the BaitRunner as one of the most significant advances in tackle design of the last century, and I am in full agreement.

In spite of all the very real advantages offered by small and medium threadlines, they have one major drawback in that there is no satisfactory way to free-spool them to feed line to a fish when using natural baits. When the bail is left open, a short run by a fish results in loops of line spilling up into the guides. When the bail is closed to strike, the angler is out of contact with the fish until the slack from the coils is recovered, which produces a hit-and-miss situation, with the angler virtually striking blind most of the time.

The BaitRunner system provides a lever at the rear of the reel which can be used to take the spool out of gear while the bail remains in the closed position. This means that direct contact with the fish can be maintained at all times. When the angler wishes to strike, a small forward movement of the crank handle engages the gearing and the angler is again in direct contact with the fish.

LEFT- AND RIGHT-HAND REELS
In the small to medium threadline classes, most experts agree that a reel for a right-handed person should have the handle on the left side of the reel. This is mainly because when fighting a fish, the single-handed threadline is often held clear of the body with no real support at the butt from body contact. It therefore follows that you use your stronger hand to hold the rod, and your weaker hand to perform the simple task of turning the reel handle.

There are other benefits, such as not having to swap the rod from hand to hand when opening the bail before casting, and being able to snap the bail shut when a casting weight is still in full flight to bring it down on a particular spot (done by using the fingers of the left hand on the spool). Fishing like this may seem a little awkward at first, but when you watch a good right-handed angler working this way, you will soon see that it is the best way to fish threadline tackle.

LOADING LINE ON THREADLINES
The way you wind the line on a threadline reel is of the utmost importance. When filling the reel with line, the line spool must be held side-on to the reel so that the loops coming off the spool are being laid down in the same direction on the reel. In other words, your bail arm will be travelling clockwise, so it is important that the line comes off the spool the same way. Otherwise you will put a twist in the line that will cause all sorts of problems when you start to fish.

If you do get caught with twisted line somewhere along the way, the best solution is to let the line out (with nothing on the end of the line) behind a slowly moving boat and just drag it along for a while. When you wind it back on the reel the twist should be gone.

CLOSED-FACE REELS
Closed-face reels have never become popular in this country for the simple reason that they don't work all that well.

Something of a cross between a threadline and a baitcaster, they sit on top of the rod and are normally used with a pistol grip butt. With the spool cover removed you can see that they have a very narrow, front-facing spool like a threadline, but a pin located in a rotating skirt over the rim of the spool acts as a line pick-up. A cap fits over the whole spool assembly, feeding the line out through a small central hole.

Obviously, the line has to travel at the worst angle imaginable to leave the spool, moving up over the skirt, then angling down hard again to exit through the outlet hole.

When these reels are working properly they cast very well, as the centring of the line at the reel completely eliminates friction as the line passes through the rod guides. The problem is that the line tends to bunch up on the narrow spool, tangling inside the spool cover. They work best when spooled up with heavy line, which is no real help, because you would normally be fishing a light line class with a reel of this size.

OVERHEAD REELS

Obviously, overhead reels are mounted on top of the rod. The family of overheads is difficult to classify neatly, as there is some degree of overlap in every category. This is caused by the relatively small gradations of size available, and by the flexibility of many models.

The only hard demarcation line that can be drawn is between casting and non-casting reels. The casting reels start with the smallest of the baitcasters, and go on through to long-range rock and beach casting reels. The non-casting styles are generally limited to blue-water work, where strength, line capacity and a heavy-duty braking system are of paramount importance. The full game reels dominate this group.

If there is something the overheads have in common it is the general structure of the reel, which can be used to produce an enormously strong piece of equipment. The reel is housed inside a framework of end casings and cross supports that can be made as strong or as light as the job the reel is meant to do will require. In baitcasters this frame is relatively light, in keeping with the need to keep the overall weight of a single-handed casting tool down as far as possible. At the other end of the scale, a game reel may be manufactured out of a solid alloy block, giving it enormous strength.

CASTING OVERHEADS

The key to the casting reel is the operator's ability to control the speed of the spool. Unlike any other style of casting reel, the spool of the overhead spins when a cast is made, and as small wheels on a car need to turn more often than big wheels on the same car at any given speed, so the spool of a small reel revolves faster than that of a large reel when a weight is released at any given rod tip speed. It is also worth remembering that a full spool will turn more slowly than a near empty spool when casting.

The nightmare of novice overhead casters is a condition called overrun, where the reel suddenly spews forth a great mass of line that fouls up in a tangle all around the spool and sometimes up into the guides. This dilemma prevents many anglers from becoming competent with an overhead, which means that they have no hope of ever becoming really complete anglers.

The starting point is to understand how the overhead casting system works. When you cast an overhead, the reel is out of gear and you lock the spool in place with your thumb as you swing the rod through the arc of the cast. You then lift your thumb off the spool at the exact point where you want to release whatever you are casting. At that point of release the spool has to suddenly undergo tremendous acceleration to match the speed of the missile, and this is where most of the problems occur. The casting weight in flight is actually pulling line up through the guides as it travels through the air, and if the spool is

The three reels to the left are upmarket baitcasters, while the red reel to the right is an example of a reel with a slightly larger diameter spool that would be used on a double-handed outfit. Keep in mind that the bigger the reel, the larger the diameter of the drag washers, which is helpful when chasing hard-running fish.

travelling faster than the missile, you have a reel that is supplying line faster than the missile can drag it out through the guides. This oversupply has nowhere to go, and so it falls back onto the spool and tangles.

The two danger periods the angler must control are the initial surge of acceleration and the point towards the end of the cast where the missile slows down.

The reel must be set up properly in the first place. All casting reels have some mechanism to control overrun, the most basic being a nut that adjusts pressure on one end of the spool axle. Almost all modern reels now have a more sophisticated system – either an internal magnetic system or a mechanical damper system. The ultimate control is a well-educated thumb, but that comes later.

The idea is to create just enough drag on the spool for it to always be moving a fraction more slowly than the cast weight. The weight will therefore always be dragging line away from a slightly reluctant spool, eliminating the possibility of a build-up of slack when spool speed exceeds missile speed.

Whatever system you are using, start with an excessive amount of drag on the spool and *very gradually* back it off, cast by cast, until you find that you need to thumb the spool to stop it as the cast weight enters the water. In other words, with too much drag on, the mechanical control will be terminating the cast prematurely, so you should back off until the cast is going the full distance and you are providing the final spool check.

When learning to cast, concentrate on two things. Start with quite modest aspirations in the distance department. The more modest the cast, the less acceleration you are going to have to control. The second thing is to concentrate on being smooth and fluid in your movements. Do not try to snap or jerk a cast – this instantly causes a spool surge you won't be able to handle.

All this sounds much harder than it really is. If you set the reel up right in the first place, and concentrate on making short, smooth casts, all should go well. Once you get the hang of it, gradually increase your casting distance and try easing off just a fraction at a time on that friction control. Every step you take should be a small one.

For maximum casting distance, the very best spool control is provided by the thumb lightly feathering the rim of the spool. This takes practice, but once you get it right you don't have to think about it any more – it just happens.

A lot of lure fishing specialists, particularly those casting long distances, get to a stage where casting almost becomes an end in itself. They bang out one cast after another, each one just a little way short of their maximum range, and it is a very pretty sight to watch good anglers at work in this way. Their movements are relaxed and fluid, and energy expenditure is minimal.

BAITCASTERS

The single-handed baitcaster is a small overhead reel designed to cast quite light weights, ideally from the 4–30 g mark. Expert casters can handle lighter weights than this with the smaller reels, and with heavy lines and fast-recovery rods the reels can handle heavier casting weights.

Bass have always been a prime target for the baitcast specialists who like the way they can cast very accurately with this style of rod and reel.

The great strengths of the baitcaster are the way it lends itself to highly accurate casting and the fact that it is relatively easy to build a very good drag system into an overhead reel. Both of these attributes make it the ideal reel for fish such as bass, cod, barramundi, mangrove jack and other fish that can be taken by casting close to structure and cover of some kind. Lures must be cast to within centimetres of the cover in some cases, and then the fish has to be bullied if it is not to break off on the cover.

When married to the conventional short pistol grip rod, a cast is not much more than a wrist action. The natural arm position is a slightly extended one which has the reel close enough to eye level for the cast to be sighted well. A good cast with a baitcaster is one punched at the target with a flat trajectory, although experts use backhand, roundhouse and just about every other kind of action to put a lure just where they want it. The thumb on the spool allows the cast to be braked to drop the lure on target with great precision.

The physical characteristics of the system make the single-handed baitcast outfit an ideal fighting tool capable of delivering substantial power when heavy line is used. At the bottom end of the scale, a reel spooled with 3–6 kg line could be used to drag bass out of a snag pile; at the other extreme, the reel might be spooled with 15 kg line and married to a powerful fast-recovery graphite rod to try to come to terms with a hoodlum Niugini black bass in a similar situation.

There is very little penalty paid for going to heavier lines on reels with revolving drum spools. Light lines will cast better than very heavy lines to some degree, but with the line going up through the guides without twists or loops, there is virtually no friction factor to take into consideration. The greatest risk involved in fishing heavy lines on these small reels is that the reel frame or spool may become distorted if you overdo it.

Although most of the good baitcasters offer excellent drag systems these days, a light mechanical drag and a thumb lock over the spool is often the method preferred by creek anglers, who are regularly called on to stop a fish dead in its tracks at the critical moment before it reaches cover.

A double-handed grip on a short rod, a combination allowed by the design fundamentals of the baitcast outfit, allows the angler to apply more pressure on a

Somewhere between a baitcaster and a full-sized casting overhead, reels like this can be used to subdue some very big fish.

fish than does any other comparable line, rod and reel combination.

Baitcast reels use a level wind system where a guide moving backwards and forwards in front of the spool lays the line back on the reel evenly on the retrieve, which means the angler doesn't have to worry about this when fighting a fish.

A good baitcaster is one of the most rewarding styles of tackle to fish with, and is worth every cent you pay for it. It is worth buying from the top end of the market, because the baitcaster is by nature a precision tool, and near enough is not nearly good enough in this class of tackle.

MAXI BAITCASTERS

These overgrown baitcasters constitute something of a grey area, falling midway between a true baitcaster and a full-size surf reel. They are most commonly found in tropical waters as a bluewater extension of the shorter creek rod. They also get a lot of use as light beach reels in some parts of the country.

SURF AND ROCK CASTING

The largest of the overhead casting reels came into the surf and rock casting classification at a time when many people made use of the overhead's superior casting ability. They teamed them up with 3.6–3.9 m rods and used sinkers or lures weighing from 60–100 g. The advent of the sidecast reel and the unweighted – or very lightly weighted – baitfishing system put an end to the overhead's dominance of the surf, but there are still plenty of people who stick with the system simply because the outfit is more comfortable to use over long periods of time than the more cumbersome sidecast. There's also the undeniable fact that if you want maximum distance out of your casts, this is still the best way to go.

These days the majority of baitfishing work involving overheads is done in the southern states. The other major users are those who like to cast lures from the rocks for surface fish. In this context the baitcasters are referred to as high-speed spinning reels, which is a bit confusing for the newcomer, as the big threadlines also fall under that heading. Rock fishing jargon sorts this out by calling the threadlines 'eggbeaters'.

Dedicated snapper men love the overheads for their casting ability and good braking systems.

With sidecast reels eating into the overheads' territory at the light casting weight end of things, and the eggbeaters coming on much stronger with the help of the new GSP lines, there are still fundamental reasons for sticking with the overheads if you need consistent maximum range casts to reach fish.

The first is that a revolving spool reel almost completely eliminates the problem of friction drag when casting. There is a very slight initial drag from the spool as inertia is overcome at the beginning of the cast, and once the spool hits speed it is virtually throwing line up into the guides with an absolute minimum of drag on the projectile being cast. Even the angle at which the spool presents line to the guides is the optimum angle, and there are no coils of line involved to complicate matters.

The second reason is that the high reel position on the rod actually allows the angler to bring near total body power into play when casting. Good casters begin with the weight held out low before them, then start the cast by swinging back hard and pivoting the body off the thighs. Then, while the weight is still travelling backwards, in one continuous movement, the body pivots to the front, the left hand pulls down on the butt of the rod, and the high right hand drives the rod over the shoulder and forward. In the last part of the cast, the power of the pivot plus the back and shoulders all combine to deliver maximum power to the cast. No other casting system allows total body power to be brought into play like this.

As this style of reel is really an overgrown baitcaster, it also has the capacity to deliver a first-class braking system, and thumbs on the spool can be used to override the set drag and add a little extra pressure when required

NON-CASTING OVERHEADS

Non-casting overheads includes all those star and lever drag reels used for trolling and jigging, along with the complete family of gamefishing reels.

All the overhead reels considered so far have had casting ability rated as a high priority, so the actual weight of the reel has been an important factor in their design. When we get to the non-casting overheads, a different set of priorities emerge: line capacity, drag power, and strength of construction. In other words, we are now talking about a piece of machinery designed primarily as a tool for fighting big fish, and since the weight of the reel can now be supported by some kind of belt or harness, weight and bulk are no longer major considerations.

The spool is at the heart of a large-capacity reel, because enormous pressure can be brought to bear on the spool as stretched monofilament line, which has been wound on under considerable pressure, compresses on the reel spool. This is a little like having a python wrapped around your arm, constricting its muscles in the hope of crushing you. Under this sort

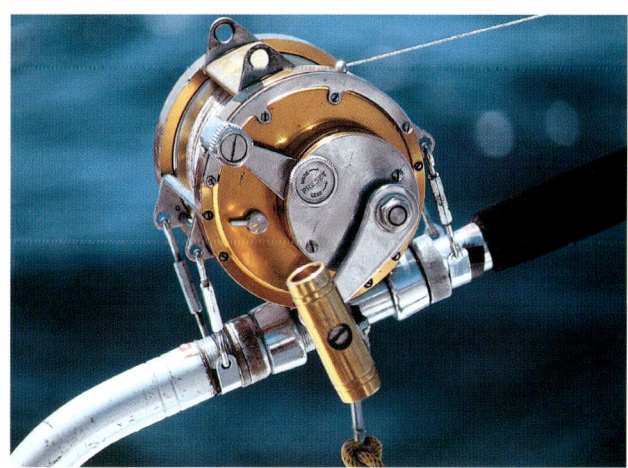

A 60 kg-class Penn International, the kind of reel required to snare the biggest of big game fish.

of punishment, any reel that is not strongly constructed will see the spool expand, the end plates pushed out of place and the supporting frame distorted. Overfishing the line class you are using can lead to the same disastrous consequences unless the reel is very strong.

Once weight has ceased to be a major consideration, the spool and housing can be made as strong as the job will require, and space can be allowed for the reel to house a really beefy set of gears and a large drag system. Heat dissipation is a real problem when dealing with large, enormously powerful and fast fish, so the surface area of the drag system is important.

This sort of reel uses the lever drag system. Instead of winding on a screw device of some kind to increase drag pressure on a series of smaller washers, pressure is brought to bear, through a lever-driven cam system, on a single large disc that is sandwiched between stainless steel plates. A small spring-loaded stop button is located towards the end of the lever's arc of travel. It is normal to set the maximum drag required for the line class to be in effect when the lever has been advanced to this point. There are many advantages associated with this system, including the fact that you can back off the drag if you feel the need, and still be able to come back to exactly the right setting by simply pushing the lever up to the stop again. You can also override the stop by simply pushing the lever past it.

Gearing varies enormously according to the job the reel is expected to do. Heavy-duty straight game gear may offer the ability to shift from a working gear down to a super-low 1:1 to break a deadlock with an oversized fish hanging deep. Even at 3.5:1 a big game reel will be recovering line at high speed if cranked vigorously. Gearing of 6:1 is frequently used by people who fish deepwater jigs a lot, but this is only effective when the jigs are relatively light and working with modest action. Sometimes a game reel actually makes

Centrepin reels have always been the weapon of choice for luderick both in rivers and on the ocean rocks.

a better deepwater jig reel than reels that have been primarily designed for jigging.

Many of these reels are fitted with heavy-duty clamping systems to lock the reel in place on the rod; if they are not locked in place they will constantly loosen the locking nuts on the reel seat. They are also fitted with heavy lugs on the top of the reel, to which harness straps can be connected with clips. Gravity alone determines that these very heavy reels will always be unstable and wanting to find their way under the rod, so support of some kind is essential.

CENTREPIN REELS

The term 'centrepin' encompasses a number of reels which are simply hand-driven direct-drive spools rotating on a central axle. In its simplest form, the centrepin is the basic blackfish reel, and has no further refinements. The next step up the ladder is to fit ball bearings to the reel to allow it to spin more freely.

The most basic fly reels are centrepins that are little more than line minders. The fish is usually played with the fly line stripped back by hand, then wound back onto the reel later. They are extremely light, which is an important factor in balancing the reel with light fly rods.

Saltwater fly reels are a more robust and complex version of the freshwater reel. They are used to capture larger sport and game fish, so they have a comparatively large line capacity and are fitted with sophisticated drag systems.

SIDECAST REELS

An Australian invention introduced by Jack Alvey, the sidecast reel is probably better known as an 'Alvey' than as a sidecast reel.

In some respects the sidecast has a lot in common with the centrepin family of reels, the main difference being the fact that it has a release lever just below the reel's foot which allows the reel to be turned side-on for casting then switched back into fishing position again after the cast is made.

The actual shape of the spool is the same as that of the handcaster, with one side of the spool coming out at a low angle to a softly turned lip over which cast line flows quite freely. The large-diameter spool is the key to the sidecast's success: to cast any given distance, considerably fewer loops of line need to be pulled from the reel than would be the case with a threadline – even a large one. The line is also laid out over a much greater spool surface, so there's less line-on-line friction at any point. Because the line flows so freely from the reel, and there is no friction contributed by moving mechanical parts, casting weights that would be far too light to be used with other systems are ideal for use with the sidecast reel.

Sidecast reels are available with many refinements these days, but it is the basic reel that completely revolutionised coastal fishing all around this country and changed the way we approach much of our fishing today.

The sidecast's great contribution to Australian fishing is its ability to cast unweighted, or very lightly weighted, baits over a considerable distance. Before the introduction of the sidecast, the need for considerable weight to cast any distance with an overhead reel restricted all land-based baitfishing to bottom fishing, and fish are not always on the bottom.

When the sidecast reel appeared, beach anglers in Queensland and northern New South Wales would use whole, unweighted garfish, mounted on a linked flight of four or five large hooks, to blitz the then prolific schools of tailor. Their catches sounded like Donald Bradman batting scores, with 100 fish per person in a competition team a standard sort of result. These days you would be roundly condemned for butchering fish on such a scale, but bulk catch competitions were all the go back then.

The Australian-made Alvey sidecast reel is still the only reel many beach and rock anglers will use.

This floating bait system also opened angling eyes to the fact that big bream and snapper were often feeding well up off the bottom, and that an unweighted bait moving around in a wash tended to find fish, and when it did, they were more likely to be hooked because there was no sinker drag on the bait to make them suspicious of the offering.

One other door opened by the sidecast led into the field of brute force fishing. Live baits, crabs and cunje could be allowed to float around in some terribly wild reef and whitewater country for jewfish, kingfish, groper, drummer and so on – large, powerful fish that would be certain to escape if given room to run. The sidecast, with its simple direct drive and virtually indestructible solid spool, was the perfect tool for the job. The anglers spooled up with 30 kg test line, flipped the bait out into the wash, then locked up on everything and dug in their heels when the bite came. The big fish that were captured this way could not have been taken with any other form of tackle available.

Rods: the long and the short of it

The illustration at right compares two extremes of the rod builder's art: an unlimited class gamefishing outfit, and the surf caster's rod and overhead reel. The surfcasting outfit is highly specialised, but does offer its owner some degree of versatility. The game rod, on the other hand, is totally uncompromising. It is the very best tool ever made for just one job, and it is absolutely hopeless for anything else at all. Between these two lie an infinite number of variations, and somewhere in the middle you might even find one single rod that is a perfect blend of those extremes. Let's take a look at why these two rods have been made the way they are.

The game rod is a tool designed to fish big marlin. It is intended for use on fish in excess of 450 kg, the old magic 1000 lb mark, 'a grander'. Anglers who put their money down for a rod like this are dedicated to achieving just one ultimate goal – the capture of a 450 kg plus billfish. Unlimited tackle is all about catching the ultimate fish.

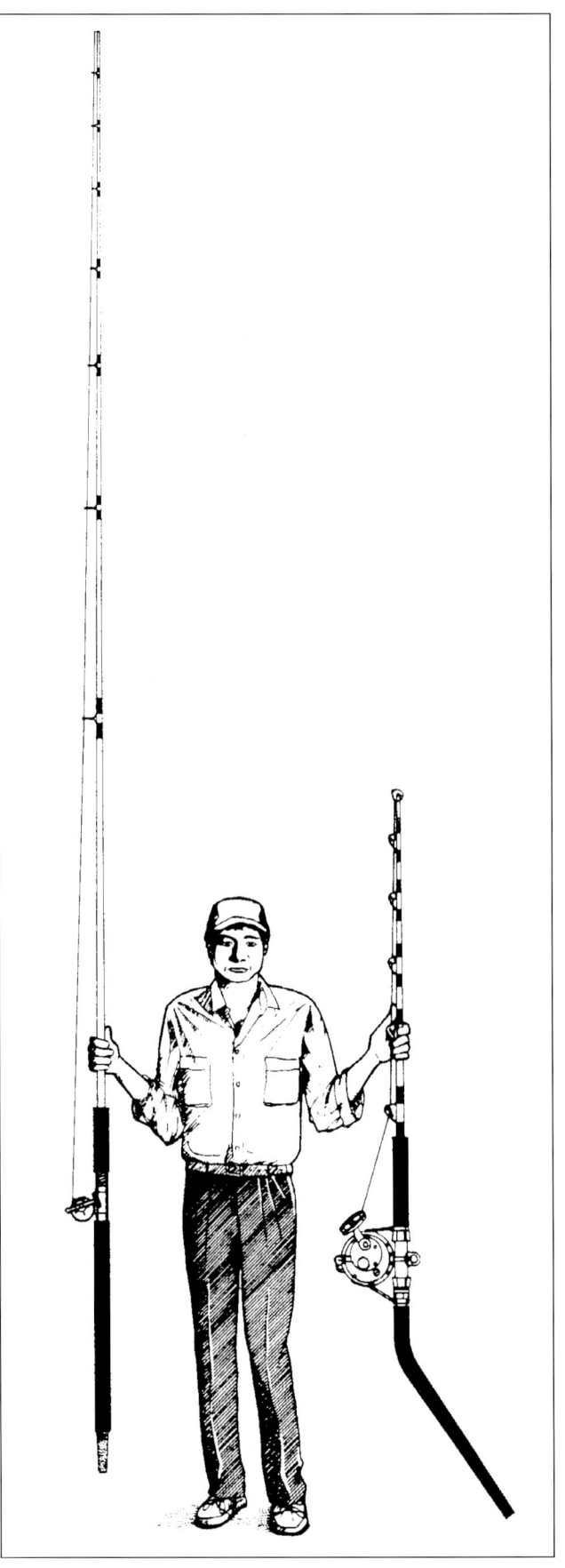

Rods of all classes have generally become shorter over the years, but many rock and beach anglers still like the reach they can get with a longer rod.

Although it is always hoped that each rod will be tested by a record fish, this rod is designed to deal with problems that arise with fish well short of the 450 kg mark: tough fish that can take line out over guides fast enough to create serious friction problems, and fish capable of getting so much line out in the water that friction from the water itself can present problems. It is not uncommon to find anglers having to make a great physical effort just to recover slack line on one side of the boat while the fish is jumping way out on the other side.

Obviously, priority one for the angler is to come up with the most powerful lever possible. The fish can't be stopped from running if it wants to, so tools that will recover the great weight of line stretched out over the open sea, then ultimately lever the head of a huge sulking fish around and force it to swim towards the boat are needed. The rod will never have to cast and

never have to register a bite. All it has to do is hold together as, with the aid of a specially designed fighting chair and body harness, anglers bring to bear every bit of strength and power they can to lever that fish up out of the depths.

The almost total lack of flex in the rod is offset by using large roller guides and the tip to eliminate friction on the line, especially at the tip, where the line passes over the end at a hard angle. It is true that the fish is often played off the reel rather than off the rod.

The bent butt is designed to get the massive reel close to the angler and to afford maximum leverage. The butt and reel seat are as strong as technology can make them. As you can imagine, the fighting chair is as much a part of this outfit as the fishing line. Nobody could stand around for long holding this tackle, even without a fish on the other end of the line.

When you think about how a crowbar works, using a long lever to bring great pressure to bear at the other end of that lever, you will appreciate that a fishing rod is a lever and the angler is always on the wrong end of the lever. To see how that works, get someone to hold a fishing rod in the fighting position, then take hold of the tip and bear down on it. You won't have to apply much pressure at all to have the person holding the other end of the rod really straining to resist the pressure you are comfortably applying. For this reason, the shorter the rod, the more pressure a fisherman can apply to the fish.

When we turn to the beach rod we see a situation where the leverage factor has been seriously diminished by the length of the rod, making it a fairly ordinary sort of a tool for handling big fish. The length has now become an advantage, though, because this is primarily a casting tool, and by describing a circular motion with the angler at the hub of that circle, tremendous speed can be generated at the rod tip, which is travelling at the outer edge of the circle. Very little effort is required at the hub to achieve this result.

Beach anglers need rod length to keep as much line clear of the surf as possible, and they need the combination of length and particular flex characteristics to achieve the long casting distances often associated with surf and rock fishing. Because the fish they deal with are relatively small, and can be played out at leisure over a clear sand bottom, there is little need for real fighting power in the rod, so its comparatively soft action creates no problems in that area. The overwhelming consideration is to be able to put the right bait and rig out into the part of the surf where the fish are likely to be feeding.

Although it is possible to generate enormous tip speed when casting with shorter rods, doing this involves radical acceleration that can tear hooks out of soft baits; it's a technique better suited to casting heavy weights. The more gradual acceleration of these rods is perfectly suited to getting baits out a long way.

A rod like this develops power evenly, all the way through from a comparatively soft tip to a moderately powerful lower section. The soft tip allows lighter weights to be cast respectable distances, and skilled casters can get quite heavy weights away over a good distance using the power contained in the full length of the rod.

Our illustrated example boils down to a power tool on the one hand, and a flexible long-range delivery system on the other. Every fishing rod ever made embodies more or less of both these characteristics.

BUILT-IN SPEED AND RECOVERY

The distance you can cast any given weight is determined by the speed it is travelling at the point of release – the end of the cast, when you actually release the line.

There are two major factors that determine how much tip speed you can generate. The first is the length of the rod, and the second is the recovery speed of the tip.

In the old days, when fishing rods were fairly unsophisticated, extra speed was generated by increasing the length of the rod. Some rods were 4.3 m or more in length, and when you consider that an expert caster may have an additional metre of so of line between the tip and the casting weight, anything around the edge of that 5 m arc would have been travelling through the air at lethal speeds. The rods did the job, but they were exhausting things to use, and the angler needed a great deal of elbow room to deliver a cast like that.

The early fibreglass rods were built along the same lines as the cane rods that went before them. They started with a fine tip, then gradually expanded the diameter of the blank as they moved down towards the butt. The tip was the least powerful, most flexible section of the rod, and the butt was the least flexible, most powerful section of the rod. Power increased, or decreased, in a smooth progression in either direction. Under load, such a rod would describe a parabolic arc.

But as builders explored the potential of fibreglass, they found ways to build more speed and power into any given length of rod. By increasing the thickness of the walls of the rod blank at various stages they were able to increase power wherever they wanted it. As rods that had the same external profile began to be able to vary in their casting and fighting actions, recovery speed became the factor determining the true character of the rod.

The best way to appreciate this is to take hold of a soft rod with a floppy tip and one that has a stiff tip. If you place the butts on the ground, take hold of the rod midway, then pull the tip back and just let it go, you will notice two things. The first is that it takes more energy to pull the stiff tip back, and the second is that the tip of the stiff rod will recover to its original position much faster than the tip of the soft rod does. That is a demonstration of 'fast recovery' at work; it is this recovery speed that determines the casting power of the rod.

When you cast a weight with a rod, at the start of the cast the rod tip has to overcome the inertia of the weight before it starts to move the weight. In that short period of inertia, the tip lags back and 'loads up', just like an archer's bow as the string is drawn back. At the end of the casting arc the loaded energy cracks the tip through, actually accelerating it faster than the rest of the rod, so additional casting power is delivered. Good casters make the most of this with a technique they call 'backcasting', where they actually swing the weight back behind them then punch into the cast as the weight is still travelling in the opposite direction, maximising the loading effect right at the start of the cast.

Tip speed and recovery have been further enhanced by the use of new materials, blended into composites, in rod blank construction. Most new rods have some graphite content – the more graphite and the less fibreglass in the mix, the faster, lighter and more powerful rods become.

For many applications, rod designers have been able to substitute speed and power, which are built into the blank, for length and still achieve the same ends. Unless they are specialising in areas where the absolute maximum casting range calls for power *and* length, rock anglers who cast lures to pelagic fish now generally use 3 m rods with overhead reels. Rod builders have even managed to decrease the diameter of blanks required to deliver a given amount of casting power, making rods more aerodynamic and easier to punch through the air when casting. The bottom line is that when you build more power into the rod, and at the same time make it lighter, you will reduce the demands on anglers in terms of energy input.

The plus with a rod like this is that it can deliver great power for casting, and the minus is that it needs a reasonable amount of weight on the end of the line before this power can be tapped.

SLOW ACCELERATORS

Having outlined the great advances made in the area of reducing rod length and increasing power, especially with respect to tip speeds for casting, a case must also be made for rods with slow-recovery characteristics.

The casting action of an ultra-fast recovery rod involves great acceleration, which in turn calls for a fairly substantial casting weight and a strong line. Casters seeking maximum distance usually use a shock trace of some kind – a short length of heavy line attached to the main line, capable of absorbing the tremendous stress generated where the line comes over the tip of the rod at a sharp angle. Obviously, only tough baits or aerodynamic lures can be cast with an outfit like this, as hooks simply tear out of anything soft and leave it behind.

Thus a case can be made for a rod blank with slow-accelerating characteristics: something with a light, slow tip, developing real power halfway through the rod. The lag at the start of the cast does not energise the rod tip to the same degree as a fast-recovery rod, so it winds up to follow the rapid arc being described lower in the rod slowly, gradually accelerating to maximum speed right at the very end of the cast.

A plus with this style of blank is that it will cast very light weights, as it does not require the drag of weight to load it with energy. You can simply whip or flick the tip of a rod like this and develop quite a lot of tip speed.

PARABOLIC AND FLAT-TRAJECTORY CASTING

Before moving on from the physical casting properties of rods, it is important to understand the role a desired casting trajectory can play in the choice of a rod style. Let's consider a few examples.

Bass and jacks are usually associated with snags and bank-side cover, and the bass enthusiast is often faced with a situation where the fish are hanging under a tree trunk, way back in under the cover of low foliage. The angler might have only a 20 cm opening above the water to get the lure through. In a case like this, an absolutely flat trajectory cast is the only way to go, and the best tool to deliver a flat trajectory cast is a light, stiff rod.

Stiff, fast-recovery rods are nearly always the best tools for casting where accuracy of placement is the prime consideration. The lure is cast with only a very short drop of line from the rod tip, and it pretty much follows right where the rod tip goes. If you punch the rod tip directly at the target, the lure should follow the same line.

The punched, flat-trajectory cast is also the best way to cast into a wind. You don't want your lure or bait hanging high in the air with a great tail of line vulnerable to the wind. If you go flat and hard you offer nothing for the wind to work on except the streamlined, fast-moving projectile you are casting.

The parabolic lob style of cast is almost inevitable with the softer, slow-action rods, but of course you can lob a cast with a fast-action rod if you wish. A parabolic arc is the path to aim for when you are casting a soft bait.

Long-distance casting involves a trajectory midway between the parabolic and the flat cast. To get absolute maximum distance from a cast, you need to keep the projectile in the air until all forward motion is spent.

Cast too high and you waste energy fighting gravity; cast too low and your projectile will splash down prematurely. A clean, low arc delivers optimum casting distance with all tackle.

Slow tips are extremely valuable when you have no backcast available to you at all, as when fishing a ledge with a cliff at your back, a common situation around the rocks. With a light tip in the rod you can still get a good cast away with a tight flicking action forward. It doesn't take much at all to load these tips, and a half arc will serve you quite well with a bit of practice.

LIFTING POWER

So far we have looked at just one aspect of fishing rods: the characteristics that allow them to meet our various casting needs. The other important consideration is the rod's role as a fish-fighting tool.

This is what lifting power is all about. The short stroker folds over at the tip end so the power is coming from a section just ahead of the foregrip of the rod. This takes some of the leverage away from the fish and puts it more in the angler's favour.

Rods are used to fight fish in two ways. Soft, springy rods are used as shock absorbers, soaking up short, sudden lunges made by the fish. Hard, more powerful rods are used as a lever to drag a heavy fish through the water, or at least to try to force it to swim in a desired direction.

The basic structure of the rod that makes it cast the way it does also determines the type of fighting tool it will make. Happily for the angler, casting requirements and fighting requirements are often complementary in a rod required for specialised fishing.

The shock absorber style of rod is the most basic rod type – this would include blackfish rods, a great many medium-length threadline outfits, and nearly all freshwater fly rods.

The shock absorber is a long, soft, parabolic rod. When loaded, it bends into an even, full-blooded curve, distributing the load over the better part of its total length. These rods usually employ a large number of line guides to help with this even distribution of stress.

The shock absorber is an ideal tool to use when the fish is relatively small, and a light line is required to catch it. The two things most likely to break a fishing line are a sudden jerk and a build-up of heat on a section of the line, which can happen when a section of line is worked hard over the surface of a guide at a radical angle. With a parabolic shock absorber, any sudden movement by the fish is simply soaked up in the even flex of the rod, and since stress is distributed evenly over a large number of guides, friction is kept to a minimum.

When fishing with a shock absorber rod, the angler simply needs to hold the rod upright, allowing the full flex to come into play, and wait for the fish to tire. As it does, the recovery in the rod itself is often sufficient to draw the fish in, and the angler can gently wind the line onto the reel until the fish is led into a waiting net.

The levers are more aggressive fighting tools. They are used to subdue larger, more powerful fish, and fish that are encountered close to cover and need to be dominated from the moment of the strike. They come in a great variety of sizes and shapes, ranging from the almost rigid unlimited big-game rod to a stiff butt section in an otherwise flexible casting rod. Any attempt to accurately describe all the characteristics of this group of rods is futile, as advances in rod blank design are taking place in months rather than years.

Suffice it to say that you can pretty much ask for any fighting characteristic you want in a rod – someone somewhere will make a rod that does exactly what you want it to do.

A high graphite content can produce very light, short rods that generate power along their entire length. Some are almost full parabolics under load, but parabolics with lightning-fast recovery. Others have quite extreme tapers, but retain a lot of power throughout the blank. This style of rod is favoured by many for bass, mangrove jack and some barramundi fishing, where what is needed is casting accuracy, backed up by a lot of power to dominate fish that are hooked close to cover.

These days many threadline rods are built on very fast recovery blanks, designed for the same tasks described above, as well as for fishing for surface and light game fish. Very fast tapers are popular with anglers who need to cope with a range of lure weights plus strong fish.

The short strokers used for bluewater sportfishing are a more radical rod design. Some of these rods are so extreme that the top half of the rod virtually folds completely over under load, leaving a straight, brutally powerful short lever from the foregrip down through to the butt. By holding the rod right at the top of the foregrip – which is usually extended – the angler can bring tremendous lifting power to bear against the fish.

Power, however, must always be traded off against other considerations. The more fighting power you build into the rod, the heavier the line you need to take full advantage of that power. The greater the casting power of the tip, the heavier are the weights and line needed to tap into that power. Fast tapers tend to offer the best of both worlds in many situations, with their combination of relatively light, fast tip and powerful butt sections. As in life as a whole, everything is a question of balance.

ROD PROFILES

In years gone by, friction was probably the angler's greatest enemy. It is now not the bogey it once was. Great advances have been made in recent years in the low-friction materials that are now being used in the manufacture of fishing rod guides.

It used to be possible to demonstrate friction between fishing line and a rod guide by threading a length of 15 kg line through the guide and then, taking hold of line either side of the guide, quickly sawing it back and forth over the surface of the guide under pressure. In many cases it was possible to reduce the line to jelly with just a few passes to and fro. The progress in the use of low-friction materials has been so great that you could do that stunt with 6 kg line and take quite a while to break the line now. Using GSP lines you might be there for most of the day.

There is a secondary friction point – where line makes contact with the rod when using overhead reels. While this is almost impossible to eliminate altogether, it can be reduced by using the correct number and type of guides. On cheaper rods the manufacturer will reduce the number of guides to contain costs, and line contact can then become a real problem.

With reels designed to be used under the rod you won't have the problem of the line rubbing on the rod, but if you have too few or badly placed guides, you may find that you have line travelling over some of the guides at a hard angle – these are potential trouble spots.

On the other hand, if you use too many guides, the weight can kill the action of the rod. There's that trade-off again.

As the rod becomes heavier, guide weight becomes less important, which is just as well, because some of the shorter rods with radical actions require a lot of high-bridged guides to keep the line clear of the rod.

In some of the short, lever-style rods it is just not possible to distribute line pressure evenly, and it is therefore not possible to eliminate potential hot spots. This is offset to a large degree by the way people fight large fish with this style of rod. When a large fish runs hard in the initial stages of the fight, there is no point in trying to hold the rod high, which produces maximum line friction on the guides. The angler reduces the friction by 'bowing' to the fish, pointing the rod towards the fish. This flattens the extreme arc in the rod, spreads line load more evenly across the guides, and reduces the total pressure across them. Much the same thing is done with game rods.

The heavier classes of game rods also produce some quite radical angles over which line must travel, particularly at the tip. From 24 kg on up it takes

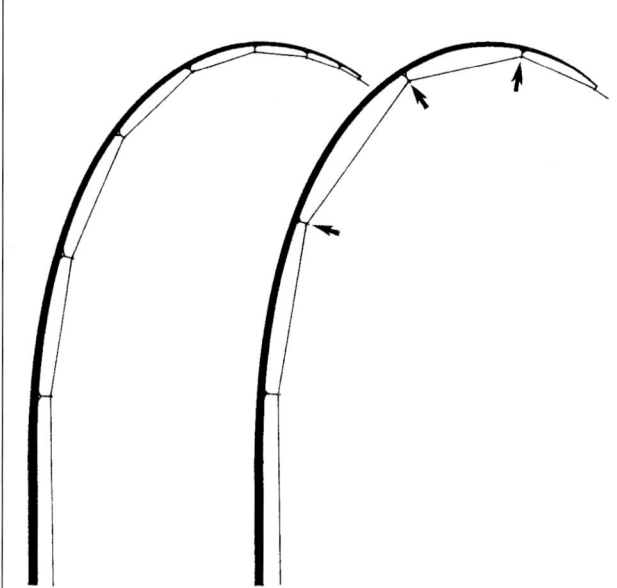

It is never possible to get a perfectly even flow of line over rod guides, but the illustration on the left shows how the spacing and number of guides has spread the load as evenly as possible. On the right, an insufficient number of guides has created three hot spots that will cause wear and tear on the line, possibly resulting in lost fish.

tremendous pressure to bend a traditional game rod, and most of this pressure is being applied at the extreme tip of the rod. As hot spots go, this one can be classified as 'red hot'. To cope with this problem, guide manufacturers produce roller guides – guides and tips that actually roll under the line – mounted in high, super-strong frames.

If roller guides are better than anything else, why not put them on all rods? Weight is the main reason, but they also affect flexibility. The roller plus its frame and feet add up to extra weight; they also require heavy under-binding to protect the rod blank, then over-binding to keep them in place. All this has a stiffening effect that goes unnoticed on a game rod but would be very obvious on anything noticeably more flexible.

ROD TYPES

Does the type of rod you choose determine the type of reel you will buy, or does the type of reel you need to use determine the rod you must buy? The answer is that it could go either way, depending on the circumstances.

Someone who fishes the surf could reasonably choose between an overhead reel, a threadline or a sidecast. Each reel would require a different guide set-up, and in each case the reel would need to be mounted at a different height above the butt. The reel would dictate the rod type. On the other hand, someone buying an outfit for yellowfin and kingfish would have a lot less to think about, because the line class and rod power required to handle these fish dictate the use of an overhead reel.

In the great majority of cases, however, the job the angler needs to do will determine rod, reel and line class as a package.

SINGLE-HANDED THREADLINES
Possibly the most universally accepted outfit of all, the single-handed threadline rod, normally measures 2 m or less, with the reel mounted some 20 cm from the butt. The most popular line size would be 2–4 kg breaking strain. This is often the style of outfit chosen by specialists wanting to fish 1–2 kg line classes.

'Single-handed' is a bit of a misnomer really, as you do have to use two hands to fish with these outfits; the 'single' refers to the number of hands required to cast.

Short threadlines are very flexible outfits, being able to cast ultra-light weights when coupled with light line and, at the other end of the spectrum, being used by sportfishing specialists to take line class records on quite substantial fish. Often referred to as 'spinning outfits', they are superb tools for casting light lures, which makes them popular for trout and bream fishing. However, they are most commonly used as a general-purpose outfit. A beginner can learn to use one effectively in minutes, which is one of the reasons for their great popularity.

The tree floating along in the background of this photograph had barramundi galore hiding in submerged branches. Tom Bethurem used a light but extremely powerful graphite rod to pull several of them out.

The introduction of GSP lines, with their low diameter to breaking strain ratios, has expanded the role of the light threadline quite a bit, although nowhere near as much as it has the larger threadline outfits. Because the line comes away from the reel in coils which create a lot of friction as the line goes through the guides, light threadlines have always worked best with soft, light lines. Now, with the GSP superlines available, you can fish a line with the same diameter as 2 kg monofilament and have 5 kg breaking strain to work with. This will no doubt lead to more powerful rods being used on large fish.

DOUBLE-HANDED THREADLINES

This category covers a wide variety of rods, ranging in length from just over 2 m to around 3.8 m. The smaller ones are among the most popular rods on the market, because they can be used to fish from the shore with bait for common light saltwater species and in river and bay fishing areas.

The more powerful versions are used with lures or live baits to sportfish for everything from mangrove jacks to small billfish.

With the reel position higher on the rod, anglers can use two hands to cast, which allows them to bring in the power of their arms and shoulders to get long casts away; two hands also allows a lot more power to be brought to bear when fighting a fish.

Line range with monofilament is normally 4–10 kg, with stronger lines reducing casting range considerably. Once again the introduction of GSP lines has transformed these outfits, making it possible to fish 15–24 kg at the top of the range, or stick with the old breaking strain and enjoy greatly increased casting distance.

A lot of anglers are specialising in these double-handed threadline rods these days and are becoming extremely efficient with them. They have developed casting skills – of a kind previously only associated with baitcaster reels – to probe snags in barra country, and are taking advantage of the range associated with GSP lines to stand well off those snags in order to avoid spooking the fish.

At the very top end of the range, with rods to 3 m and more in length, threadline outfits are used from the beaches and rocks in both lure and baitfishing roles.

Originally designed to cope with relatively small fish, the baitcaster has taken on the role of giant-killer. Here, Tim Simpson goes hard on a longtail tuna in Arnhem Land in the Northern Territory.

BAITCASTERS

Baitcaster rods are single-handed outfits designed to match up with the smallest of the overhead revolving spool reels. They measure between 1.5 and 1.8 m, employ a very short butt, and are usually fitted with some sort of trigger grip just under the reel seat.

Specialists use the smallest baitcast outfits with fine lines to cast quite light weights, but generally speaking they are at their best with line weights around the 3–6 kg range, casting lures from 7–40 g. In extreme cases they can be used with much heavier lines to deal with large tropical species lying up in mangrove roots and snags, or for freshwater heavyweights such as Murray cod.

Baitcasters are most frequently built on powerful blanks with plenty of tip speed, and are superior to anything else as a short-range, high-accuracy casting tool, which is why this is the outfit of choice when lure fishing for any species that lies up close to cover. Interestingly enough, the baitcaster is used to cast almost everything but natural bait. The term probably came from Europe and the US, where lures are sometimes called *artificial baits*, *crank baits* and so forth.

DOUBLE-HANDED BAITCASTERS

Choosing between a double-handed baitcaster and a double-handed threadline these days is pretty much a matter of personal preference. The baitcasters used to be in front because you could use lines as heavy as you liked without incurring a real casting penalty, and they had superior drag systems, but nowadays the threadlines have the baitcasters covered in both departments.

OVERHEAD CASTING

These are the rods covered in our opening discussion on 'The long and the short of it'. They used to be a major part of the fishing scene because people used overhead reels for many styles of fishing, but now the threadlines and sidecast outfits have reduced them to the highly specialised roles of long-range casting with baits and land-based spinning for surface fish.

SIDECASTS

The sidecast rod is a classic case of the rod being designed by the reel. Unlike the threadlines, the sidecast reels get better as they get bigger, and the 16.5 cm sidecast reel is close to the backbone of Australian surf and rock fishing these days.

These big reels throw line up into the guides in big loops when casting; to contain these loops with a minimum of line-on-guide friction, the first guide (called a stripping guide) is usually a large one set well away from the reel. All the guides are placed on around half the length of the rod, which is unusual. Because the reel is heavy, it is placed quite low on the butt, where it achieves some sort of balance.

Sidecast rods are usually long and fairly slow-tapered, with relatively soft tip sections. This is because they are popular with surf fishermen, and one of their great strengths is that they can cast unweighted baits, or only lightly weighted baits, over good distances.

BLUEWATER AND GAME RODS

Many of the rods we've already discussed could come into this category: the double-handed threadlines and baitcasters, for example. But apart from them there are rods that are designed to be used exclusively out on the bluewater. Many of these boat rods can be used for a variety of jobs; only the straight game rods can be classified as true single-purpose tools.

With double-handed threadlines looking after the casting chores, and straight game reels taking care of trolling and live baiting for the bigger game fish, fast-taper overheads with plenty of tip speed and a lockup point just ahead of the foregrip serve in many roles. They are used for trolling and live baitfishing, for

Long rods like this give the land-based angler additional reach to clear rocks and the longest possible casting range. The drawback is that they are too long to be efficient fish-fighting tools.

bottom fishing with bait and for deepwater jigging. Some people don't bother to go to the expense of dedicated game rods, and they use these short stroker rods for everything except the light lure casting which is the specialty of the threadlines.

These short levers (stand-up rods) have become very popular, probably because they are far more comfortable than any other form of rod for pumping big fish up out of the deep. Using any kind of long rod

The heaviest game-class tackle in action against a marlin in excess of 450 kg. Note how far the angler has been lifted off the seat as the fish uses the advantage of being on the right end of the lever (the rod).

the angler is on the wrong end of the lever, and that lever can do a lot of damage to the lower back when you are fishing straight up and down, as you often are out on the bluewater. With the short stroker style of rod the angler can almost use a straight-arm pull to the top of the foregrip, using upper back and body strength to lift the weight rather than allowing the vulnerable lower back to be stressed.

While game rods and reels are generally cumbersome and heavy, the stand-up rods are generally reasonably light, as are the medium-sized reels used with them.

FLY RODS

The major purpose of the fly rod is to cast an unweighted fly as far as possible. The casting weight is in the fly line itself.

With their beginnings in the folklore and rampant mysticism of trout fishing, fly rods tended to be, in the past, incredibly pure. Not only were they designed simply to cast a line; also, each rod was designed to cast one weight of line. This meant they had very little, if any, flexibility as a fishing tool.

As fish-fighting tools, the freshwater fly rods were as basic as a fishing rod could be – simple parabolics possessing very little muscle with which to maintain a serious argument with a determined fish.

What the system had going for it was finesse. By adding a succession of traces of diminishing size to the end of the coarse fly line, the final tippet could be rolled over at the end of the cast to deliver something the size of a gnat in front of the trout's nose without causing a ripple. That was the name of the game.

These days the young Turks on the frontier of sportfishing are saltwater fly specialists, and they are using equipment that has precious little to do with trout wands to take some impressive fish. They have taken full advantage of the great power-to-weight advantages offered by current rod-making technology – the very fine profiles of the new rods are a great asset to anyone who is going to ask their wrist to wave a powerful rod back and forth all day long. The new rods also have the fish-fighting power that was missing from the old rods.

The reel is always mounted as close to the butt as possible for three reasons: first for balance, second with a view to completely eliminating the possibility of the reel having any effect on the action of the rod, and third to stop coils of line looping around the butt of the rod.

THE ROD-BUILDER'S ART

Blackfish rods, land-based game live bait sticks, southern land-based snapper rods ... the list of special-purpose rods goes on and on. Even the descriptions of mainstream rod styles offered here is of necessity brief, and I have intentionally avoided the subject of rod blank design and materials. The manufacture and design of fishing rods is a complex art these days, and the subtleties understood by the best designers lie far beyond the scope of this book. It is also true that new materials are constantly changing the rules of the game; monthly magazines are best suited to offering advice on state-of-the-art happenings in this field.

By all means look into building your own rods, but be warned that it can easily become an obsessive and expensive activity. Do not ever look upon it as a way of getting rich.

It is, in my opinion, better to buy one good rod than three cheap ones. A rod that does the job for which you bought it, and does it well, will last you a long, long time, and will give you much pleasure. A rod that does not deliver will cost you fish and cause you a great deal of frustration.

Fly rods are primarily designed to do one thing – cast a fly line. When you pit them against a tough fish, in this case a kingfish, you need to have patience.

Hooks

You might be surprised at just how complicated the subject of fish hooks can become, with specialist anglers going to great pains to get hold of a particular hook pattern that, to the novice, may not look very different from one you can buy in the supermarket. This level of focus on a particular hook is normally the result of an angler fishing for a particular fish over a long period of time – a process of trial and error has led the angler to one hook that outperforms all others. Sometimes the hook really will be much better; at other times most of the difference will be in the angler's mind. Always be prepared to experiment with something new and see how it works for you.

There are a few things about hooks that need to be kept in mind at all times. The first of these is one of the most important details in fishing for any fish, anywhere in the world. This is that most hooks are blunt until you sharpen them, and blunt hooks will miss more bites and lose you more fish than any other problem you are ever going to encounter. Take the attitude that there is no such thing as a sharp hook in a box or pack of fish hooks – some hooks are just less blunt than others.

This problem has been addressed to some degree by the introduction of chemically sharpened hooks, which come out of the packet with a point as sharp as most anglers could create with a stone on a normal hook – perhaps even sharper. So sharp, in fact, that you need to handle them with some care.

You also need to keep in mind that sharp hooks, even chemically sharpened hooks, don't stay sharp forever. It pays to check your hooks from time to time, especially when you are casting to cover with the occasional hang-up in the timber (see the following section for correct sharpening methods).

Another thing to keep in mind when you are trying to present a natural bait is that hooks represent weight, and some of the strongest hooks can represent a lot of weight. This may make a critical difference when you are trying to get an unweighted bait to drift back down a berley trail in a natural manner.

Weight may also be a major consideration when you are changing hooks on lures. Many of the imported lures we use in this country are fitted with fine wire hooks, and they are nowhere near strong enough for much of the lure fishing we do here. It is

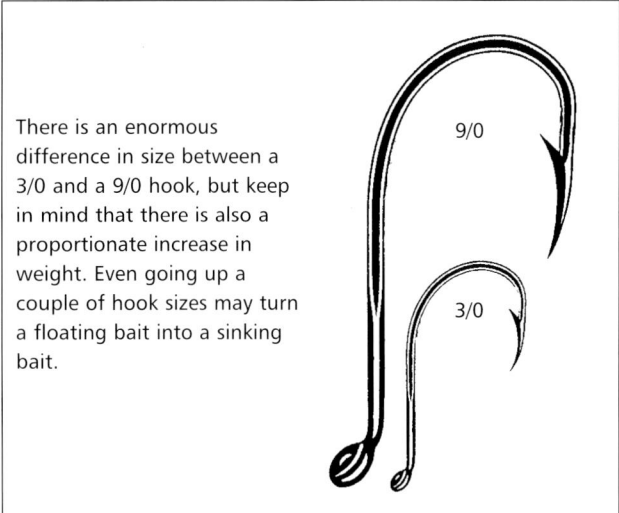

There is an enormous difference in size between a 3/0 and a 9/0 hook, but keep in mind that there is also a proportionate increase in weight. Even going up a couple of hook sizes may turn a floating bait into a sinking bait.

common practice to remove the wire hooks and replace them with much stronger and heavier stainless trebles, but when you do this you may well upset the balance and swimming action of the lure. Some lures are very sensitive – you may find yourself stuck using light hooks that need frequent replacement, or you may find that you can get away with a smaller size in the stronger hooks to offset the weight factor. It is always a good idea to do a 'before and after' test swim of the lure to see if your change creates a problem.

SHARPENING HOOKS

If you examine the head and jaw structure of some of our most popular species you might start to wonder how they ever get caught on a hook at all. Bream and snapper, for instance, have dental work that seems to form the greater part of the mouth area – there is precious little opportunity for a hook to find purchase anywhere in there.

If you take a random selection of hooks from various packets and run the points of the hooks over the palm of your hand at a 45° angle, you may be surprised at

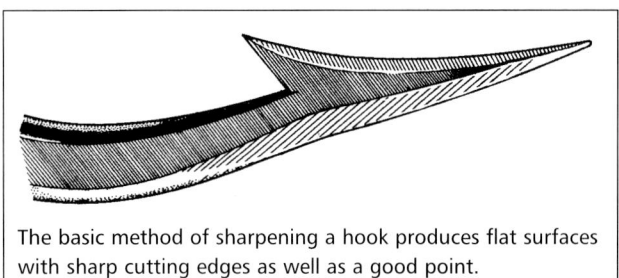

The basic method of sharpening a hook produces flat surfaces with sharp cutting edges as well as a good point.

how many times you can do this without having the point of a hook catch on your skin. Fine wire hooks will generally do better than more robust hooks.

The real test for sharpness is to repeat the same exercise on the surface of a thumbnail. Even fine wire hooks will usually just skid across the nail. When you do this test and the points of your hooks dig in straight-away, without any slip at all, you are fishing with sharp hooks. You may also find that you are starting to hook a lot more fish.

You need to carry a small whetstone for sharpening small hooks, and a diamond sharpener or file for the larger ones. You can buy diamond sharpeners with a groove in the side for sharpening hooks: these are very good, as they don't allow the point of the hook to skid off the surface and find a finger if your concentration wanders a bit.

For heavy hooks, an appropriate file is usually required.

Very fine hooks normally only require a few strokes on the whetstone to achieve a decent point – and the nail test will tell you when they are right. When the point of the hook is large enough for you to actually see

what you are doing, you should be aiming to achieve a triangular point. The great virtue of the triangular point is that as well as achieving a good point this way, you also make three cutting edges along the hook point.

Take care not to oversharpen your hooks by creating too long a point. This can actually weaken the hook – the whole point may break off. If you use the same hook for any length of time, check the point every now and then. Hook points come into contact with all sorts of hard surfaces, and your very sharp hook may have its point removed or bent over on the first cast if it comes into contact with a rock.

Always have a look at your hook after you've been snagged, and check the trebles on lures after every fish has been landed. Even small fish can get enough leverage on trebles to twist them into all sorts of funny shapes.

HOOK PATTERNS

There must be literally thousands of different hook shapes, and variations on those shapes, available around the world. Out of that enormous variety, most anglers end up choosing just a few patterns, and then a variety of sizes of those patterns.

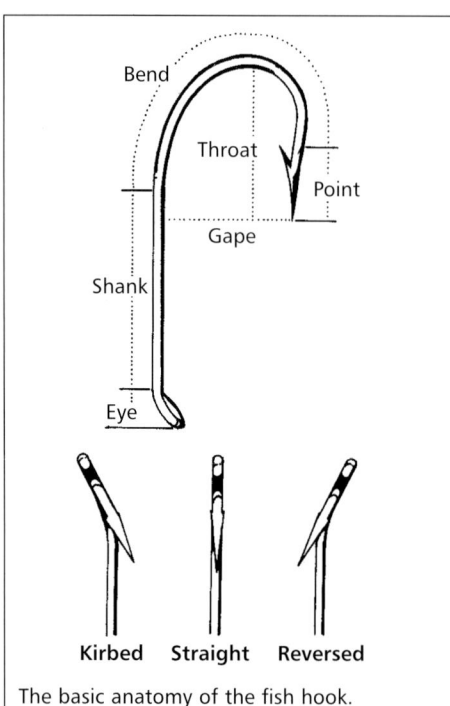

The basic anatomy of the fish hook. Reversed and kirbed points need to be thought about with some care, as having the bend going the wrong way can result in the point being buried in the bait, reducing the chance of a hookup.

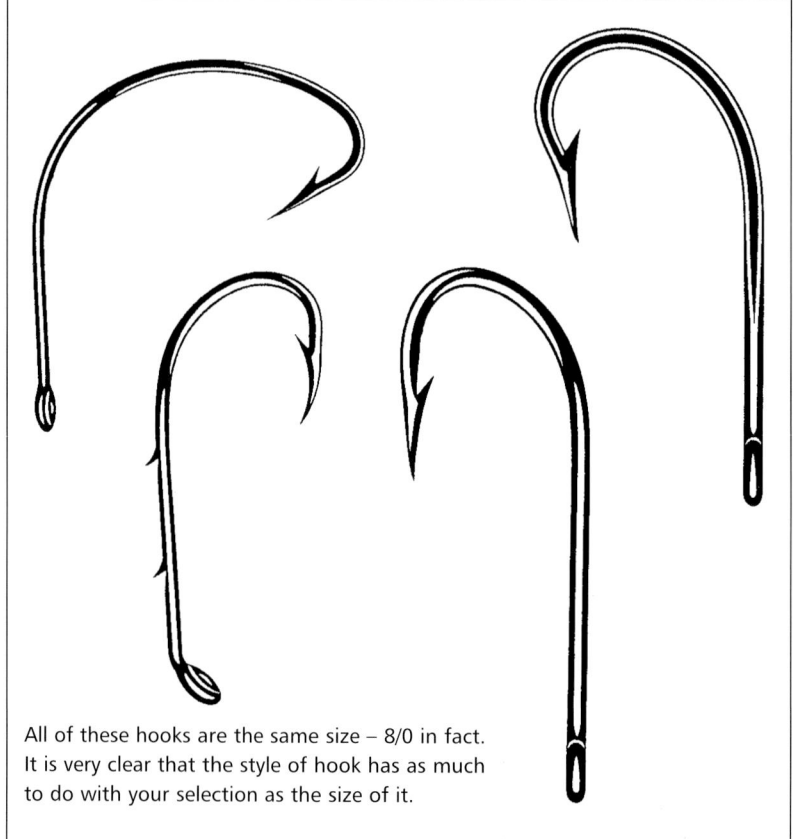

All of these hooks are the same size – 8/0 in fact. It is very clear that the style of hook has as much to do with your selection as the size of it.

Hooks have many different types of points; they vary greatly in the shape and gape of the bend; they have variation in the length of the shank; they have different kinds of eyes (and sometimes no eye at all); and they come in a variety of weights and strengths.

Then, on top of all that, most hooks are also available in stainless and non-stainless finishes, although stainless hooks are not quite as popular these days for the simple reason that non-stainless hooks quickly break down from rust if left in fish that are hooked and lost, eventually dropping out of the jaw, while stainless hooks stay put. Some stainless hooks are the best choice in areas of game fishing, or in other areas where the particular pattern or strength will make a critical difference, but if you have a choice, try not to use them.

So where do you start when you just want to buy a few hooks to go fishing?

Choosing a hook for a particular situation starts with you deciding what sort of fish you plan to catch. In an estuary where bream are a pretty safe bet you will be fishing for relatively small fish, using small, soft baits and fishing with light line. This will mean you don't have to consider strength in the hook – you can select light, fine hooks. Remembering that these baits may be quite soft, you might lean towards those hooks that have a sliced shank. This produces a little barb or spur on the shaft of the hook that can be a help in keeping a soft bait in place.

The size of the fish you are after dictates the size of the hook, and as a general rule it is safer to have a hook that is too small than one that is too large. If, for example, you had a mixture of bream and whiting on hand, it would not hurt to go down to a small, long-shanked hook to make allowance for the whiting.

If, on the other hand, you were still going to fish for bream, but wanted to do your fishing in rough water from a rock ledge some 5 m above water level, swinging the fish up to your spot with a relatively powerful rod, you would obviously need to use a stronger hook.

Don't complicate things by saying to yourself, 'But what if a big flathead or jewfish comes along?' If a big flathead or jewfish scoffs your little bream bait you are in trouble anyway, and there's not much you can do about it. If you start trying to make too many compromises, you will end up with a rig that won't

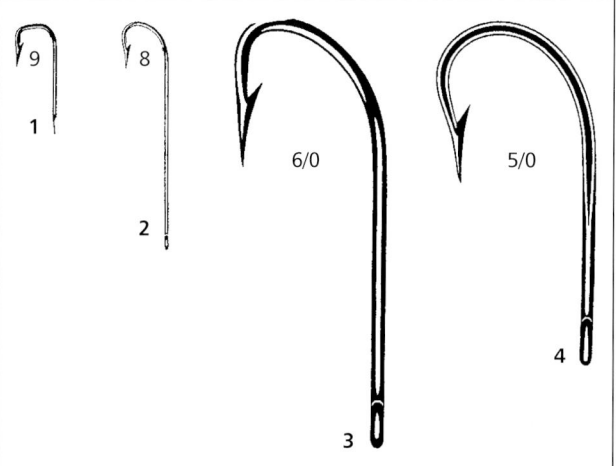

Different hook shapes make them ideal for a variety of jobs. The flattened eye and squared bend of the sneck (**1**) makes it popular with luderick anglers presenting weed baits. The long-shanked Kirby Kendal (**2**) is the choice of whiting anglers, especially when fishing with worms. The Mustad Limerick (**3**) is a strong hook ideal for use with heavy lines, and it comes in a variety of finishes. A similar strong hook, but with a shorter shank, is the Tarpon (**4**).

catch anything. If you want to catch a flathead or jewfish, put out a live bait on a heavier line with a bigger hook, and just trust the big fish to find the line aimed at it.

Going back to long-shanked hooks, these were once very popular – particularly the larger sizes – with flathead anglers. The idea was that the long shank would stop the flathead biting through the line. This all dates back to a time when fishing lines were nowhere near as good as they are today. The system had an inherent weakness: a decent flathead can probably swallow the longest long-shank hooks ever made anyway.

The idea with flathead is to use the best hook for your bait, regardless of shank length, and to use a short length of heavier monofilament line for a trace – 10 kg would be ample. A hook with a particularly wide gape would be more suited to a fish with a mouth as large as the flathead.

A truly weird-looking hook that some flathead specialists are coming to favour is the Mustad wide-gape 37140. The enormous gape on this hook is particularly well suited to finding a grip on that cave of a mouth, and I like the way the point can stand well clear of a large live bait.

Flathead do not bite through monofilament line, they saw through it when they shake their heads vigorously when brought to the surface. When fishing for them it is advisable to use a heavier mono trace, but you can also overcome the problem by keeping the head of the fish in the water until it is netted.

Flathead do not bite through a line – they saw through it with their fine teeth when shaking their head. Nine times out of ten this happens at the side of the boat when an overanxious angler pulls on the line and lifts the head of the fish from the water, which actually helps the fish by stretching the line nice and tight across its jaws. If you keep the head under the water and net the fish under the water, you won't get your line bitten off by any flathead.

Long-shank hooks in very small sizes are the right thing to use when presenting worms for whiting, and

they can be good for touchy bream. They are invaluable when catching live bait, which should be handled as little as possible. With the baitfish over the tank, simply hold the hook by the shank and the fish will usually shake itself off and drop into the tank without being handled.

The style and size of bait you use will have a lot to do with the style and size of hook you choose. Live yabbies dictate a fine, light hook – otherwise the bait may be ruined by being put on the hook. Worms are also best presented on a fine hook, often a long-shank hook. Strip baits of fish flesh with the skin still on often call for a hook that is of medium weight, very sharp, and one that has a relatively small eye if you are going to pull the hook right through the skin; otherwise, once again, the bait can be ruined when you try to get it on the hook.

If the bait is to be presented with the point of the hook just passed once through the tail, with no further threading, you would probably be able to get away with a very heavy gauge of hook if you thought you needed it. A crab bait is an example of a bait that can be effectively used with the heavier gauges of hook.

It is particularly important to keep hook sizes appropriate to the bait when fishing any kind of live bait. You might get away with a heavy 6/0 hook in a strong 15 cm yellowtail, whereas an 8 cm poddy mullet could call for a light 2/0 hook, or something even smaller. When you use live bait, don't think in terms of *live* bait, think in terms of *lively* bait. A lively bait will always be the first thing to be taken, and sometimes it takes a very lively bait indeed to get a strike at all. Don't make the hook any more of a handicap to the bait's swimming action than it has to be.

If you use a hook with an offset point, ensure that the point will be facing away from the bait if the shank is laid flat along the side of the fish. Check this by actually turning the eye of the hook down to face towards the tail of the bait, at which time the point should be turning away from the bait. If you take the hook through the bait so that the point turns in, the point of the hook is likely to catch in the side of the bait, ensuring that you can't possibly hook anything that takes it.

Offset points on hooks can also cause a bait to spin; they are never used with any sort of lures for the same reason. If you favour offset points on your hooks, make sure you use a swivel above them.

Heavy-gauge hooks are only called for when the rest of the tackle is heavy enough to test the strength of the hook. You can only apply as much pressure to a hook and a fish as your line and rod allow. Fishing with 3 kg line on an appropriate rod, there is precious little chance of even a light hook being straightened. As most people underfish any given line class to a large degree, you could probably stretch that to 6 kg line. If you were about to indulge in a little knock-down, drag-out fishing with some tough customers like groper or drummer, using tests of 10 kg up, then hooks in the double- and triple-strength class are called for, and are appropriate to the tackle.

Something well worth keeping in mind with the heavier hooks is the ability of your tackle to actually drive the point and barb in and set the hook. Even a very sharp xxx hook takes a lot of setting in the exceptionally tough jaws and lips of some of the rock species. In a small, light fish, the hook may actually push the head of the fish away before it penetrates.

If you know nothing at all about hooks, put your trust in the tackle store experts. They will certainly get you started with a good average selection of hooks for the area you plan to fish. Buy a wide range of hooks rather than a lot of one pattern until you have your own preferences established. Whatever else you do, experiment! Bites missed do not always indicate tiddlers too small for your hook. Large fish often mess and fiddle with a bait if it is not to their liking, and a large hook in the bait will soon become obvious to them – it may be enough to turn them away. Sometimes a small hook will get a result in such a situation.

Very large fish can be taken on small hooks, but a small fish will not be able to take a hook that is too big. You rarely have anything to lose by fishing a small hook, so when in doubt, think small.

Hooks must also be kept in proportion to the bait, and baits need to be kept in proportion to the hook. Unless you are using a super-soft bait such as bread, dough, or perhaps a soft-flesh fish bait that will simply fall apart as a fish takes it, *you must always have the point of the hook standing clear of the bait*. By all means hide as much of the hook as you can, if you think that helps – and sometimes it is important – but always try to have the point standing clear. That often dictates the size of hook you must use with a particular bait.

Small hooks for big fish should also be a consideration when fishing a floating bait down a berley trail. All hooks have weight, and a hook of any size, plus the drag of the line, will cause a bait to sink at a faster rate than the berley around it. A big hook in a floater could have your bait passing under the fish every time, particularly when fish are hanging back from the boat. A small hook just caught in the very end of the bait's skin will probably do the job, even on big fish.

Hook preferences are largely dictated by the area in which you fish, but I find myself drifting towards a very simple selection of hooks these days, with a definite preference for straight-point, short-shank hooks with a comparatively wide gape to a very wide gape. With the exception of a few heavy hooks for the odd big fish live bait situation, I am also moving towards smaller hooks, especially when fishing any kind of floating bait, where the smallest hook that can stand a point clear of the bait is the choice most of the time. This is, of course, purely personal, and most people I fish with work with a larger selection of hooks, and are very particular about using particular patterns for different jobs.

DOUBLE AND TREBLE HOOKS

Double and treble hooks are specialised hooks that are used most often with lures. All multi-hook arrangements allow strong-jawed fish to exert leverage that may damage the hooks, and sometimes enable the fish to lever the hook right out. Doubles are particularly bad in this regard, so when you can choose between doubles and trebles, choose the trebles. If the choice available allows for single hooks, it is usually better to choose a single.

GANGED HOOKS

Ganged hooks have their origin in tailor fishing, but these days they are one of the most versatile rigs available to the beach and rock angler. They are also used a good deal by small-boat people working shoreline washes, offshore islands and bomboras. When baited with blue pilchards or fresh sea garfish, they account for an extraordinary variety of fish species.

Hooks are ganged by either closing the barbs with pliers to get the hook through the eye of the next hook in the gang, then re-opening it or by using Mustad

4202 open-eye hooks, which are closed with pliers after ganging. The alternative is to open the eyes of the selected hooks yourself by using sidecutters to force the bend of the eye away from the hook shank.

When ganging hooks, it is most important to remember that the eyes must be bent in to an angle of 45° with pliers (if the eyes are not already turned down); otherwise the hooks tend to lock up and it is impossible to manipulate them when baiting up. Locked hooks also lever themselves out of the bait when cast.

Fishing big baits such as pilchards and garfish, the hooks will be from 3/0 to 5/0 in size, depending on the size of the bait. The size of the bait will also determine the number of hooks used in the gang. Most anglers make up a quantity of ganged hook rigs, covering a range of hook sizes, at home. It is easier to remove a hook than to make up whole gangs when you are out fishing, so err on the side of too many rather than too few hooks in your rigs.

You will become adept at judging hook sizes and the length of rigs you need for particular sized baits after a while, but if you are new to it, the most important hook of the lot is the one that goes through the eye of the bait. Lay the flight of hooks along the side of the bait, with the centre of the bend of the top hook in the gang (the one the line is tied to) sitting right over the centre of the bait's eye. Ideally, the last hook in the gang should then be sitting slightly above the fork of the bait's tail – this hook should penetrate the bait where the centre of the bend of that hook falls. Put the last hook (the one nearest the tail of the bait) in first, remembering that it is vitally important for the hook to go directly in and straight through the bait at that exact point. Each subsequent hook should go into the bait immediately below the centre of the eye of the hook preceding it.

If you allow the hooks to go through the bait at an angle, or if you do not ensure that they go straight through the bait at the exact point where they should be, when you cast, the hooks that are badly aligned will tear loose and you will probably throw the bait away before you get a fish on it. If you are spinning with the bait, a bait with badly set hooks will twist and probably swim in an unnatural manner, or spin.

The best way to get a gang of hooks in right is to carefully line the hooks up on the bait, then press firmly on the bend of the last hook with your thumb. On pilchards and garfish, this leaves a slight impression in the flesh, and it is then easy to see exactly where the points should be going in.

Some anglers extend the use of ganged hooks very cleverly by linking small hooks – to be used with very small baits – together. Small mullet and whitebait, along with strips of any good bait flesh, can be every bit as lethal as whole pilchards, which are probably better suited to reasonably large fish. I watched West Australian angler Ross Cusack catching whiting on whitebait mounted on a flight of six No. 10 Tarpon hooks, and came away thinking it one of the most flexible rigs I'd ever seen. Small baits like this are more commonly rigged on three slightly larger hooks. These tiny rigs are fiddly things to make and use, but consider the range of fish a rig like that will cover!

Sydney fisherman Dave Harrigan uses Mustad 7766 Tarpon hooks in sizes from 1 to 4, in flights of three or four, to fish lightly salted strips of pilchard in similar situations, and he often takes big whiting, along with other species, on these rigs. You will find hook preferences varying from one location to the next, which may well reflect the advice of the local tackle shop.

Sinkers

In a perfect world we would never have to use a sinker on a fishing line. We would always have just our bait on a razor-sharp hook and be able to fish with lots of slack line, so that when a fish picked up that bait and inspected it before swallowing and turning away, the bait would feel as natural and weight-free as any other naturally occurring morsel in that particular area.

Sadly, we live in a world that is less than perfect, and our rigs will nearly always be less than perfect because we need to use some lead to get baits out to where the fish are when we cast, and we often need to use lead to get a bait down into deep, turbulent or fast-running water. We have to accept this state of affairs, but the right attitude towards setting up a rig for any kind of fishing is this: no lead is perfection, so every gram of lead you add to the rig takes you one more step away from the ideal. If you rig up with this attitude in mind, you will be well on your way to becoming a much better angler.

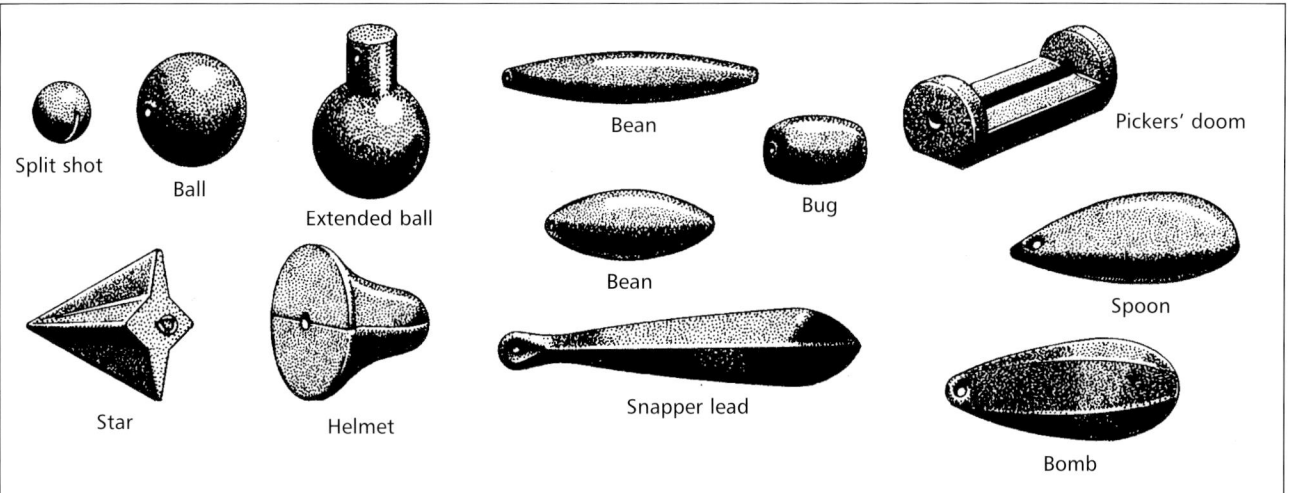

Split shot

Ball

Extended ball

Bean

Bug

Bean

Star

Helmet

Snapper lead

Pickers' doom

Spoon

Bomb

Weighting a line to take a bait below the surface of the water is just the primary purpose of a lead sinker. The sinker selected can make or break a terminal rig, and you need to understand which particular sinker will serve you best in each situation you have to deal with. The cross-section presented here covers the most frequently used styles of lead.

Before we go further into the subject of sinkers, we should look at ways and means of cancelling out their side effects. Whenever you can, use running sinkers; you should be able to use them whenever you are over a good bottom of any kind. As long as you have no knot, swivel or ring above a sinker, and you allow some slack line for a fish to run with, all sinkers that have the line threaded through them are running sinkers. Generally speaking, though, the hole through a sinker is usually small and is often choked with sand or grit, so there could be quite a bit of resistance when line tries to slide through it.

The best way to set up a running sinker is to use a spoon, a snapper lead, or any kind of sinker you can tie on a short dropper, then tie this to a ring. The main line is then threaded through the ring so that it can slide quite freely. Sinkers that have a clip swivel embedded in the lead, so that you can change sinkers quickly by running the line through the swivel's eye, are now available. You can do a similar thing for yourself by attaching spoon sinkers on a clip – the swivel would stay on the line, which is threaded through the ring end, and the clip goes through the eye in the sinker.

The pickers' doom is an old favourite with bream people, who use it to fish fast-running rivers. This funny-looking little sinker, with its arches at either end, is the best running sinker of them all. It is usually held in the hand while the bait is dropped over the

side and slack line is fed into the current. When enough line is out the sinker is then dropped over to work its way right down the line to the hook. When the sinker is judged to be all the way down to the bait, and if there is no fish on the line, it is retrieved and the process is repeated.

The alternative method is to fix the sinker behind a very long trace, up to 6 or 7 m long. In this situation the sinker acts as an anchor point, with the long trace allowing the bait to move freely about in the current. It can be a lethal fishing system at times.

Novice anglers often use far too much lead because they want to anchor the line to the bottom and keep a tight line between the rod tip and the bait so that they can 'feel' the bite. This is a dreadful mistake to make, because many fish take food into their mouths by expanding their gills and virtually inhaling it, along with water that is then expelled through the gills. A fish has no hope of inhaling something that is firmly anchored to the bottom, and if it does go to the trouble to inspect it with a direct bite after that initial turn-off, odds are it won't go on with it if it feels weight there. After all, if you went to pick up a 5 cm prawn and it weighed 100 g, you'd be more than a mite suspicious of it too!

Sinkers come in a great variety of shapes and sizes, and some do particular jobs better than others. There are sinkers that are designed to cast well, others where priority has been given to gripping power, and yet others that set out to be a combination of both.

BALL SINKERS

At any size, the ball presents casting weight in a very compact and aerodynamic shape, yet the very shape that makes it easy to cast is a drawback in terms of holding power. The ball is easily rolled about the bottom by surge and wash; if it is used over a rock bottom it will roll around until it finds a crevice to roll into.

Having said that, there are occasions when we want the terminal rig to move, and this is when the ball sinker is an obvious choice. An example might be when fishing a tidal run in relatively shallow water, when the bait is cast up-current and allowed to swing back in an arc with the run of tide. You need to get the bait down, but you don't want anything to impede it and stop it moving naturally with the current.

Ball sinkers are most often used these days in rigs that require only a very small amount of lead, and in semi-floating rigs that are not intended to work on the bottom. Small ball leads are generally rigged to run right down the line and sit on top of the hook.

BEANS AND BUGS

Bean and bug sinkers are an improvement on ball sinkers in that they are both good casting shapes and they both have much better bottom-holding profiles. These, and other flat-sided sinkers, are also a good choice when hand-lining in boats, as they don't roll around the deck tangling coils of line that are lying there.

The bean is just that, a bean-shaped sinker, which means that it can roll from side to side but in no other direction. It is another sinker that is favoured where the bait is fished as a sinking floater; it is also a good casting lead.

Beans in large sizes are often the lead of choice with people fishing deep water where the rig calls for a sinker on the main line above the hook rather than any type of dropper rig. Sometimes their combination of mass and a reasonably slim profile means that they work better than anything else when there is a strong current working on the line.

Bugs are something of a favourite with many anglers, especially in the small sizes – around 10 mm in length and smaller. A bug could be described as a bean someone has stomped on, because it has a flatter profile. The result is a lead that will sit on the bottom quite well in anything other than a strong surge. Bugs are very good when allowed to run right down onto the hook in a light bream rig.

BARREL SINKERS

The barrel offers the slimmest profile of all the leads, which makes it particularly useful when a trolling line needs weight, although this is not done very often. It also has some value when used on a drift rig, in that it moves through sand and gravel with a little less drag than bulkier sinkers do.

SNAPPER LEADS

The snapper lead is the sinker of choice when maximum casting distances are needed, or when bulk weight is required to reach the bottom in deep water or hard-running currents. It has the best casting shape of any of the sinkers, and that shape – with the eye at the opposite end of the lead from the maximum weight, which will become the leading edge in flight – makes it an easy sinker to rig for clean casting. Happily for the angler, the rigs that cast well are also the rigs that allow line to run freely when a fish takes the bait.

The real long-distance casting specialists use variations on the snapper lead, such as the 'bomb'. This is a six-sided lead, slightly squatter in shape than the conventional snapper lead, and with the hole in the body of the sinker rather than in an extended neck, as is the case with the standard lure. This provides a more streamlined shape and eliminates the possibility of line fouling around the neck.

STARS, HELMETS, SPOONS AND OTHER BEACH SPECIALS

Because beach fishing sees anglers trying to work the most user-unfriendly environment of them all, that area of fishing has spawned quite a number of specialised rigs. It is interesting that the environment that gave birth to a fascinating array of leads, all designed to anchor a bait firmly to the bottom and keep it in one place, also gave birth to one of our hottest fishing systems – the unweighted bait fished on ganged hooks! This system worked well because it was not anchored to the bottom.

The style of sinker used for beach fishing is dictated by prevailing conditions. When fishing normal surf, where most of the water is moving either towards or away from the beach, conventional sinkers will do just fine, for it is often an advantage for your bait to be moved about by the surf. If your targets are tailor, bream or whiting, you might even go down to very small leads so that your bait will move about a good deal.

When water movement is on a large scale, though, or when a powerful cross-current sets in, it is time to dig to the bottom of the bag for the beach specials that will hang on in the worst conditions. There are also, of course, times when you might want to anchor in one particular spot because that happens to be where the fish are and you are having trouble staying there – on the sloping beach-side edge of a sandbar, for instance.

Spoons are not the best casting leads in the world, but they do have a nice flat profile that allows them to cling to the bottom. They are a good lead to use in any surf conditions, and suit running sinker rigs very well. It would take quite extreme conditions, or perhaps a need to make maximum casting distance as well as having to hold bottom in bad water, for an angler to look for something more efficient than a big spoon.

Stars, helmets and pyramid types are all contenders in the heavyweight division, and choosing one over another is a personal thing. A lot of anglers, myself included, feel that all the fun has gone out of surf fishing by the time you need to get into this type of terminal rig, but the true enthusiasts will hang in as long as they can keep a bait in the water. Beach fishing being the kind of waiting game it is, this sort of perseverance often pays off.

SPLIT SHOT AND SHEET LEAD

These forms of weight are very much the province of the luderick angler, who has to get into finetuning at times to get a delicate float to behave just so. When fishing any kind of float at all, the idea is to enjoy the benefits offered by the buoyancy of a float without suffering the drawbacks of that buoyancy, which come in the form of resistance offered to a fish when it tries to swim off with the bait. The art is to weight the float to the point where it is just floating, where the slightest additional weight or downward pressure will make it slip beneath the surface.

Expert specialist luderick anglers can enjoy years on end arguing the relative merits of either split shot or sheet lead, and I will make no attempt to buy into that debate here. One thing worth noting, however, is that the rule of using the least amount of lead possible is reversed when you rig a float. When you fish a float, the lead offers no resistance to the fish, but the float does, so you should always use the *maximum* amount of lead the float will carry.

Swivels

The primary reason for using a swivel in a terminal rig is to allow various parts of the rig to spin without twisting the whole line. Most baits, for example, will spin when retrieved through the water.

A swivel will only do this job when it is placed *above* the spinning component of the rig. Anything that is spinning above the swivel will still twist the main line. It is also worth noting that bigger is not automatically better when you choose a swivel, especially when you are dealing with anything other than the expensive ball-bearing game swivels. Brass swivels, for example, do not always rotate easily, and when a big swivel is used with fine line, the line simply does not develop enough energy in the twist to turn the swivel.

Some of the very small swivel sizes look extremely fragile, but this can be misleading. If you have doubts as to whether a swivel is strong enough to stand up to the tackle you plan to use, simply tie it into a length of line, tie the line off on a fixed object and subject it to a direct pull with your hands. If the swivel doesn't give under this load, there is no way you will pull it apart with the pressure you can apply through a fishing rod.

When a swivel is going to be used primarily as a connection in a rig that is likely to be subjected to

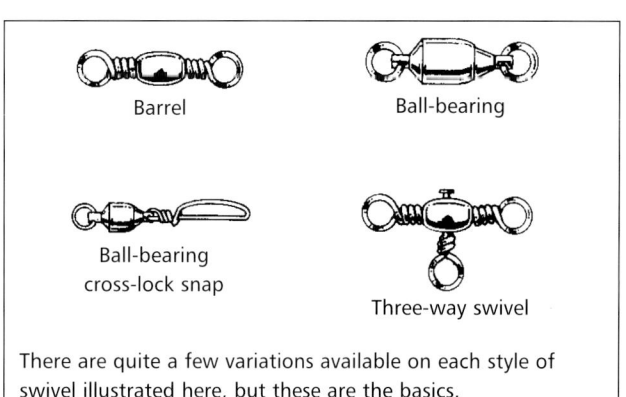

Barrel

Ball-bearing

Ball-bearing cross-lock snap

Three-way swivel

There are quite a few variations available on each style of swivel illustrated here, but these are the basics.

extreme stress, remember that a solid ring will make the strongest connection – unless you are using top-quality game swivels.

Swivels are also often used as connectors in places where an appropriate knot would suffice. In cases where the swivel is going to sit at the top of your terminal rig, you need to take care when winding in to ensure that you don't keep slamming the swivel into the top guide, because this could eventually displace the guide liner, which could cost you a fish, and maybe even a day's fishing.

BARREL SWIVELS

By far the most commonly used swivel, the barrel is cheap, available everywhere and good enough for most jobs involving lines of breaking strains to 15 kg. Beyond that point the strength-to-size ratio gets out of hand, although bottom bouncers fishing with very heavy line and enormous sinkers can get away with huge barrels without suffering any penalties in rig efficiency.

BALL-BEARING GAME SWIVELS

There are all sorts of ball-bearing swivels on the market these days, and they vary considerably in price and quality. The way to look at this range is to consider what you are going to tie on the end of your line, and what you hope to catch. If you are going to tie on a lure worth $40 to $100, rigged with hooks worth several dollars apiece (and perhaps be up for a few hundred dollars' worth of fuel, or charter fees, as well), it makes sense to pay a few dollars for a top-quality swivel that won't pull apart. If, on the other hand, you are trolling cheaper lures for smaller fish, you may well be able to get away with brand X ball bearings. Strength, as well as perfect performance as a swivel, is what quality ball-bearing swivels are all about. Any time heavy tackle is fished to the limit, top-quality ball-bearing swivels should be in the rig.

SNAP SWIVELS AND SNAPS

Most novice anglers are seduced by the way snap swivels can reduce the labour involved in rigging, especially when the style of fishing may call for frequent changes of terminal gear – when you are spinning with lures, for instance.

All snap swivels, with the exception of the very expensive cross-lock and 'Coastlock' snaps that go with ball-bearing game swivels such as Sampos, should be avoided. They come undone and fall apart. Generally speaking, by the time you get one strong enough to trust, you are using a swivel much larger and more cumbersome than you really should be using.

They are absolutely the worst way you could devise to attach a lure to your line, as their weakness could result in the loss of an expensive lure. Gamefish-quality snaps are used to effect quick trace and lure changes in line classes up to 37 kg and sometimes heavier.

The only time snap swivels are really useful is when they are used to attach running sinkers to a line. Traditionally, running sinker rigs were made up with a trace from the sinker tied to a ring sliding on the main line. Attaching the sinker with a snap allows a quick change of weight to be made; if you use a snap to connect to the main line you can quickly change the trace rig, sinker and all. The rule is to keep snap swivels out of the direct path between your main line and your fish.

It is important to distinguish between snap swivels and the very much more effective snap connectors. Snap connectors do not have the swivel section, and are designed with a rounded form in the actual snap area – this is quite strong, and is generally reliable. The rounded form also allows them to be used satisfactorily as a direct connection to lures that would otherwise need to be attached with a loop.

THREE-WAY SWIVELS

Three-way swivels are something of an oddity, and they don't get much use these days. They are designed to be used where a dropper is to be attached to a line, but the majority of anglers rigging this way prefer to fashion droppers from the main line itself.

Gaffs and nets

If you have ever talked with an angler for any length of time, you will have heard about the fish of a lifetime which was at the side of the boat but was lost because the angler had no net, or the handle of the gaff was not long enough. Whatever the variation, it all boils down

If the fish is big enough to be throwing a pressure wave like this when still completely submerged, you need to start thinking about what you plan to do with it alongside the boat. A bad time to realise you only have a tiny net on hand.

to much the same thing – the angler had no way of getting the fish out of the water.

Even when your line has the strength to lift the fish you catch straight out of the water, you should never do this, for several reasons: the line may be frayed and not as strong as you think, the hook may straighten and drop out, or (even more likely) the hook may simply tear free. Wherever it is possible and practical, use a landing net or gaff to actually remove the fish from the water.

Landing nets and gaffs are not generally interchangeable items. Nets have their place, as do fixed-head, flying-head and cliff gaffs. It is important to know just which tool to use for the job at hand.

It is also important to understand that none of these devices is intended to be used to shorten a fight with a fish. All of them are only aids to removing an already played-out fish from the water. (See 'Landing

fish' in Chapter 7 for detailed information on the correct way to use gaffs and nets.)

LANDING NETS

Landing nets were, in the past, used for the smallest of the fish that are too big to be lifted into the boat on a line, which to my way of thinking is just about anything worth keeping. Quite large fish can be landed in quite small nets if the fish is swum into the net headfirst. Never try to scoop a fish from below with a net. As long as the fish will fit into the net, use a net rather than a gaff.

These days, with the increased popularity of sportfishing for flathead, and the understanding that what used to be trophy-sized fish are the valuable breeding females, huge nets that are half canvas and half mesh are used to allow these fish to be netted,

A net with a big opening like this will handle quite large fish. Nets are a much safer proposition than gaffs with fish under 10 kg.

handled and released without inflicting the damage that can be caused to the fish by the mesh of a net.

Buy the biggest net you can comfortably handle and store; if storage space is a problem (and it can be with nets), go for a collapsible net.

The Japanese make considerable use of nets on long telescopic handles when fishing the rocks – this sort of thing would seem to be a good idea for our rock anglers as well.

FIXED-HEAD BOAT GAFFS

Fixed-head boat gaffs range from homemade gaffs with a hook not much bigger than a large fish hook all the way through to very expensive aluminium poles fitted out with high-quality stainless steel hooks.

Many valuable fish, such as a big snapper, fall into something of a no-man's-land between the net and the gaff with regard to landing. A gaff will only work when it has some weight to work against, and the bigger the gaff hook, the more inert weight will be required to drive the point in. This is particularly true where scaled fish are concerned, as the point has to find its way between the scales. Unless you plan to carry a comprehensive range of gaffs with you – and many boats do just this – it is better to have your gaff a little too small than a little too large.

It is hard to find an ideal lightweight gaff on the market for this type of work. The best bet is to make your own with a small gaff hook (these are available from any tackle store). The method of making the gaff is illustrated here, and you will find that the rather soft steel used in the manufacture of these heads allows a long, needle-sharp point to be fashioned – this is ideal for working with smaller fish. In our work boat we use this kind of gaff for fish to around 10 kg, although the same size and type of head in a long-handled rock gaff can be used on fish up to a little over 20 kg.

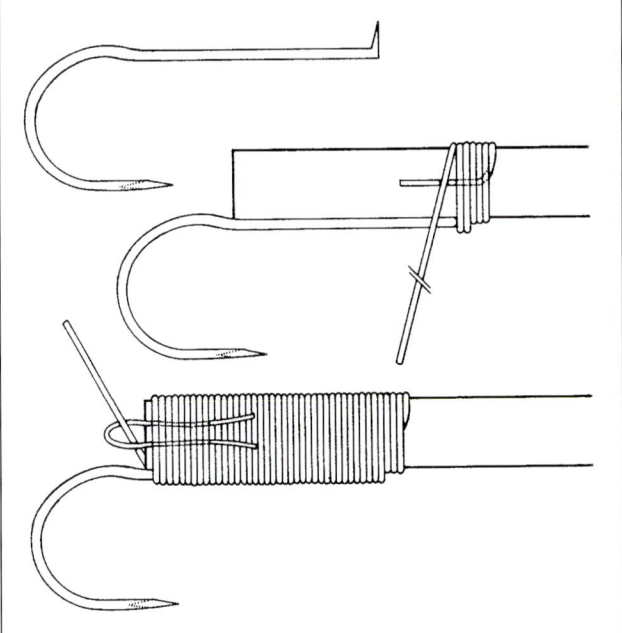

This is a simple and cheap way to make a light gaff. For a short gaff use a length of dowel, and for a longer one use an old broken surf rod, or, if you can get one, a Rangoon cane. Bind the hook in place with sash cord then soak the cord with Araldite.

A homemade gaff can also handle surprisingly large fish, but as you work your way up to powerful fish with some bulk and weight to them, you need a stronger hook and also a larger gape in the hook. However strong a hook, if it has a small gape it will simply fail to get enough bite to lift a big fish, and you will have problems with the hook tearing out. And a wide-gape hook without the strength will probably straighten out under pressure. If you are after fish big enough to justify a large gaff hook, spend the money and get a good one.

Something else you need to consider, especially when you are making your own gaffs, is the length of the handle. A small gaff can have a short handle, because you need to have all the weight of the fish over the point of the gaff to give you your best chance at penetration anyway. If you reach out and try a shot where the hook has to be pulled towards you, the fish may simply be pushed through the water without the point biting.

When gaffing a big fish, though, you will invariably be going over the top of the fish, and it will have enough bulk in its body to allow pressure to be applied from the side. This means that you can reach well out to take a gaff shot. There is something to be said for taking a shot at a fish before it comes right alongside the boat, where a last burst of energy might see it go under the boat, or straight around propellers and rudders. While you can take a close shot with a long gaff, you can't take a wide shot with a short gaff.

When dealing with large, powerful fish, there is sometimes debate about who is going to end up owning the gaff, and more than one expensive gaff has gone to the bottom with an escaping fish. Big cobia are great gaff snatchers, sometimes coming quietly to the side of the boat as if beaten, then absolutely exploding when pricked with the gaff. Some people like to attach a leather loop to the end of the gaff to go over the wrist, but there is obviously an element of risk associated with this approach. The Aralditied sash cord grip used with a homemade gaff in the illustration provides an excellent positive hand grip, and can be successfully added to an aluminium handle. Use a fairly coarse grade of cord, as it is the ridges between the turns of cord that provide most of the grip. If a fish is strong enough to take that off you, you may be better off letting it run around for a while to tire itself out some more.

LAND-BASED GAFFS

Rangoon canes were once the basis for all land-based gaff handles, but they are hard to come by these days. A few places still stock them, and if you are into anything less than big game from the rocks, they do make an excellent gaff when fitted up with a medium-sized hook. For fish over 20 kg you probably need to be looking at something more substantial, or two gaffs, but don't tell that to the old anglers of the north coast of New South Wales who landed 30 kg jewfish from tough rock situations with Rangoons. On the long-range boats working out of southern California, where the deck is as high off the water as most of the rock platforms, Rangoon cane gaffs are used to get the reach required, and fish of 140 kg are lifted from the water using multiple gaffs.

Aluminium gaffs, some with screw-in extensions, are available (at a price) – these are the gaffs normally used by those seeking larger fish from the rocks. Some aluminium gaffs with a threaded head, which allows the angler to fit the appropriate head for the occasion, are available now. You can even attach a flying head in some cases. One of our best fishing writers, Ted Clayton, came up with an idea for a very useful belt gaff. It was the same thing as the do-it-yourself gaff illustrated here, but with a handle just long enough to provide a hand grip. It is invaluable when you are fishing at water level and need to recover a fish quickly, or if you find yourself dealing with a fish too large to handle with a one-handed grip. If you get a short length of plastic tube to fit over the hook so you don't gaff yourself, you can wear the gaff on your belt.

FLYING GAFFS

A flying gaff is used to control the largest of game fish. With a flying gaff the hook is separate from the handle and secured to a length of heavy rope. The rope in turn may be secured on a cleat; in big-game boats it may be secured to the base of the fighting chair.

The hook base slots into the end of the gaff pole, the handle being nothing more than a positioning

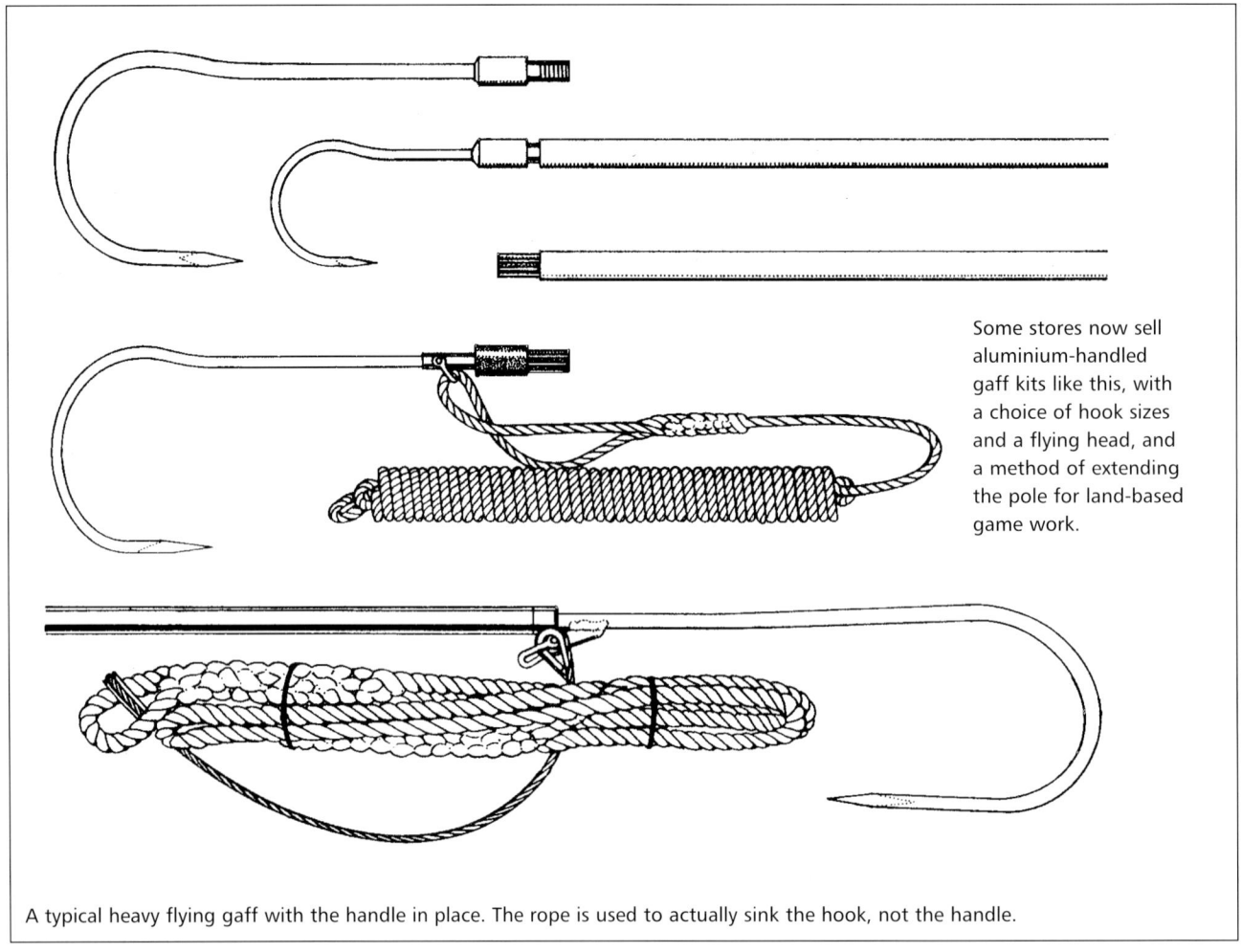

Some stores now sell aluminium-handled gaff kits like this, with a choice of hook sizes and a flying head, and a method of extending the pole for land-based game work.

A typical heavy flying gaff with the handle in place. The rope is used to actually sink the hook, not the handle.

device. As soon as the hook is in, the handle is withdrawn and the fish is worked off the rope.

Remembering that the end of this rope is going to be anchored to some part of the boat, small-boat operators should use flying gaffs with great discretion. There have been some hairy incidents where large sharks tied off on the stern cleats of small boats have been powerful enough to drag the back of the boat under water.

It is important to keep all gaff hooks sharp, but it is particularly important with large gaff hooks, where you are trying to sink a piece of metal with a substantial diameter. As with fish hooks, the points should be sharpened to a triangular or diamond shape, the edges of which can be made razor sharp.

CLIFF GAFFS

Rock anglers can access some interesting, and possibly lightly fished country if they can fish from high ledges and cliffs. Fishing high offers both advantages and drawbacks.

On the credit side of the ledger is the great benefit offered by height when it comes to dealing with reef dwellers who like to dive for cover as soon as they are hooked.

The great disadvantage is the difficulty associated with getting fish out of the water. The cliff gaff shown opposite solves the problem, enabling the angler to lift quite large fish up high cliffs.

The gaff is attached to a strong rope, and then secured to the fishing line using clips or rings. The gaff is allowed to slide down the line to the fish, which is then jagged with the hooks. Care needs to be taken not to slam the gaff down so hard that it dislodges the fish from the line.

Silver rope or sash works better than nylon rope, which twists on the main line and can create problems.

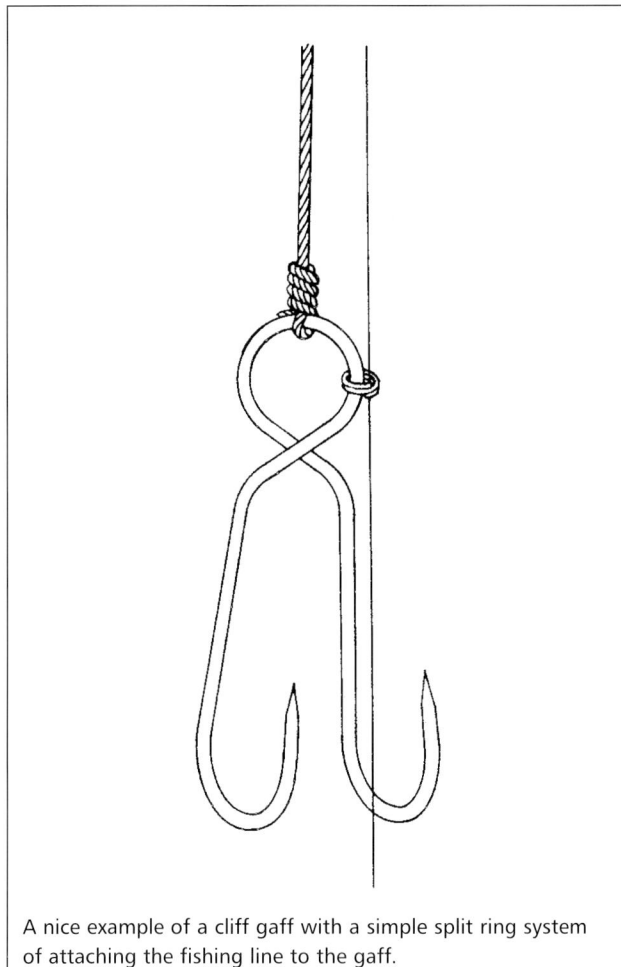

A nice example of a cliff gaff with a simple split ring system of attaching the fishing line to the gaff.

Floats

Floats come in many shapes and sizes, and can be broadly classified as either a means of suspending a bait off the bottom or a casting aid. Very often the float does both jobs – this is the case if you are luderick fishing from the rocks, for example. With just a tiny leaf of cabbage weed on the hook, the luderick enthusiast depends on the float to provide casting weight.

Floats fall into four categories: the classic stemmed float, the bobby cork, the bubble float, and a fourth hotchpotch group which includes party balloons, helium balloons, bits of foam, plastic bottles and just about anything else a desperate live-bait person might lay their hands on. To this you need to add the herring 'blob', which is half float, half berley.

All floats are rigged in one of two ways. Either the float is built into the rig on the main line as a fixed or running unit, or it is attached to the line so that it will break away and be lost when a fish takes the bait. In the latter case, a float can obviously be any crude device that will support the bait and keep it where the angler wants it to be. The most important thing is to ensure that it can break away easily. A big, powerful fish, tearing down into the depths towing a float, is going to subject the line and terminal rig to all sorts of extreme stress, which is not what you want at all.

In all other forms of fishing that involve any kind of float remaining on the line, the art of float fishing is to reduce the buoyancy of the float until it is just floating, and that's all. This is something of a relative term, in that a float that is just floating in dead calm water will be weighted to the point where a stern glance would put it under the water, whereas a big bobby cork fished in a rough ocean surge might have quite a bit of buoyancy left in it even when it is carrying as much ballast as conditions will allow.

FIXED OR RUNNING FLOAT?

Wherever float anglers gather you will hear argument as to whether a fixed float is better than a running float in this or that situation. In fact, when you need to fish deeper than the length of your rod, and you also need to cast, you have very little choice in the matter: you have to use a running float, and that's that. Apart from the casting limitation, it is hard to think of an objection to the use of a fixed float. A fixed float generally allows the bait to be fished at its full depth in rough conditions where wind and waves may be pulling the main line above the float about. In a similar situation, a running float could be sliding up or down the line, lifting and lowering the bait, and you would never know where you were.

Since it is often important to be fishing at a particular depth when float fishing, you should usually choose a rig that gives you your best chance of doing just that. Sometimes a fixed float will provide the answer, but at other times it might be a matter of going to a larger float that will support a lot of lead used down near the bait.

Floats may be fixed in any number of ways. Balloons and the like are simply tied to the main line, where required, with light cotton. Stemmed floats normally carry plastic or rubber sleeves to secure the line. Bobby corks are sometimes fixed, with a match jammed in the hole to wedge the line, or given limited movement by having a stopper knot above and below the cork. There is a gadget on the market that places a fixed bead wherever you want it above a float – this does away with the need for stopper knots.

Running floats have eyes fixed to the stem (stemmed floats) or a hole through the centre (bobby corks). A stopper knot is tied onto the main line at the desired depth, and because the knot can travel freely through the guides and down onto the reel, the stopper can be placed anywhere on the main line, allowing the bait to be fished at a considerable depth if desired. Since the hole or eye on the float or cork is often of a large diameter, it is frequently necessary to have a small bead with a fine-diameter hole running on the main line between the float and the knot.

One word of warning here. If you do use a running float and have the stopper knot going past the guides when you wind in, remember to check the depth setting from time to time. If the stopper knot is not absolutely locked tight, it can be pushed down the line as you wind in, and you may end up fishing much shallower than the depth at which you originally set the float.

STEMMED FLOATS

Stemmed floats are generally associated with light tackle fishing, with the great majority being used by luderick anglers. So fastidious are these people about their floats, and the way they are used, that almost all of them manufacture their own. There is, as a result, virtually no market for commercial luderick floats. Estuary luderick people are easier to please than their counterparts on the ocean rocks, where eye of newt and the claws of Mongolian toads may well be used in spells cast to make floats work just so.

Stemmed floats range from the straight, unadorned quill to the stem with an attached buoyant body of cork or foam. The float may, or may not, have eyes attached to facilitate the use of a running rig. Straight stems often have a small piece of rubber tubing on the stem; this is slid down to hold the line fixed in place on the float. Others have a little sheet lead wound around the base of the stem as basic ballast.

One of the virtues of the stemmed float is that the shape offers little resistance to water. A very shy fish

taking a bait presented on a properly weighted stemmed float, or quill, will be dealing with the next best thing to an unweighted slack line. The other great virtue is the fact that the stem can readily be seen even in very choppy water and when rugged conditions have produced foam several centimetres deep on the surface.

Straight-stemmed floats, or quills, are used a lot by anglers fishing for garfish and mullet, and they should be used a good deal more than they are by anglers trying for bream along rocky breakwaters.

BOBBY CORKS

The name 'bobby cork' dates back to the time when these floats really were made of cork, with sometimes a little lead already attached to the base of the cork. The floats were quite heavy, and could be cast a long way without the use of any additional lead.

All bobby corks sold these days are made from foam, and are as light as a feather. They have buoyancy out of all proportion to their size, and are capable of supporting a lot of lead. This works in favour of the rock angler, who can end up with a very handy casting weight on the line by the time enough lead has been added to counter most of the cork's buoyancy.

An angler sensitive to the need to keep a terminal rig as unobtrusive as possible may be put off by a well-balanced bobby cork rig set up to fish rough water. It

Stemmed floats are normally used for sensitive fish like luderick as it requires little effort to take them under the water. Rock blackfish like this are an incidental catch when fishing for luderick from the rocks.

will have a great lump of lead above the hook trace acting as primary ballast, and then another small ball or bean sitting right on top of the hook. It looks awful, but in the wild white water around the rocks where the use of a bobby cork can really pay off, you don't find too many sensitive fish. The fish don't have time to fool around in an environment like that, and the strikes are normally thunder-and-lightning affairs.

Rock hoppers generally carry a range of sizes in corks, from wine bottle cork size for calm conditions and sensitive fish, through to tennis ball size for long-range casting and rough water. Always choose the smallest cork that will do the job in the prevailing conditions.

BALLOONS AND DISPOSABLE FLOATS

There are two classes of balloon: the conventional disposable float type and the gas-filled balloon, which is used much the same way as a conventional kite – to dabble a live or dead bait right on the surface of the water – and is mostly aimed at Spanish mackerel and sailfish. The latter is a highly successful technique, but you have to add a cylinder of party gas to your gear. You also need to have offshore wind working for you, if you are working from land. Boat anglers, who have the ability to create their own breeze, might find it easier to use a kite. Gas balloons don't exactly come under the heading of float fishing, but they probably get a bait out to where it's wanted faster than anything else when there is a strong offshore wind.

An ordinary balloon is a good option where an offshore wind, an outgoing current or backwash, or a combination of both, lets you carry a bait out from the shore. Balloons offer another advantage as a float in that they normally self-destruct as soon as a big fish tries to drag them under the water. Balloons will also self-destruct if you blow them up too much, because the heat from the sun will cause further expansion as they sit on the water.

THE BLOB

The blob is a specialised wooden float used by herring anglers. It is made from timber, and has a channel through the centre from top to bottom and a recess in the centre which you pack with berley. The blob

provides all the casting weight necessary for the rig, and when it is cast out it starts to disperse its berley load as soon as it hits the water; the berley then filters down around the baited hook below.

The same system can be used for mullet and garfish, although the herring's aggressive nature and large mouth make it the best target of all for this rig. Generally speaking, a small, fine float is a better bet for garfish and mullet.

Lures

If the introduction of GSP lines can be considered a revolutionary step in the development of fishing tackle, then the advent of soft plastic lures at the beginning of this century is at least as important an event. I am specifically talking about the new wave of lures here, not the long tails and double tails that date well back into the 20th century.

The new plastics are based on ultra-chewy slimy materials, have a powerful scent component, and come in an extraordinary range of colours – some even have holographic images impregnated into the body. What is possibly as important as all those things put together is the fact that they have come into being alongside a wide range of jig head weights and shapes that allow the plastics to be presented to fish with great

Soft plastics are cheap, they don't take up much space in the tackle box, and they work!

My son Alex can barely restrain himself as professional guide Harry Watson shares the secrets of his tackle box. Acquiring tackle is half the fun of fishing.

finesse at any level of the water table, when and as required.

At one end of the scale, you can fish a tiny unweighted slider grub on ultra-light line; at the other end, you can lob heavily weighted fish styles into deep bluewater and fish them as jigs.

Selling for around half the price (sometimes less) of the cheapest hard-body lures, and around a third the price of the more expensive hard bodies, price has played a very important role in their popularity. But the thing that has rocketed them to the top of the lure hit parade is the fact that fish of all kinds just love them. They seem to have accounted for at least one of every species, and when you have lots of fish around they produce staggering results.

Still, hot as they may be, the soft plastics are still only one option available to those who fish with lures. Bibbed lures, stick baits, poppers, fizzers, metal jigs,

skirted trolling lures and more can all be the right tool for the job – at the right time and place. The soft plastics just mean that the angler's arsenal has been greatly expanded.

Some 40 years or so ago, lures of all kinds were referred to as artificial baits, and although the term seems to have drifted out of the modern angler's vocabulary, the description is still a reasonable one, and still covers many of the lures manufactured in the world today. When you are not fishing with a live, or dead, version of what a fish might eat in the wild, you can use a creation that, in some way, matches up with natural food.

Although the imitators of natural food of one kind or another are possibly the most prolific of lures, a lure does not have to look like anything a fish eats to draw a response. In the case of a territorial fish, hiding up in the mouth of a cave or under a log, a noisy, brightly coloured lure cast onto the front doorstep can trigger extremely aggressive behaviour, resulting in a positive strike. Some surface poppers are ripped across the surface in the same way that a panicked garfish, or perhaps a flying fish, might skitter across the surface in a desperate bid to escape. In such a case the predator strikes at the source of the disturbance without ever really seeing the lure.

One of the most commonly used lure forms in the world today is the minnow. Minnow-style lure bodies start at around 4 cm in length and go up to 30 cm monsters. The little lures really are intended to represent the many types of minnow-like baitfish present in most environments; as the lures increase in size they could be mullet, salmon, pilchards, mackerel, small tuna or any one of dozens of species that share that same general cigar-like profile. Swimming action varies considerably from lure to lure, as does the speed at which they can be worked and the depth to which they will dive when retrieved.

The action of the lure has a great deal to do with the way a fish will react to it. It may be important for a lure to look right when a fish spots it, and 'looking right' may mean either looking natural or looking unnatural. As we learned when discussing the senses of fish, they have a sonar system which allows them to monitor vibrations set up by other fish swimming – or a lure moving – through the water. It is entirely possible then that certain vibrations a lure creates could trigger a response that is keyed to a particular swimming action. Many good minnow-style bodies, for instance,

have a tight, pulsing action which would probably create vibrations similar to those made by a small, panic-stricken fish trying to escape.

When fitted with a plastic or metal 'bib' at the front of the head, a minnow will 'swim' and dive. The shape and angle of the bib determines both the swimming action and the depth to which the lure will dive. Minnows with a small bib set at a steep angle will run shallow and have a tight swimming action; those with larger bibs set at a shallow angle will dive hard, the depth achieved being determined by a number of factors, including bib angle and the point at which the line is attached to the lure. Many lures now carry an indication of their depth potential on the packaging, but you need to remember that the actual depth achieved may well be determined by the diameter of the line you are using. The finer the line, the deeper the lure will dive.

Not all minnow bodies are fitted with bibs. Fizzers have blades fitted to the front and back of the body, and these spin when the lure is moved. Stick bait-style minnows may or may not have a bib, and they depend on rod tip work to give them their appeal – to make them behave the way an erratic, perhaps injured bait would behave.

All swimming lures with a built-in action should be attached to the line by either a loop or a metal snap with as round a gape as can be found.

SOFT PLASTICS

A special section for soft plastics is now essential for this book, as it is very difficult to include them in a general discussion on lures. Perhaps the major difference between the soft plastics and any other kind of lure is the fact that they fall somewhere between bait and completely artificial offerings. Although we know very well that these creations are made of plastic, fish don't always seem to share that understanding. Soft plastics are often attacked by a fish while the lure is lying still on the bottom, and it is not at all uncommon when fishing them to have a fish come back to the lure several times if it is not hooked on the first attack.

Soft plastics come in an extraordinary range of body shapes, colours and scents. You can buy spiders, crayfish, frogs, prawns, worms, fat grubs and shads. You can choose lures that have no action, lures that have long curly tails that wriggle enticingly when the bait is

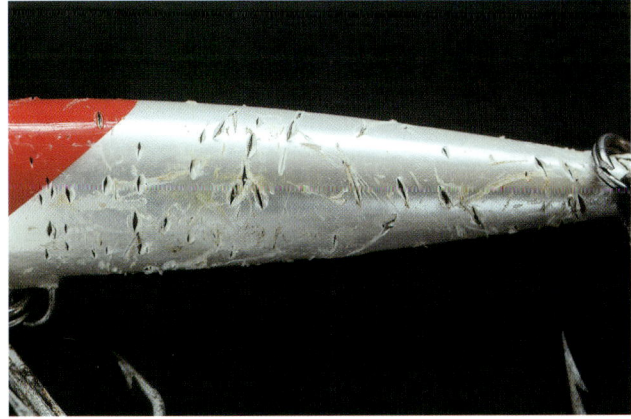

Is this a good lure or what? Most effective lures start to look a bit second-hand after a few encounters with toothy critters.

You can catch just about anything on soft plastics. This sample includes (clockwise from above left) venus tusk fish, sharks, giant herring, flathead, bass and bream.

Soft plastics that imitate every creature you are ever likely to find in the water, and then some, are available. The most common types are the paddle tails in the top row and the curly tails and worms seen below. Of these, the paddle tails are the most popular.

moved, or paddle-tail shad lures that vibrate with a very tight action. And these are only the most popular styles!

One thing that makes these slippery critters so effective is their productive time in the water with each cast (or drop, if you are jigging them). Their swimming action is effective at such slow retrieve speeds that they are usually overfished by those who are not used to using them. It is a very good practice to spend a little time with new lures in clear water to determine just what happens at what speed. Most of them will burst into life with any movement at all – you will find yourself doing all the work with the rod tip, with the reel simply being there to collect line.

The plastics make a very strong case for the use of specialised tackle, with light but fairly rigid rods being a popular choice. You don't want a soft rod that will buckle as soon as you lift the lure. You want something that will not flex much at all, as you need to be directly in touch with the lure at all times. Fish often take the plastics on the drop, or come up under them, which can create enough slack to cause you to miss the bite. Plastic specialists all use GSP lines because of the direct contact they offer.

You need to experiment a lot with the plastics you buy and the areas you fish. Fishing flathead, we let the lures sink to the bottom then use a couple of short rips of the rod tip, then allow the lure to sink to the bottom again. Flathead simply can't resist this technique with the paddle-tail shad types, but an amazing variety of fish will happily compete for these offerings. In fact it's easier to list fish that won't take them than fish that will.

If you are fishing for bass, lightly weight a paddle-tail slider-style grub, let it sink slowly to the bottom, then lift it very slowly, then let it drop again. Underline the word s-l-o-w-l-y, because you really do have to slow things way down for this style of fishing. After all, when was the last time you saw a worm sprinting?

Another reason for the plastics having become so popular is, of course, the sorts of results they deliver. It is possible to produce excellent results with them even in hard-fished locations where baitfishermen are regularly missing out altogether. They also move efficiently between fresh water and salt water, impoundments and rivers, inshore and offshore. They have a fairly good working life unless you run into a school of toothy critters, in which case it would be wise to revert to hard-bodied lures.

I have a thing about fishermen getting the best results from those lures they spend the most time fishing with. In the case of my son and I, we have become focused on shads between 55 and 65 cm long, and we get very good results with black backs and coloured sides. Mind you, we spend around 90 per cent of our fishing hours using those lures, so it's not surprising that we catch more fish on them than on anything else.

When rigging the plastics, make sure they are lying straight on the hook, and that your hooks are razor sharp. If they are not, your catch rate will be way off.

Having the correct-size weight and hook with which to rig the soft plastic is an important part of the operation. The lightest weight that will do the job will always bring out the best action in soft plastics and allow the angler to work the lure very slowly if required.

LURE SIZES AND SHAPES

Having lures the same shape and size as common baitfish suggests that in order to work well, a lure should look like a baitfish. But take another look at that group of baitfish lures. They are fluorescent pink, bright orange, black and purple, gold and green! Some have been coloured to look like the real thing, but not very many. When you go beyond the minnows and check out the lure display in any large tackle store, you will find that most lures, at first glance, seem to have little in common with anything you have seen in real life – but most of the successful ones you use will seem to appear real to the fish. The art of understanding a lure lies in knowing which element the fish will react to.

For a start, the fish cannot always examine the lure in detail. If the predator is one of a school of fish, it might be a case of 'first in best dressed' – hesitation resulting in another fish getting to the offering first. In this sort of situation the lure only needs to be visible to the fish – and have a swimming action similar to either a healthy or a wounded baitfish – to become a priority target.

The outline and size of a lure is often more important than the details. To a predatory fish working a school of bait from below, a silhouette close to the size of the school fish, moving overhead at a pace either matching or at odds with the prevailing bait, will be a member of the school as far as the predator is concerned. The speed or swimming action discrepancy can work in the lure's favour, convincing the predator that the lure is a wounded fish that will be a sure kill. It is usually the stragglers and those that are in some way the 'odd ones out' that are first hit when predators attack bait. In fact, at those times when potential prey and predator are peacefully inhabiting the same patch of water, erratic behaviour from a single baitfish will almost always attract the attention of the potential predator.

When there is a great deal of any one kind of bait in the water, especially if that bait is small, matching the exact size of that bait can be the critical factor. You can switch from one colour to another and still get strike after strike, but you can rarely vary the size of the lure at all. This sort of situation often arises when casting to some of the tuna, or to tailor or salmon.

In the winter months, mackerel tuna often turn up in great numbers along the central to southern New South Wales coastline. When they first appear, these fish are often feeding on plankton of some kind, or very small baitfish, and although they are splashing and crashing all over the surface in a wild feeding spree, they cannot be taken on any sort of lure. A little later in the season they appear to shift onto larger bait, and at this time anglers with enough know-how to keep their boat well clear of the mack tuna schools, and enough casting skill to place small metal lures just in front of or to the side of fast-moving fish, can start to get hookups. Towards the end of winter, land-based anglers will be catching them on big lures that would have never taken a fish a few months before.

THE ROLE OF COLOUR

The ability of a predator to see the bait has a great deal to do with the way lures are coloured and patterned. There is a never-ending argument as to whether fish can see colour or not, but what they see and how they see it is largely beside the point. Whatever they see, and however they see it, there is no doubt that colour often plays a major part in successful lure fishing.

It would seem that the most important role played by colour is in making it easier for the fish to actually see the lure. Many successful lures have colour schemes that include sharp contrasts and hard-edged patterns. There are no fluorescent fish in the sea, but fluorescent colours reflect a great deal of light, which could account for the popularity of fluorescent lures.

A lure collection should not only include a wide range of colour options, it should also give you a wide choice in lure body sizes, enabling you to roughly match the profile of bait in the area.

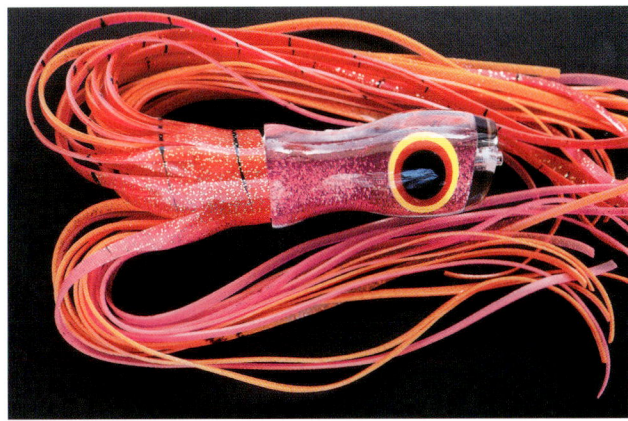

TOP Sometimes colour will be the most important element in lure selection. Lures of every kind now offer an extraordinary range of colours and reflective surfaces.

ABOVE This picture teaches one of the most important lessons you will ever learn about colour – that fish don't see things the way you do! Mullet that would be a shiny silver–white in sunlight disappear as their scales become mirrors of the environment around them. On the other hand, the human legs with no reflective surfaces stand out like beacons.

Conversely, in some clear-water conditions anglers may find more subtle colours more effective. Even transparent-bodied lures with very little in the way of colour may become highly effective.

There is no doubt that colour contributes to a lure's effectiveness, but it is difficult to come up with hard-and-fast rules about colour. I remember spending a day trolling for small tuna with three rods rigged with lead-headed jigs dressed with feathers. One was white, one was red and white, and the third was lilac and white, and I fished the same three lures from the same rod holders in the boat the whole time. First thing in the morning the white lure took all the strikes, then as the sun rose higher in the sky that lure took no more fish and the bite shifted to the red and white lure. The last few strikes, around midday, all came on the lilac and white, which had not been touched up to that point. It is very hard to believe that fish can't differentiate between colours after an experience like that.

At the time of writing I have undertaken to sift through what will become thousands of replies to a survey conducted by a national fishing magazine. The survey sought to establish the most popular lures used in different fishing environments, and the colours preferred by anglers buying those lures. The first few days of sorting produced a list of around 130 colours and colour combinations in one category alone, suggesting that the list will contain several hundred colours and combinations, perhaps many more, by the time the job is finished.

A similar survey carried out a number of years ago showed blue, then silver and pink to be far and away the most popular colours with anglers trolling on salt water; green, followed by yellow and black, stood out in fresh water. Many people nominated metal lures, probably because they flash a great deal in the sunlight. With metal, though, you have to learn to differentiate between reflective surfaces, which will simply mirror the colour and light around them, and silver-coloured lures, which will reflect a great deal of light and flash.

It would seem reasonable to suggest that once we work out what colours are easiest for the fish to see, we should be able to fish with those and enjoy success every time we go fishing. Wrong! Mother nature protects her creatures better than that. Colour preferences change as conditions change.

As the sun rises in the morning, moves across the sky and then sets in the evening, light enters the water at a range of angles. First thing in the morning light will be coming into the water at a shallow angle, and predatory fish are likely to be near the surface, looking at the sides of our lures. As the sun moves higher into the sky, predators will begin to move away from the surface, especially when the water is calm – then they will likely be looking at surface lures from below. The light will be penetrating further into the water, so the colours of deep-running lures will also be important.

The condition of the surface, the clarity of the water, the depth of the water and the nature of the bottom all affect the way fish see things. A weed bottom will absorb light and a sand bottom will reflect it. It is an interesting fact that baitfish over either kind of bottom will change colour to blend in better with the natural colour scheme. Even if there is not any obvious weather change to alter the state of the water, the arrival of a current that varies just a few degrees in temperature from the water it replaces is enough to bring about a dramatic change of colour and density of the sea in any given place.

People who are deep jigging with polished metal lures can catch a good many fish at times. This suggests either that fish do not see lures the way we do, or that they don't need to see a lure very well in order to find and take it. After all, they are sometimes feeding at 30 fathoms (55 m) at night, eating fish that are coloured to blend into the background even when there is a bit of light about!

It seems that a case can be made for the use of bright, very dark or contrasting colours when visibility is poor because of either water or light conditions, and more subtle colours and tones when visibility is good. Lures that create flash on matt reflective surfaces, combined with the right colours, are very popular with bluewater anglers. It is notable that both very bright and very dark colours work when there is poor visibility, but this does make sense: bright colours that reflect available light are easier to see from the side, while dark colours that are fished at the surface stand out when viewed from below even when overhead light is poor.

THE ROLE OF SOUND

The sonic effect of lures is a fascinating subject. Poppers have been the most popular style of sonic lures for a long time now, but few Australian fishermen ever come to terms with the subtleties that can apply to fishing lures that rely on a sonic effect for their ability to switch fish on. Basic pencil poppers are used a great deal in our tropical waters, where they are dragged across the surface at speed to draw strikes from queenfish, giant trevally and mackerel. This is a crude and fundamental use of noise – the effect is that of bait trying to escape by skipping across the surface.

A popper is obviously a sonic lure depending on a loud splash and popping noise to attract fish. Few people think of the spinner bait as a sonic lure, but it makes plenty of noise that fish are sensitive to.

The pencil poppers are a pretty good imitator of a natural event, but it is hard to imagine what a fish thinks when he hears a concave-faced blooper at work. A blooper is like a very fat cigar with the face scooped out to create a concave surface. These lures are usually worked with one hard stab of a rod tip that creates a loud 'pop' or 'bloop' sound. They are then allowed to simply sit on the surface of the water for a while before another movement creates another short, loud noise. Because they are out there for so long on each cast, a loud blooper can draw fish in from quite a distance away, which means that apart from their fish-catching value, they can be used to get scattered fish to congregate in the casting zone, where other lures can be used to catch the fish. A really good blooper is worth its weight in gold, and I have seen fishermen cut the barbs and points off the hooks so they can't lose an old favourite to a large reef dweller.

Rod Harrison is a fisherman of outstanding ability, and he is particularly well tuned in to the sonic value of lures. Working a blooper on a glass-calm sea in New Guinea, he had dogtooth tuna and Spanish mackerel rocketing metres into the air as they came screaming up out of the depths, trying to take a lure that was spending most of its time sitting in one spot doing nothing.

Rod also gets an amazing response to his 'fizzer' technique, which utilises even less lure and rod action.

Fizzers are pencil-shaped or elongated cigar-shaped lures with rotating propellers on either one or both ends. They can be chugged across the surface in much the same way as a popper, but their greatest asset is their ability to drive fish mad when they are worked with great subtlety in the one spot. Rod makes the blades of a fizzer spin with just the slightest rod movement – it is almost line movement doing all the work. The lure doesn't seem to move, but the props go 'fizzzzzz', just like that.

After we had peppered the mouth of a small run-off with all of our sure-fire barra lures for quite some time, Rod sat a fizzer out there and worked the blades as described above. He worked it once, then twice … then all hell broke loose as a big barramundi exploded from the water to monster the little lure right at the side of the boat. After that the area simply switched on, and we were able to troll up a number of big fish.

Another form of sonic lure is one where rattles are built into the body of the lure. Rattles can be added to almost any moulded lure body, but they don't all work. Why this should be remains something of a mystery.

Fish have extremely good hearing, and it is possible that in trying to create sonic lures we produce something that makes too much noise. There is an enormous amount of noise going on at any one time in a fish community, and we can only assume that all of that has as much meaning to individual fish as the morning cacophony of sound does to birds in the bush. We hear noise because vibrations travel through air and impact on the sensitive receivers which are our eardrums. Fish have a second hearing system – the lateral line down the side which allows them to monitor vibrations. It's a sort of short- and long-range sonar. Almost anything that moves in their vicinity will move molecules of water that the lateral line can monitor and probably evaluate as to size, speed and direction of travel.

Even though we can't hear it, every kind of lure we use – sonic or not – probably produces its own sound signature. Hook chatter against the body of a lure, any sort of spinning blade, and perhaps just the body flutter of a tight swimming action from a minnow will be making its own special noise as far as the fish is concerned. Just because we can't hear it doesn't mean it isn't happening.

THE ROLE OF SPEED

Speed is often a critical factor in lure presentation, whether the lure is being cast and retrieved or trolled behind a boat.

Most lures, and especially those that have any sort of action built in, have a speed at which they are at their most effective. If you take any of the lures with bibs and retrieve them at a variety of speeds, you will observe that each has a particular speed at which the tip of the rod will begin to bounce in a steady rhythm, reflecting the pulsing action of the lure. If you want to make a faster or slower presentation for some reason, you should change the lure rather than try to make a lure do the job at a pace at which it was not designed to work.

Consider the extremes of speed. At one end you have the pelagic fish, the hunters of the open sea. Although lures are normally presented to them at 7 to 10 knots (13 to 18 km/h), many game boats travelling home at speeds in excess of 20 knots, trailing high-speed lures, find game fish willing to hit those lures. Whipping lures in with big reels geared at 6.2:1, I have noticed that Spanish mackerel actually zigzag the last couple of metres in to the strike. This probably has something to do with range finding, but the fact is that the fish still has pace to burn when pursuing the fastest offering we can present with casting tackle. Most of the tunas can also run rings around our fastest retrieves,

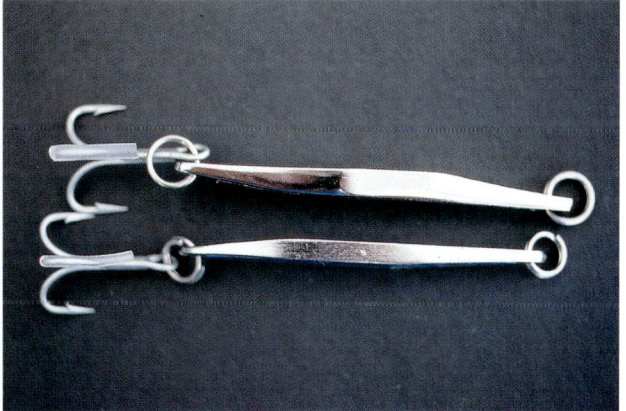

Do these lures look the same to you? Look again! They are quite distinctly different in terms of surface contours and weight distribution, both factors that will determine how well the lure will cast and what it will do as it moves through the water.

and it is often the case when casting to longtail and mackerel tuna that only the swiftest retrieves of all, with lures that offer minimal resistance to the water, have any chance of being hit.

At the other end of the scale you find the soft plastics and small poppers. With the plastics it is almost impossible to fish some of the patterns too slowly, and most will from time to time be taken even when they are sitting still on the bottom.

Fishing with poppers is something of a game of nerves, as the pause between movements of the lure is often as important as the moves themselves. You get situations where a good, noisy popper will draw a fish in from some distance away, and you really need to keep the lure in the strike zone for as long as possible. Ten seconds between short movements of the lure is by no means too long.

Anglers describe evening fishing for bass with any kind of surface popper, fizzer, paddler or chugger as being one of life's most nerve-racking experiences. Fishing these lures properly involves an absolute minimum of action and an absolute maximum of heart-in-the-mouth waiting. The whole point is to fool the bass into thinking that a large insect has fallen onto the water and is struggling at the surface. The lure is dropped onto the surface with a 'splat', then just left sitting there for as long as the angler's nerves allow. Below the water, perhaps 5 m away in a snag pile, the bass hears the noise, tunes in and moves towards the source of the disturbance. As it moves into the general area, the angler gives the lure the slightest twitch, just enough to disturb the surface and send rings radiating out from the lure. Now the bass has something to home in on. Seconds later the fish has moved immediately below the lure, and is looking up to the surface, where he sees a small dark shape that could be the source of the disturbance. It twitches just once more and … bang! After what seems an eternity of silent waiting, with nerves stretched to breaking point, the boil and crash of a surface strike from a bass is like a lightning strike for the angler. Hit or miss, such a strike on a dark, silent creek is a truly memorable event.

Time plays a major part in the whole operation. The bass needs time to react, time to zero in on the target, then more time to decide that it's the real thing and line it up for a strike. The numbers of misses on

these lures, despite the overwhelming enthusiasm of the attack by fish that normally get a good deal of surface feed in their diet, is probably down to the buoyancy of the lure. Most fish inhale their food along with a lot of water, which they then expel through the gills. The lure has so much flotation that it is probably often just pushed away by the head of the fish bulging the water ahead of the take.

THE ROLE OF DEPTH

If fish see or hear a lure that really interests them, they may come from near and far for it. Our concave popper is a good example of a noisy attractor style of lure. Marlin anglers talk about certain boats being good fish attractors – they believe that the particular pulse of some diesel engines will bring marlin and other game fish up out of the depths to check out the boat, which of course also puts them in a position to see lures the boat is towing.

Anglers generally think about depth in fairly broad terms – surface lures, deep divers, and jig-style lures which can be fished anywhere between the bottom and the surface. In many cases this approach may be good enough, but there is a definite advantage available to the person who can appreciate the subtleties of getting lures working at very precise depths.

Some years ago I fished Lake Michigan in the United States for steelhead trout, a coastal species (originally) that grows to a considerable size. The

The bib on a lure and the location of the towing point on that bib determine both the depth to which the lure will dive and the way it will swim.

world record for steelhead at that time was 19 kg, and the fish we were catching were in the 4–6 kg range. We were using downriggers, a system in which the line from the rod is connected to a heavy lead ball on a steel cable by a quick-release clip. The ball is lowered to the depth required, with the lure streaming out a few metres behind the ball. The two advantages associated with downrigger fishing are that you can use any lures you like, because the lure does not have to achieve depth by itself, and the lure can be placed and kept at any depth the angler wants to fish.

Using first-class echo-sounding equipment, the skipper of our boat was able to see the actual downrigger balls, and the fish he was trying to catch. He would see fish on the sounder then call for depth adjustments of as little as 20 cm to place the lures exactly where he wanted them in relation to the fish, and when we got that right we often took a strike. Allowing for the fact that echo sounders show you fish that are off to either side of the boat as well as those that are directly below it, after three days of this sort of fishing I was prepared to believe that 20 cm could be a critical depth difference when fishing for these lake steelhead.

Another real-life example came in a barramundi tournament in the Northern Territory. The barra were suspended just above a weed bed, and one angler had been taking fish after fish in the spot. The word got around that he was using a particular brand and type of lure, so everybody got out on that same weed bed the next day, but it produced very few fish. When they quit and went on to try their luck in other spots, the original angler went back to the weed bed and started to pull barra out again. After the tournament had finished he revealed that he had not adopted the usual practice of replacing the hooks on these lures with heavy-duty trebles, while everyone else had. The result was that his more buoyant lure was travelling along above the weeds, where the fish were, while the less buoyant lures were dragging through the top of the weed beds, where the hooks were fouling with weed. Hook weight was the critical difference.

Still in barra country, casting to structure catches fish, but the lure is often only in the strike zone for quite a short space of time. When the same lure is trolled, on the other hand, it remains at a constant depth, and providing the depth is appropriate, will be

Professional bass guide Harry Watson makes his own spinner baits and fishes them with deadly effect on bass and Murray cod.

in the strike zone for longer periods. The trade-off here is that the fish may be spooked by engine noise; because of this, you should always try casting before trolling.

Bass specialist and lure maker Harry Watson uses his own spinner baits to make a long cast and achieve a constant depth on retrieve. Harry uses quite heavy spinner baits with large blades and constantly racks up impressive bass – impressive in terms of both size and number. Harry makes a long cast, then lets the lure sink to the bottom. Once it's there he gives it a brief burst of speed to lift it just off the bottom, then retrieves at a steady pace that keeps the lure moving along at the same depth. As Harry points out, a spinner bait fished this way stays at the desired depth for the entire length of the cast, whereas a bibbed diving lure will only retain maximum depth for a short time before it starts to plane back towards the surface.

There can be a critical difference between deep-running lures and deep-diving lures. Deep runners are lures that generally rely on spearhead-like metal bibs, or no bib and flat surfaces on the head, and plenty of speed to run at a constant depth. Unless trolling specifically for marlin, where the hooks used with these lures are unsuitable, it is always a good idea to have one or two deep runners in the lure spread to pick up deep-swimming fish.

Deep divers, on the other hand, rely on large bib areas to dive and generally only work at much lower speeds. Any forward motion at all will cause them to dive sharply. Their place in the scheme of things is to enable the angler to fish deep around structure. The usual system is to cast the lure alongside the target – say, the trunk of a downed tree – then snatch the rod tip hard, causing the lure to crash-dive on the spot. Once it's down, the retrieve can be backed off to the point where the lure will swim alongside the cover at depth, where it can be seen by fish sheltering under the cover.

You don't want any speed in a lure for this style of fishing: the slower the lure will work, the longer it is going to be in that critical strike zone. A lot of fish caught this way are not too keen on moving far from cover, so catching them involves being able to put a lure right on their doorstep.

The floating deep diver has one great advantage over the sinking lure: you can fish your way through some real tiger country without hooking up on the timber and losing your lure. You can cast right over a submerged tree trunk, diving your lure on the far side of it then backing off and allowing the lure to float to the top to be slowly swum across the timber, then diving it hard once again on the near side. A good angler can fish some horrible snag piles this way, but can also be tested to the limit when hitting a fish in that sort of territory.

The increasing popularity of soft plastics has also increased the angler's options in terms of how and where a lure is to be presented. Recognising that time spent in the strike zone is a major factor when fishing lures, having a lure that requires very little movement to do the job is clearly an asset. One of the great things

about most of the plastics is the fact that the body and the weight are separate, interchangeable elements.

Fishing flathead in a deep channel the other day I started with a very light jig head on a plastic shad, moving up in weight from time to time as the tidal run increased. As the run backed off I went back down on the weight. The heaviest weights killed the action of the shad to a degree, but the bonus was the fact that the weight kept me down where the fish were – right on the bottom. Because I could back the weight off, I spent a similar time on and near the bottom, but I also picked up a bonus in that the shad had a slow drop back to the bottom after having been jigged, thus presenting a more attractive target to the fish.

In really calm water you can fish with a jig head that weighs not much more than the hook, and then you can really work a lure at sleepwalking pace. Any movement of water at all over the body of a plastic will cause the tail to shimmer and paddle, and that's all it takes to bring on a strike. On the other hand, all of the bibbed hard-body lures require some measure of speed to do their job, and therefore must spend less time in the strike zone.

It is cynically said in the tackle trade that it is more important that a lure be designed to catch anglers than fish. There is probably some truth in that remark, for we all tend to fish most with those lures we have the greatest faith in. And because we have those lures in the water more than lures we are not quite so keen about, you get a self-fulfilling prophecy where the

Jigs like these are designed to be used in deep water, where they are simply dropped to the bottom then bounced there, or retrieved with a series of rips with the rod tip.

favoured lures do catch more. Another rarely recognised truism about fishing is that the angler who catches the most fish is the one who spends the most time on the water.

Here is an interesting exercise. Think about the range of environments you regularly fish, then lay out the contents of your tackle box and ask yourself how well equipped you are to exploit the range of options those environments present. Colour range, working depth levels and speed options all come into it. At the same time, look for those areas where you have duplicated tools, or where you are carrying lures that simply don't apply to what you are doing.

SERIOUS METAL

Not altogether tongue in cheek, I sometimes refer to the fishing business as a 'fashion industry'. Like the length of dress hems and hair, today's fishing 'must have' is often tomorrow's 'wouldn't be seen dead in'.

A lot of great lures and fishing styles are introduced from time to time, and as often as not they are soon left behind, not because they stop working, but because something else grabs our fancy and we forget about yesterday's tools and techniques. But lures that work are like yo-yos. Like summer and blowflies at a barbecue, you can be absolutely sure they'll be back sooner or later.

Over the years, metal casting and jigging lures have been the craze on many occasions, with lures ranging from ultra-light metal spoons through to thundering great metal bars that plummet to the bottom in 50 m of water even with lots of current in play.

For these tools to be a fashion item is just plain ridiculous. There are many, many situations where serious metal is the only thing to be using. In a high-speed spinning situation from the rocks, absolutely nothing casts into the teeth of a gale like a metal hex bar or a basic metal slug. They don't have much action in the water, but belted back with a high-speed retrieve, they don't always need it.

A step further up the ladder come the coffin-shaped, flat-bodied lures that may, or may not, have a twist in them. These lures are not quite as good a casting weight as a slug or bar, but they have two very important things going for them. The first is that they generate terrific action coming through the water, and

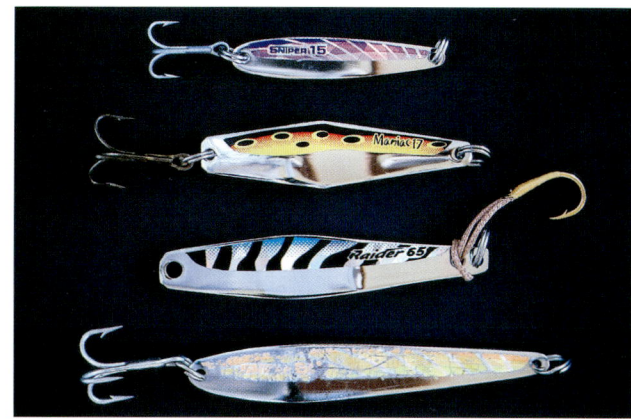

A range of spoons and metal casting jigs should be in every saltwater tackle box. From the Spanyid collection the top lure is a 15 g Sniper, ideal for casting in wind and capable of fast retrieval speeds. The 17 g Maniac also casts well but has a wild side-stepping action at lower retrieval speeds. The Raider 65 is unusual in that this deepwater jig has the hook swinging from the same end of the lure as the ring to which the line is connected – strange but it really works. The 80 g Sniper pictured at the bottom can be cast or jigged. This one has been seriously worked over by queenfish and mackerel.

the second is that they can generate that action at relatively slow speeds. Smart fishermen working a wash can back right off the retrieve in a backwash and let water movement work the lure. That adds up to more time in the water per cast, and nothing is more important than the amount of time you can keep any lure in productive water.

Another point in favour of these action metal lures is the fact that they make great jigs and are ideal for vertical fishing in deep water. In a versatile fishing situation they can be cast to surface-feeding fish, then dropped to the bottom to exploit deep fish schools.

Available in a range of sizes that allows them to be cast to anything from fussy fish feeding on whitebait through to big cobia or great trevally, they are among the most useful lures ever devised and should be in the tackle box at all times.

LURE-FISHING TIPS

I could write – and in fact am writing – a book on this subject. The following information touches on a few of the fundamentals.

- Many imported lures, particularly those of European origin, are designed for light freshwater fishing. Some of them are quite lethal in our salt water, but you may have to change the hooks and rings to something stronger. Ask for advice on this when buying lures, because refitting with unsuitable hooks may well kill the action and effectiveness of the lure. The majority of Australian-made lures are sold with appropriate hardware in place.

- Bibbed lures, and in fact any lure where the whole body swims or wobbles through the water, will probably need to be tied to the line with a loop connection of some kind, or a solid snap connection with a generous bend in the head of the snap. If you are unsure about how to make the connection, use a loop to be on the safe side. This allows the lure to move about freely and achieve its maximum action.

- Stiff wire trace can hamper the action of a lure, so where a trace is required for a lure to be cast, use the single-strand wire with a haywire twist loop. Some anglers like to use plastic-coated wire, simply taking a number of twists in the wire then fusing the twists in place by melting the plastic coating with a lighter flame. If you go this way, change traces regularly, because the old wire will eventually rust and lose its strength.

- When fishing with any kind of trace, use the finest diameter that conditions and commonsense will allow. When fishing where abrasion is going to be a factor, go the other way – use a high-diameter trace. In the tropics this might mean 24 kg breaking strain or more, but this will only need to be for a very short length of line. There are times when you simply have to put up with super-heavy trace material, but if you can fish lighter, do so.

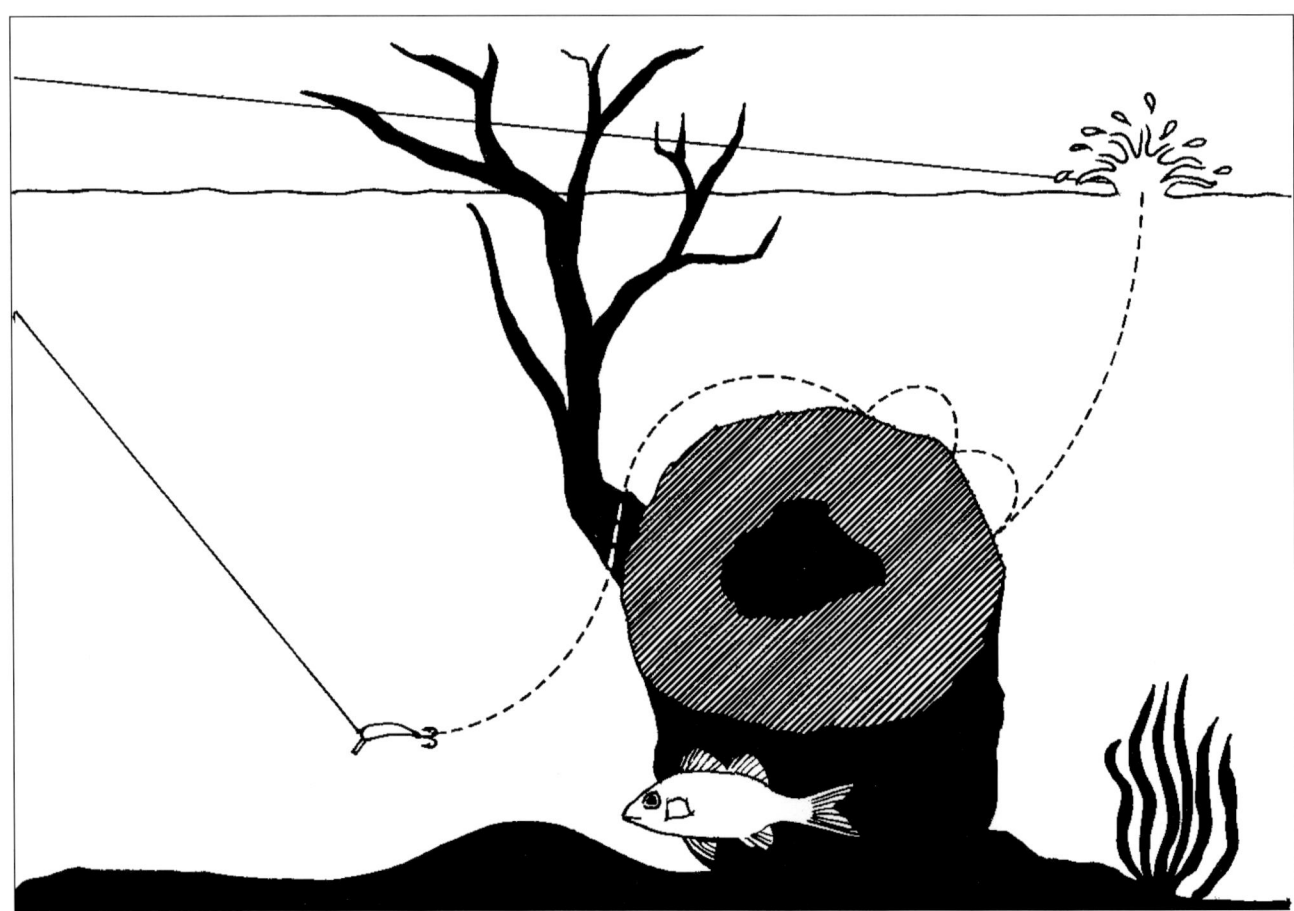

A hard-diving floating lure can be worked all over cover by simply stopping the retrieve when it hits something and allowing it to float up over the obstacle before being dived again.

- With more than one angler fishing in an unknown situation, make sure you choose different lures and presentations until something gets a result. There's no point having two or three people proving the point that the fish will not take a particular lure.

- When sinking lures over deep water, especially when fishing over a rough bottom, count the drop to the bottom after the lure hits the water. You can be quite accurate if you count 'one hundred and one, one hundred and two' and so on – you'll then know exactly how many seconds it takes for the lure to reach the bottom. If you start your retrieve a few seconds short of the bottom, you will be able to fish lures very deep without getting snagged. It pays to vary the drop when fishing from the rocks with sinking lures, but make sure you count, because you will want to know where the lure was if you take a mid-water strike. A great many strikes occur when the lure is sinking or when the retrieve first starts.

- If you can see fish following a lure but not striking, try these tricks. First, crank the lure a little faster for a moment, then stop dead for a second before starting the retrieve again. Another trick that sometimes works on curious fish that are not taking the lure is to have one angler cast out the biggest popper on hand, then start popping it with as rapid a retrieve as possible. Then cast in behind the popper with regular lures and retrieve. Some anglers carry a huge popper with no hooks, or with capped hooks so that big fish can't hook up on it and break off with the precious popper still in their jaws. A good one is worth its weight in gold at times.

- When trolling on the open sea, experiment with your lures and make sure that you only use spreads that work at a common speed. If you are setting up for this style of fishing, ask for expert advice the lures used for this work are all expensive, so you need all of them to be productive.

- Try to get as much variety in your lure spread as possible. Think about colours, actions, and whether the lures will run shallow or deep. Vary the length of the drop back in the pattern and try to place lures on the face of any pressure waves your hull is creating. Do not hesitate to have at least one lure in close to the propeller; fish are sometimes

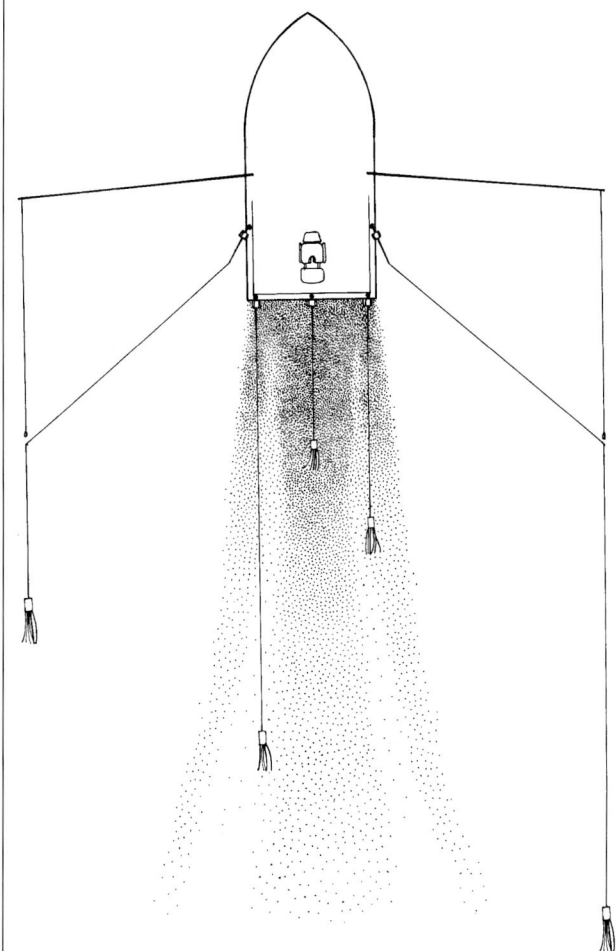

A staggered spread of lures allows the boat to be turned without tangles. This one exploits the prop wash, the clearing area of wash and the clear water well to the side of the wash and boat. If they were surface types, the lures would be placed so that they were running on the face of waves created in the boat's wake.

attracted to the source of the prop wash. This is especially true when you're running a 4-stroke outboard.

- Always keep a sharp eye out for any sign of the fish demonstrating a preference for colour, lure size, lure type or depth of presentation. If the red lure is attracting attention, consider using more of the same colour, but also be aware that it might not be the colour – it might be the size or some other factor that is working for this lure. The same thing goes for how far lures are being dragged behind the boat. If the long drop works, put another lure back there. If it's the short one that's working, bring the whole spread in closer.

- Large boats can keep lines well separated because they have plenty of beam, but even then they sometimes use outriggers to increase the spread. Fouled and crossed-up lines can be a real problem in a small boat. In addition to having your lures staggered, it can be a big help to also vary the heights of the lines. It is important that the forward rod holders be angled outwards to give the greatest possible outwards reach with the rod tips. The aft deck holders can point straight astern. It is also a good idea to add a rod holder in the centre of the transom if space permits. Further variation can be added by lowering the towing point of a couple of the rods. This is done by taking the line down from the tip to the reel, or a cleat, and fixing it there with an elastic band. Avoid doing this with very light lines.

- When a strike is taken by a boat trolling, retrieve the remaining lures, starting with the lines that are furthest away from the boat and bringing them in as fast as you can wind; this will often produce another strike. A group of good anglers who know what they are doing may have casting rods rigged with metal lures ready to cast back behind the strike. Allowing them to sink and then retrieving them fast is another way to cash in on a single strike, but it can get really messy with lines all over the place at times.

Lure fishing is very much a thinking person's way of fishing. You will catch a few fish with the 'chuck and chance it' approach, but you will catch many more if you are prepared to experiment and enjoy the endless challenge lure fishing presents.

Flies

Just as lures were designed to imitate the bait big fish eat, so flies were originally made to imitate the various insects and other stream life that make up the diet of freshwater fish, mainly the trout family.

Lures presented no special problems to the angler, as they were large enough to be fished off existing tackle. Flies, however, were another bag of tricks altogether. Much of the trout's natural diet is provided by a variety of tiny insects, and to further complicate the matter, a lot of those insects float on the top of the

water. This presented the angler with an interesting problem. Almost anything small enough to look like the trout's natural food would be impossible to cast and fish on conventional tackle. Of course quite a bit of fishing was done with natural insects that were large enough to fit onto the hook, but the problem remained – trout often feed obsessively on insects far too small to be easily presented on the tiniest of hooks.

These considerations inevitably led anglers to create and perfect fly fishing. Fly fishing started out as a very practical way to catch what at times could be a difficult fish, and then went on to become, for many people, a way of life, a religion, a reason for being on Earth. All of that side of fly fishing can safely be left in the hands of the high priests and mystics; we will just concentrate on the more realistic and practical elements of the business.

In fly fishing it is the line itself that is cast, not the bait. The line contains the casting weight, so the bait can be as light as human ingenuity can make it. Not only can the line be cast, it can also be made to sink or float, and the weight can be biased towards any part of the line or largely removed from any part of the line. With this sort of casting system available, the stream angler is able to put in front of the trout a pretty good imitation of just about anything it eats, and has quite a range of choice as to how to present it.

Saltwater fly fishing is a fairly recent innovation, and it probably came about through experts wanting to test their skills against bigger game. Initially, the

Floating and sinking flies were originally designed by anglers trying to imitate insects that form a large part of the trout's diet. These days flies are available to imitate the food of just about any fish, and that includes marlin.

popular view of saltwater fly fishing was that it was a little like building full-size bridges out of matchsticks. In other words, finding the hardest way possible to do the job, then doing it just for the satisfaction involved in completing a difficult task. Remember, the saltwater people had none of the problems that sent the original freshwater people looking for a new fishing system.

But saltwater fly fishing has exploded in recent years, and this has been largely due to two things. The first is that increasing numbers of people are looking upon angling purely as a sport; they have little or no interest in the food value of the game. Many release everything they catch, and a lot more are into tag-and-release, with just the odd fish being kept for the table. If you take this attitude, you might as well go for the branch of the art offering the greatest challenge, and saltwater fly fishing does just that.

The second reason is that the saltwater flies themselves often present a better representation of natural bait than hard-bodied lures, and there are times when the fly will activate fish that will not look at anything else. One major asset common to many of the flies is their ability to pulse in the water as the dressing opens and closes with water pressure variations. Even when you know darned well that they are made out of feathers and animal hair, it is hard to believe, with some of the better flies, that they are not live, swimming creatures.

Walking along the beach one day I noticed a most beautiful small baitfish lying at the bottom of a pool. I reached down and picked it up, only to discover that I was holding a saltwater fly somebody had lost.

These days fly fishing has spread throughout just about every fishing environment, and many anglers take a fly rod along as a matter of course, no matter where they are going to fish.

One of the greatest attractions for the fly anglers, working any kind of water, is the joy of tying and fishing their own flies. Many people look upon fly tying as an end in itself, and few serious fly anglers rely entirely on commercial fly tyers for their flies.

FRESHWATER FLY TYPES

Dry flies are those intended to be fished on the surface of the water, and they range from minute offerings

TOP a collection of wet flies designed to be retrieved below the surface, and **ABOVE** a couple of dry flies which perch on the top of the water.

sitting high on the surface film through to bulkier models intended to look like larger insects that have come to grief falling into the water.

Wet flies are representations of drowned insects, live beetles, crustaceans and small fish. They are fished below the surface.

The only level of stream life remaining to be covered are the larval stages of many of the creatures whose adult forms are the subject of dry fly patterns called nymphs. Many stream insects lay their eggs in or on the water, and when they hatch they are streambed creatures until they eventually sprout wings and fly from the water. Although a specific group in themselves, the nymphs are also a wet fly.

At top are streamer flies, which are tied in an incredible variety of styles and materials. The extreme fly in the middle is a Dahlberg Diver, something midway between a popper and a true diving fly. The monsters above are flies designed for marlin, which can also be fitted with a foam buffer at the face, allowing them to be used as poppers.

SALTWATER FLY TYPES

Streamer flies are probably the most important group in the saltwater arsenal, as they are a baitfish imitation, and therefore a fly with universal application. The classic Lefty's Deceiver, a swimming fly of great versatility, has achieved almost legendary status in the fly fishing world, its name now being known throughout sportfishing circles.

Popper flies do all the things the hard-bodied poppers do, but on a smaller, more subtle scale. Where the hard-bodied poppers attract attention through fairly outrageous behaviour, the fly version gets a lot closer to the behaviour of real baitfish in trouble.

Bluewater baitfish flies are superb imitations of the tiny baitfish so often responsible for the obsessive, single-minded feeding behaviour of quite large saltwater fish.

In addition to the pure fly styles mentioned above, saltwater people are coming up with flies for special applications, some of which are carrying enough weight to be cast on a light threadline outfit. Flies intended to be presented to billfish are in this category.

Saltwater fly fishing also has its classification of flies intended to fish deep, or close to the bottom.

Fishing systems

To give you an idea of the way in which some of this tackle comes together, the following pages show how a few outfits are used. Extending from the tip of each rod is a sample range of typical rigs that might be used with the outfit. The idea here is not to show you everything you could do with an outfit, but to give an impression of the range of jobs the combination can handle.

You will notice that some of the terminal rigs are duplicated, especially with the big threadline and sidecast outfits. These represent areas of function overlap. Some of these jobs are better performed with one outfit than another: for detailed information in this area turn to the specific section in the book where the rod and reel types are dealt with in depth.

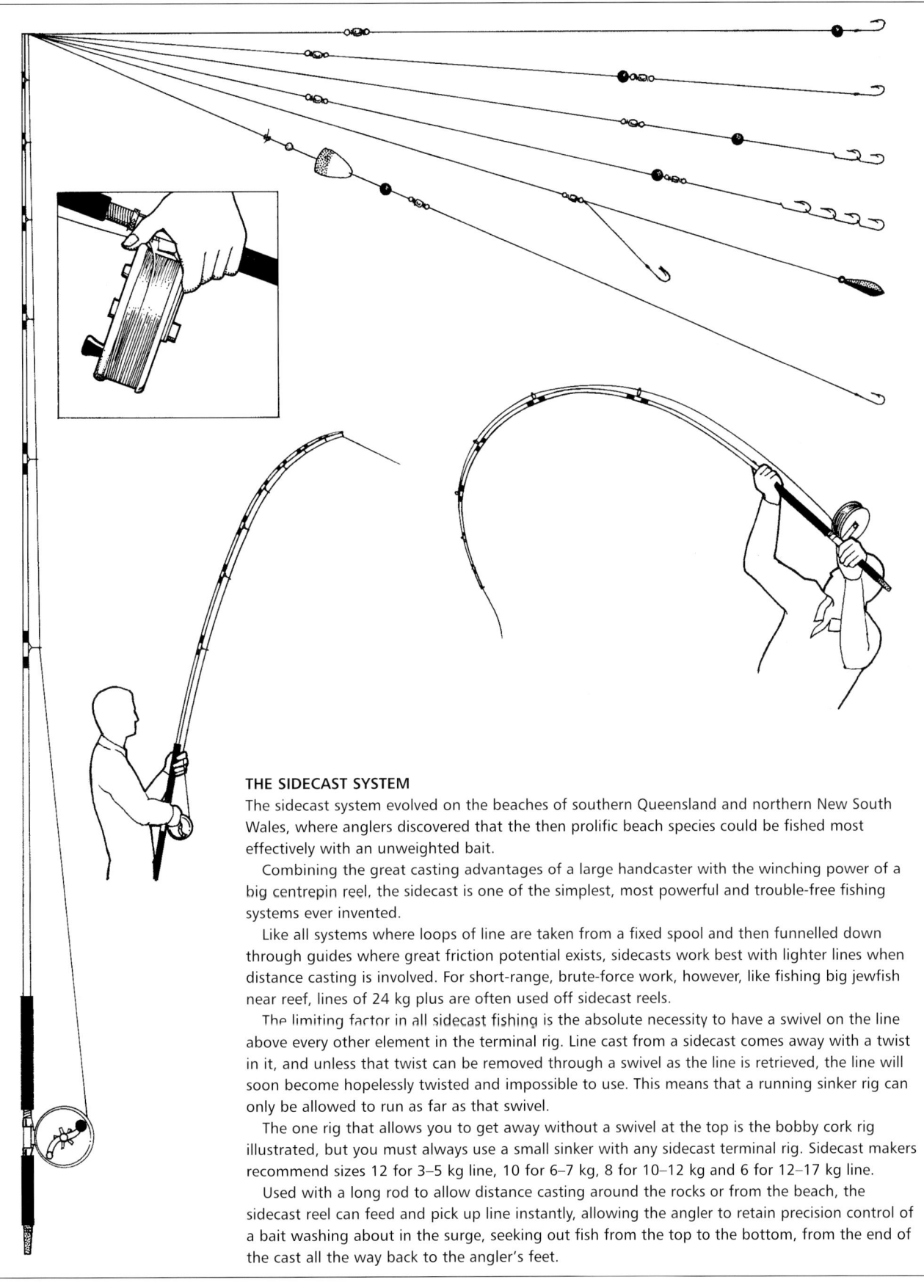

THE SIDECAST SYSTEM

The sidecast system evolved on the beaches of southern Queensland and northern New South Wales, where anglers discovered that the then prolific beach species could be fished most effectively with an unweighted bait.

Combining the great casting advantages of a large handcaster with the winching power of a big centrepin reel, the sidecast is one of the simplest, most powerful and trouble-free fishing systems ever invented.

Like all systems where loops of line are taken from a fixed spool and then funnelled down through guides where great friction potential exists, sidecasts work best with lighter lines when distance casting is involved. For short-range, brute-force work, however, like fishing big jewfish near reef, lines of 24 kg plus are often used off sidecast reels.

The limiting factor in all sidecast fishing is the absolute necessity to have a swivel on the line above every other element in the terminal rig. Line cast from a sidecast comes away with a twist in it, and unless that twist can be removed through a swivel as the line is retrieved, the line will soon become hopelessly twisted and impossible to use. This means that a running sinker rig can only be allowed to run as far as that swivel.

The one rig that allows you to get away without a swivel at the top is the bobby cork rig illustrated, but you must always use a small sinker with any sidecast terminal rig. Sidecast makers recommend sizes 12 for 3–5 kg line, 10 for 6–7 kg, 8 for 10–12 kg and 6 for 12–17 kg line.

Used with a long rod to allow distance casting around the rocks or from the beach, the sidecast reel can feed and pick up line instantly, allowing the angler to retain precision control of a bait washing about in the surge, seeking out fish from the top to the bottom, from the end of the cast all the way back to the angler's feet.

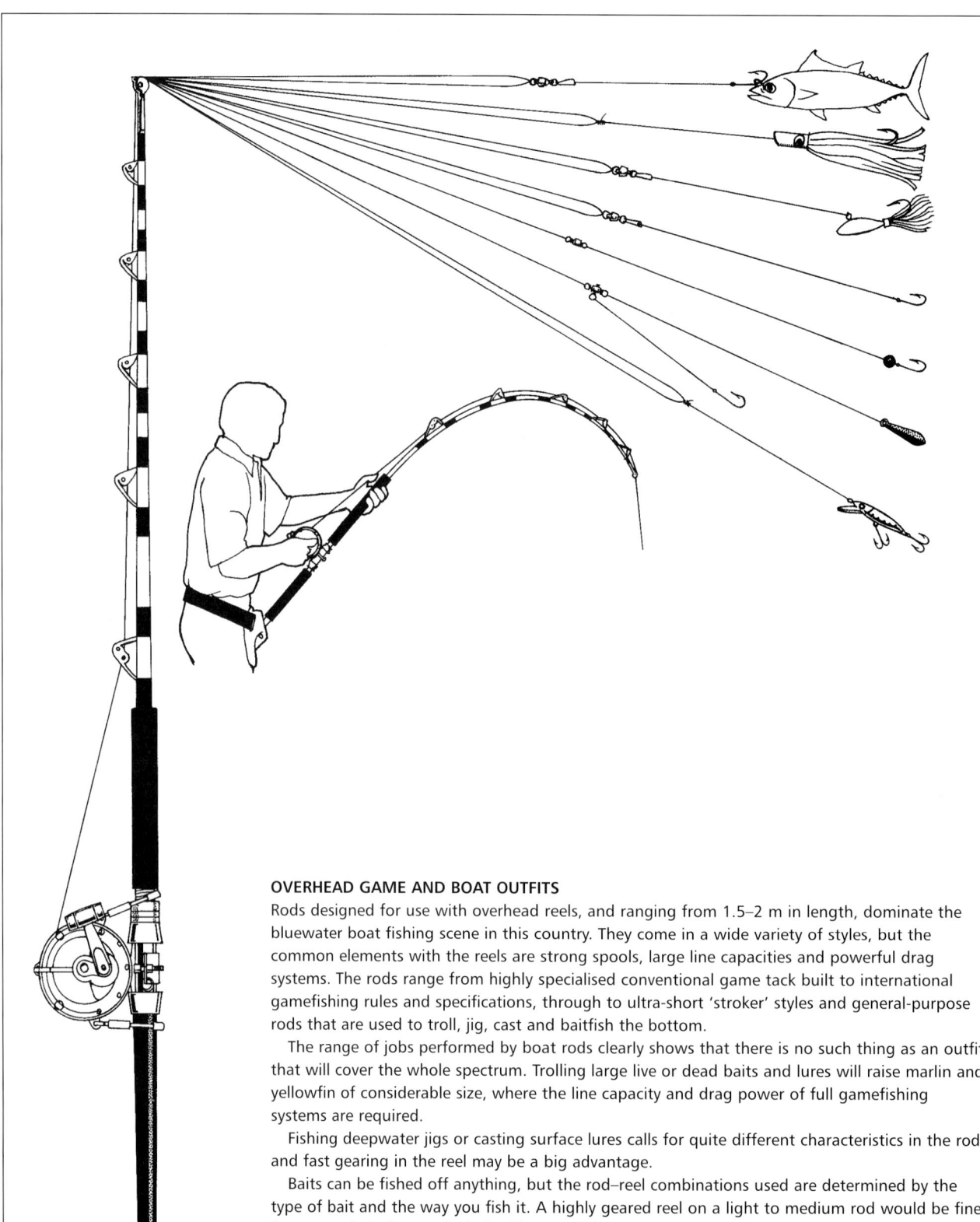

OVERHEAD GAME AND BOAT OUTFITS

Rods designed for use with overhead reels, and ranging from 1.5–2 m in length, dominate the bluewater boat fishing scene in this country. They come in a wide variety of styles, but the common elements with the reels are strong spools, large line capacities and powerful drag systems. The rods range from highly specialised conventional game tack built to international gamefishing rules and specifications, through to ultra-short 'stroker' styles and general-purpose rods that are used to troll, jig, cast and baitfish the bottom.

The range of jobs performed by boat rods clearly shows that there is no such thing as an outfit that will cover the whole spectrum. Trolling large live or dead baits and lures will raise marlin and yellowfin of considerable size, where the line capacity and drag power of full gamefishing systems are required.

Fishing deepwater jigs or casting surface lures calls for quite different characteristics in the rod, and fast gearing in the reel may be a big advantage.

Baits can be fished off anything, but the rod–reel combinations used are determined by the type of bait and the way you fish it. A highly geared reel on a light to medium rod would be fine for some of the bottom bait rigs illustrated, but you would be asking for trouble putting out a reasonable-sized live bait on such an outfit.

The argument against using gamefishing gear all the time to 'be on the safe side' is weight. The price you pay to have a reel that will carry a lot of line, not distort under great pressure and have gears that will not collapse under the strain is a lot of weight that can be very uncomfortable to handle in an active fishing situation.

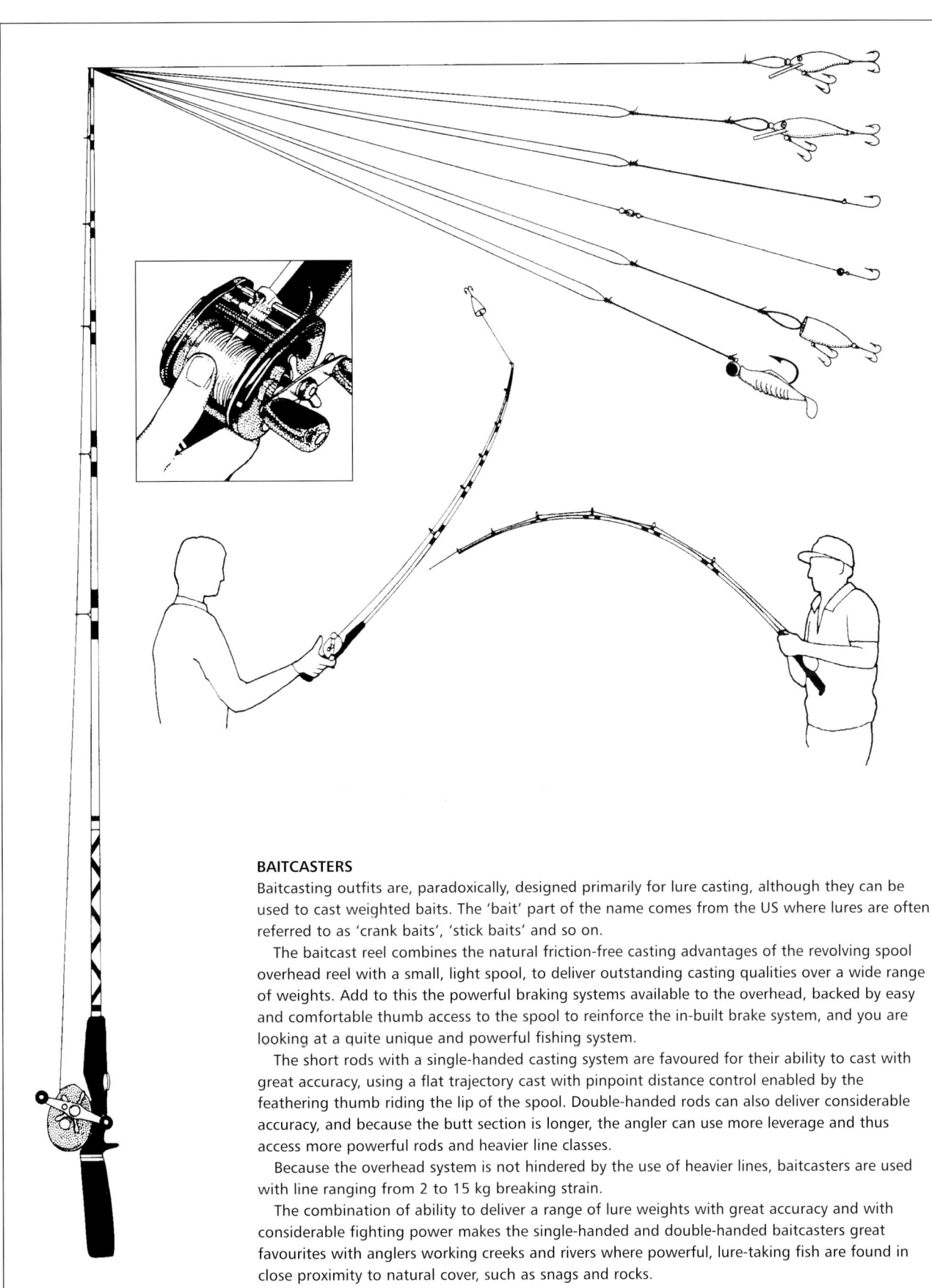

BAITCASTERS

Baitcasting outfits are, paradoxically, designed primarily for lure casting, although they can be used to cast weighted baits. The 'bait' part of the name comes from the US where lures are often referred to as 'crank baits', 'stick baits' and so on.

The baitcast reel combines the natural friction-free casting advantages of the revolving spool overhead reel with a small, light spool, to deliver outstanding casting qualities over a wide range of weights. Add to this the powerful braking systems available to the overhead, backed by easy and comfortable thumb access to the spool to reinforce the in-built brake system, and you are looking at a quite unique and powerful fishing system.

The short rods with a single-handed casting system are favoured for their ability to cast with great accuracy, using a flat trajectory cast with pinpoint distance control enabled by the feathering thumb riding the lip of the spool. Double-handed rods can also deliver considerable accuracy, and because the butt section is longer, the angler can use more leverage and thus access more powerful rods and heavier line classes.

Because the overhead system is not hindered by the use of heavier lines, baitcasters are used with line ranging from 2 to 15 kg breaking strain.

The combination of ability to deliver a range of lure weights with great accuracy and with considerable fighting power makes the single-handed and double-handed baitcasters great favourites with anglers working creeks and rivers where powerful, lure-taking fish are found in close proximity to natural cover, such as snags and rocks.

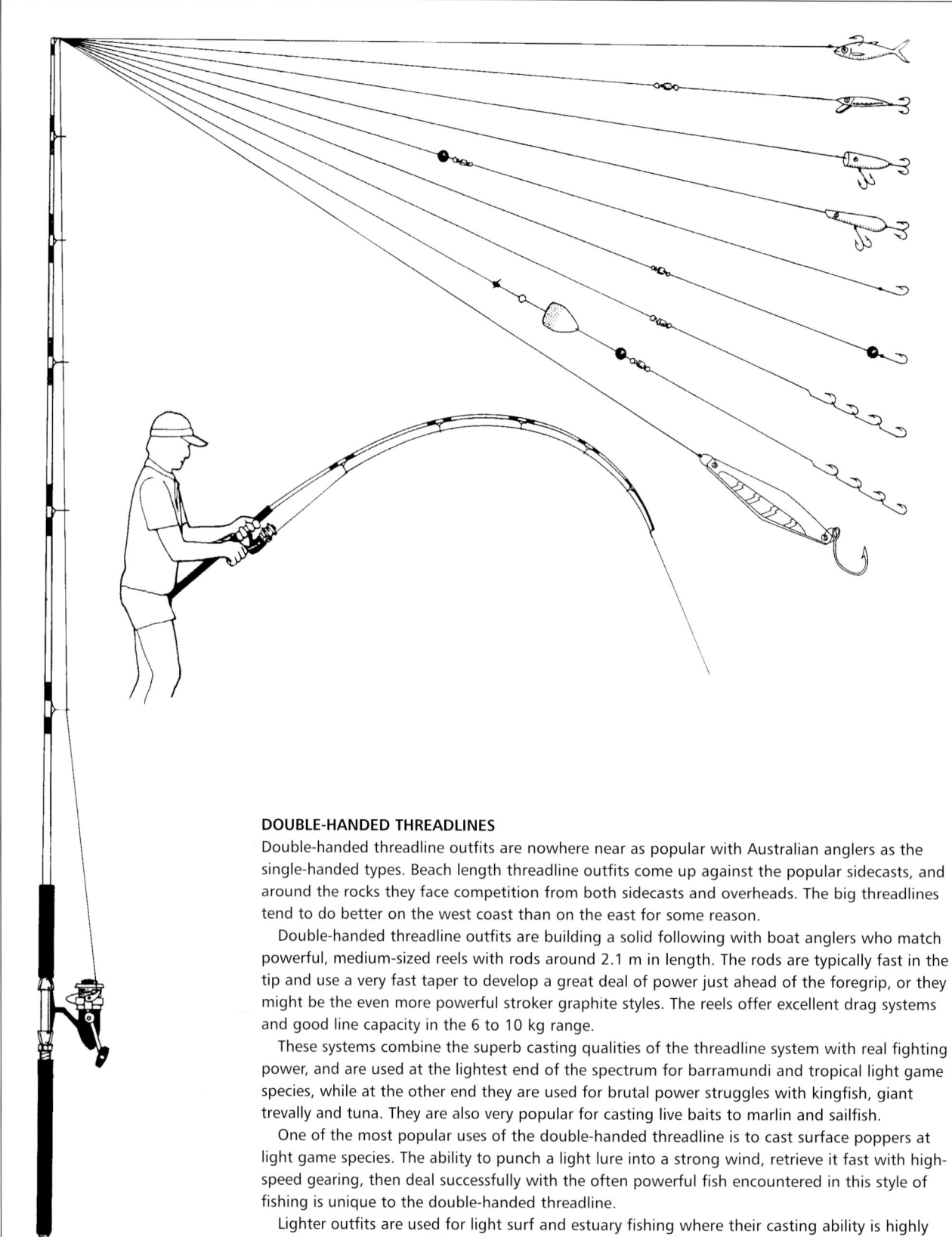

DOUBLE-HANDED THREADLINES

Double-handed threadline outfits are nowhere near as popular with Australian anglers as the single-handed types. Beach length threadline outfits come up against the popular sidecasts, and around the rocks they face competition from both sidecasts and overheads. The big threadlines tend to do better on the west coast than on the east for some reason.

Double-handed threadline outfits are building a solid following with boat anglers who match powerful, medium-sized reels with rods around 2.1 m in length. The rods are typically fast in the tip and use a very fast taper to develop a great deal of power just ahead of the foregrip, or they might be the even more powerful stroker graphite styles. The reels offer excellent drag systems and good line capacity in the 6 to 10 kg range.

These systems combine the superb casting qualities of the threadline system with real fighting power, and are used at the lightest end of the spectrum for barramundi and tropical light game species, while at the other end they are used for brutal power struggles with kingfish, giant trevally and tuna. They are also very popular for casting live baits to marlin and sailfish.

One of the most popular uses of the double-handed threadline is to cast surface poppers at light game species. The ability to punch a light lure into a strong wind, retrieve it fast with high-speed gearing, then deal successfully with the often powerful fish encountered in this style of fishing is unique to the double-handed threadline.

Lighter outfits are used for light surf and estuary fishing where their casting ability is highly prized, and our range of rigs shows just how versatile and powerful this system can be.

The fighting illustration shows how the longer butt and a higher foregrip position allows some real leverage to be brought to bear through the rod.

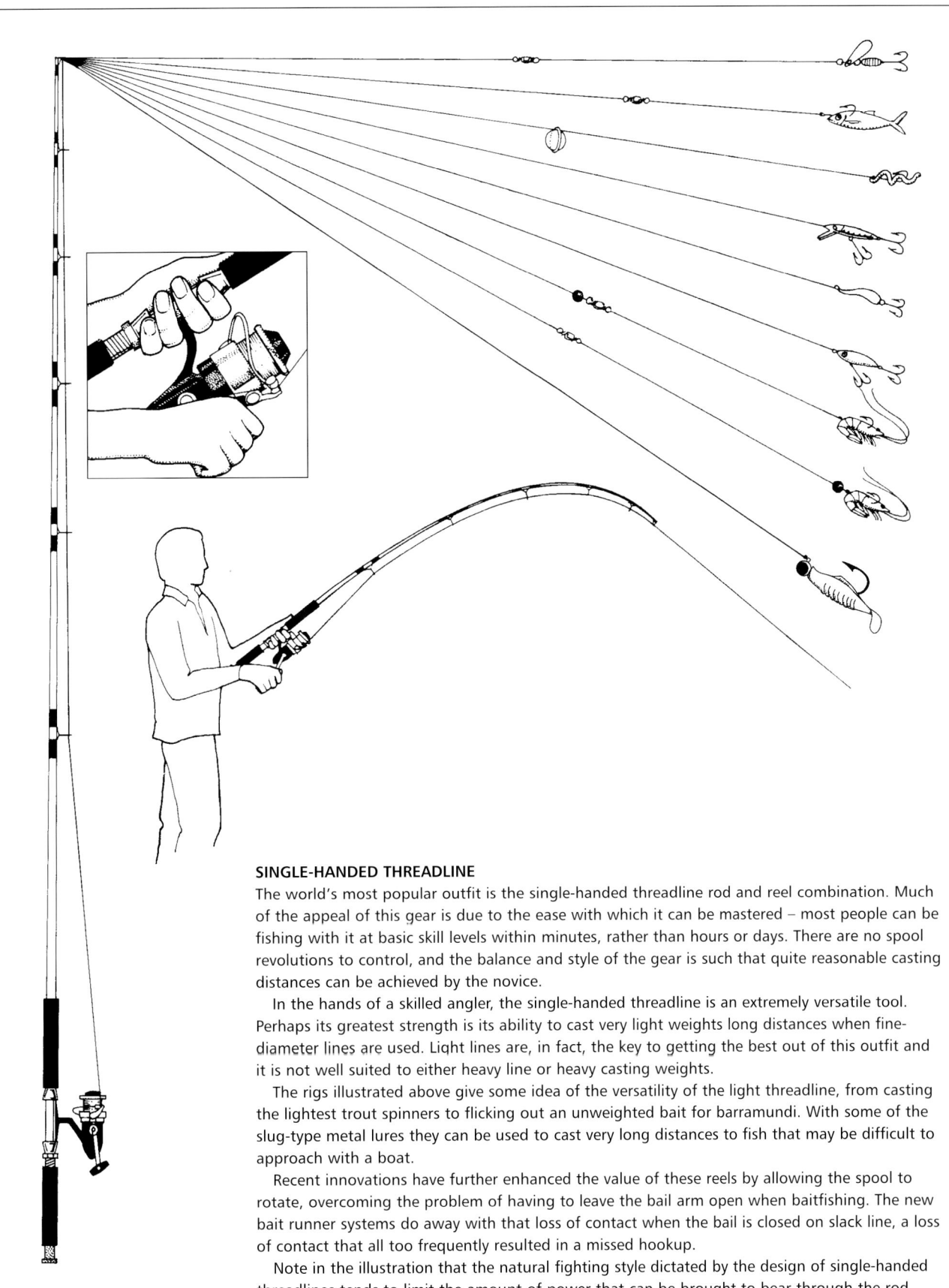

SINGLE-HANDED THREADLINE

The world's most popular outfit is the single-handed threadline rod and reel combination. Much of the appeal of this gear is due to the ease with which it can be mastered – most people can be fishing with it at basic skill levels within minutes, rather than hours or days. There are no spool revolutions to control, and the balance and style of the gear is such that quite reasonable casting distances can be achieved by the novice.

In the hands of a skilled angler, the single-handed threadline is an extremely versatile tool. Perhaps its greatest strength is its ability to cast very light weights long distances when fine-diameter lines are used. Light lines are, in fact, the key to getting the best out of this outfit and it is not well suited to either heavy line or heavy casting weights.

The rigs illustrated above give some idea of the versatility of the light threadline, from casting the lightest trout spinners to flicking out an unweighted bait for barramundi. With some of the slug-type metal lures they can be used to cast very long distances to fish that may be difficult to approach with a boat.

Recent innovations have further enhanced the value of these reels by allowing the spool to rotate, overcoming the problem of having to leave the bail arm open when baitfishing. The new bait runner systems do away with that loss of contact when the bail is closed on slack line, a loss of contact that all too frequently resulted in a missed hookup.

Note in the illustration that the natural fighting style dictated by the design of single-handed threadlines tends to limit the amount of power that can be brought to bear through the rod.

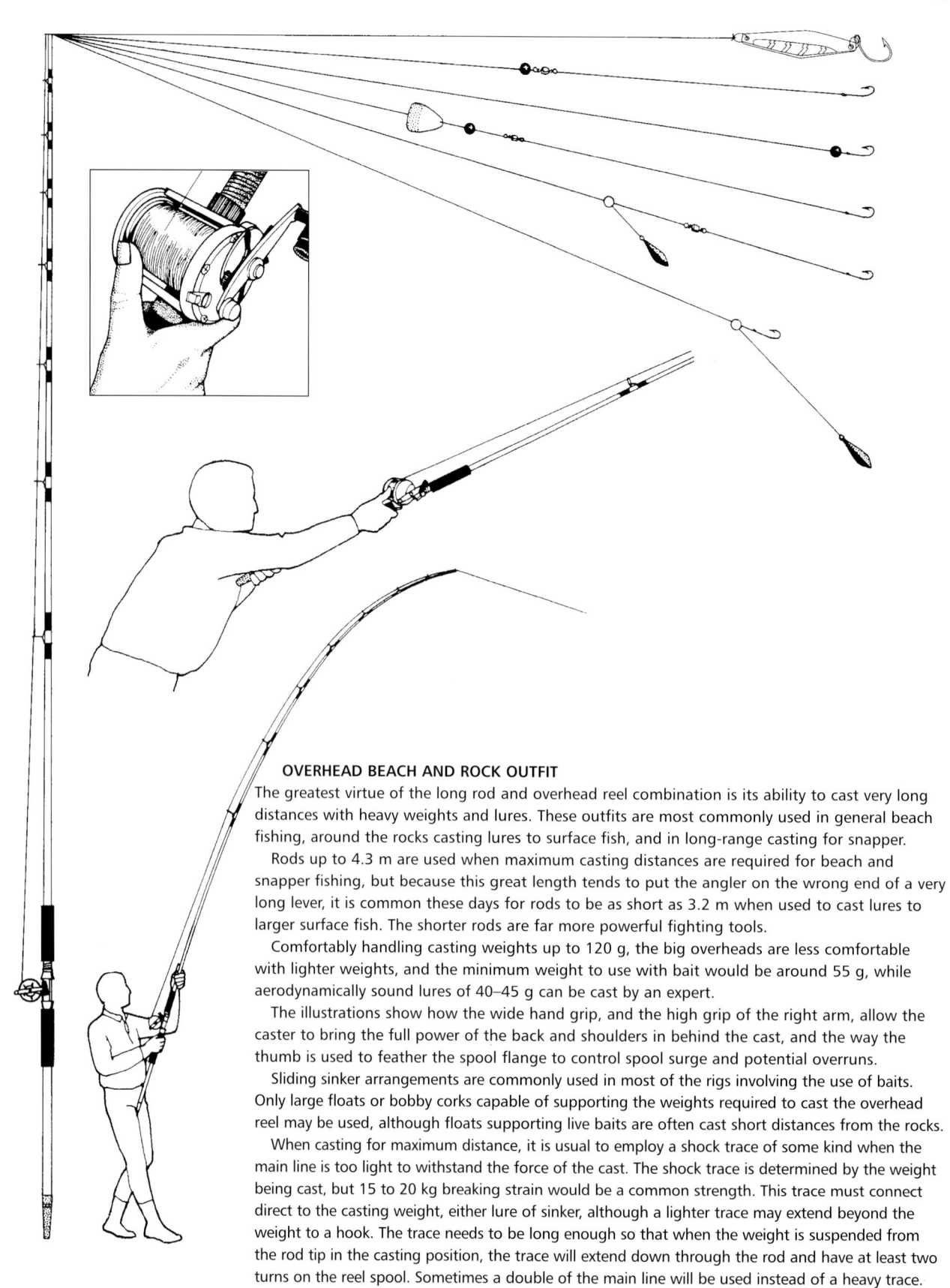

OVERHEAD BEACH AND ROCK OUTFIT

The greatest virtue of the long rod and overhead reel combination is its ability to cast very long distances with heavy weights and lures. These outfits are most commonly used in general beach fishing, around the rocks casting lures to surface fish, and in long-range casting for snapper.

Rods up to 4.3 m are used when maximum casting distances are required for beach and snapper fishing, but because this great length tends to put the angler on the wrong end of a very long lever, it is common these days for rods to be as short as 3.2 m when used to cast lures to larger surface fish. The shorter rods are far more powerful fighting tools.

Comfortably handling casting weights up to 120 g, the big overheads are less comfortable with lighter weights, and the minimum weight to use with bait would be around 55 g, while aerodynamically sound lures of 40–45 g can be cast by an expert.

The illustrations show how the wide hand grip, and the high grip of the right arm, allow the caster to bring the full power of the back and shoulders in behind the cast, and the way the thumb is used to feather the spool flange to control spool surge and potential overruns.

Sliding sinker arrangements are commonly used in most of the rigs involving the use of baits. Only large floats or bobby corks capable of supporting the weights required to cast the overhead reel may be used, although floats supporting live baits are often cast short distances from the rocks.

When casting for maximum distance, it is usual to employ a shock trace of some kind when the main line is too light to withstand the force of the cast. The shock trace is determined by the weight being cast, but 15 to 20 kg breaking strain would be a common strength. This trace must connect direct to the casting weight, either lure of sinker, although a lighter trace may extend beyond the weight to a hook. The trace needs to be long enough so that when the weight is suspended from the rod tip in the casting position, the trace will extend down through the rod and have at least two turns on the reel spool. Sometimes a double of the main line will be used instead of a heavy trace.

TACKLE STORAGE AND EQUIPMENT

TACKLE BOXES

It would be hard to imagine a size or shape of tackle box that is not already available. There are miniature pocket-sized boxes for flies at one end of the range, and multi-drawer monsters capable of gobbling up more lures and terminal tackle than most of us could ever afford to own at the other.

The largest of the tackle boxes on sale are tempting things, as they seem to offer a quick solution to organising all your gear. Experience in the field suggests otherwise. Most anglers try this approach at some time or other and find that the boxes are cumbersome to carry around, and are often difficult to

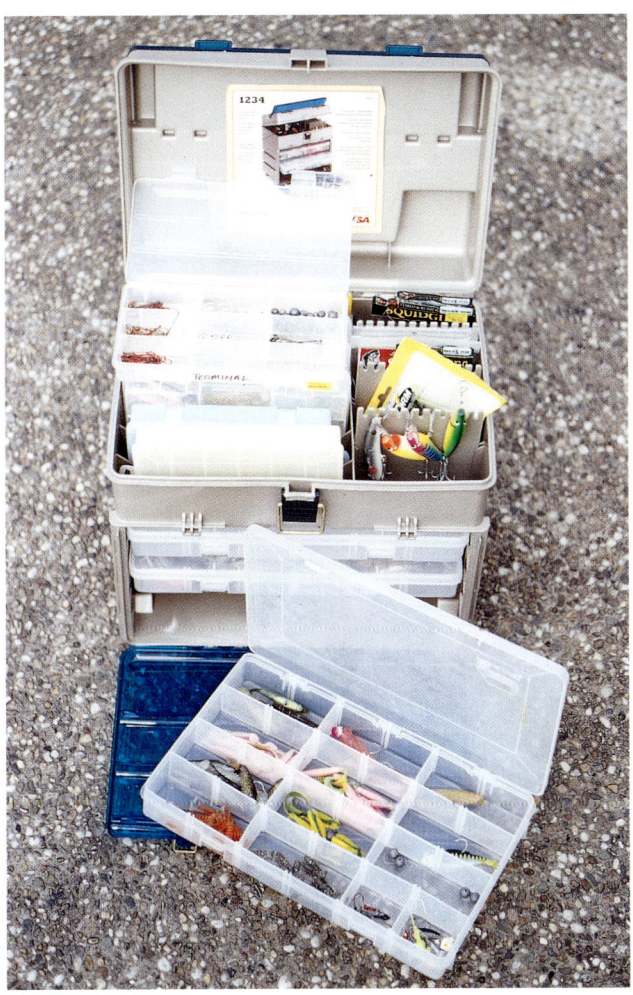

The current trend is mega-tackle boxes with interchangeable mini tackle boxes rather than the traditional fixed drawers. It's a great system for people with a lot of lures.

use. Those with two stacks of large, multi-level trays that rise up as the lid is lifted are notoriously unstable in boats, and in many small boats they demand more space than is available. If water gets into them, everything you own gets wet.

The alternative style – a flat box with a lid front and back – is more convenient. These boxes don't fall over, are easy to carry, and if you have a lot of gear in a boat, they can be stacked to save space. It makes more sense to spread your gear over two or three of these boxes than to have everything you own exposed every time you open a lid. If you give a bit of thought to the way you organise the boxes, allocating gear to the various sides according to the amount of use they get, the system can work very well.

The range of tackle boxes currently in vogue have some of the old-style fixed storage shelves with lure compartments for larger lures, but they also offer big areas designed to take small plastic tackle boxes with snap lids. You can buy any number of these small boxes and set up your big tackle box with whatever set of smaller boxes you expect to need on a particular trip.

My boy currently uses one of these. It even has a space on top of the lid where you can throw lures that have been used in salt water until you have a chance to wash them down in fresh.

The type of storage you need varies greatly according to the type of fishing you do, but many anglers share my view that it is better to have tackle stored in a number of small containers than to have everything in one large one. Bulk supplies of hooks and lures are best stored at home, with just enough of everything in the box to get you through the trip at hand.

The tackle boxes I use when travelling by road are two large Tupperware containers with snap-seal lids. I carry small tray boxes in these to handle items of terminal tackle, with lures left in the boxes they come in. I generally work out of one container and have backup gear in the other. A big plastic fish box houses everything in my boat, and within that box separate Tupperware-style boxes keep everything pretty well organised.

When storing gear, remember that some of the soft plastic lures and worms we use these days are made of a strange material that eats other plastics. The great majority of storage boxes these days are worm-proof, but if you dig out some older plastic boxes, make sure they are worm-proof before you use them. If you're in any doubt, keep soft plastics in individual snap-lock plastic bags and do not mix one type with another. They can make a shocking mess in the tackle box, as they reduce everything they touch to a sort of plastic slime.

Rod Harrison used to wander the world with a huge fish storage box fitted with a tightly fitting lid, with everything he owned more or less housed inside in an assortment of plastic bags and containers. None of his lures was fitted up with hooks when he was travelling. There is nothing like a few long-range fishing trips involving air travel to make you come to terms with what you really need and what can safely be left at home.

Rod also had the words 'DANGEROUS SNAKES' printed on the side of the box, which greatly reduced the interest airport thieves were likely to show in this particular piece of cargo. Generally speaking, the less your gear looks like fishing tackle, the longer you are likely to keep it.

Over the years you will find that you tend to waste hooks if you carry too many with you. They invariably get exposed to salt spray and go rusty before you use them. Plastic 35 mm film canisters and vitamin and pill containers are good for storing hooks. The film canisters are particularly good because they fit neatly into one of the lure compartments in the average tackle box.

The latest tackle boxes house a number of these flat tackle storage boxes in which compartments can be adjusted to fit large or small items. An angler might have terminal tackle and lures in any number of these small boxes, which makes it easy to fill the big tackle box with just the things you need for a specific fishing trip.

If you fish in a variety of environments, it is a good idea to make up several of the flat compact containers, each with terminal gear appropriate for a particular area.

Pre-rigged trolling lures are best stored and carried in individual snap-lock plastic envelopes, which in turn can be dumped in a large soft bag. Take a large plastic bag with you and make sure all the lures that get used go into that for washing and drying when you get home. Carry one flat plastic box with compartments for all your hooks, swivels, trace materials and so on.

If you keep all your lures in their packages until you actually want to use them, you can then dump all your backup supply into the bin area in the bottom of the box without fear of tangles. Carry an empty plastic box with you and put all the used lures in there until you get a chance to wash them. Keeping wet lures out of a tackle box saves an enormous amount of wear and tear on your gear.

Another solution to bulk lure storage is to just carry the lure bodies in the trays of the box, rigging them as needed with trebles. This doesn't take long to do, and you will be amazed at how many more lures will fit in a tackle box when the treble hooks have been removed. Spend a bit of money on a decent pair of split-ring pliers to take the fuss out of the job.

ROD TUBES

There seems to be little point in anyone manufacturing a commercial rod-carrying case when the PVC tubes we all buy from the nearest plumbing supplier work so well. Some of the telescopic commercial tubes are, however, certainly attractive.

When you go to buy some PVC tubing, buy it in a length that will leave some space at either end when the rods are loaded in, and buy a diameter just a little too large for the number of rods you plan to carry. This will give you room to get at least one thickness of cotton sheet or something similar between your rods. Ideally, the fit should be a snug one when you slide the rods into the tube. It is a good idea to tie the rods together before they go into the tube, and to do this with butts and tips mixed, butts protruding beyond the tips, if possible. The bit of space at either end is where your socks and underpants travel, to ensure that the rod tips are not broken. Glue the base cap into place, then screw on the top cap and secure it with masking tape.

PVC tube also makes an ideal map case, and will considerably extend the life of expensive marine charts that are carried in a small boat.

THE EXTRAS

CHOOSING A TACKLE STORE

Fishing tackle is sold in all sorts of places these days, and not all of them employ fishing enthusiasts as salespeople. If you know what you want and are just looking for a bargain, go for your life and buy where you think you are getting the best deal. If, however, you are going to need guidance in the purchase of expensive equipment, you would do well to check out a few shops before you start parting with too much money.

It is rare to find people in the retail tackle trade who are just there for a fast buck. Most of them are smart enough to know that anglers never stop buying tackle once they start, and they generally do their best to keep you coming back to their store. That means looking after you to the best of their ability. The amount of interest they express in what you actually want to do before they start to recommend gear is a good indication of just how genuine they are.

Your main job is to locate people with a real interest in the sort of fishing you want to get into; this is particularly true of those areas requiring expensive high-performance tackle, such as game fishing and fly fishing. There are stores around that specialise in these fields, and it can be worth your while to deal with them, but your local person might have a good knowledge of your area of interest, so always try there first.

For any of the regular forms of fishing, the local person is usually the best bet, as they should be up to the minute with the things that are working in your fishing area. In addition to selling you gear, you should expect them to be a source of tips on spots to fish, as well as methods and bait. If they are tight-lipped about such matters, go spend your money somewhere else.

I lean on my local tackle store for all sorts of things, and as the demands of business leave me less and less time for my tackle, I look towards the tackle store people to service reels and repair my rods. As a matter of fact, some of the gear is becoming so complex that I feel it is a darned sight safer to have them do it for me.

TRACE MATERIALS

If you plan to do any amount of serious game fishing, you will need to set yourself up with a kit for making a variety of traces. The type of trace materials you need will vary greatly according to the area you fish. Tropical anglers use wire of various kinds, while most southern anglers, with the exception of those into serious specialised shark fishing, lean towards special-purpose heavy monofilaments. If you are going to get into game fishing, you will need heavy traces, crimps and crimping pliers. It is important to have the correct sizes in crimps for your traces, so if you don't know how to use crimps – especially those used with mono traces – ask your tackle person to show you how to do it properly. Also get their help selecting the appropriate traces and crimps. It is very important to get all this right.

For anything short of game fishing, it is useful to carry a few spools of trace materials of various strengths in the tackle box. Mono traces of 30 kg breaking strain are a popular choice for tropical creek fishing, where a short trace is used to the lure. Some people opt for wire; if you go this way, use as fine a wire as you can get away with.

Once away from the tropics and its many toothy critters, traces to baits (alive or dead) do not need to be especially heavy, and size is largely a matter of personal choice. Some will opt for heavy trace, while others will fish the main line straight through to the hook, believing that this produces more strikes. Adherents of both schools of thought are dogmatic in defence of their beliefs: try both approaches for yourself before closing your mind on the subject. Large diameter and a hard surface are good characteristics in a monofilament trace, so take care not to buy one of the high-quality lines where a high breaking strain is achieved in a fine-diameter line.

If you are going the opposite way and are looking for a fine trace for presentation to sensitive fish, you should give preference to high-quality line with good diameter to breaking strain characteristics. In a subtropical estuary the diameter and colour of a trace may make a big difference to the end result. There is obviously an incentive to fish a heavy trace to an expensive lure, but there is less incentive to fish a heavy trace to a bait. Keep in mind that the trace is the part of your terminal tackle that the fish is going to look at closely. In lightly fished areas where

A strong gaff is the only way to go when dealing with fish that are not to be released – toothy critters like mackerel and other species that are just too large and boisterous to be handled in any other way. Gaffs are not recommended for lighter fish that lack the body weight and substance required to allow a gaff point to penetrate.

competition for food is fierce, fish may not be worried by a heavy trace, but in heavily fished areas an obvious trace should be avoided.

Don't forget that your tackle is only as strong as the weakest link. Don't go too hard on a fish when you've gone to light trace to get your bites, and don't forget the strength of your main line when you are using a heavy trace.

A few packets of galvanised or multi-strand wire take up little room in the tackle box. If you live in the southern half of the continent you may find that you never use it, but in waters where mackerel and wahoo tend to be thick, fishing with wire becomes a matter of course.

The rule with wire is don't use it unless you have to, and when you have to, use the lightest wire that will do the job. When fishing with bait in marginal situations, go to linked hooks rather than wire.

KNIVES

Knives are an interesting subject, but they can get you into numerous arguments, so I will restrict myself to some fundamental points.

There are basically two types of knives: those made from hard steel that hold an edge for a long time, and those made from soft steel that lose their edge very quickly. Knives that hold their edge longest take forever to re-sharpen; those that lose their edge quickly also accept a new edge quickly. If you have nothing better to do with your time, buy a quality hard steel knife and revel in the joys of using and sharpening it. If you are like me, buy soft steel and be crude enough to sharpen knives by rubbing two blade edges together, or buy yourself a sharpening steel or stone. They all get the job done. The advantage of having a soft steel knife is that you can have a good edge every time you use it.

You need two knives, one for general knockabout work and the other for filleting. A good filleting knife should have a thin, pliable blade that can be flexed to lie flat along the backbone of a fish, and it should accept a good edge without too much trouble. Good filleting knives are treasured items in most fishing households, and they should only be used for the filleting job. The knockabout knife is used for all the heavy cutting work.

The knockabout knife is defined by the individual's particular needs, but try to resist Rambo-type bad guy

Two good-quality sharp knives are essential items. The fillet knife (at top) has a thin, flexible blade which allows the cutting edge to work over and around bones with ease, while the heavy-duty blade will only be required by people who have the specific need for a strong blade with a good edge.

killers with those enormous, heavy, hooked blades, as they are not much good for anything other than making Rambo movies. If you can find what you want in a fairly short blade you'll be well ahead, because a short blade resists snapping better than a long one.

You don't want the blade too thick, as it will take a lot of sharpening, but it obviously needs to have a reasonable amount of meat in it. Rock anglers often need a heavier blade than other folk, especially if they cut cunje.

Pay special attention to the handles of your fishing knives, as your hands will usually be quite slippery when you are working with them. Most handles are just plastic these days, but if you can find something offering a better grip, it is an asset.

SCALERS

Although you can scale fish with a knife, nothing scales a fish as well as the old-fashioned scalers that have a metal ring with a serrated top and those little wooden handles. Perhaps it is just my clumsiness, but I always manage to skin and puncture my fingers on dorsal fins and pectorals when I scale with a knife. People seem to invent scalers at the rate of a new one every week, but I've never seen a system to beat the double pass of sharp points you get with every stroke of the old-style scaler.

PLIERS

Pliers are used for all sorts of things in the fishing scene, and it's probably a good idea to buy a special pouch that allows you to carry pliers on your belt, where they are always within reach. You can even buy double pouches that allow you to carry two pliers at once.

Most anglers carry a set of long-nosed pliers for removing hooks from fish; side-cutters are also handy to have around when you are working with heavy traces and wire. Anglers who work a lot with lures carrying treble hooks prefer specialised split-ring pliers.

Pliers are also very handy for flattening the barbs on hooks; I will look at this again later, in the section on safety. Getting hooks out of yourself can be a nasty business, especially in remote areas (geographically and personally speaking), and more and more lure anglers are flattening the barbs on their hooks in anticipation of the inevitable. A lot of anglers question the value of barbs anyway, quite a few believing that the difficulty of driving the barb in offsets any value it might have in holding the hook in place.

For the less substantial mono lines, to around 50 kg breaking strain, nail-cutters (fingernail, that is) are a great thing to have in your pocket, especially for tidying up the loose ends on knots.

This little collection of odds and ends is very handy to have close at hand when fishing. Superglue can be used to smooth over bulky knots and repair all sorts of things, and also to attach soft plastics to jig heads. You can hang a strong nail clipper around your neck with a piece of fishing line and use it to trim knots. A good pair of side-cutters may be required if wire is being used. The Leatherman series of multi-purpose tools are expensive but worth every cent. I never go fishing without the larger of the two attached to my belt.

SUPERGLUE

Superglue might seem an eccentric extra to have in the tackle box, as might nail varnish, but both are handy items. Superglue can be used for all sorts of running repairs, and to cement knots. It can also be used to create a smooth external shell around a knot, as can nail varnish. This is handy when knots need to travel back and forth through guides, and when you are trying to minimise bubble trails produced by your terminal tackle. Wahoo love to snap at the source of bubble trails, and this is often a lumpy knot in your rig.

If you carry a small roll of sash cord-type string as well as your superglue, you can fix an awful lot of broken gear in the field. If you decide to replace a guide, though, don't forget that the job will be permanent if you have used superglue.

ELASTIC BANDS

People who do a lot of trolling can go through plenty of elastic bands: they are used to secure lines to cleats and reels to lower the towing point. They are also very handy for securing loose ends of line on reel spools and handcasters. Some game anglers refuse to use elastic bands on their lines, claiming that they don't always break, but I have not experienced problems in that area, and I only ever fish light tackle. Once again, try it for yourself.

FILES AND HOOK SHARPENERS

Files and sharpeners should be everywhere throughout your fishing gear and boat. You can buy diamond sharpeners with a pocket clip like a pen, and these are very handy. Diamond sharpeners in general are excellent sharpeners for hooks right up to those sizes where a file becomes a more practical tool. Small stones are best for the small, fine, wire hooks.

PLASTIC BAGS AND TWIST TIES

Keep a collection of plastic bags and twist ties on your boat and in your backpack. Life is so much easier when all the day's rubbish goes into the one bag for easy disposal, and life is much nicer for all those who follow you if you get rid of your rubbish in a thoughtful manner. Lazy anglers have a lot to answer for in some areas.

As mentioned earlier, it is also a good idea to toss all the used hooks and lures into a separate bag to be washed in fresh water and dried before they go back into the tackle box.

FISH KEEPERS

A good keeper net takes up very little space in a pack or tackle box, and having one on hand will enable you to keep your fish fresh when you don't have ice on hand. Some people argue that fish kept alive deteriorate in quality, due to distress, but I can't say that I have noticed this.

In wilderness areas and at sea, keeping fish over the side of the boat is not always such a good idea. Sharks and crocodiles in the back country are not always as cautious as those in the more heavily trafficked areas. Fishing a remote creek out of Darwin with some friends once, a giant stingray staked a claim on a live bait keeper left hanging over the side of a dinghy, and then pressed its claim with quite remarkable persistence. We were all glad it was not one of the toothier critters known to inhabit the area.

When you don't have ice and are unable to keep fish in the water, remove the gut and gills from the fish, leave the scales on and hang your fish up in a shady place. This system is only good for a few hours, so don't kill a lot of fish under these circumstances.

GLOVES

Most rigging methods for big fish involve the use of a long, heavy leader of some kind, which means that this long trace can be taken by hand to control a fish for gaffing. At least one full wrap of line is taken over the hand, and if this wrap is allowed to slip, the hand can be cut to the bone very easily. You should always wear heavy gloves when fishing this way.

Heavy gardening and industrial-style gloves are okay for this work, but they are usually stiff and cumbersome. You can overcome this to some extent by leaving the gloves in water when they're not being used. These days you can also buy special tracing gloves that are light, pliable, very strong, and have an external surface that offers excellent grip – they are well worth having in any offshore boat that will be mixing it with big fish.

These sure-grip gloves can also be very handy for dealing with big flathead. If you stick your thumb in the mouth of a small flathead and your first finger under the jaw, you can immobilise the fish as long as you keep the tail in the air. Don't do this with bigger flathead, though, as they have a couple of rather nasty cutting teeth at the front of the mouth, and if they do start to jump around they can really make a mess of your thumb. With bigger fish, use the glove and you will be okay.

Do not use cotton gloves or light gardening gloves, as a good fish taking off with a heavy leader over your hands will cut or burn you badly right through these.

To land a fish like this, every tiny detail in terms of sharp hooks, correct leaders and appropriate main line needs to be right.

Chapter Seven

Skills and techniques

Casting

Learning to cast is fundamental to being able to fish, but most novice anglers get badly hung up on the notion that long-distance casting equals good casting. There are times when being able to wring a few more metres out of a cast makes the difference between catching and not catching fish, but it is more often the case that accurate casting is far more important than long-distance casting. A land-based snapper angler would argue in favour of the former, a bass angler in favour of the latter, but in the wash-up it's pretty much like the game of golf. You won't do much good trying to play a golf course with either a putter or a driver – you need both.

Good casting requires good tackle in a good state of repair. You can make do with a lot of things in fishing, but you can't cast well with inadequate tackle. The weight and diameter of your line will have a great deal to do with the way you cast, as will the design of the rod and the size and placement of runners. The rod, reel and line must be in keeping with the weight you want to cast. As with everything else, when you start to talk fishing tackle, the first thing you need to consider is what you want the tackle to do for you. You then tailor the tackle to that primary need.

Not all fishing tackle is designed to cast well. Sometimes the fighting task required of an outfit will compromise its ability to cast well, and at other times the mix will go the other way. Jig rods tend to lean in favour of fighting characteristics, although they are commonly used to cast lures, while fly rods are a classic example of a rod that is designed as a delivery system, with everything else coming a poor second.

The following sections examine the casting role of various outfits, and how to cast with them.

SINGLE-HANDED THREADLINES

The single-handed threadline is the obvious starting point, as it is the most used, and abused, outfit of them all. The problems usually start when the new reel is taken out of the box, then overfilled or underfilled with line that is far too heavy for it. The thick line has difficulty getting up out of the spool to start with, then produces all sorts of friction going over the lip of the spool, then more friction as its stiffness creates bulging

coils that have to fight to get out through the guides. The only way to overcome this problem is to use more lead to actually drag the line off the rod with brute force, but even this does not work because the big lead then overloads and kills the action of the rod.

Good casting starts when you buy the outfit and work out what class of line it is designed to be used with. Some threadline manufacturers offer advice that is so far off the mark as to be quite bizarre, so you should check whatever they say with the people in the tackle store. Around 90 per cent of these single-handed outfits will average out on 3 kg line, being capable of going down to around 1.8 kg and up to 4 kg.

If you want to be able to cast maximum distances with your outfit, have a look through the brands of 3 kg line on offer in your local store for the one with the smallest diameter. On the label you will see two figures: one gives the breaking strain in kilograms and the other states diameter in millimetres. The finest diameter line will probably be the most expensive line on offer, but if you want distance off a threadline, fine-diameter line will make a noticeable difference to your casting distance.

Having a correct line load on your reel is also vitally important to being able to cast well. If you overload

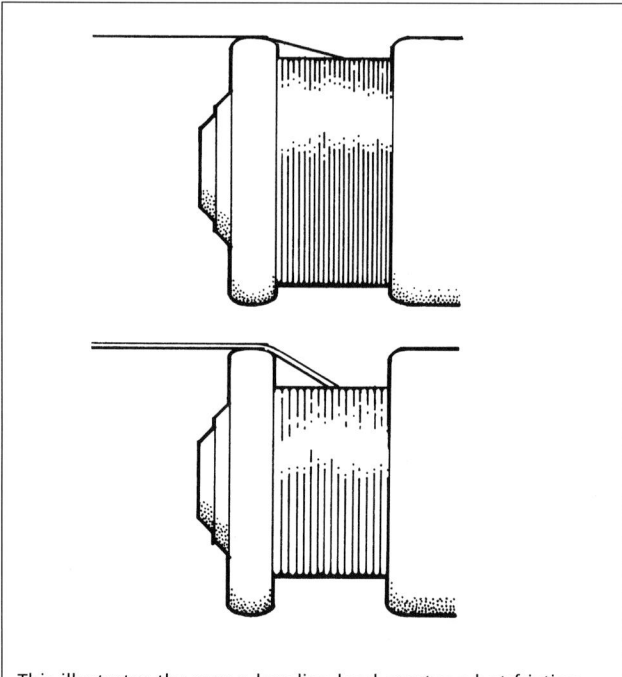

This illustrates the way a low line load creates a hot friction point over the lip of a threadline reel. This can cost real casting distance.

the reel so that the line load is level with or above the spool lip, a whole bunch of coils might well release at once to jam in the first guide in a great tangle. If you underload, and have the line load too deep on the spool, you will have the line going over the lip at a hard angle that creates friction and reduces casting range dramatically. An ideal line load would see the spool filled to within around 2 mm of the lip, with the line wound onto the spool under firm tension, not crushed on under maximum tension.

If, after using a threadline for a while, the line on the spool has become loose, wind the top 50 m or so off onto another reel and then rewind it – this should get you a firmly packed line load. If you lose line and end up in a position where you still have quite a lot of expensive line left on the spool, but the load is getting too far down from the lip, remove a little more then join a fresh length of line and top up. Some anglers anticipate this problem when they first spool up by filling the bottom half of the spool with a cheap backing line, then just topping up the working half with top-quality line. This makes it much cheaper to use top-quality line and to change it as frequently as you should for top-performance fishing.

You will always be rigging to use the smallest lead you can get away with under the prevailing conditions, but it is a useful exercise to take a handful of leads and try casting each one off your outfit, just to see what happens. The smallest lead will hardly deflect the rod tip when you cast, whereas the biggest will have your rod tip bent over and straining even before you attempt the cast. The *optimum* casting weight will just be bouncing the rod tip a little when you hold the rod out and allow the weight to swing free in the air, and it will be capable of loading the rod when you cast.

There is no real way to explain accurately what correct loading means – you just have to learn to feel it. If you take the unrigged rod and make a casting action, the rod will not deflect much at all, and you can feel that. The small lead will deflect the tip a little, and you can also feel that. The weight that is too heavy will have the tip hauled too far back at the end of the cast and the rod will feel overloaded. The optimum weight will pull the tip back into a full-blooded back curve, but just before release the power of the rod will have overcome that inertia and the rod tip will be powering through and moving the casting weight forward itself.

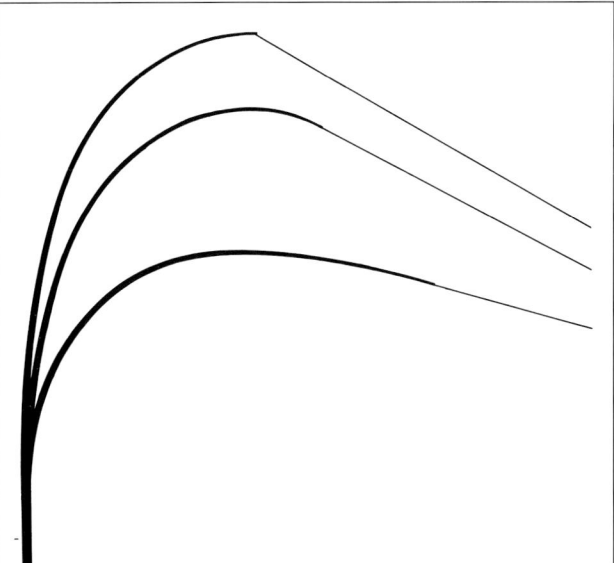

Three loads on the same rod blank. At the **top**, the blank is loaded well below its potential. In the **centre** it is perfectly loaded to the point where the tip is pointing straight at the point of pull. In the third example the rod is overloaded and a big section of the rod has been flattened by the load and is no longer working. This example is relevant to most types of rods, but not to the radical tapers where the top half of the rod is meant to fold over, leaving the whole point of leverage to occur at a hard angle somewhere down the rod length.

The basic threadline casting routine is to have the stem of the reel gripped between the second and third fingers, with the line picked up over the index finger. The bail of the reel is opened with the other hand, then at the end of the casting arc the line is released by straightening the index finger.

It is always easier, at first, for right-handed people to cast with the right hand, then swap hands so they can wind the handle with the right hand and hold the rod in the left. It takes a little while to get used to the idea of winding with the left hand so that the rod can stay in the right, but believe me, as I mentioned earlier, it is worth the effort. The hand-swapping involved when you want to wind with the right hand is only a minor nuisance – rod in right hand to cast, then swap to left to fish. The real drawback comes when you find yourself in combat with a big fish in a fight that requires a little bit of effort from your rod arm. There you are, stuck with the rod in your weaker hand, while your stronger, better-educated hand is relegated to the menial task of turning a handle around in a small circle. That's silly.

So why is it that right-handed people use the left hand on just about every other kind of rod? All other kinds of rods allow the butt of the rod to be supported against the body, and in most cases the power of the shoulders can then be brought into play to support the arm. When you fish a single-handed threadline you get no body support, and very little support from any part of the body beyond the wrist. Your wrist will tell you all about this the first time you find yourself fighting a big fish.

The length of line, the 'drop', between your casting weight and the rod tip makes quite a difference to the way things work out in the cast. If you want to make a lob cast, where the weight describes a big parabolic arc to plop down into the water at the end of the cast, you use a long dropper, which could be 50 cm or more; if you want to make a flat-trajectory power cast you would use as little as 5 cm off the tip – at most, a 10 cm drop.

What's the difference? The long-drop parabolic arc of cast involves slow acceleration, which is ideally suited to casting baits. As you want plenty of speed at the time of release, but not too much acceleration (this pulls hooks out of baits), you use a long dropper, then extend your arm to send the projectile through the longest arc you can describe in the wind-up to the cast.

The alternative style of cast is most often used with lures, where you want all the acceleration you can get to fire that lure away flat and fast. Why flat and fast? Two reasons. Most lures are not as aerodynamically sound as sinkers, and, given a parabolic cast, they are inclined to plane on the air and lose forward momentum. When they are fired hard and flat they penetrate the air better – the idea is to minimise the part of the cast at the end of a lob, where the projectile is in free fall without much forward thrust. The second virtue of the flat cast fired off a short dropper is that the angler has much better control of direction and length with this style of cast. In other words, you can be much more accurate.

When you are casting for accuracy, use a short dropper and minimal arm movement in the cast. You sight your target with the forearm extended away from the body, then whip the rod tip back in a short back-stab, then hard forward. This is a wrist action, and the idea is to be stabbing forward when the lure is still going the other way. This pulls a maximum load into

the rod tip in a minimum arc of travel, which allows you to easily keep the rod oriented towards the target. It is important also that the arc be on a vertical rather than a horizontal plane for this style of cast.

DOUBLE-HANDED THREADLINES

Once you go to a two-handed threadline outfit, most of the rules relating to casting with a double-handed overhead apply as far as body movements are concerned, particularly with beach and rock-sized overhead tackle. The next section covers this technique.

There is some middle ground to be explored with the light two-handed threadline outfits favoured by sportfishers and a good many barramundi anglers. I personally stick with my left hand on the crank, because I feel comfortable with it, but I know a lot of anglers who fish single-handed rods the way I do, then go to the right hand on the crank as soon as they go to a double-handed rod of any kind. The arguments either way are not as compelling once you get the length in the butt that allows you to rest it on your body and get that pressure off the wrist.

OVERHEAD REELS

Overhead reels deliver the longest casting distances because there is very little friction involved in getting the line off the reel and into flight behind the projectile being cast. The inertia that has to be overcome in the stationary spool and line load is the only resistance, and this is overcome right at the point of release.

Understanding this inertia factor is at the heart of coming to terms with casting overheads, and appreciating the relationship between the casting weight and the weight of the line and spool combined is half the battle.

You have a dead weight in the form of the spool and line, and then out at the end of the casting arc you have a projectile travelling at enormous speed. During the arc of the cast, the spool is locked in place by the angler's thumb, but when the thumb is lifted the spool will instantly be required to accelerate to the speed of the projectile, and in that fraction of a second, at the point of release, there is great potential for mischief and disaster.

In an ideal cast, the missile will continue away from the rod tip for some time at the speed of release, and

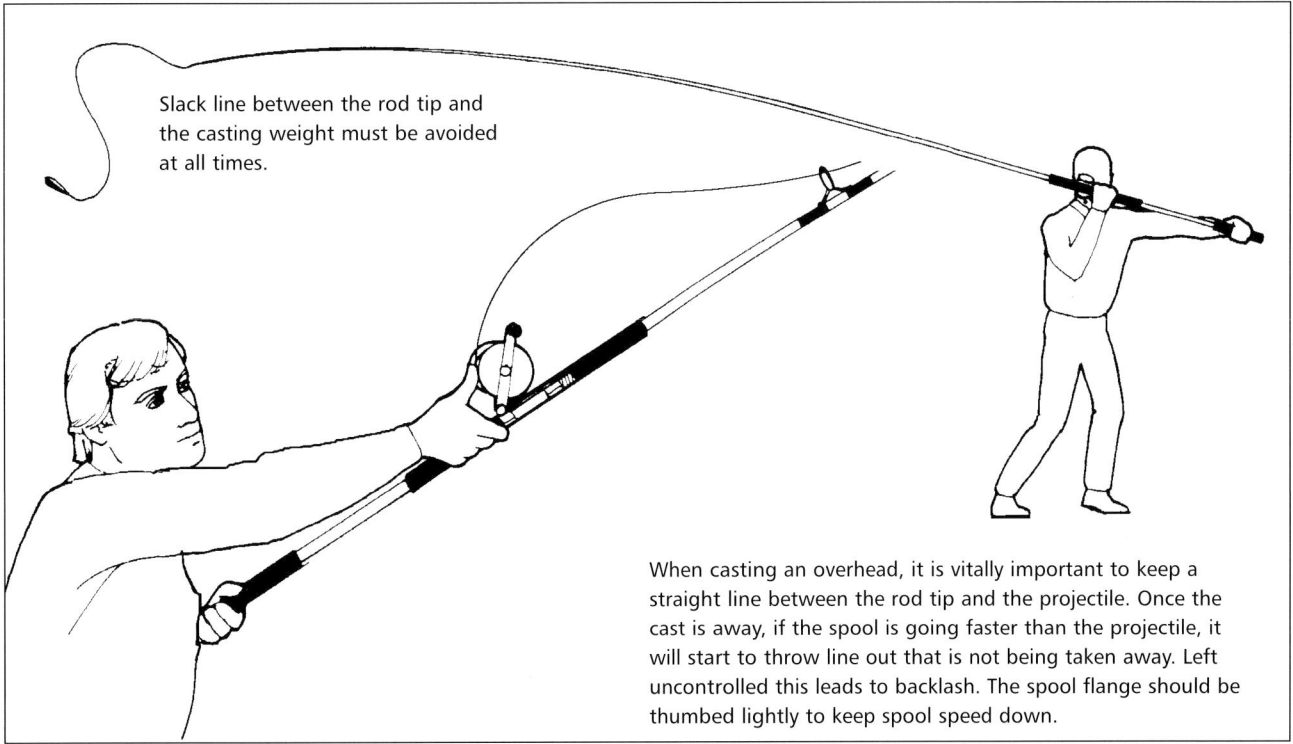

Slack line between the rod tip and the casting weight must be avoided at all times.

When casting an overhead, it is vitally important to keep a straight line between the rod tip and the projectile. Once the cast is away, if the spool is going faster than the projectile, it will start to throw line out that is not being taken away. Left uncontrolled this leads to backlash. The spool flange should be thumbed lightly to keep spool speed down.

the reel spool will accelerate to exactly the same speed and no more. When this happens, the missile is pulling line up through the guides at the same speed the reel is feeding it away, and there is a steady tension between missile and reel spool at all times. As the missile begins to slow down, spool speed should slow down accordingly, so that the missile continues to keep the line tight, and a fraction of a second before touchdown an educated thumb should clamp down on the spool to terminate the cast cleanly.

The easy way to ensure clean casts every time is to add drag to the reel spool with some form of mechanical damper, or by 'feathering' the lip of the reel spool with the thumb. Both systems will reduce maximum casting distance either a lot or a little, depending on how much damping you apply to the spool. The standard approach to damping is through a cap in the side plate of the reel that allows pressure to be brought to bear on the spool spindle. The more sophisticated methods involve internal friction devices and magnetic controls.

Damping avoids some difficulties, but many problems associated with casting overheads can be avoided in the first place by choosing appropriate casting weights. Remember, success depends on that missile continuing to pull line away from the reel at the speed the reel is feeding it out, so you can't afford to have a projectile that fades away rapidly after it leaves the rod tip. For this reason, unlike the threadlines, the overheads have very clearly defined minimum casting weights; these will be heavy enough to punch through the air and some breeze without suffering a rapid loss of speed.

Leaving double-handed baitcasting rods out of it and concentrating on full-sized overhead beach/rock/jig-sized reels, 70 g is a good average weight to use, with 55 g getting down into the expert area, and 110 g looking like the top end for the majority of people. That weight will vary according to the actual combined weight of the spool and line, so a lightweight spool designed for small line capacity could be expected to handle lighter weights than a reinforced spool with a big line capacity.

'Line capacity' and 'line load' are terms that should not be confused. 'Capacity' is the line load when the reel is properly filled to within a couple of millimetres of the lip, and 'load' is whatever amount of line happens to be on the reel. To release any given amount of line a reel will have to turn faster when it is underloaded than when the line load is at maximum diameter, so an underloaded reel will always be harder to cast and control than a fully loaded reel.

You also have to think about the nature of the projectile. If you want to cast a great floppy cut bait out into the surf you should add a bit of weight to the lead to overcome the drag this aerodynamic disaster will create. Also consider the shape of the projectile. Something with flat sides will float on the air and not pull as well as a ball- or pear-shaped object. The snapper lead is said to be the most aerodynamic shape of all, with its weight bias forward – this is obviously the lead to choose when maximum casting range is called for.

You can do two things to take much of the pain out of learning to cast. The first is to choose a weight from the optimum (70 g) to the mid-top end of the range and stick to casting aerodynamically friendly rigs, and the second is to add just the right amount of damping at the reel.

There is trial and error involved in getting magnetic dampers just right, so go for maximum damping and work your way back from there. With the end plate cap system, screw the cap up tight, then put the reel out of gear and very slowly back off the tension on the cap. You will arrive at a point where there is just enough tension on the spool ends to allow the casting weight to sink slowly to the ground – that is exactly right for practice casting. If you are about to make your first casts with an overhead, crank on another quarter-turn.

Learn to cast on a beach, or in a park where you have all the back-swing you want. For your very first lessons go early in the morning, before the wind gets up, as a strong wind can complicate things considerably. If you are casting into water, try an aerodynamically sound metal lure to learn casting with – lures are the easiest things to cast and you might also score a fish while learning.

Use a drop of 50 cm or so from the rod tip, and lay this out on the sand behind you. Take a step forward until you feel the weight dragging on the rod tip, then bring the cast through in a big, round lollipop cast *with absolutely no attempt at distance whatsoever*. The idea of the step forward is to create a drag on the projectile so that you have something to cast against. It is vitally important when casting overheads that there is no slack between the rod tip and the missile, so this step forward with the weight dragging on the sand is quite important. Focus your concentration solely on describing a smooth arc throughout the cast. The arc that normally produces the fewest problems is when you come over your shoulder at an angle of 45° or so. For the time being, avoid going directly over your shoulder – this can increase the possibility of getting some slack between the projectile and the rod tip.

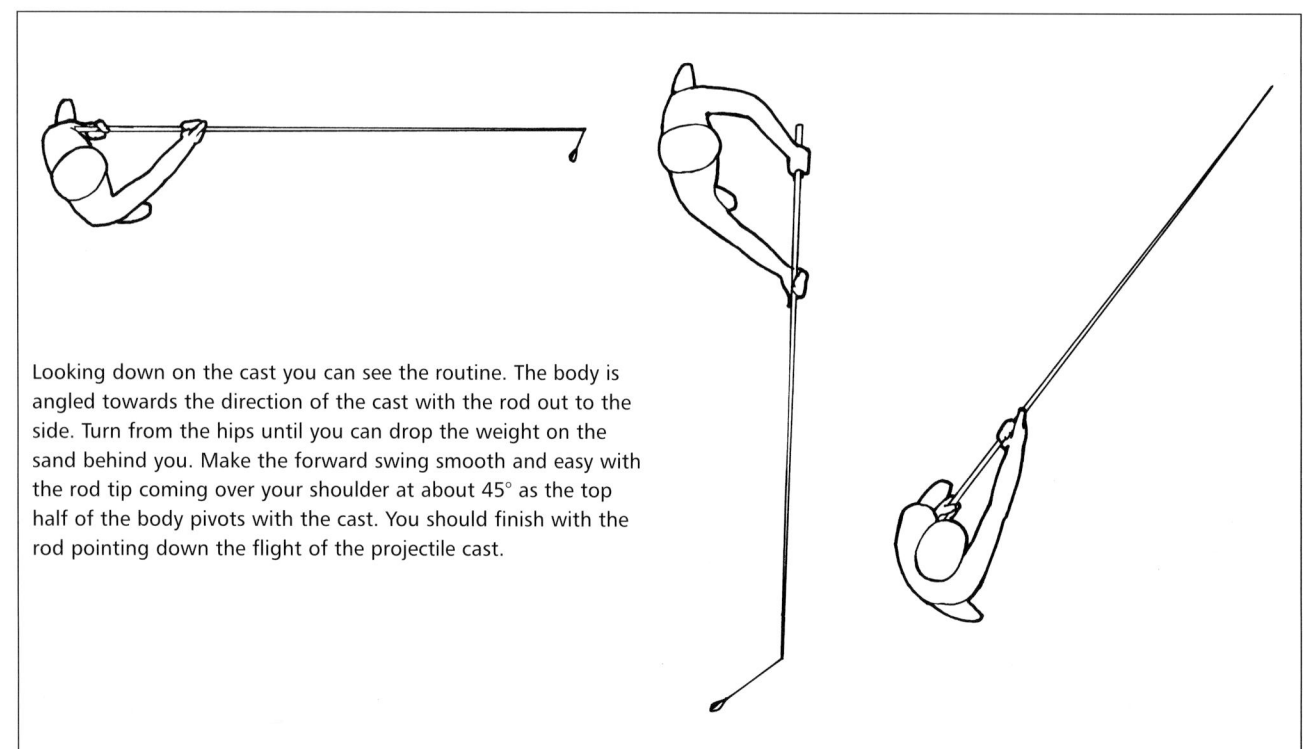

Looking down on the cast you can see the routine. The body is angled towards the direction of the cast with the rod out to the side. Turn from the hips until you can drop the weight on the sand behind you. Make the forward swing smooth and easy with the rod tip coming over your shoulder at about 45° as the top half of the body pivots with the cast. You should finish with the rod pointing down the flight of the projectile cast.

Rest your thumb on the lip of the spool to lock the spool before release, and only ease off the pressure at release – don't remove the thumb altogether. Just before the weight touches down, lock down firmly with the thumb to terminate the cast.

Keep the casts short until you can make continuous short casts without a backlash, then gradually extend your distance. What you are doing at this stage is educating your reflexes in a controlled situation.

You want the thumb and brain to work together without having to think about what is happening, because by the time you think about it, it's all over. As you go for more and more distance, that relationship between thumb and reel spool becomes a critical, delicate thing, and you will find yourself exercising control to a point where the barest contact will mean the difference between your maximum distance and total disaster.

As a fantastic example of control, watch a good long-range caster with a great hump of line sitting up in the air between the reel and the first guide as a cast goes out. The reel will have accelerated marginally beyond projectile speed at the point of release, throwing a belly into the line, and the angler will be just feathering it out rather than clamping down and cutting the cast short. Such skill is available to anyone who is prepared to practise.

Distance casting is achieved by bringing the whole body into the cast. Instead of taking the basic step forward, the caster now stands almost side-on to the cast with the left foot (assuming a right-handed person) pointing in the direction the cast is to travel. The cast starts with the rod pointed out in front of the body roughly at waist level, then the projectile is swung towards the rear, with the top half of the body pivoting to follow this backcast. Before the projectile has completed the full arc of the back-swing, the body swings forward from the waist and the arms start driving forward and over the shoulder, with the bottom hand pulling down on the butt as the top hand drives against the reel. By the time the bottom half of the rod is over the shoulder and powering into the final part of the arc that will end with the lower two-thirds of the rod pointing exactly at the point of release, the back, shoulder and right arm should all be driving in a flowing line into that forehand. The final forward movement is a snap right at the end of the fluid pivot,

and in that snap the lagging tip accelerates through to impart the final burst of speed to the rod tip. The end of a perfect cast is almost like sighting down the barrel of a gun, with the arms and rod extended forward in front of the body, the tip of the rod pointing to the path of the missile, and the whole body in line behind that cast. It is rare to find video of people casting these overheads, but if your video library still carries the old Fisherman's World series, get the 'Spinning For Spaniards' tape out and you will be able to watch some pretty good casting technique on show.

As your skills develop, go out and do some spinning from the rocks or the beach. Casting is a sport and an art in itself, and there is tremendous mental and physical satisfaction to be found in belting out one perfect long cast after another. Go for about 80 to 90 per cent of your best range all the time and you will be amazed how long you can keep it up.

The majority of jobs done by this type of tackle involve making parabolic casts over a distance. However, there will be odd times when you will need to make a flat trajectory or limited arc cast. A flat trajectory cast is easy enough to make: simply keep your elbows in close to your body and limit the casting action largely to the push-pull of the hands on the butt. A very tight arc producing a true parabolic flight path and quite impressive distance can also be described by taking your arms over your head, pointing the rod and weight straight down behind you, then coming down hard on the butt to bring it straight into your stomach at the moment your top hand punches a very hard and tight arc on the foregrip. Both methods involve quite ferocious acceleration rates that in turn demand pretty advanced reflex control of the spool.

One last word of advice for the developing caster: don't go for broke with your first cast of the day, even when you have become good at it. A cold reel with cold lubricant will not cast anywhere near as well as a warm one, so pop out a few easy warm-up throws to start with – unless, of course, you are baitfishing in which case every cast will be a 'cold' one.

BAITCASTER REELS

When you use a baitcaster reel on a two-handed rod, most of the above principles still apply. The only major

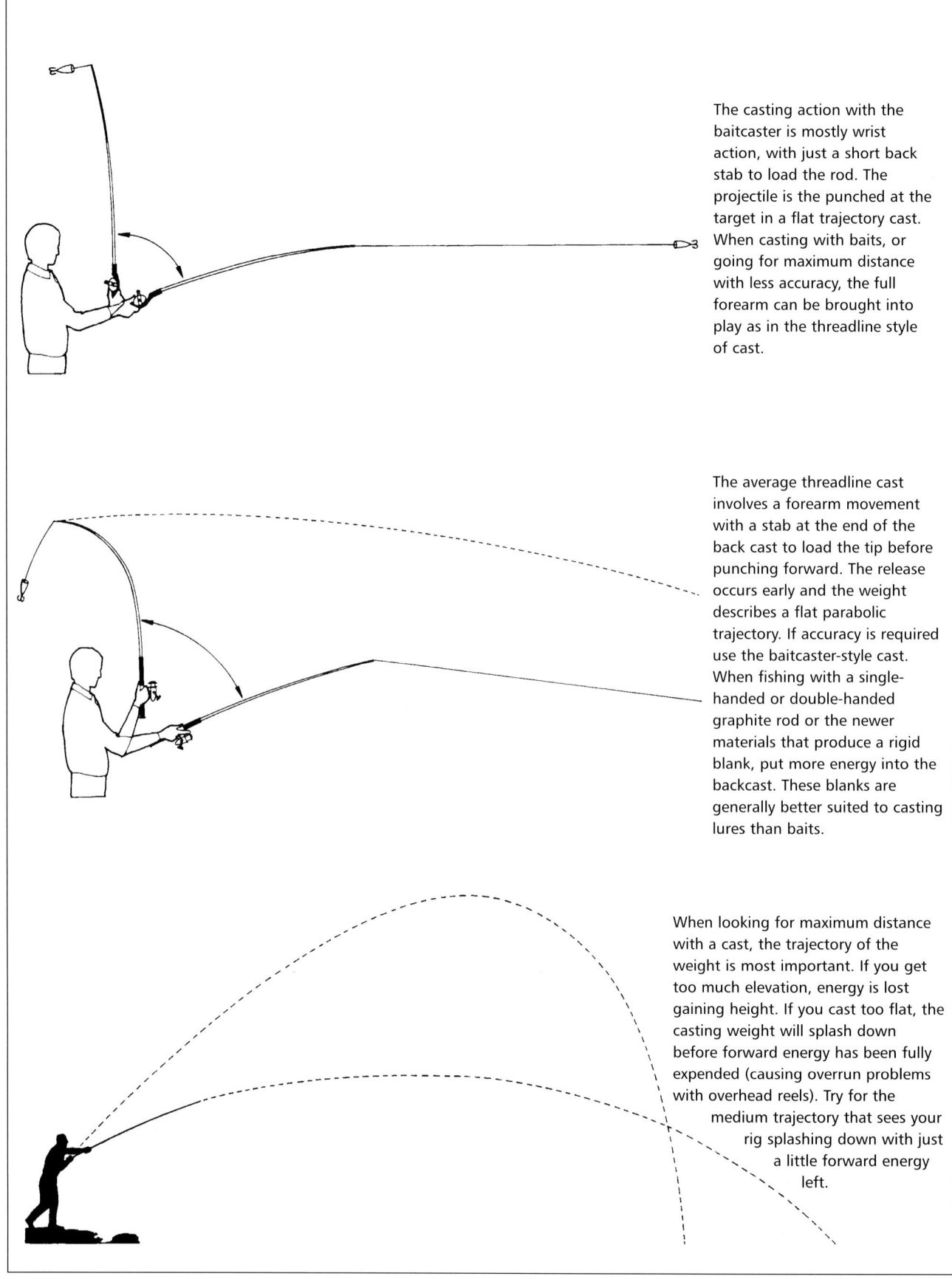

The casting action with the baitcaster is mostly wrist action, with just a short back stab to load the rod. The projectile is the punched at the target in a flat trajectory cast. When casting with baits, or going for maximum distance with less accuracy, the full forearm can be brought into play as in the threadline style of cast.

The average threadline cast involves a forearm movement with a stab at the end of the back cast to load the tip before punching forward. The release occurs early and the weight describes a flat parabolic trajectory. If accuracy is required use the baitcaster-style cast. When fishing with a single-handed or double-handed graphite rod or the newer materials that produce a rigid blank, put more energy into the backcast. These blanks are generally better suited to casting lures than baits.

When looking for maximum distance with a cast, the trajectory of the weight is most important. If you get too much elevation, energy is lost gaining height. If you cast too flat, the casting weight will splash down before forward energy has been fully expended (causing overrun problems with overhead reels). Try for the medium trajectory that sees your rig splashing down with just a little forward energy left.

difference between the two reel types is that the single-handed baitcast rod is primarily an accuracy casting tool.

Nothing else delivers a flat trajectory cast quite like a baitcast outfit, and no other outfit allows for quite the same pinpoint precision in lure placement. The cast is set in flight much the way a flat trajectory cast off a threadline would be, with almost all the power coming out of the wrist alone. The big difference between the two outfits lies in control of the flight path. You can control the height and range of the cast on a threadline by lying a finger alongside the lip of the spool and interfering with the coils of line as they come away, but you can't do this with any kind of finesse. Feathering the rim of the rotating spool on the baitcaster, however, lets you drop a cast where you want it with very great precision. If you want to become good at using a baitcaster, start by placing a bucket on the ground at a reasonable distance, say 10 to 12 m, and practise dropping casts into it. Next, place the bucket on its side and practise firing casts into it. Finally, just when you think you are getting pretty hot at this, put the bucket under something with lots of nasty branches and little twigs waiting to eat your lure, and see what this does for your confidence. This is the best kind of practice, because most of your real-life targets will be difficult places like this.

In addition to providing accuracy, remember that the baitcaster, being an overhead, will not be handicapped by heavy line, which makes it the obvious tool to use when you have to cast well to fish that are close to cover and tough enough to present you with real handling problems.

SIDECAST REELS

The sidecast reel is probably the easiest reel of them all to use, but it does have its little quirks and foibles.

First off, you need a rod designed for a sidecast reel, and this puts the reel down very close to the butt of the rod. This in turn means that you end up with a wide spread of the hands, and that the lower hand is involved in a rather odd grip that reduces some of the reel's power to put snap into a cast.

The sidecast works much the same way as the threadline in the cast, in that the spool is side-on to the rod guides and line comes off that spool in a series of loops. The most popular sidecast reels are the big ones, with diameters of 15 or 16.5 cm, which means that the loops of line coming off that reel are large and cumbersome. There is great potential for friction problems in this situation, which is why the first guide on a sidecast rod is placed almost midway between the tip and the butt. This distance allows the coils to have taken on a more elongated shape before they need to be funnelled down into the guide system.

The sidecast is at its very best with medium to light lines and medium to light casting weights. It can't match an overhead for maximum casting range, but it will throw a light weight further than anything else, and that goes all the way down to unweighted baits. The great majority of 16 cm sidecasts in use in this country would be spooled up with 6 to 7 kg line, although you also get plenty of people using the brute winching power of the sidecast to handle large fish in nasty places with 24 kg line. This is usually fishing at virtually point-blank range, where casting performance is not an issue.

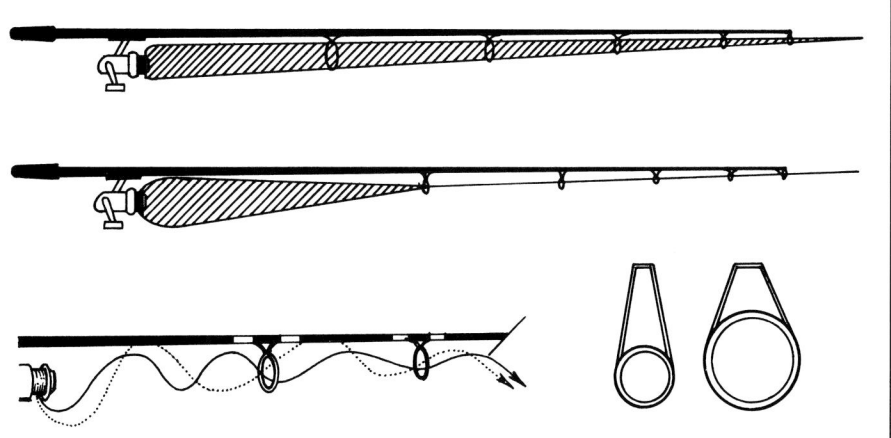

There is a long-standing argument as to how you should fit guides for a threadline or sidecast rod. The Fuji guide manufacturing company offers this example showing the need for guides to funnel the line efficiently. In the case of the lower rod, huge guides are allowing the line to flog the blank. They argue for high-mounted guides to funnel the line quickly.

The manual supplied with most sidecast reels suggests a casting style that has the rod held over the head to start the cast, with the caster then whipping the rod through a full-blooded arc, but the nice thing about the sidecast is that you can actually whip a cast off from just about any position, depending largely on the style of rod you are using.

The line is picked up over the fingers of the left hand as the thumb unlocks the reel, then the fingers turn the reel back to the cast position and the grip is transferred so that the thumb pins the line while the palm and fingers now wrap around the rod butt. It sounds odd, but it's actually an intuitive action and you get used to it quickly, which is one of the reasons sidecasts are so popular in this country. You really can learn to use one in minutes.

The traditional beach and rock rod used with the sidecast reel has for a long time been a parabolic, around 3.8 to 4.25 m long. Faster taper rods and new blank materials have brought many rods ranging from 3 to 3.8 m into use, but the bigger rods are still the ones most often used when long casts are called for.

Because there is no spool inertia to overcome, and because line comes away very easily off the big spools, a tip movement of just a metre or so is enough to pop out quite a decent little cast with a sidecast. This makes them particularly popular with rock anglers, who sometimes work tight against cliff faces with no backcast available at all.

Casting tips

When the angler needs to make maximum distance with the cast, details become very important. For example, if you fish regularly at a land-based snapper spot that calls for a genuine gut-busting cast every time, it might pay you to set up a rod just for this type of work, and a prime consideration would be the guides on the rod. There is an enormous difference in friction properties between the best and the cheapest guides on the market, and if you are sending 100 m of line out through six to eight guides and a tip when you cast, you are talking about a significant friction factor. Friction would be less on an overhead than with a sidecast or threadline reel, but it would still need to be considered.

Line diameter and spool load are critical to long-range casting on sidecasts and threadlines, and the lightest line that will handle the fish you seek is the one to be using. You don't have to worry about the possibility of break-offs with light line when power casting, as it is common to use a shock trace to absorb the power of the cast. The shock trace would be long enough to go from the casting weight all the way through to the reel, where it would allow for two or three turns on the spool. This line can be any weight at all, although if the discrepancy between the trace and the main line is too great it can be difficult to get a good join in the knot – 10 to 15 kg lines are good shock trace material for most situations.

Using a heavy shock trace does not mean that you have to have a heavy trace to the hook. The shock trace only need go directly to the casting weight, and a light trace can then extend off to the hook. (See 'Basic rigs' on pages 98–104 for examples.)

Line weight is not as important when using an overhead, although you do need to consider that wind friction will be increased on larger-diameter lines, and also that any given cast with a large-diameter line will reduce spool diameter marginally more than a cast with a light line.

When casting for accuracy with a baitcaster or threadline, think the way you do when you toss a rock at something – you concentrate on throwing *at* the object, and not just *towards* the object. This is the only difference between people who hit targets and people who consistently miss them. I find I get better accuracy if I push my wrist forward with my forearm as I make my cast. It's just a slight movement, but for me it adds considerable accuracy to a cast.

When you practise, keep in mind that most of your single-handed rod fishing will be done in confined spaces, such as in a canoe or a punt with other people close by who will not thank you for sinking treble hooks into the backs of their ears. Nor will they show much interest in lying down every time you want to make a cast. This is why you should get into the habit of practising backhand, vertical and underarm casts. Even place yourself hard up against something that will not allow you to cast comfortably, and practise that way.

When you need to cast a heavy weight off any outfit, use the longest possible arc for your cast and employ gradual acceleration. Threadlines and sidecasts

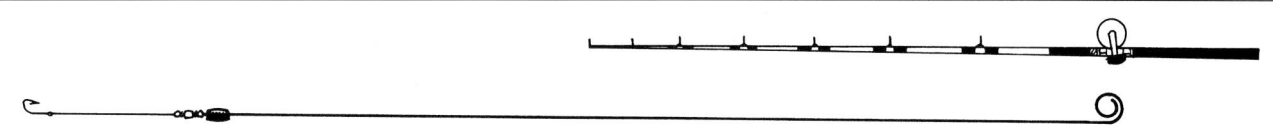

This illustration shows a shock trace placed beside a rod to demonstrate how you need enough for the required casting dropper when you have one and a half to two turns of the trace on the reel at the other end. The shock trace terminates at the swivel and a light trace has then been used down to the hook.

are not the best outfits for casting heavy weights, although sidecasts are better than threadlines. That line over the finger can really hurt when you are releasing a heavy weight at the end of the cast.

When casting light weights, the flat and hard approach to casting is the way to go, using a lot of tip in the cast. The short back-swing and hard forward stab is the best method with a medium dropper from the rod tip.

When casting unweighted baits, slow acceleration is the key to stopping your hooks tearing out of the bait. This means using the biggest casting arc you can get when space is available; when it is not, get your bait moving easily, then whip the last part of the cast. Rods with light tips are always the easiest for casting unweighted baits.

Good casting is primarily an exercise in mind and body control. Your mind controls your reflexes, and it also controls your level of physical relaxation. Casting is not a brute force thing, although it is often a power exercise. The power comes out of flowing movement and timing. Make a mental picture of the Tai Chi expert and think of the way their body flows. That is what casting is all about – fluid, controlled movement. The more relaxed you are, the more powerful you become, and the further you will be able to cast.

Trolling

Some people look upon trolling as a hit-and-miss fishing method, which is far from the truth. In some situations trolling would be the worst approach to the fish, but in other situations it is the *only* way to catch fish. Perhaps the key question to ask yourself is, 'How critical is the noise of the engine going to be?'

It is not easy to evaluate the noise and disturbance factors associated with a boat and engine. If you take a

boat anywhere near a school of mackerel tuna, nine times out of ten they will sound and be gone long before you get a lure anywhere near them. On the other hand, striped tuna will take lures just a couple of metres beyond the propellers, as will wahoo and the odd marlin. I have an image indelibly printed in my mind of a wahoo passing up six lures trolled well back from the boat, then taking a mighty leap into the prop wash to monster a lure trolled right up close to the transom!

When you can see fish at the surface and it is possible to catch them by casting to them instead of trolling them, this is always the way to go. Trolling is for catching fish you can't see, and for times when you don't really know just where fish are likely to be in a big body of water.

Good trolling practice starts by having the rods properly organised at the back and side of the boat. Big boats with a wide beam have rod holders right across the back of the boat and a couple more placed in the cockpit side-decks, but the great majority of Australian boats are built with a rod holder either side of the boat in the aft side-deck, then holders forward of that angled slightly outboard, still in the side-deck. This set-up is basic to the point of being seriously inadequate, but that's the way most boats are sold, and that's the way most boats stay.

The minimum set-up for anything larger than a creek boat is the four side-deck rods plus one or two holders on the transom. The propeller is a real attraction to some fish and it is vital to have rods located so that lures can be placed in tight on the prop wash.

The best small-boat set-up for offshore work, in my opinion, uses the stern-quarter rod holders as a mounting point for a rocket launcher. This launcher is on legs that simply drop into the aft rod holders, and has a series of rod holders welded onto its base,

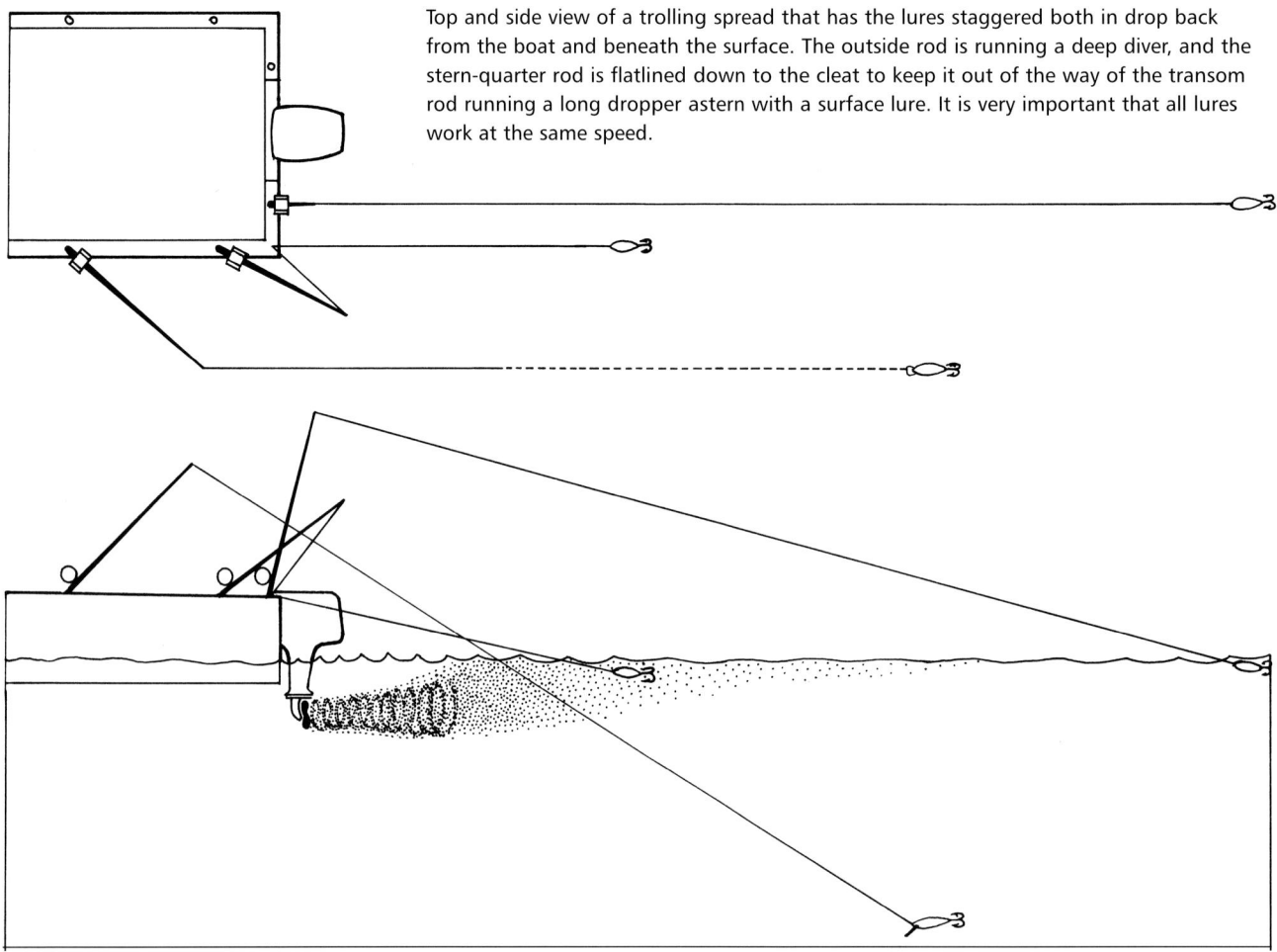

Top and side view of a trolling spread that has the lures staggered both in drop back from the boat and beneath the surface. The outside rod is running a deep diver, and the stern-quarter rod is flatlined down to the cleat to keep it out of the way of the transom rod running a long dropper astern with a surface lure. It is very important that all lures work at the same speed.

fanning the rods out from the centre of the cockpit. This allows up to five rods to be used on the back of the boat, and you can still use the forward side-deck holders to come up to seven rods in all, or you can run high lines off a Targa. That's not a bad spread, and you can use it on boats as small as 5 m.

In a set-up like this, the centre holder puts a rod right over the top of the outboard in the prop wake. The next two holders are angled out to put lures either side of that centre wash. The stern-quarter holders are then spread wide to run lures outside the hull wake. These outside lines are dropped well back, and then you can either use the side-deck holders to handle lures in line with the aft-quarter lines, but held back in closer to the boat, or perhaps with deep-running lures that will sit back under the close-set lures. Anglers often use rods high set in Targa rod holders for shotgun sets, with lures way out behind the boat.

It is the usual practice to try to stagger the drop backs of lines off the back of the boat to avoid tangles when a turn is made; this also helps avoid hassles when you put a rogue lure out that wants to wander from side to side.

Another good organisational ploy is to vary the vertical levels at which the lines are streaming astern. When rods are placed close together in a small boat you can run one line off the rod tip and pull the next one from the tip down to the reel and fix it in place with a rubber band. I even take lines down to the ski eyes, low on the back of my transom, to get a tow point close to the water line. This is called 'flatlining', and many people do it just to get a low tow point for lures that spend too much time popping out of the water.

Outriggers are very handy, especially when trolling baits and lures that are best presented at the surface, but they can be a real pain on a small boat. They are always in the way when they are folded down the side of the cockpit, which means that you have to put them up whether you need them or not.

The more lures you can put out the better, but the lures need to be compatible. For example, if you put out a spread of trolling heads that like to be dragged around at 10 knots, there's not much point in also dropping out a little minnow and slowing the boat down to suit the minnow. A host of high-speed, deep-running solid-bodied lures are now available that allow multi-level spreads to be presented from dead slow to quite high cruising speeds.

Some anglers have raised lure placement behind a boat to a high art, and they get results commensurate with their skills. You need to be extremely observant and prepared to constantly adjust positions to get the best out of your lures. Different boats produce different wake wave shapes, and there are times when a following sea will make wake waves unimportant, but the idea is to have surface lures working in the face of the wave, not on the back of it. Quite apart from the fact that the lure works better on the face than it does on the back, a lure on the face of a wave is a perfect target suspended against background light. Think about it.

Don't get caught in the trap of wanting to get your lures out a long way from the boat. By all means have something back there, and there will be days when that will be the strike zone for some reason or other, but most days you will have fish swimming right by those wide offerings to take something they fancy up closer to the boat. Never overlook the possibility that fish come up from the depths to look at the boat and the wash, and only then see the lures. Put the lures too far away from the boat and these fish could miss them altogether.

While you need to choose your boat speed to suit the lures that are in use, you also need to consider what sort of presentations you should make for the conditions of the day. For example, in very big seas you would need high-speed patterns, simply because it becomes virtually impossible to slow the boat down when it is being pushed along by fast-moving swells. On a bright, calm day it might pay you to choose mostly deep-running lures, and if it's wild and windy, and the surface is in turmoil, shallow and surface runners might be the order of the day. Good average conditions would allow you to mix the spread to cover as many options as possible. Until a pattern reveals itself, mix the colours and lure sizes as much as you can.

There is, of course, a lot more to trolling than dragging a bunch of lures around at the right speed. Much of the art lies in keeping the lures where they are likely to do the most good, and skilful skippers produce far more fish than the hit-and-miss merchants.

On the open sea, lures presented along the edge of a current line are well located, as are lures trolled above an underwater structure, even when that structure is many, many fathoms below where the lures are being presented.

When fish are sighted on the surface, the art of trolling them is to try to keep the boat as far away from the schooling fish as you possibly can. This usually involves having the lures well back from the boat, then passing the school with the boat off to one side, and cutting sharply across behind the school to angle the lures in to the fish. You don't need to have the lures pass through the school, so a nice presentation right along the side of the school is ideally what you should be aiming for.

A really smart skipper will anticipate the path of travel of the school if they are on the move, and work the boat well away from the school, with the lures aimed to intercept the path of the fish.

Working a stream, the bank-side rods should always be hand held so that the tips can be pushed in under bank-side cover, allowing lures to go where the boat can't. I have been fascinated to observe how often fish come out of a shallow weed bank right behind a boat to strike a lure trolled close by. This leads me to believe that steady, consistent sound arouses curiosity in many fish, and that you can troll into some very skinny water effectively as long as you don't stomp on the bottom of the boat. A 4-stroke or electric trolling motor is a definite advantage here.

This corner-cutting technique can also be used to great effect to work dangerous white water off rocks and reef. The boat can be kept well away from the shallows while the lures are dragged right along the rock face.

Downriggers are another tool to consider, especially in big bodies of fresh water, where fish often work temperature layers, suspending themselves beneath the reach of the deepest diving lure but well above anything presented on the bottom. The

Trolling a school of fish, the dotted line represents the path of the boat and the solid line shows the path the lures will travel. It is terribly important to keep your boat as far away from the fish as possible.

downrigger system involves a heavy weight attached to a wire line, worked off either a manual or power deck winch. The winch is a complex thing which normally includes a depth meter of some description, allowing the angler to determine where to set the weight. The rod is placed in a holder associated with the deck winch, and the line is clipped to the downrigger weight by a simple release mechanism, with sufficient trace to the lure to allow it to swim freely, well clear of the weight.

The beauty of this system is that the lure can be located with great precision, and because the lure is not required to do any diving of its own, you can present a shallow runner or a fly at 30 m, if that seems to be the right thing to do.

The weights of the downriggers usually make a great target for an echo sounder, so the angler is normally in a position to see precisely where the lure is being presented and to make sure that this is in the zone the fish are working.

Hooking fish

The difference between getting plenty of bites and getting plenty of fish lies in your ability to hook fish, and this has little to do with the way you hold your tongue in your cheek, or with any secret tricks with the rod tip when you get a bite. Most of the tricks that make all the difference between hooking and missing fish have to do with the hook you use, the condition it is in, and the way you put a bait on it.

It cannot be said too many times that hooks rarely come out of the box sharp enough to be a useful device for catching fish. Most hooks need to be sharpened, and sharpened properly. A few rubs with a stone is not good enough. You have to actually sharpen the hook until it is a positive menace to everything it comes into contact with. That goes for hooks on lures as well as hooks to be used with bait.

You can now buy chemically sharpened hooks that are dangerously sharp, but they do not stay that way forever and a day. You need to check them now and then to ensure that they are still sharp.

Having properly sharpened the hook, the next thing to do is to put the bait on in such a way that the point of the hook either remains exposed or is under such soft meat that it will come through at the slightest pressure. This means giving some thought to the shape and nature of the bait as well as to the way you put it on the hook. It also means thinking beyond the way the bait looks when it is in your hands: you have to ask yourself what is going to happen to it when you cast it, and how it will stand up to a few nibbles by pickers.

When you have the hook and bait combination right, give some thought to how the fish is going to attack the bait. The great majority of small baits are sucked in with a mouthful of water. The water is then expelled, and the fish is swimming away as it begins to swallow. If the hook and bait combination is right, 99 fish out of 100 will hook themselves, providing you leave them alone – it's inevitable. If the take is not clean, and you are getting rattles and bumps on the bait without a clean hookup, you may be dealing with fish too small to take the bait in, or you may be dealing with fish that can see what you're up to because your line is too heavy, your sinker is too heavy, or your bait and hook presentation is just too clumsy. Before you give the spot away, try a fine trace, a smaller sinker, and a neater bait on a smaller hook, and see what happens. You might just prove the point about tiddlers, but there's an outside chance that you might start hooking decent fish.

It is absolutely essential with the majority of fish to give them slack line with which to take the bait. Think it through again and imagine what is going to happen to that nervous type who wants to keep a tight line to the bait, fearful of missing a nibble. A big fish sucks it in on the run, which is the way they usually take it, then before it gets anywhere, and while it still has its mouth full of water, it comes up against the pressure of that line. Whoosh! Out goes the water, bait and all. It's as quick and easy as that for the fish. You must give a fish slack line with which to run until that water is expelled. If you watch experienced people at work you will see them giving a fish plenty of room to move before striking.

There are odd fish that need to be struck at, and whiting fit into this category. They tend to want to eat a bait on the spot much of the time, and you actually have to strike to hook them. Much the same thing can be said of float fishing, and fishing in the surf, where there is often a lot of belly, or slack, in the line between the fish and the rod tip. The strike removes the belly and sets the hook.

Some of the surface fish, such as tailor, attack a bait with their jaws opening and closing so fast that a strike always gives you a fifty-fifty chance of hitting when the mouth is wide open, which will of course pull the bait and hooks straight out. The best approach is to continue a steady retrieve, which will put sufficient pressure on the first hook point to find a grip, which will in turn ensure a solid hookup.

A case can be made for a solid strike when heavy hooks are being used, and even a sharp point may need some help to penetrate beyond the barb. Which raises an interesting point. In recent years, many people heavily into catch-and-release fishing have been filing the barbs right off their hooks. It was originally thought that the barb was the only thing that kept a fish on a hook point, but experience shows that this is not the case. The barbless hooks hold fish just as well much of the time, and many think that because such hooks can penetrate more easily, they score more hookups in the first place.

I trust you never have the opportunity to try this for yourself, but after having a hook driven into their own flesh, most anglers think it is going to slip out easily if the barb has been cut off. What a surprise they get when they find that this is not the case, and that in fact the flesh manages to hang onto that hook as if it were superglued in place. I demonstrated the affinity of flesh for metal in a big way once when I had a large gaff go all the way through my hand. It actually took one man holding the hand down and another pulling on the hook to eventually dislodge it. So give some thought to trying a little barbless fishing: it may give you a better hookup rate on the fish and a slightly less painful personal experience if your own hookup is one of those where the barb would have stayed under the skin.

When you get up to really big hooks in trolling and live bait rigs for very large fish, you need to consider the ability of the line class to set the hook. These fish hit trolled lures and baits with tremendous impact, and if that impact does not meet with fairly stiff resistance, the hooks will not be set. Putting your biggest lure on a light outfit is not the way to go.

I have always fished all my big baits, including live baits, with the reel in free spool and the ratchet on, but I now make an exception to this rule when fishing live baits off the rocks under floats. I found that I missed a good many hookups until I went over to fishing the reel on a strike drag, and then I rarely missed a fish. I put this down to the way fish hit the bait when they are in close to the shore like that – I feel they may be particularly uptight and cautious in this situation. I am referring here to small baits carrying a relatively large hook: I would still use a free-spool approach with a large live bait.

Fighting fish

It is only in fairly recent times that we have started to talk about 'fighting' fish rather than 'playing' fish. While neither word seems to me to be totally accurate or appropriate, 'playing' certainly is the better of the two to describe what goes on between the hooking and the landing of a fish. It would be more correct to say what 'should' go on between the hooking and the landing, for not many anglers really understand what playing a fish is all about.

Tackle stores do a lovely little business in reel repairs, especially on threadline reels – these are made necessary by the way the majority of anglers abuse and misuse this tackle. They buy a small reel, put line on it that is far heavier than the manufacturer ever intended the reel to be used with, and then screw down on the drag setting until the spool is completely locked up. This means that they can now apply pressure to the little machine far beyond anything it was designed to cope with, and it is only a matter of time until it breaks.

Some years ago, *Choice* magazine decided it would test some threadline reels. Because the packaging said that this reel would take so many metres of this breaking strain and so many of that breaking strain, to test the reel they filled it with the heaviest line – say it was 10 kg – clamped the leg of the reel in a vice, locked the drag and then applied 10 kg of pressure direct to the reel. The folk at *Choice* had never heard that these reels are fitted with a slipping clutch so that there is never more than a third of the breaking strain applied directly to the reel, so they concluded that this was a dud product when they managed to snap the leg off the reel. A lot of anglers, like the people at *Choice*, do the same thing.

Very few people understand what the breaking strains of lines really mean in terms of power. You don't need 10 kg line to land a 10 kg fish unless you actually plan to lift that fish out of the water and take all its weight directly on the line, in which case you will probably need 10 to 20 kg line to do the job. Load up some 3 to 6 kg line on your rod, tie it off on a fence, and then go ahead and try to break it. You will be amazed at just how difficult it is to break even light line over a fishing rod.

Think about this. If you take a piece of light line, or cotton, and take a few turns of line around each hand and then slowly move your hands apart in an effort to break that thread, there's a good chance it will hold together long enough to do some damage to your fingers. But if you snap your hands apart, the thread will break without effort. That's one lesson about fishing lines: everything has to happen smoothly to avoid the sort of showdown that has a way of finding flaws in anything.

The second lesson about fishing lines is that since people first started using them, they have gone out of their way to come up with methods of avoiding brute force confrontations with their quarry. Since the old handline-only days, the best method ever devised has been to use a slipping clutch system of one kind or another, allowing the pressure to be reduced at one end of the line whenever the pressure at the other end comes anywhere near the breaking strain of the line. A good handliner with sensitive hands does this by holding the line over their index finger, checked by the pressure of their thumb. When the fish applies too much pressure, the angler just eases up on the thumb a fraction and lets line skid over their flesh under slight pressure – a primitive but highly effective drag system. These days that slipping clutch is built into the reel, and can be preset with great precision on a good-quality reel.

I will come back to that in a moment, but let's now consider some of the elements you should allow for immediately after you get your bite, and then get the hookup that takes you into combat mode.

All you know at this stage is that you have a fish on the line. You don't know what kind of fish it is, how big it is, and most important of all, you don't know where, or how well, it is hooked. You also don't know much about its fitness or personality. Like humans, fish vary in fitness, strength and willpower. If you are going to use all the power of your equipment and muscle against this fish from the start, you can immediately write off anything that is lightly hooked, because you will tear the hook out. Even fish that are quite well hooked are sometimes lost this way: too much muscle flexing at the human end of the conflict enlarges the hole in the fish's jaw, leading to the hook simply dropping out when the fish is right at the point of being landed. You also need to be mindful of the strength of the hook itself – hook considerations are another reason for taking it easy right from the beginning.

Pedal-to-the-metal, head-on confrontation is the only way to go with fish that will use cover or structure to break the line if you let them near it. Otherwise, a more tactical approach might be prudent.

The third reason for taking things gently is that you don't know how much power you are going to come up against. It makes no sense at all to get into a head-on confrontation until you know what you're dealing with. As long as a fish is still on the end of your line, it is not going anywhere. There is absolutely no reason to stop it running about out there unless you are dealing with one of the species that works from cover and will try to make its way back there at the first opportunity, but that's another subject (which I'll get to in a minute). For all the clean-fighting species, and that is the great majority of fish, the sensible thing for the angler to do is to protect their tackle and allow the fish to use up its strength running against a *controlled drag*. When the fish tires, you then begin to quietly work it into range of a gaff, net or whatever you are using to actually get it out of the water.

It seems to me that many anglers become filled with blind panic the moment a fish begins to struggle on the end of the line. Convinced that it is getting away, they do everything they can to help it by trying to stop it dead in its tracks and skull-drag it straight out of the water.

Playing a fish properly starts when you set up your tackle to go fishing. When setting up gamefishing tackle, where there is always a good chance that the tackle could be pushed to the limit, drags are normally carefully set against scales so that the drag will begin to slip line when pressure equal to one-third the breaking strain of the line is applied at the reel. Note carefully that I said 'at the reel', which means that you are pulling directly against the spool of the reel, not over the rod. A lot more stress than that needs to be applied on the rod tip to produce that pressure on the spool of the reel. You can set up any reel this way, but for most fishing reels you can use more 'rule of thumb' approaches, such as rigging up the outfit, tying off your line on something solid, then loading the rod and adjusting the drag until line slips just beyond the point where the rod is fully loaded. As you get a feel for drag systems, you will eventually get to the stage where you can set a drag quite accurately simply by pulling line off the reel by hand until you have the drag just where you want it.

It is necessary for drags to be set with great accuracy on gamefishing tackle, because that drag may be called upon to operate at maximum efficiency for prolonged periods of time under great stress. It is nowhere near as important to have a maximum drag setting on reels that are to be used in more normal fishing situations, and the rule of thumb is to underset rather than risk oversetting a drag. A drag can always

be instantly beefed up by simply placing a finger or the palm of the hand on the rim of a flying spool, but if you have too much drag on in the first place, you may lose the fish before you can do anything about it.

The position of the rod also has a great deal to do with the amount of drag on the line. When a fish bolts on you, and builds up too much pressure on the line, you can take the heat straight out of the situation by pointing the rod at it. This takes all additional friction off the line and brings you down to a situation where no more than one-third the breaking strain of the line can be applied before the drag slips and begins to feed line back to the fish. Once it stops its big run, raising the rod increases the pressure from your end as friction over the guides backs up the drag on the reel. If you are underset on your drag, you can up the pressure even more by locking the reel spool (very cautiously), with a finger or thumb.

The load on the angler's rod means that friction over the rod and guides will be added to the drag setting to put a lot of pressure on the fish.

In an extreme situation, where half or more of the line load goes out with a real long-range runner of a fish, you might have to think about backing off on the drag, or simply pointing the rod at the fish to minimise drag. What happens is that the drag you set when your reel is full of line will increase quite dramatically as that line load reduces. This happens because the line is now trying to turn the reel from a point close to the axis of the spool, which greatly increases the amount of leverage required to turn the spool, and the spool is also required to turn more revolutions in order to surrender a given length of line. There is also a good deal of water friction along the length of line between rod and fish, and this can be a big danger when fishing with light line. This sort of extreme situation is most likely to confront someone game fishing, particularly someone land based.

There are, of course, plenty of times – when dealing with pan-sized fish – when a drag system never comes into the fight. The flex and bounce in the rod itself is sufficient to absorb the struggles of the fish, and the rod does all the fighting for you. The reel is rarely used to bring a fish in. This is always done by 'pumping' the fish with the rod, with the reel simply storing the line recovered by the rod. The rod is used to drag the fish through the water towards you on the up stroke, then on the down stroke the reel recovers the line won. It is vitally important that the down stroke be smooth and easy, with the reel winding against constant pressure all the time. You have to avoid getting slack line between the rod tip and the fish, and the easiest way to do this is to ensure that the rod always remains bent. Most of the upper part of the rod will bend as you lift against the weight of the fish, but be careful to keep a bend in the tip on the way down. The changeover from the up to the down stroke is the real danger spot here.

It is generally good practice to work a short rather than a long arc when you are pumping a fish, especially with a long rod. When anglers take a great long up stroke, the tip of the rod tends to end up back over the shoulder where the angler has no control at all over the situation, and it is then almost impossible to avoid dropping just a bit of slack into the line. Better to keep the pumps short and frequent.

You may get away with long strokes when dragging in a small, completely exhausted fish, but you will get into trouble with a strong, lively fish, because it has a good opportunity to get its head around the other way while you are picking up line on that equally long down stroke.

When you are playing a strong fish, think in terms of controlling the head and you will be on the right track. After the initial strike and run there is a deadlock period when the fish will be turned away from you, or side-on to you, and you just have to keep the pressure on and wait for it to turn. When it does, you want to keep it coming, and you can only do that if you keep control of the head. If you slack off it will be turned around and off again before you know it, but if you keep a steady pressure on, it will usually find it easier to go with the flow, so to speak.

There are times when you are faced with fish that you simply can't play out, such as bass, kingfish, groper, rock blackfish and other species given to burying their heads in snag or rock piles. When dealing with these species, the seconds immediately following the hookup are usually critical – they decide the outcome of the encounter. With the exception of the kingfish and giant trevally, most of the problem fish let everything go in one great explosive burst of energy on the hookup, and if you manage to survive that you usually come out on top.

You obviously need to gear up for fish like this, and there's not a lot to be gained by going in after them with light tackle. You really do need to be able to stand on the brakes and bully them into submission, but having said that, the master angler will still be giving and taking in subtle ways. For instance, when a fish makes a bolt towards cover and seems to stand a fair chance of getting there against your maximum set drag, you are obviously going to have to override that drag, even lock up completely, and get into that head-on confrontation we try so hard to avoid. When there is no alternative to the lockup, there is still room for some subtlety that might save the day.

If you remember how line snaps more easily with a quick jerk than with steady pressure, you will appreciate why I suggest sliding into that spool lock, rather than simply clamping down suddenly. Also, just when you do this, extend your rod out to one side and get as much radical side pressure on that fish as you can. Fish will sometimes instinctively go with a release of pressure, and you at least give yourself a chance of bluffing it into turning side-on at the last moment. This will dissipate the head of steam it has built up and bring it back to a standing start, which will be a lot easier to deal with than a full-blown stampede for the sticks.

With the smaller fish, and especially when you are fishing with lures, the main thing is to try to keep the fish coming out on the strike. The fish has to be swimming out from cover to some degree to take the lure, so you have it pointing the right way at the time of the strike, although we are talking hundredths of a second here, between hitting the lure and going in the opposite direction. It is critical that you have the rod tip down and pointing at the lure on strike – this allows you to bring pressure to bear in an instant by simply lifting the rod tip. Reflex actions are everything here, and anglers given to daydreaming tend not to be very effective in these situations. It will be all over before the strike is registered.

When fighting very strong fish, such as kingfish, cobia and trevally – or any large game fish, for that matter – their great endurance forces many anglers into error: the anglers start to hurt quite badly themselves, and then make the mistake of trying to force the issue prematurely. These fish are wearing themselves out almost as much when they are just on their side lugging against the line as when they are bolting off at speed. You can afford to take a breather and simply let the fish work against the pressure for a while as you catch your own breath, given that you have pumped him up out of the real danger zone, which is down deep.

When you are fighting the real toughies, keep the pumps as short as possible, all the way down to keeping a deep bend in the rod, and simply work within that bend to take up one crank on the reel at a stroke in a series of short, powerful pumps. This is called short stroking, and it has the advantage of allowing maximum pressure to be maintained on the head of the fish *all the time* – the line is wound back onto the reel under full drag pressure, with no slack at all.

The art of playing fish is to keep telling yourself that time is on your side. Everything you do to force the pace of the fight shifts the odds in favour of the fish. If you remain calm and keep all your actions fluid and smooth, only bad luck, or oversights and ill-considered actions in the past, can rob you of your prize.

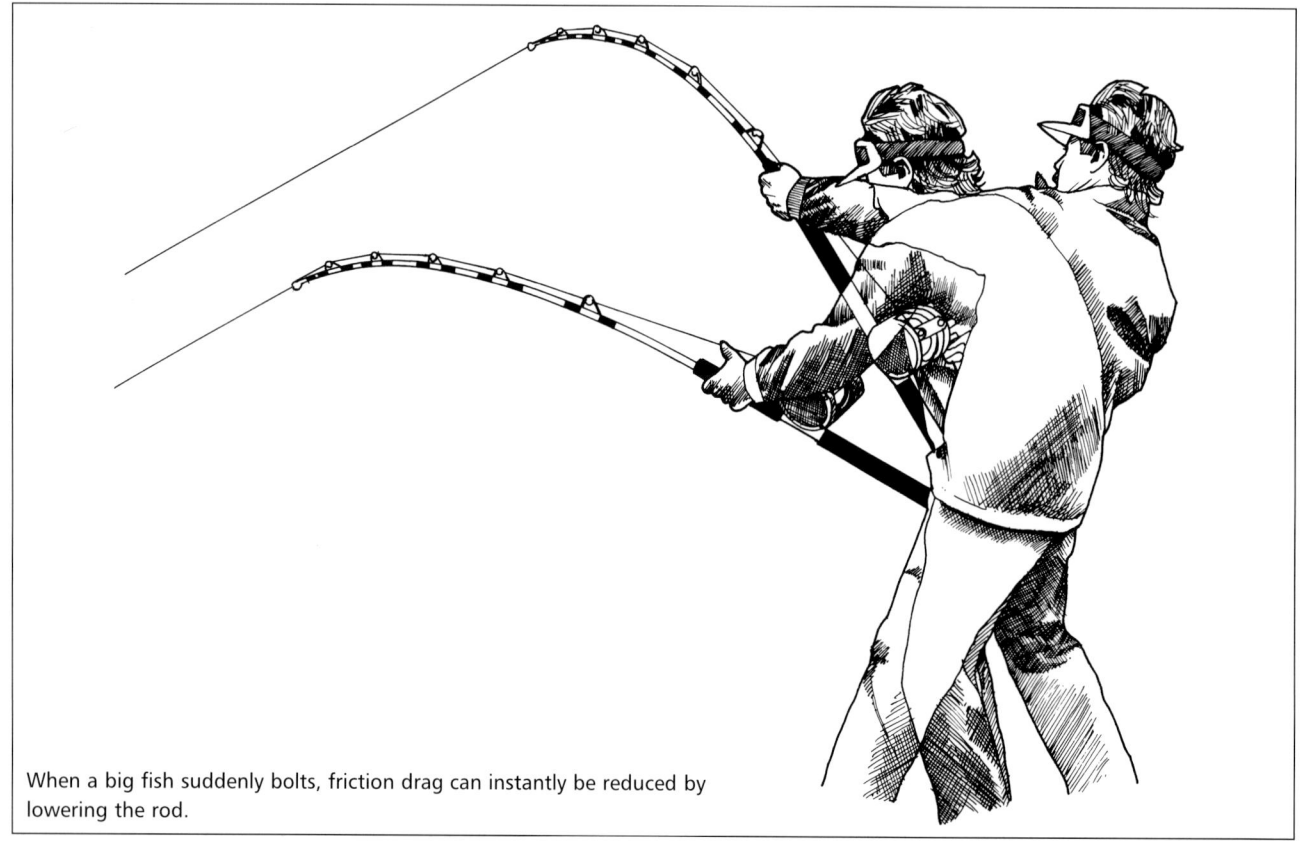

When a big fish suddenly bolts, friction drag can instantly be reduced by lowering the rod.

Oversights and ill-considered actions in the past? Well, things like a total failure to maintain your gear do make you a tad nervous when you suddenly find yourself attached to the fish of a lifetime. Being careless about your knots is another chicken that comes home to roost when a fight goes beyond the half-hour mark, then the hour mark. You also spend quite a bit of time pondering the wisdom of saving money on line when the knot joining your new line to the old rubbish you use for backing goes sailing out through the guides to become the weakest link in the chain. Much of the fun tends to go out of your life right then, and it stays out until you have that knot well and truly buried back in the spool again. The fish you want most is inevitably the one that will be lost. Softly but firmly is always the best approach, and time spent on the homework side of fishing is never time wasted.

Landing fish

No fish has ever been captured until it has been safely removed from the water, and the business of getting fish out of the water is fraught with danger. Don't ever use the line to lift a fish from the water if you can possibly avoid it. This is when hooks pull free and lines break.

Problems begin when the fish comes into view. The angler sees a prize catch and determines not to let that fish get away. This is the time when the sight of the shore, or a boat looming up, will cause the fish to use every last bit of strength it has in one final lunge for freedom. This sudden burst often catches the angler off guard, allowing the fish to break the line, or perhaps foul the leg of an outboard motor. The shorter the fight has been, the more reserves the fish will have to put into this last burst. The flathead is the grand-master of this tactic, and many a trophy flathead has found freedom by saving its best until last.

A smart angler will always back the drag off the reel a bit when a big fish is alongside, relying on finger override on the spool (unless we are talking about a lever-drag game reel), as this can instantly be backed off in an emergency. The angler should always be ready to shove the tip of the rod straight down into the water the instant a fish takes off in any direction other than directly away from the boat. When you get the rod in

An exhausted fish will lie on its side. This is the time to land the fish, or attempt a release.

all the way up to the foregrip, at least you have the line cleared of obstacles, no matter where the fish decides to go (except in the case of a roller tip rod, where you have to make sure the line does not go over the side frames rather than the roller). This could result in a lost rod if the drag is still full on, which is just one more reason for having had the foresight to back the drag off as the fish came alongside. Obviously, you don't want deadwood standing between you and your bolting fish when things go wrong, so onlookers should be in the centre of the cockpit, not hanging over the rails and in the way.

The best and safest fish to land is the one that is falling on its side with exhaustion, but you don't want this situation if you are planning to release the fish, of course. For release fishing you break all these rules and cut every corner you can, making it part of the game to see just how fast you can get to the fish and get it off the line. The longer you fiddle about with it, the greater the chance that it will eventually die, or at least be terribly vulnerable for a long period after release.

Fish recovery problems vary according to the area you are fishing. Even on the beach, anglers are advised to wear a short-handled gaff on their belt. The standard method of working the fish to the edge of the wash then walking backwards up the beach with the next big wave to strand the fish is a good one, but big fish tend to strand well down the wash, and it is nice to be able to whip down and secure them with a

gaff in the gills or lower lip. A hand grip there is fine if you have the time to sort it out, but you do see the odd person take a nasty wound on their hand trying to rush this. Nobody should rush gilling a big flathead or jewfish.

The knack here is to be ready to back off and let the fish go back with the wash if you don't get it far enough out on the first try. Trying to hold a bulky fish against a strong backwash is inviting disaster. Landing fish on a beach with the help of a wash – or even harder, on a stillwater shore where the angler gets no help from the water – involves considerable judgement. You need to pick a moment when the fish is not only close to the shore but also swimming towards the shore – then you will be simply accelerating the fish in the direction in which it is already travelling, rather than trying to force the issue. Remember, always go with the flow.

Landing fish from the rocks is perhaps one of fishing's greatest challenges. It is the time when anglers risk losing not only the fish, but also their life.

Given a shallow ledge, the basic landing technique around rocks is much the same as that used on a beach. The fish is brought up on a swell, then stranded as the water recedes. The angler gets down onto the ledge, recovers the fish, and gets back up again as quickly as possible. Because the trip down to a low ledge is often dangerous, the short-handled gaff is again worth considering, as it allows you to get hold of the fish a little faster.

Long gaffs are the main method of getting larger fish out, but a few anglers use landing nets on long handles. The nets deserve more use, because it is a lot safer to swim a medium-sized fish over a net than to try to gaff it. Fish need to have bulk and weight to make good gaff targets, and a lot of fish are lost on gaffs.

Cliff gaffs in a variety of shapes and sizes allow anglers to work terrain that otherwise would be quite impossible. The fish should be played out to the point

of exhaustion, then simply held at the surface of the water. The multi-prong gaff, which is secured on a rope, is then attached to the main line either by clips or rings, and slid down until it comes into contact with the fish. It is then jiggled on the rope until one of the points finds a hold, enabling the fish to be hauled up the cliff. Western Australian anglers have made cliff fishing something of an art, and they land huge fish from high cliffs using these gaffs.

If you are working from a boat, anything that can be netted should be netted. In other words, if the fish is small enough to fit into a net, it is too light to be safely gaffed. The golden rule is this: if you want the fish, net it – if you don't want it, try lifting it into the boat. There is also the irrefutable law which ensures that stingrays and catfish never fall off the hook when you lift them into a boat without a net, but every fish you desperately want to eat will.

Netting fish

Getting a fish into a net is something of an art. An unrushed approach is called for here. If the person wielding the net is getting a wild-eyed look and their nostrils are starting to flare at the sight of the fish, take the net and do it yourself. This job calls for cool calculation, not rampant blood lust.

A fish has to be tired and slow to be securely netted. A net or gaff is not a means of shortening a fight; it is simply a method of getting a beaten fish out of the water safely. With the fish tired and completely under control, put the net in the water and lead the fish over it, tilting the net up at the last minute so the fish will actually swim down into it. You don't sweep a fish up with a net, nor do you chase it about as if it's a butterfly.

Gaffing fish

Most serious anglers working with gaffs carry more than one, because the smallest gaff that will do the job is always the one to be used.

To explain this: the bigger the diameter of the gaff hook, the harder it is going to be to drive it into a fish, especially a scaled fish. Since the real danger period in

OPPOSITE Grippers like those pictured here do very little harm to a fish, and immobilise it to a point where hooks can be removed and the fish released with a minimum of harm. Wet your hands before you actually touch a fish that is to be released. The acids on your skin remove its protective slime.

a gaffing sequence is when the attempt is made to actually get the gaff in, it is essential that the hook used be the one most likely to go straight in. This suggests that we should always use a fine hook, but fine hooks often straighten out under the stress of holding and lifting a big fish. The rule is to use the smallest gaff head that will hold the fish in question. In a small boat this probably means the basic tackle store gaff hook, set up on a suitable length of dowel. This is so cheap to make that it pays to carry a couple, just in case a big fish takes one from you, or you get lucky and strike a two-gaff fish. These gaffs are ideal for snapper and jewfish, where you want something that will get in under scales. If you fish offshore, you also need to carry something that will cope with real weight – you can use this as a primary gaff on a large fish, or as a second gaff to cope with weight after a big fish has been secured with a finer gaff hook.

Larger boats working primarily with larger fish and game fish will carry a range of aluminium-shaft gaffs with heavy-duty stainless steel hooks, and perhaps some flying gaffs.

Flying gaffs are a system where the gaff head is attached to the boat by a heavy rope, and the handle is only used to take the hook to the fish. The hook normally has some sort of receiver, into which the gaff pole is fitted, then held in place with the rope. The hook is taken to the fish on the pole and then pulled into the fish with the rope, after which the handle is withdrawn. Flying gaffs are normally only used on

Jaw shots with a gaff are not recommended. It is too hard a target for one thing, and there's a good chance of fouling hooks and line to produce an unintended premature release.

very large fish such as marlin and sharks, where there is serious doubt about crew being able to hang onto the fish with conventional gaffs.

Before using a flying gaff, make sure that your boat and transom are up to the stress the fish may apply to them. A large shark on a flying gaff that is tied off on a stern cleat can easily swamp a small boat.

Some rock anglers are also using flyers these days, as the heavy rope gives them their best chance of hanging onto some of the huge fish they are bringing in. Some of the yellowfin and marlin being hooked up would be a handful from a boat, let alone from the hairy rock platforms on which these people operate.

Gaffs, like nets, are not a means of short-circuiting a fight, although some gaff people have a remarkable ability to pluck speeding fish out of the water, and take great pride in their skill. The problem is that when a gaff shot is botched, the line is often caught up on the hook and the fish is lost.

Always come over the back of a fish with a gaff – any touch under the belly will send it wild. Aim for the bulkiest part of the fish, which is the shoulder. Always try to get the gaff *behind* the fishing line, so that if you miss, the line will travel away from the gaff, and never lean over the line for your shot.

It isn't easy, but if you are gaffing a scaled fish and get the chance, try to bring the hook in at an angle to give the point a chance to go *under* the scales. Never

It is usually safe to handle a barra with a thumb in the mouth grip, but not when the lure is still in place.

stab at fish with a gaff – this usually leads to disaster. Wait for the target to be comfortably within range, place the hook accurately without touching the fish, and then come into the fish firmly, only jabbing when you have the weight of the fish against the hook.

Tracing fish

In game fishing, where long and very heavy traces are frequently used, it is customary for a crew member to don heavy gloves and take the trace by hand when it comes within reach. The fish is then dragged to within reach of the gaff. This procedure is sometimes necessary because the trace is attached to a swivel which will not go through the rod tip guide, and the length of trace from that swivel to the hook is too great for the angler to be able to bring the fish within gaffing range. I don't like this system much, because after working a big fish carefully for ages, it makes little sense to me to then skull-drag it by hand when the hook is often just hanging in a considerably enlarged hole in the jaw. The fish – especially if it is a yellowfin – can break free under these circumstances. The system is fine if the person doing the job is sensitive, but the drama of the moment tends to bring out the

Trevally can be lifted from the water by grabbing them just ahead of the tail. A glove can save wear and tear on the angler.

Rambo in deckies, with blood being pumped away from the brain to inflate the muscles.

I personally prefer the system used on the American long-range boats. They use gaffs with extra-long handles to secure fish wide of the boat, minimising the need for trace handling. Having said that, however, tracing is still the only way to go when the fish is to be released.

Chapter Eight

Handling and cooking fish

Handling your catch

Many amateur anglers refuse to eat fish bought from a fish shop, claiming that they wouldn't eat that old rubbish when they can provide fresh fish themselves. To be completely honest with you, I would put fish from a good fish shop, or a packet of frozen crumbed fillets from the supermarket, way ahead of the fish produced by the average amateur. Very few amateur anglers carry ice with them to keep the catch fresh, and the average amateur-caught fish ends up being badly handled and bruised. In addition, most people leave fish lying around un-gutted in the heat, which is just asking for trouble.

The Japanese set the benchmark for careful handling of fish at the landing stage. For instance, they insist that a tuna intended for sashimi be rendered unconscious with a blow to the head before it is brought into the boat. This way the fish will not bruise itself trying to swim against the hard sides and the cockpit floor. Once safely in the cockpit, a special tool is used to remove a core of meat, allowing access to the spinal column, then another tool is used to sever the spinal nerves. This both kills the fish instantly and removes the possibility of reflex nervous action damaging the flesh.

I don't think we need to go to these extremes in the handling of our catch, but between the Japanese approach and our own there is a lot of useful ground to be explored.

Many people are cautious about handling fish, fearing cuts and punctures from spines, and even being bitten. Bites are very rare, but anglers often suffer injuries from spines and gill covers, and also frequently hook themselves as they remove hooks from fish.

Poisonous fish

SOMETIMES POISONOUS

The fish that are most likely to cause us harm are those that are only sometimes poisonous; this group includes some of our most popular tropical table fish, such as the coral trout and mackerel. Any tropical reef fish that eats other fish is potentially dangerous as a source of ciguatera poisoning, but the mackerel and coral trout are the ones that are most often the culprits, because they are the species most commonly consumed and they can poison you if you have a single big meal. Ciguatera is not completely understood, but most authorities agree that the *actual* quantity of the fish consumed is a key factor. Big fish are the ones most likely to have accumulated toxin in their bodies, and big fish are also the ones most likely to induce humans to indulge in a feast. If alcohol accompanies the feast, the effect of the poison will be increased considerably.

Ciguatera can also accumulate over a period of time in a person regularly eating small fish meals.

The effects of ciguatera vary a lot, with tingling sensations in the extremities at the mild end of the spectrum and death at the other. In between lie sensations of hot and cold, nausea, loss of muscle coordination and balance, and muscular aches. Mild sensations can either indicate a mild dose of poisoning or announce the onset of something more serious.

Take the hint and get a suspected victim to a doctor, fast. If the symptoms are strong, induce vomiting and be prepared to use mouth-to-mouth resuscitation if respiratory difficulties arise. Those experiencing a mild dose of ciguatera should avoid eating reef fish altogether for at least six months – this is the time it takes for the poison to dissipate and the symptoms to disappear.

The correct approach to tropical fish is to try to stick with the smaller fish, and if the opportunity to indulge presents itself, have a small portion of a number of small fish rather than one whole fish. You should definitely avoid eating large amounts of a single large fish.

From time to time kingfish and snapper will feed on toads, and at such times it would be as well to avoid eating such fish. A friend and I once took a good haul of snapper and kingfish at Montague Island, and were intrigued to note that all of them had been feasting on green toads. We ate a good many of the fish and both came down with a dreadful dose of vomiting and diarrhoea that lasted over a week. While it is possible that a seemingly innocent hamburger consumed around the same time may have been the real culprit, no fish that has been eating toads will ever be eaten by me again.

ALWAYS POISONOUS

All of the toadfish family should be avoided, but these are rarely a problem, because they are known to be poisonous and few people attempt to eat them. The box fish is another rather nasty customer. It comes in a wide variety of shapes and colours, a few of them disturbingly similar to some of the more ornate leatherjackets. All of these fish are highly toxic at all times.

Most of the poisonous species are either ugly, highly decorated in garish colours, or both. When you catch something you can't identify, and you are even the least bit suspicious about it, it is best to discard it. *Fishes of Australia* by E.M. Grant (E.M. Grant Pty Ltd, Scarborough, Queensland, 1987) is a guide to common Australian species that clearly identifies those that are always or sometimes toxic, and is a handy reference for those not familiar with the dangerous species. There are some other excellent guides listed in Further Reading on page 246.

DANGEROUS TO HANDLE

All spined fish are dangerous to handle to some degree, and a spine puncture from the most innocent of our common edible species will produce a painful wound, usually followed by some minor infection.

Flathead have spurs protruding from the outside edge of the gill covers, and these spurs have razor-sharp sides. A flathead can whip its head from side to side with considerable speed and power, and if your fingers are within range, these spurs can deliver a painful cut which will probably become infected.

David Angus became the catfish king when he hauled in this whopper. Large, sharp and very strong spines on the pectoral fins and in the dorsal fin can inflict severe injuries if these fish are not handled with great care. Wounds will also become badly infected if not treated properly.

The barramundi has some very effective cutting plates located on the outside of the gill covers – this area should be treated with considerable caution. In fact, barra have a habit of bursting into frantic contortions at the most unexpected moments, so they should always be handled with great care. The dorsal spines and gill covers can deal out some very nasty injuries.

Many tropical fish have quite spiny gills inside the covers, so do not take hold inside the gills to immobilise the fish while removing hooks unless you know that the fish in question is safe to handle this way. I put my hand in one once and left a lot of skin behind getting it out.

A whole family of scorpion and scorpion-like fish, including the firefish or butterfly cod, red rock cod, stonefish and the fortescue, are equipped with spines on the head, or down the back, that are extremely poisonous. Ironically, northern anglers call some of these fish 'happy moments', but being stung by any of them will lead to anything but happy moments. A stonefish sting can cause death, but even the least venomous of these fish delivers a very painful sting – these stings usually require medical attention.

The common denominator with all these fish is that they *look* dangerous: even the most innocent of them have some form of spikes or spines on the head, particularly over the eyes.

Parents need to watch out for children catching fortescue – they are sometimes caught around weedy or rocky edges in rivers and bays. These fish are just 4 to 7 cm long, and with their dull brown colouring they do not look particularly offensive, but they are dynamite. Warn the kids about them and make sure that they understand not to touch them. They should not be left on the bank where they can be trodden on.

Most of the stingrays have quite dangerous spines on their tails, but this is again a case of well-known danger, and few people put themselves at risk. Catfish also need to be handled with the utmost caution, as they too have some very nasty spines on the pectoral and dorsal fins.

In the case of an injury inflicted by any of these fish, immediate treatment involves immersing the affected area, usually the hand or foot, in hot water for up to 2 hours. The water should be the hottest the patient can tolerate without scalding the skin. To make allowances for the intensity of the pain in the poisoned area, do this testing of water temperature with the unaffected hand or on another person. Medical aid should be sought as a matter of urgency.

HOW TO HANDLE FISH SAFELY

Some of the very poisonous fish, such as the red rock cod and the fortescue, are often caught by anglers. They need to be handled with extreme care. The safest method is to simply hold the fish away from you while you cut the line and get rid of the fish. Many anglers,

This jaw grip is a reasonable way to handle non-toothy critters such as bass and barramundi. Obviously, you need to be sure about the dental status of the fish before putting your fingers in there. Incidentally, the gill covers of both these species have horribly sharp edges that need to be avoided at all times.

however, like to eat the red rock cod (also known as mouth-almighty and flower pots); if you want to keep one, the best approach is to take a good grip on the lower jaw with pliers then use a hook remover or second set of pliers to remove the hook. It is also quite safe to hold the fish by taking a grip on the lower jaw with the thumb inside the mouth and the curled index finger outside, but if you do this, make sure that you are holding the fish clear of everything, as it is only the weight of the body that keeps the mouth open when you do this. This method is not recommended with most other species of fish.

Northern anglers often use this grip on the jaw to remove hooks from barramundi before releasing them, and southern anglers use the same grip for bass. The drawback is that the fish can quite suddenly explode into action, causing the hooks to be transferred to the angler's hands and fingers. In the worst case, some hooks stay in the fish – which continues to kick frantically – while others find their way into the angler. Experience doesn't help much, and some of the best barra anglers I know just accept regular hookings as part and parcel of barra fishing. If you don't feel as tough as that, use a jaw gripper to hold the fish while you remove the hook with pliers, or handle the fish with a landing net. If you are releasing, do all this outside the boat, in the water, or bring the fish into the boat and handle it with a wet cloth or towel rather than your hands – this will do less damage to the fish. (The acids on our skin harm fish by removing their layer of protective slime.) If you are keeping the fish, use the towel to hold it, and then use pliers, preferably long-nosed hook removers, to get the hooks out – and be prepared to move fast when the barra bursts into action.

Pan-sized fish can usually be handled safely by simply holding them aloft by the line until they settle a little, then sliding the other hand down over the head with a loose but firm grip, folding the fins down under the hand as you go. Bigger fish can be handled by placing the palm of the hand at the back of the neck, with the fingers gripping just behind the gills on one side of the body and the thumb in the same spot on the other side. Just make sure that your palm is not coming down over an erect dorsal.

Very large fish are generally handled by taking a grip in behind the gills from the belly side. The thumb goes into one side and the fingers into the other side of that narrow bridge of flesh and bone that joins the belly to the head. This grip is also the best way to handle a flathead, as it enables you to avoid those nasty gill case spines.

All these hand grips have some risk associated with them, especially if you use them tentatively. With all of them, be firm and get a good grip that won't slip.

The safest way to handle any fish is with a towel and pliers, and that's the way to go when you are not experienced. When you plan to eat the fish, but do not intend to keep it alive until you are ready to clean it, kill it immediately, either by giving it a sharp hit on the head right between, or above, the eyes, or by breaking that bridge across the throat, and then turning the head back and breaking the neck. The latter has the advantage of also bleeding the fish, which can be advantageous with some species.

To kill or keep alive?

It is nearly always advisable to keep fish alive as long as possible. This can be done by keeping them in those nylon mesh swim bags you can buy anywhere these days, or by tethering them by running a cord through the lower jaw; this system works well with larger fish. If you can't keep the fish in the water, then you should kill it immediately – to prevent bruising to its flesh and for obvious reasons of humanity.

Care of the catch

In the ideal situation you would have ice available, in which case you would remove the gut and gills from the fish, along with any obvious blood in that area, but *leave the scales on*. The scales trap moisture in the flesh and do a good job of keeping the meat moist and fresh. If you keep the fish moist and do not let it dry out, the scales will be easy to get off later. They only become difficult to remove once the skin has dried out. Wash the fish thoroughly to remove external slime, then put it straight on the ice. *Do not use plastic bags to store the fish at this stage.* Only use plastic bags if you are keeping other food on the same ice. Drain the water off the ice regularly so that the fish are not floating in

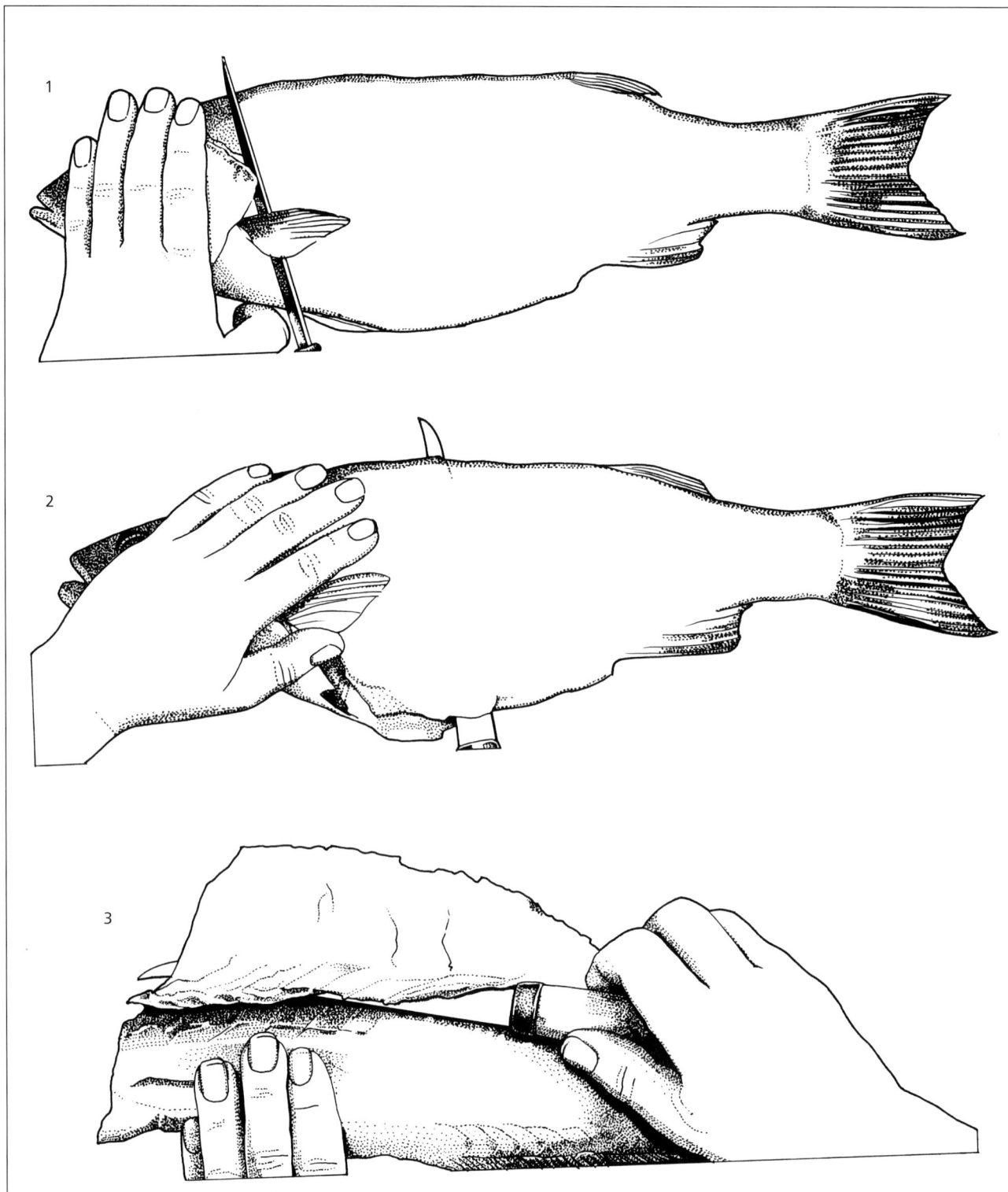

This is the basic filleting technique. Start by (1) going under the pectoral fin and angling the knife towards the head, cutting down to the backbone. Then (2) turn the blade of the knife around and, with the blade flat on the backbone, cut back towards the tail with a sawing motion. In the next step (3) you remove all the rib cage by sliding the knife along under the bones. When both sides are done (4), using either the fillet knife or a special skinning knife (one with a flat, flexible but dull blade), make a cut at the tail between the skin and the flesh so that you can take hold of the tail end of the skin with your fingers. (5) Keeping a tight grip on the skin, saw the knife back and forth in the one spot and draw the fish to the blade by pulling on the tail end of the skin.

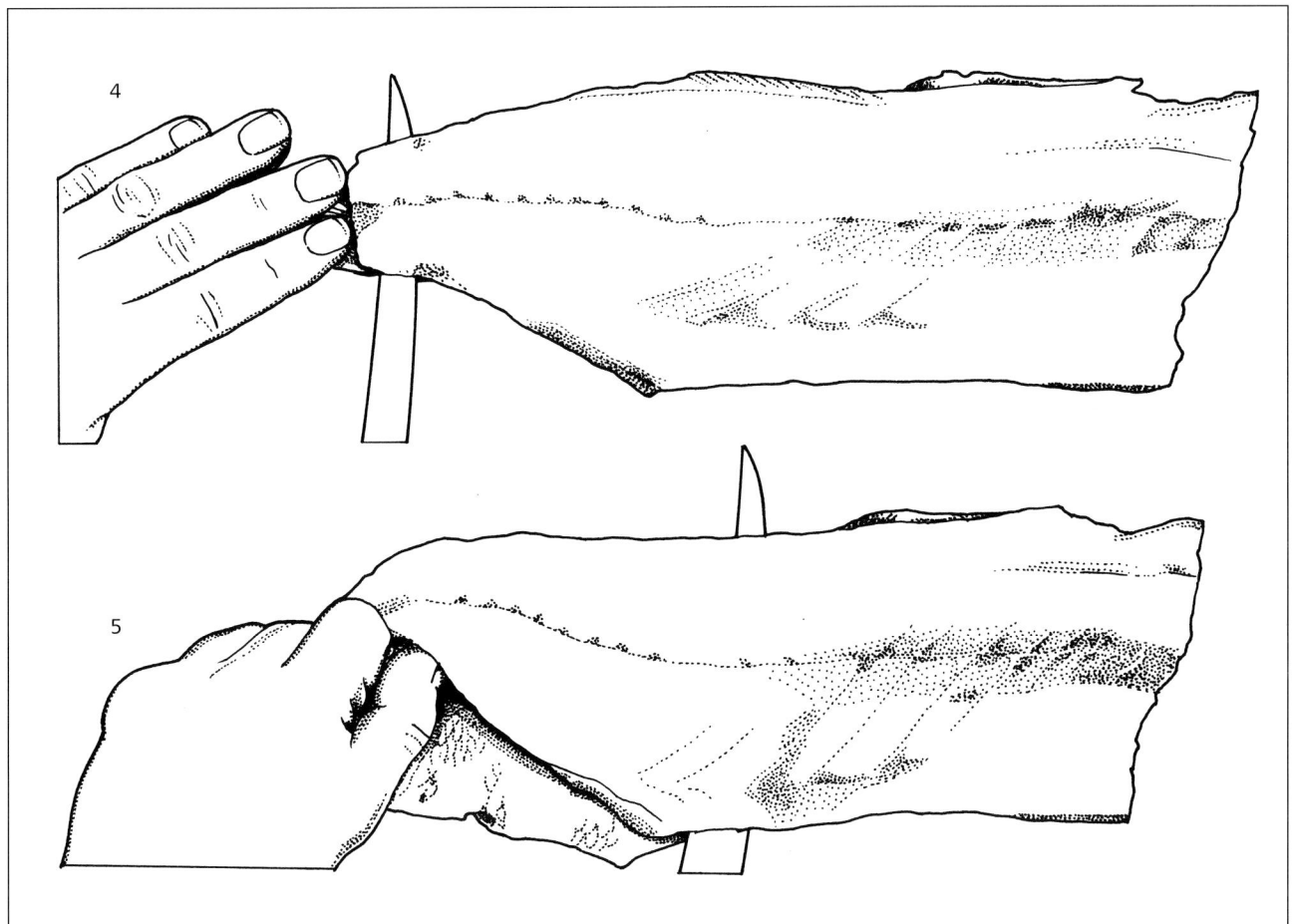

slime and blood – if you have managed to thoroughly wash your catch so that the ice water is clean, this will not be necessary.

If you don't have ice on hand, try bush refrigeration. Keep your fish in a wet hessian bag in a shady place, preferably hung so that air can circulate around it. After you clean the fish, as outlined in the following section, wash the bag thoroughly to remove all traces of slime and blood before you use it for the cleaned fish. Hessian seems to retain moisture better than most other materials, and it is the passage of the breeze through this material that keeps things cool. If you don't have a hessian bag, gut the fish and simply hang it in a shady place. Wetting it now and then will help keep it cool, but it is surprising how well a fish can survive on even a hot day as long as it is cleaned immediately and the scales are left on. Even a wet towel or piece of cloth wrapped around the fish will make a big difference to the way it keeps.

Cleaning fish

The job that everyone hates can be made a lot less painful if you set yourself up with the proper tools in the first place. What you need is a work knife with a strong but not too thick blade, and a filleting knife with a fine, very flexible blade. Anglers who skin most of their fish add a third knife – one with a flexible but rather broad flat blade – but you can skin a fish with any knife if you take a little care. Finally, you need a proper scaler; I think the old-fashioned circular metal scaler is still the best thing I've ever used.

I prefer knives with soft steel blades to the hard stainless types. The hard steel keeps an edge longer, but it is difficult to re-sharpen. Since you need a keen edge for this sort of work, the best bet is to have something that will take an edge quickly, with just a couple of strokes on a diamond sharpener or steel. You might have to sharpen your knives frequenly, but you will always be working with a good edge.

Gutting a fish is simply a matter of taking the point of the blade in through the anus, then cutting forward to the throat. Take the blade in at a shallow angle to avoid cutting into the gut itself – you don't want to rupture the gall bladder and let all that acid and bile loose on the flesh. Remove the gills by hand. They are pretty firmly connected to the roof of the throat, and in the case of a big fish you might have to remove them one section at a time. Take care with this, especially if you have to keep the fish for a time before it is eaten. Those gills are loaded with blood, and the more blood you can get rid of the better.

With the gut and gills removed, turn the fish over to allow yourself good access to the gut cavity, and use the point of your knife to scour along either side of the backbone. Most fish have a pocket of blood along here that can either be scraped away with the knife or easily removed by scrubbing with a stiff nailbrush. How much trouble you go to with all this will depend on how long you need to keep the fish before you eat it (or prepare it for longer-term storage) and whether you intend to fillet it or cook it whole.

If you are cleaning the fish in the field and want to keep only the fillets, this is the time to introduce plastic bags. Remember, plastic bags do not breathe, so heat builds up in them. You want to have your fish as clean and bacteria-free as you can get it before it goes into plastic; if you don't, it will quickly deteriorate.

Before you put any fish into a plastic bag, wash it, wash it, wash it, then dry it, dry it, dry it. It is essential to get rid of the blood and slime before you store fish, even if it's only for a day or so. The fish should be as dry on the outside as you can get it. When you have done this, drop it into the plastic bag and *roll the bag* closed to exclude as much air as possible. You have a choice as to whether you scale your fish before you fillet it or not. Skinning a fillet removes scales as well, so if you don't plan to cook the fish with the skin on you don't have to scale. Fish are easier to scale when they are in one piece. Take special care of those areas close to the fins and spines that many people avoid doing because they fear puncturing their fingers on a spine. Just take it easy with this job and keep in mind that it is a potentially flesh-bruising operation.

There are two basic approaches to filleting. Either you take the knife in behind the head and cut all the way through from head to tail, taking ribs and all with the fillet, removing the whole side in one slab, or you make a cut right down the back alongside the dorsal ridge then gradually work your way along the backbone in a series of long strokes from head to tail. Professionals generally opt for the first method. When you make the first cut the knife will be at an angle that takes the cut high into the neck meat, angling back to exclude the pectoral fin. You also tilt the knife a little to angle in towards the head, and cut right down to the backbone. You then turn the blade towards the tail, lie it parallel to the backbone and cut towards the tail with a sawing motion. Hold the fish by the head with your free hand to get the cut started, then, once the cut is underway, place your free hand flat on the side close to the area where the knife is cutting.

Once you have the side off, turn it over and cut the whole rib cage out. Discard that. When you do this, cut with some upward pressure towards the bones if you want to retain the belly flap meat. I throw the whole rib section and belly flap away, as I find it is often tainted and never as good to eat as the rest of the fish.

Finally, to skin the fillet, take hold of the tail with your fingernails and bring the knife in and down to the skin at an angle before turning the blade to lie it flat on the skin. This is a fiddly bit and you may need to change your grip a few times until you have a big enough piece of free skin to get a good hold of it. Then pull firmly on the skin as you saw the knife blade back and forth. Do not try to do this by moving the blade forward. Keep it going back and forth in the one place and pull the skin along the blade.

The second method of filleting, which is the best one to adopt when you have a fish with a bulky, nobbly backbone and heavy ribs, is to start right behind the head with a shallow cut, then carry that right down the back to the flat tail area behind the second dorsal fin. Go back to the head and keep running the blade down the same cut, with the blade flat to the backbone. Lift the fillet with the other hand as you go until you hit the spine. At this stage, work the blade up over the rib cage in a series of short strokes, then make a cut across the tail and saw forward until you hit the rib cage again. At this point you should be able to lift the fillet and finish the job off by cutting through the layer of skin along the belly of the fish. This method takes a little longer, but it is a good one for people who are not skilled with a fillet

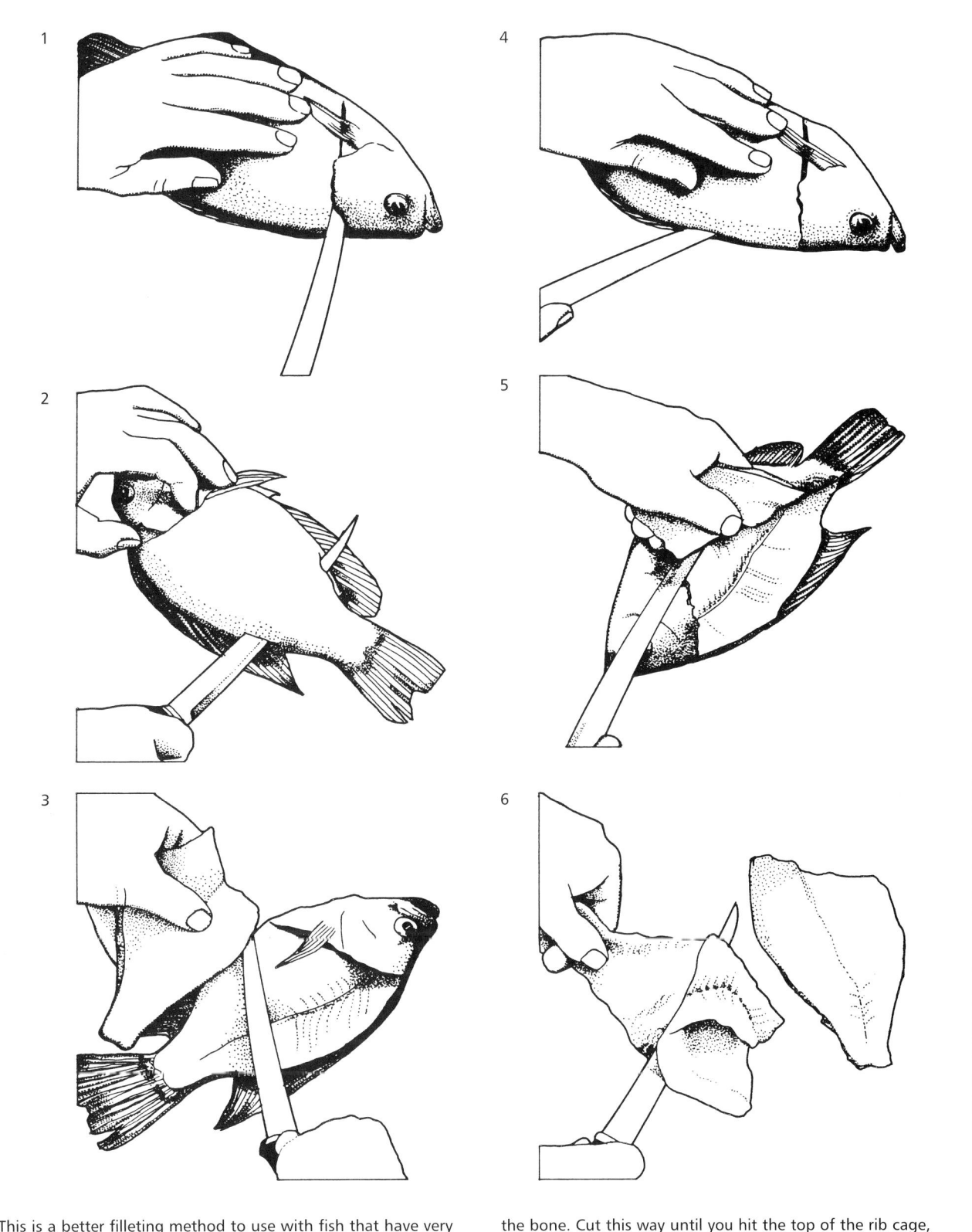

1

2

3

4

5

6

This is a better filleting method to use with fish that have very strong bones in the rib cage. (1) This time you have the fish facing away from you when you make the cut behind the head. (2) Now turn the knife and instead of using the length of the blade, just use the point to cut right down the back along the bone. Cut this way until you hit the top of the rib cage, then (3) push the blade right through and cut the fillet free at the tail. (4) Now slide the knife over the rib cage bones, finally (5) cutting through the stomach skin to free the fillet. (6) Skin the fillets as in method one.

knife and who want to get every scrap of meat off the backbone.

When you have filleted a big fish, there can still be a good deal of meat left on that backbone, so check out your cookbooks for some fish soup recipes. Fish soup can be delicious.

Some fish carry a lot of oil in their skin. This oil is released into the flesh when you cook them; this is one of the reasons for skinning fillets. People who have in the past discarded some of the weed-eating fish, such as luderick, should try them skinned and with the whole gut and rib area removed. They taste completely different when handled this way.

When you have a really big fish to handle, say, something upwards of 6 kg, you might want to cut it into steaks. This involves a series of cuts down to the backbone either side of the fish, spaced as wide apart as the size you want each steak to be, then cutting the backbone through with a saw. The other way to do this is to freeze the fish whole, then take it down to your friendly butcher or fishmonger and ask for it to be put through the power saw. This will cost you a steak or two, but you'll get a great job.

Mind you, you don't *have* to cut a big fish into steaks. All you are doing when you slice up a fish is reducing the meat to portions you can handle and easily cook. Some people, myself included, prefer to fillet even the biggest fish, then cut those fillets up into strips which can be varied in size and shape to suit different dishes.

Storing fish at home

When you get all that fish home, the first thing to do is wash and dry it again, because this will be your first chance to do it properly. Paper towels are great for this job, as they really pull the surface moisture out of the fish. My Japanese teacher in this area suggested that the fish is ready to store when you can press it with a clean paper towel and not get any stain or moisture on the towel. Drop each piece of fish into a plastic bag and carefully roll the air out, then secure the bag with an elastic band to keep it airtight. If you think all this is excessive, do an experiment on two lots of fish. Prepare one this way and simply place the other fish on a plate with cling wrap over the top. Give them both a couple of

days in the fridge and then apply the nose test. Neither fish should be off by any means, but the fish stored dry will have virtually no odour compared with the other.

There is a second reason why the Japanese go to all this trouble rather than just wolfing the fish down fresh. A storage period of several days allows the muscles that have gone into spasm at the time of death to relax and tenderise. The difference is not as noticeable if you compare cooked fresh and tenderised fish samples, but if you try both types raw you will notice quite an appreciable difference in texture.

For short-term storage, say, a day, simply dry the fish and leave it on a paper towel on a covered plate in the fridge. That will be fine.

Fish needs to be handled with great care if it is to be frozen, and different approaches are advised depending on whether the fish is intended for short- or long-term freezing. For short-term freezing, fish prepared as described above is ready for the freezer – just ensure that as much air as possible has been squeezed from the package and that it is completely sealed.

For long-term freezing, save your old plastic ice-cream containers and those handy little plastic cartons you get takeaway food in these days. Put one meal of fillets in a container and then fill it to within a few millimetres of the top with ice water (the space allows for the expansion of the water as it freezes). The faster you freeze any food the better, so if the fish is cold and the water is close to freezing when you fill the container you are doing the job right.

If you have a considerable amount of fish and no containers, try placing the fillets in a flat cake tin, or in a shallow layer of water in the bottom of a baking dish. Freeze the lot, turn the ice block out of the dish, wrap it in foil, then pop it in a heavy plastic bag.

When you freeze fish, make absolutely sure that you mark the outside of the container with the date plus the number and type of fillets. This will guard against you serving the guests salted fillets intended as bait.

Fish can be kept frozen for a maximum of six months; it is a good idea when using domestic refrigeration to keep fish for a maximum of four months. The best approach is to consume frozen fish within a month.

We found with tailor, a soft, oily fish with quite a high blood content, that the fish improved out of sight if it was frozen for just a couple of days after having lemon squeezed all over it. This might be worth trying with some of the trevally, which have similar flesh.

Thaw your fish with care, melting the ice off the blocks under a running tap or in a big bowl of cold water and allowing the final defrost to take place in the fridge on a covered plate. Give yourself plenty of time with this, as a fast defrost will spoil the fish.

Microwave defrosting is excellent. Thaw away the external ice in water, then follow the directions for your particular machine.

Cooking fish

Cooking fish begins with the inevitable question: 'Is it fresh or not?' Apart from the obvious nose test, you can look at the eyes of a whole fish, which should be bright and not milky, and if you push the flesh with your finger the flesh should recover. If the flesh reacts like soft putty, retaining the dent from your finger, you might be looking at a candidate for the berley pot.

Sometimes the only difference between successful and unsuccessful fish cookery is the way the fish has been cut before cooking. Fish flesh is delicate, and should never be overcooked. If you make the pieces too thick, you will end up overcooking the outside to ensure that the centre is cooked. Thin fillets will be

If the fish has good colour in the eyes it is probably very fresh. Another test is to prod the flesh with your finger. If the impression of your prod remains in the flesh it is probably not fit to eat.

fine just as they are, but a thick fillet might be better cut into smaller finger shapes or wedges to allow the heat to penetrate from the sides as well as the top and bottom. When a fish is to be cooked whole, it is a good idea to make several deep cuts at the shoulder to allow this area to cook through properly.

FRYING FISH

When frying, you have a choice between deep frying or pan frying, and a number of choices regarding coatings for the fish. For pan frying it's good to be able to get your hands on one of those heavy iron pans. Around 1 cm of oil in the bottom is enough, and this should be heated until it really spits when a drop of water lands in it. This is also the temperature you should maintain. If you let the oil cool off the fish will become soggy. Overfilling the pan with cold fish pieces will drop the oil temperature, so add them a few at a time and don't try to cook too many at once.

Dry the fish to remove all moisture, then roll it in seasoned flour and place it in the pan. Allow it to cook without moving: 3 to 5 minutes for a whole fish, 60 seconds for small fillets, and as little as 30 seconds for small chunks of fish. If you try to turn the fish too soon it will stick to the pan. (That's also the secret for good shallow-pan chips – leave them alone.) You walk a fine line here, because it doesn't take much to overcook fish, which will make it dry and chewy.

When you turn the fish it will require less cooking on the second side. You can test a whole fish by digging a fork or knife into the back next to the backbone in the thick part of the shoulder and giving it a little twist. If it's cooked, the flesh will come away from the bone easily. When the fish is done, drain it on paper towels and serve it straightaway.

To coat the fillets with crumbs, dip them first in cold milk or water. You can mix a beaten egg in with the milk or water if you wish. The egg helps the mixture to stick to the fish, but you tend to get a fairly heavy coating.

To make a really light batter for up to 1 kg of fish, beat the whites of two eggs until stiff peaks form, then stir in half a cup to a cup of ice-cold soda water. Gradually add 1 cup of sifted plain flour, stirring until the mixture is smooth. Adjust the quantity of soda water so that the batter is just liquid enough to coat the fish easily.

This light, fluffy, tempura-style batter is best suited to small pieces of fish, which only need to be cooked for a minute or so. I was introduced to it by Rod Harrison, who proved it was a no-sweat way of cooking by producing mountains of succulent mangrove jack and barramundi fillets in a remote Northern Territory camp one night.

GRILLING FISH

If your fish is thick, or if you are grilling whole fish, cut it deeply (to the backbone) into the thickest sections, with slightly shallower cuts as you go to the thinner sections of the body or fillet. This ensures that all parts of the fish are cooked through at pretty much the same time – otherwise the tail will be cremated while you are waiting for the shoulder to cook. Lightly brush oil over the exposed surface of the fish (use a pastry brush), then put the heat on high and the fish as far away from the heat as your griller will allow. This allows the fish to cook right through without burning and drying the outside, giving you beautifully moist, lightly browned fish.

Once the fish is almost cooked, if you like it to have more of a tan when it goes on the plate, just take it right up under the heat for a minute. Keep a close eye on it when you do this. A tasty addition is to mix a little light soy sauce into the oil before brushing it on the fish. When you do this the fish comes out golden brown and the soy usually does away with the need to add salt. People on salt-free diets can use salt-free soy, which still gives a salty taste.

Most of the oil melts off the fish as you cook it this way, so the fish has no oily taste or feel to it at all, but it does stay beautifully moist. The oil also helps to give it a slight crispness on the outside.

ABOVE Here's a truly remarkable sight. Ashley Bauden, chef on the mother ship *Tropic Paradise*, guarantees fresh fish by catching it himself. **OPPOSITE** A very short time later sashimi is served.

STEAMING FISH

For those on fat-free diets, try steaming skinned fish. You can use almost anything to steam fish, from a proper steamer through to a wok or standard kitchen saucepan. All you need is a rack to keep the fish above whatever liquid you use. Steaming drains much of the oil out of fish, so even if it's not sufficiently fat-free when it comes out of the sea, steaming will make it a dieter's dream.

You can steam over plain water if you have a delicately flavoured fish that you wish to appreciate just as it is, or you may wish to add flavours to spice things up a bit. One cunning move is to add onions and chopped vegetables to the water, so that you have something you can pour back over the cooked fish when you serve it. My favourite is to steam fish over a mixture of water, soy sauce, finely ground fresh ginger and crushed garlic. Fish done this way is delicious served on a bed of stir-fried vegetables. This is also a great way to cook crabs.

Steaming requires a little more cooking time than frying and grilling, but you should keep checking your fish. Allow around 10 minutes for a whole fish, say, 5 minutes for fillets, and less than that for strips, which is the way I steam fish.

OVEN AND FOIL COOKING

Cooking fish in a covered dish or wrapped in foil in the oven is a method that works well for the complete novice cook and the expert, for it is difficult to overcook and dry the flesh when you work this way. You can use either a covered baking dish with a heavy, well-fitting lid, or an open dish with the fish sealed in foil. It's best to use heavy foil, so that you minimise the risk of tears.

There are a number of approaches, but the most common one is to place the fish in a small amount of base liquid and then add some chopped onion, tomato and perhaps a little celery or parsley. I think that straight white wine is a little too strong for delicate fish, and prefer to use a mix of wine and water, or just plain water. A soy and water mix is also excellent, and if you go this way, why not add some garlic and ginger and create an Asian taste. I once ate trout that had been baked in peach juice with sliced peaches, onions and small potatoes thrown in too. It was outstanding.

When you use foil for this, make a little boat out of the foil with the ends tightly sealed, then roll-seal the top after everything has been popped inside. You can check progress from time to time by simply unrolling the top and having a look, but fillets generally cook fairly quickly. Twenty minutes in a moderate oven should see the job done.

When you want to bake a whole fish it is a good idea to leave the scales on, as they hold the moisture in the flesh. You can still slash the shoulder meat by going in at an angle with the knife to get under the scales. When the fish is cooked, the skin will come away in one piece, taking all the scales with it. Make sure the baking dish is well sealed and contains enough liquid to ensure that the fish does not dry out. It will take about 20 minutes to bake a fish up to 1 kg; allow an additional 10 minutes for every additional 500 g in body weight.

QUICK AND EXOTIC

I am not much interested in cooking fish in elaborate sauces, preferring the taste of fish just the way it is. An argument can be made in favour of a little exotica from time to time, though, such as when you find yourself eating a good deal of fish and need some variety, or when the fish itself is a second-rate table fish.

A quick and easy approach is to whip up an Italian-style tomato sauce by frying chopped onion and garlic, then adding a tin of peeled tomatoes, half a cup to a cup of white wine, a heaped teaspoon of sweet basil and a quarter to half a teaspoon of curry powder, although that's optional. Also optional is as much chilli as you fancy, or a big handful of black olives. When the sauce is prepared, simply drop fish cut into strips in it and gently simmer until cooked. This will only take a few minutes

Curry is also an option, if you find yourself with a lot of fish meat such as marlin, yellowfin, jewfish, or anything else that can be cut into chunks. Fry chopped onion and garlic, then add a tablespoon of curry powder, some cumin, turmeric and a good shake of coriander, plus chilli if you like it hot. Stir all this together in a pan with a cup of chicken stock, then pop it in the blender with some plain yoghurt and cream the lot. For something really special, peel a couple of sweet apples and blend these into the yoghurt before you add the curry sauce. You can then simply pour this mixture over steamed or grilled fish, if you want to preserve the flavour of the fish, or you can use it for poaching if the fish is of the mundane variety.

If you live near a Japanese supermarket, or a store that sells Japanese groceries, here is something very special. Buy yourself a bottle of mirin, which is a sort of sweet rice vinegar. Don't tell the Japanese what you want it for, as they don't use it this way at all and will think you are mad. You also need soy sauce for this — a light variety such as the Tamari sold in health food stores. You use small pieces of fish for this recipe, which is also great with prawns and scallops.

Put a huge dab of butter in the frying pan and melt it, then drop the fish in and cook it gently. When you turn the fish over, add half a cup of mirin and about a dessertspoon of soy sauce, stirring them into the butter to make a light brown sauce. The fish will be cooked by the time you have done this. Serve the fish with rice, pouring the sauce over the top. This sweet-salty sauce dish has never failed to convince people that I am a great cook, but it is a little rich for a main course. Serve it as an entree before something a little more basic.

FIELD COOKING

Some of the dishes mentioned above can easily be prepared in the field. Neither frying nor foil cooking presents any problems. The Italian sauce is particularly handy because it is a one-dish special and you can use it with pasta to produce a big, delicious meal. If you want to prepare some of the more fancy dishes in the field, mix your spices before you leave home and carry them in a couple of little jars instead of having to bring half the kitchen with you. It is also a good idea to precook and freeze a few exotic items and use these as your ice for the first day or so out, eating them as they thaw. If you chill everything before you put it in the ice box, and wrap the frozen food well in newspaper, you will be surprised at how long it stays frozen.

The best way I know of cooking fish in the field is to bake it in newspaper; foil runs a poor second. Light a good fire that will produce plenty of embers, then leave it to its own devices for a while as you prepare the fish.

Leave the fish whole, with the gut in, unless you have had to gut it earlier to keep it fresh. The gut will shrivel up into a hard little ball inside the fish as it cooks and can simply be discarded later. The idea is to keep the fish as well sealed as possible. Wrap the fish in a couple of sheets of newspaper, then dip the package in water (salt water if possible), and press the paper down onto the fish. Add a couple of sheets at a time, pressing them down and working them as you go to form a sort of cocoon of pulped paper around the fish. Use up to a dozen sheets of paper altogether, then pop the parcel into the embers of the dying fire. If the fire looks like losing all its heat inside the 20 minutes it will take to cook the fish, just build more fire on top of the fish parcel.

When you dig your fish out at the end of the cooking time, if all has gone well most of the outer layers of paper will have burned away, and the inner layers will be charred and stiff. When you peel these off, the scales and skin of the fish should come away too, leaving you with the most perfectly cooked fish you could imagine – fish that has been completely sealed to cook in its own juice.

RAW AND MARINATED FISH

Much of the art of preparing raw fish is contained in the earlier section that was devoted to preparing and storing fish. I had taken us as far as having perfectly cleaned, thoroughly dried pieces of fish wrapped tightly in plastic bags, which were to be left in the fridge for two to four days to tenderise. After that, take the fish from the fridge.

Prepare a bowl of water with plenty of ice in it. Remove the fish from the plastic bag, wash it under the tap, then wash it in the ice water. (If you want to do the full Japanese thing here, the person preparing the fish should also immerse their hands in the ice water until they are well chilled.) The fish is then once again thoroughly dried before being sliced at a low angle to produce quite thin slices.

Raw fish, when eaten in the Japanese manner (known as sashimi), is dipped in a mixture of soy sauce and wasabi (green horseradish paste) before being eaten. You can instead mix in a little chilli sauce with your soy instead of wasabi, or simply use plain soy.

The tunas are well suited to sashimi treatment, but any fish that cooks well will also be excellent raw. Whiting, snapper and bream are hot favourites with me.

Fish can also be marinated and pickled, but most of the marinade and pickling systems are so completely overpowering that the poor old fish doesn't get much of a look-in after a few hours sitting in the stuff. My preference is for white fish, thinly sliced, tossed lightly in a salad bowl – plastic or glass, not metal – with a mixture of onion rings and the juice of a couple of fresh lemons or limes. You should eat this straight-away, or leave it for a few minutes at the most. If you leave fish too long in citrus juice it will begin to pickle and you will lose the raw fish taste. Prawns are also delicious done this way; I like to add some crushed chilli to the juice before tossing. If the dish just happens to be standing somewhere close to an ice-cold gin and tonic, or perhaps a nice Chablis, life will generally look fairly rosy.

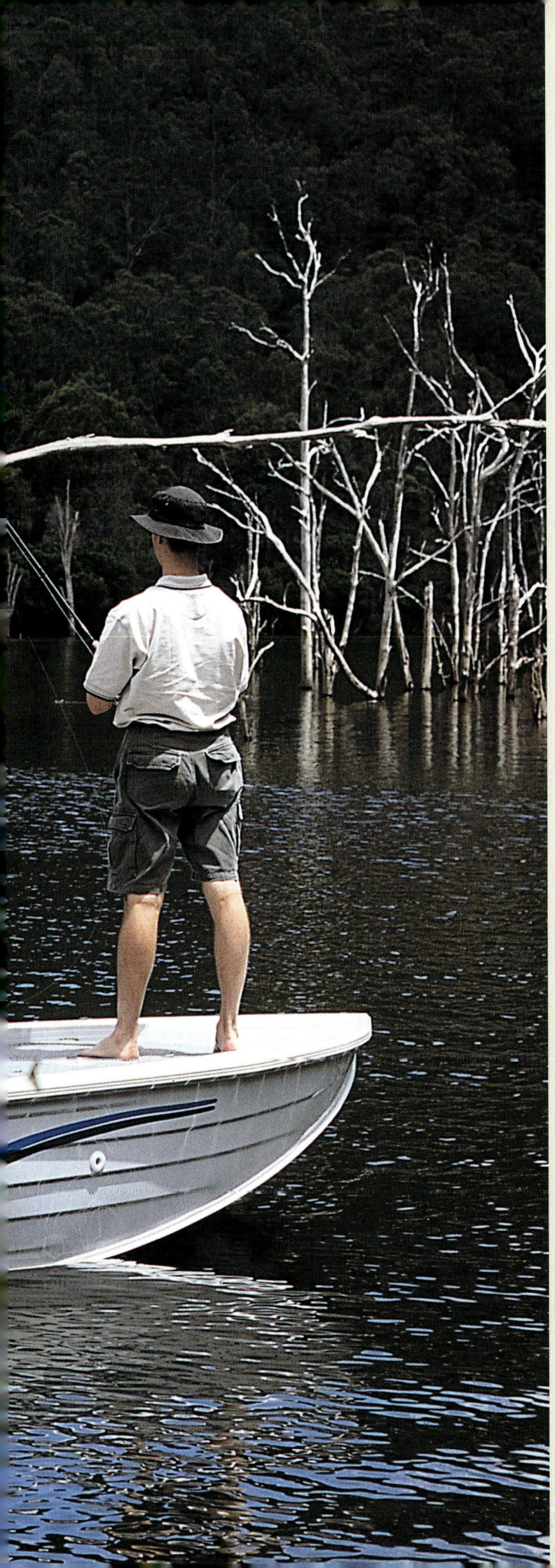

Chapter Nine

Hints for safe fishing, family fishing and travel

First aid kits

No matter how or where you fish, the first thing you should think about is what you would do if there were an emergency. Believe me, you will do all your best thinking about emergencies *before* they occur, not after. Because fishing is often done in remote and sometimes dangerous places, being in the habit of working out an emergency plan in advance is a good investment in your future.

I have owned quite a few first aid kits in my time, and hardly used anything out of any of them. You carry them around for years without using them, then suddenly first aid is required and you find that the thing you need most is not in the kit. That's just life, I guess. The experience has not turned me off first aid kits altogether, but it has taught me to carry in my kit only the things I am most likely to actually use.

Band-aids are always required for some little thing, and a tube of good antiseptic cream goes hand in hand with the Band-aids. The great majority of fishing wounds are superficial, but they can become infected and turn quite nasty if you don't get something on them right away.

The other fundamental is a bottle of antiseptic solution. You only need a small one, because one little bottle will do for even a serious injury. The only wound you can really do much about in the field is a cut, and the only thing you can do with a big cut is to get a pressure pack over it to control the bleeding and keep the wound clean until you can get the victim to professional help. So take a couple of substantial dressing pads and a big roll of wide sticking plaster.

None of this will be any good to you, though, if someone squashes the tube of ointment and it soaks through all the plaster, making it unsticky, at the same time reducing the dressings to a soggy mess. What you need is a good heavy plastic container with a tightly fitting lid. Put the ointment and bottle of antiseptic into a smaller rigid plastic container inside the big one; you might even decide to put all the individual items in their own snap-lock plastic bags. If you go to this little bit of trouble, when an emergency does occur your kit will be in good condition and easy to use.

Dealing with fish hooks

The thing all anglers dread is finding themselves on the hook instead of the fish, but if you go fishing long enough, the odds are that you will find yourself impaled sooner or later.

One of the things you can do in advance to make de-hooking yourself a little easier is to file down, or flatten with pliers, the barbs on your hooks. This is particularly true when you are using big-game and trolling hooks that often have needle points and razor edges filed on them, but a good argument can be made for cutting the barbs right back on any hook. Anglers using hooks with cut-down barbs say that there is no difference in holding power between these and regular hooks, and that they are far superior in terms of initial penetration.

When a large game hook goes in, it is best to visit the local hospital, because these hooks are big enough

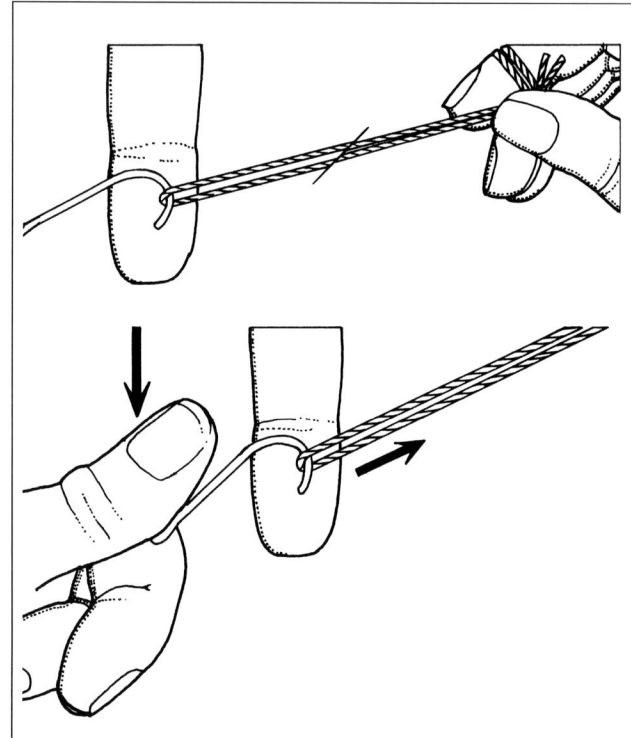

The downward pressure on the shank of the hook is most important when removing a hook that has the barb embedded in the flesh. This pressure forces the outside of the hook bend to press upwards into the wound as the hook comes out, allowing the barb to travel cleanly through the hole already created in the flesh. It sounds bad, but it works.

to cause quite severe nerve and ligament damage if they are not handled properly. However, you could find yourself in a situation where that is not an option. I heard of one incident where, arriving at a remote reef two days out from the mainland, well beyond helicopter range, the first fish to come on board left a crewman with a 12/0 stainless hook in through his wrist, with the point and barb concealed deep inside the palm of his hand. With gangrene a distinct possibility if the hook were left in for the two-day trip home, it was obvious that the hook had to come out right there and then. Fortunately, this proved to be relatively easy, and the victim was back fishing the same day. The fellow I spoke with, who actually removed that 12/0 hook, said he just couldn't believe how easily it came out.

The system for getting a hook out is the same whether it's large or small. The only difference in approach with regard to barbs is that you should cut the barb off first if it is protruding. The illustration shows exactly how to proceed, but it is important to remember to push down hard on the hook shank, and to make a very positive pull on the cord *in the direction in which the hook shank is pointing*. The bush surgeon on the job must understand that there is no room here for delicacy, and the big hit is the one that is the kindest to the patient.

It is also most important to ensure that the cord or line you use is up to the job and won't break, sending you back for another try. If you only have light line on hand, use four or five lengths together to ensure adequate strength.

A channel as wide as the hook and barb combined will have been cut when the hook went in, and the idea is to make it come back along exactly the same channel on the way out. The downward pressure on the shank brings pressure to bear on the outside of the hook bend, which has the effect of taking the barb right into the centre of that existing channel. Horrific as the system may sound in the telling, when it's done properly the hook comes out without resistance, and often the victim of the hookup feels little or no pain during the operation, or afterwards.

A great many hookups occur in the back of the neck, and in the scalp, ears and cheeks, all of which makes a very positive argument for wearing a broad-brimmed bush hat perched on the back of your head.

Human hookings really are a minor injury, and with a helpful mate on hand, a bottle of antiseptic and the right mental attitude, there's no need to waste more than a few moments of precious fishing time on such incidents.

Dealing with seasickness

Seasickness is a sickness of the head that manifests itself in the stomach. When we think we are going to get seasick, we do get seasick, and people who don't think about it usually don't suffer from it. While this is something of an oversimplification, it's not too far from the truth.

The right time to do something about seasickness is at least 24 hours before travelling. Whatever medication you plan to take, start taking it then to give your system time to adjust. Almost all such preparations will make you sleepy, so make the most of it and catch all the sleep you can.

New preparations come onto the market all the time. You can now take your drugs in tablet form, or buy little sticky patches that you put on your neck like a Band-aid, which allow the chemicals to seep into your bloodstream through your skin.

It is most important to believe that the medication you choose will work for you – I hold the conviction that this is every bit as important as the chemicals themselves. I am not in any way downgrading the effectiveness of the chemicals, but rather acknowledging the power of the human mind.

The more closely you follow your normal routine, the more likely you are to deal well with motion sickness. In other words, if you normally have three eggs and four pork chops for breakfast, eat three eggs and four pork chops before you go to sea. Don't have your stomach all out of gear before you hit the water. Whatever you do, eat! Fishing trips often have us heading off hours before we would normally have breakfast, so get something down that your stomach will feel comfortable with at that time of the day, and make sure you have plenty of sandwiches, dry biscuits or whatever to nibble steadily on all day long. Drink lemonade or any other lemon drink, but take care not to have more fizzy drink than you would normally have. I like to drink Coke at sea.

If you enjoy thinking about death and would like to know more about what it is like, spend the night before the trip out on the booze. Rum and red wine in quantity are recommended. I absolutely guarantee that you will see major benefits in being dead long before you return to shore.

Am I sounding like a wowser? I'm not really, and I frequently enjoy a few drinks in the company of friends and when making the most of a good meal. But I know it won't matter if 30 to 40 knots of southerly wind hammer the walls of my home when I've had one or two too many. My home can't sink, and there's no way I'll be leaving it to go to sea the morning after.

Exhaust fumes from boat engines are a major cause of seasickness, and although most people recognise diesel fumes as a regular culprit, some oils used in outboard fuel can also make people feel ill. I have conducted experiments on some unfortunate souls (who did not know at the time that they were helping the cause of inexact science), and can report that Valvoline oil was tolerated much better by some real basket cases than other oils that are often used to mix outboard fuel. It is well worth experimenting with fuel mixes if you have a family member or fishing mate with a serious seasickness problem.

There are a couple of things you should do the moment you start to feel a little off. First, don't delay – seasickness always gets worse, then hopeless, unless you do something positive to deal with it. Get yourself away from the engine fumes and into clean air; this normally means going from the back, where the exhaust is being released, to the front of the boat. Even though you may be well ahead of exhaust outlets in a big cockpit, there is usually a suction effect at work in a boat that pulls fumes back in over the transom. Get your head up, lock your eyes on the horizon, and suck in huge deep breaths of clean air.

Interestingly enough, if you can beat this initial onset of seasickness, you will usually be right to hop back into the cockpit after a while, and you will find yourself hoeing into the chocolate cake for morning tea and happily breathing in the same fumes that made you sick earlier. I never get sick in small boats, but often have an unsteady settling period in big boats, and the clean air and steady horizon works every time.

Rock fishing to stay alive

Rock fishing produces an extraordinary number of casualties: every year several people are swept to their deaths from rock platforms. Thousands of words of advice have been written on the subject, and the dangers have been well documented, but all such advice and warnings are ignored by the few who make up the frightening statistics.

To stay alive on the rocks you need to recognise just two facts: most anglers are swept from the rocks by ordinary waves, not freak waves, and anglers who are swept from the rocks are fishing spots where they are vulnerable to the sea, having made the decision to risk fishing in marginal or dangerous conditions.

That's all there is to it. They go down to the rocks and either don't bother to check the sea before they start fishing, or are aware of the danger and decide to chance it.

I have talked to witnesses of such fatal accidents, and they say the same thing over and over again. They express disbelief that the anglers involved could have been stupid enough to be fishing where they were in the prevailing conditions, and they marvel at the speed with which the drowning took place. The latter is particularly interesting, because even good swimmers seem to drown quite suddenly, sometimes after coming to the surface and appearing to be in good shape. My theory about this is that rock anglers are so totally unprepared mentally for an accident of this kind that they go into shock, and simply don't fight for their lives. There is a lot to be said for taking the attitude that you *could* go in whenever you fish the rocks, and working out how you would cope with the situation. Any survival plan at all in your mind would stand you in good stead.

The other thing that can make the difference between living and dying is knowing what the people on shore are going to do to save you. If your fishing group has a rescue plan worked out beforehand that is understood by all, the person in the water has something to hang onto, and their rescue will be effected a lot faster. If there is no plan, shock can render onlookers useless for some time: I have seen an onlooker who was required to help collapse in shock after seeing his mate go in. They were, by the way, fishing where no person in their right mind would have been fishing on the day. Same old story.

There are two kinds of sea conditions that create problems: local and distant storms. Of these, distant storms are by far the more dangerous. Local weather is obvious, with strong winds and a sea that *looks* rough. Distant weather can deliver huge swells out of perfectly calm and sunny conditions. The big trap is that these groundswells may come through in sets that are several minutes apart, so you could get a couple of modest sets in the first 10 minutes, with calm water in between, then a massive set in the fifteenth minute. An angler who had observed the sea for just the first set could be cleaned up in a big way by the following set. A newspaper would refer to these as freak waves, but they would have been just part of the wave pattern for that day.

Statistically, rock fishing is one of the world's most dangerous sports. Those who lack respect for the sea tend to have short careers as rock anglers.

Local rough weather is fairly easy to read; deep groundswells are not too hard to recognise, but they are very tricky to read. If you go down to the rocks and see marginal or doubtful conditions, keep in mind that the last bloke who drowned from the rocks saw much the same conditions as you are looking at, but decided to give it a go!

Skin care and sunburn

Anglers have a tougher job than most avoiding sunburn, because not only are they out in the sun for long periods of time, but they are also working on or near water, where there are reflected rays to cope with. Reflected glare sometimes does more damage to your skin than direct sunlight.

The angler's first line of defence is to cover up as much skin as possible with a broad-brimmed hat and a long-sleeved shirt. The sunscreen comes after that.

You need to pay quite a bit of attention to sunscreens – they are not all created equal, despite the claims printed all over the tubes. You need an SPF30+ broad spectrum product, and you need something that is as waterproof as you can get. My surfboard activities have allowed me to experiment with a lot of different sunscreens, and most that claim to be specialised swimming or surfing sunscreens wash off in the first few minutes. Having worked my way through all but the real El Cheapos, I have settled on the Hamilton brand, because (1) it stays on, and (2) the doctor who regularly cuts skin cancers out of me tells me to use that brand.

To get the best out of any sunscreen, apply it and rub it well into your skin 20 minutes before you go out in the sun, and then put it on again when you are out in the sun. That seems to work really well.

If you have been fishing for years, and whether you have or have not been taking a lot of care of your skin, I strongly recommend that you go and get a skin check. A lot of serious problems can be avoided with early intervention, and there are very effective creams that can be used to treat early stages of skin damage.

If you have really made a mess of yourself but not developed cancers that require surgery, there are ointments available that will clean up your skin. This treatment takes two to three weeks, but is more of a nuisance than anything else. You should try to avoid social engagements in the middle weeks, as you tend to be a rather colourful sight by that time. The end result is well worth the fuss, though.

Having skin cancers detected on your own personal hide also tends to give you greater incentive to adopt sensible sun habits.

Clothing

Fishing clothes used to be easy to identify – they were the oldest, most threadbare, moth-eaten things we owned. One fisherman who was famous for his shorts, which were rigid with blood and solid-baked fish slime, eventually had them forcibly removed by other fishermen, who could no longer bear to share a cockpit with the offending garment. They threw the shorts over the side of the boat, where they were gratefully ingested by a shark.

Now that we are all much more careful to avoid sunburn, being aware of the risks of skin cancer, we tend to be more thoughtful about what we wear when out fishing. On trips when I am going to be in the sun for long periods of time I now take along some light, long-sleeved shirts with a decent collar. Old cotton business shirts are ideal, or you can buy the army-style shirts popular with bushwalkers. Purchase them one size larger than needed, because the loose fit allows air to circulate freely inside. It helps to leave the sleeves down, with the cuffs unbuttoned. Alternatively you can buy those incredibly expensive specialised fishing shirts you see in fishing magazines these days – the ones that have loops and pockets and air vents from one end to the other. I had a couple given to me which I use to extend the life of my ex-business shirts.

Another interesting garment is those supershorts that come down past the knees. They look ridiculous but they do keep the sun off your knees when you are seated in a boat. You should also wear deck shoes, because toes, I have been told – by the man who is whittling me down to a human twig – are real hot spots for sun cancers.

Cold-weather anglers may be interested in another budget alternative to high-performance specialised outdoor wear. Apparently the single most important element in a garment's ability to keep us warm is the

thin layer of inert air on the inner surface of the material. Consider then, how much more effective than a single extra-bulky jumper would be the same thickness made up of sweatshirts! You might manage to cram on six layers of insulating air skins with them, where the jumper offers you only one. Furthermore, with the jumper you only have the choice of having it off or on. With the multi-layer approach you can adjust your temperature with great precision, which is useful when you start fishing in the dark, and then fish on past sunrise when things get gradually warmer. I

The author modelling this season's elegant fishing attire. A serious hat protects the neck, ears and face from direct sunlight, and Hamilton's sunscreen has proved to be the most waterproof and sweat-resistant product on the market. The prescription polaroids not only help to see the fish, they also keep stray hooks out of the eyes. Long sleeves and a collar that can be turned up complete the outfit.

have proved this system right for myself in the past, simply because I don't own any really warm clothes and have taken the multi-layer approach out of sheer necessity. It works!

The most waterproof coats are also, unfortunately, rather airproof, and you tend to get very hot and sticky in them after a while, particularly in warm weather. Stores specialising in outfitting campers and back-packers now sell wet-weather gear in all sorts of lightweight space-age materials that cost the earth but are, I feel, worth it, as they breathe quite well.

A lot of anglers wear hats for their fashion statement value, especially caps with all sorts of advertising logos stitched on the front. These are largely useless as protection from the sun – I strongly recommend wide-brimmed cowboy-style or gardening hats. The most effective of these make you look like a right nana, but you can do what the racing drivers do. They go racing in huge protective crash helmets, but the minute the serious stuff is over they slap on the sponsor's cap. Taking a leaf from their book, you can fish in your protective hat then take it off and slap on your spunky little fishing cap when you catch something worth having your photo taken with.

Try to avoid being a fashion statement when you go fishing and focus on the protective value of the clothing you choose. Years down the track you will be glad you did.

Footwear

Footwear is as important to the angler as it is to the athlete. The wrong footwear can be extremely dangerous, as is no footwear at all. An old barefooter from way back, I am now firmly in the camp of those who give a lot of thought to what they are putting on their feet before going fishing.

Obvious arguments in favour of footwear can be made by people who have had fish spines and large hooks in their feet, and by the many rock anglers who have gone for long slides on green weed and ended up in the barnacles. Even barefooters, when forced to spend a really hot day hopping from one foot to the other on a cockpit floor that is ready to fry the catch as it comes in over the side, see the value of deck shoes as the day wears on.

Anglers who like to fish right down close to the water from the rocks need to get themselves into the most specialised footwear of all – soft shoes or sandals fitted with cleats. The cleats are bolted into the sole of the shoe from the outside, so the angler is actually walking on a series of metal cutting edges that go right through the weed to take a grip on the rock below. Cleats are almost as specialised as ice skates, and do much the same job. Like ice skates, they are outstandingly successful when you are working in the environment for which they were designed, but pretty hopeless elsewhere. The biggest argument for wearing cleats, apart from the fact that they will stop you falling over all the time, is that you can actually run over a slippery surface when wearing them, and people who fish way down on those slippery weed ledges need to be able to run like hell when a big swell looms up.

Running shoes with those wonderful treads that athletes love are just about useless for all forms of fishing. They are fine when used for the constant, fluid forward movements involved in running, but when you perform various foot actions on a constantly changing surface, and especially on a surface with a lot of grip, such as you often get around the rocks, they actually tend to trip you. Boat skippers also hate them, because the treads pick up and tangle fishing line that a flat-soled shoe would have simply lifted straight off. Not surprisingly, deck shoes, with their low-profile sole patterns, are the very best things to wear in a boat, and the cheap ones are pretty much as good as the ones people pay through the nose for.

Socks have a minor value – they can help control sunburn across the tops of your feet and around your ankles. You can get an awful dose of burn in these areas in a boat, especially in small boats, where you are often seated with your feet poked out in front of you all day long.

If you are going for your first freshwater trip, remember that the beds of freshwater streams are usually covered in smooth, slimy stones. They are murder on bare feet, and footwear that provides good grip, plenty of ankle support and doesn't mind being wet all day is what you need. This could be just the time to dig out those old running shoes.

Thongs are no good for anything, although I do recall one time I would have killed for a pair. We were in an aluminium boat with a bare, heavily grooved aluminium floor, and we pounded into a 2 m breaking-head sea for 12 hours straight. I was barefoot, and by the middle of the day I could hardly bear the pain coming up through the soles of my feet as they absorbed one brutal shock after another. By the end of the day the soles of my feet were purple with bruising, and the next morning I had to be carried out to the car and carted off to the local chiropractor for a good stretch-and-crack routine. This did my spine and neck some good, but it was weeks before I could comfortably stand on my feet for any length of time. The most basic pair of deck shoes – even thongs – would have saved me all that grief.

My son Alex and his friend Michael Green are a formidable pair in a fishing boat. Far from asking for help, they constantly offer advice to their fishing seniors and, as often as not, out-fish them.

Family fishing

Whenever you think family fishing, you must have one overriding priority firmly established in your mind at all times, and that is safety. Safety first, second and third. The most awful stories to come out of fishing are those where some foolish person has caused the death of their own child by taking their family into a dangerous situation. Let's face it, enthusiasm for fishing borders on madness in many people, but a line must be drawn at endangering children, who rely entirely on your judgement for their wellbeing.

In my view, and I have a few healthy young anglers in my care, no-risk fishing is the only kind of fishing for kids. Beaches, river and lake banks and sheltered bodies of water in safe boats are fine, but the boats are only fine when the kids wear approved life jackets that fit them, and when they are constantly supervised by adults. If you can't afford life jackets, you can't afford to take your kids out onto the water. It's as simple as that, and there's no room for argument.

On the subject of life jackets, the law says you must have approved life jackets for your kids. But most kids simply won't wear the great, bulky, horse-collar things that are approved. You may have to have them in your boat, but I suggest that if you really care for your kids, investigate waterski or other types of personal flotation jackets for them. They don't mind wearing them and that is half the battle won. One more case of laws being drawn up by officials who don't know the front and back end of a boat from the horns and backside of a bull.

Some family groups grow into quite awesomely proficient fishing teams, but until they reach that stage, full-on serious fishing trips and family trips are best viewed as quite different outings, with you there with the family as guide rather than angler on family days.

Estuaries are undoubtedly the best places for family fishing, along with some of the sheltered freshwater impoundments. In fact, the new dams opening up great freshwater fishing along the east coast are proving so popular that they are actually turning the tide of fishing tourism. Years ago, inland anglers waited all year for the chance to go to the coast for what was perceived to be the best fishing, but now coastal anglers are going inland to enjoy superb impoundment fishing.

The best locations for family fishing are those that allow the children to fish for as long as they want, with the option of doing something else if they get bored. Beaches are good this way, and boating trips are also fine if there are plenty of opportunities for getting restless people ashore.

GETTING KIDS STARTED

The only sensible way to teach children to fish is to let them teach themselves. If you try to force the pace and make them do things *properly* before they are ready to do things that way, they will get bored, and will probably switch off altogether. They may even conclude – rightly – that 'fishing just makes the parents angry', and decide that it's best avoided.

Kids will start by playing at fishing, and you have to let them work through that at their own pace. If you are lucky enough to have a good population of tiddlers or toads around, let them get stuck into those for a while, with a heavy accent on the fact that the fish are babies that need to be returned to their mothers. Kids understand that. You may have to dodge the fishing inspector once or twice with marginal fish that junior is prepared to kill for, because to him these tiddlers appear huge and completely edible. We have only just passed through the stage of filleting with a magnifying glass at our house.

My youngest responds to being able to see something. Catching fish out of featureless water is all right, but wandering around a sand flat where he can actually see fish swimming is much more appealing. He has come through the stage where poking about in pools, or trying to work a yabby pump bigger than himself, filled his day, and the stage where he was happy winding in little tailor I trolled up. Now, at six,

Children are happy catching anything at all. As they get into fishing it pays to give them something more than basic gear, as they tend to learn very fast.

he wants to put his own baits on, is not bad at casting his own threadline outfit, and can hook and land a fish by himself. Short of watching carefully to ensure that he never lets a hook go anywhere near his eyes, I don't worry much about him sinking a hook into himself. That's not the end of the world.

Adults tend to get frustrated when they see children happily fishing the wrong way, perhaps hanging an oversized bait down into a cloud of tiddlers off the edge of a wharf. You have to back off and understand that if the child is not complaining, they are completely satisfied, and if you butt in you are going to spoil things. When they're not happy with what they are doing you will hear about it, and the only real reason for anyone to go fishing is to make themselves happy.

In our affluent society, quite a number of kids start fishing at gamefishing level in expensive boats, using very complex tackle. A number of top anglers have observed that these kids miss out rather badly by not working their way up through the more basic fishing styles, where many of the fundamental truths of fishing are better absorbed.

TACKLE FOR KIDS

Most children are bought threadline outfits to start off with, but there's an argument in favour of even more basic gear for the real beginners.

The plain plastic centrepin, which is the simplest, cheapest reel there is, should be given consideration for a number of reasons. The first is that it is virtually indestructible, so you only need grit your teeth and look the other way when children drag it through the sand or drop it in the water – they can't really hurt it. The second reason is that children find these reels very easy to use because the deep spool allows line to be retrieved without the need for fancy finger grips to stop it tangling around handles and other things. These reels don't produce tangles, and kids can cast with them simply by pulling a bit of line off by hand then tossing their bait a short distance. The reels are even better off wharves and out of boats.

When a child advises you that they don't want a kid's reel any more, that's when they're ready for something more complicated, and at this point you should probably buy something reasonably good.

Tackle can be roughly divided into three categories: junk, good, and the best. I would buy good tackle for my child, as the best often represents a quantum leap in price that is out of proportion to the increase in performance.

When buying tackle, bear in mind the physical limitations imposed not only by strength, but also by the actual shape of the little body involved. The right winch mount height for you on a threadline rod is likely to be unworkable for a child's shorter arms. Let your child handle the outfits under consideration, and give some thought to having a cheap custom rod made, one with a low reel-mount position.

Small boats

It is a little hard to define what is meant by a small boat. A 5 m boat designed for offshore work would be a big boat on a dam when a strong wind was giving the local punts a hard time, but the same craft would be a toy crossing a bar on a big day.

Most of the boats manufactured in this country meet very high safety standards, and most people who have spent a few years operating small boats in a sensible fashion come to the conclusion that those boats can handle far worse conditions than the owner would ever want to take them out in. So why have so many people drowned in boating accidents over the years? Most drownings are directly related to alcohol. People who have been drinking too much when operating a boat do something stupid because of the alcohol, and then, once in the water, they drown in a fraction of the time it would take a sober person to drown. That is a plain and simple fact.

Drownings occur quite frequently on bars at river entrances, and as with rock anglers, you have to put the majority of these fatalities down to operators deciding to take a chance. The odd boat is lost on a good day when somebody just gets their timing wrong, but most accidents occur when a skipper goes out in a sea capable of completely overwhelming the boat, and pushes the odds just that little bit too far.

Novice skippers should regard all bars with great caution, and only take them on in the most favourable conditions. Work the bar on the run-in tide only, and make sure you are back in before the tide starts to run off. It is possible to go out in the morning with a low swell hardly producing a bump over a bar, and then find, a few hours later, when the onshore wind has come up and the tide has turned, that the swell is standing up in 2 m waves that are breaking with only a few metres between them. When you are in a new area it is a good idea to watch a bar right through the top and bottom tide shifts to see what you are going to have to deal with. You can't come to any worthwhile conclusions by looking at a bar at one time on one day.

It is also very important to remember that your boat doesn't stay in the one place inside or outside a bar. You can pull up for a look, with the wind in your face, only to find out that you are being carried into the wind at a rate of knots by the tide.

One little trick is to note where the main body of water carries on out to sea beyond the bar. You can usually see this quite clearly – it is the path displaced sand will be taking when the tide runs out, and it will be the area where you could get waves popping up out

The term small boats means different things to different people. On a bass lake a small tin boat (top) is just fine, but on a working bar even a solid fibreglass offshore model (above) can suddenly seem rather small.

of the blue well clear of the bar. It is a good idea to try to get clear of the run of tide at the first opportunity after you clear the main surf line.

The last big problem area is the way boat anglers ignore weather forecasts. Boats go missing in howling gales, and you find that a gale warning had been out for 48 hours. Weather forecasting is an inexact science, but you have to be a colossal fool not to check the forecast before you plan a fishing trip, and then again immediately before you leave. If you are planning an extended trip over a period of days, a radio capable of picking up local weather updates is essential.

Offshore winds – those blowing off the land and out to sea – are the most dangerous. In quite strong winds it can remain reasonably calm close to the shore, but the further out you go, the stronger the wind gets and the rougher the sea becomes. A lot of people have died when their boats have broken down within a few hundred metres of shore in calm water, then ended up 20 km out in mountainous waves. In fact, you can almost count on a drowning somewhere along the coast every time we experience an offshore gale. A 27 MHz radio is an essential part of the basic fit-up of any offshore boat, as is a substantial anchor, a good length of heavy chain, and a realistic length of rope. By realistic, I mean a length of rope that will give you some chance of holding bottom in heavy weather. That translates to at least 3 m of length for every metre of depth; 4 or 5:1 would be a better margin.

Few people have any idea how to judge their distance offshore, or to estimate roughly where they are in relation to a known landmark. These days, most boats have a compass and an echo sounder on board, and if you use the compass to take a bearing off any obvious landmark, and then take a reading off the depth sounder, you can give rescuers a pretty good idea of where you are. They will know that if they come off that landmark and head out along the given bearing until they have your depth reading, they are likely to find you.

Of course you can't beat GPS, which allows you to radio in your exact position.

But none of that works if your problem is a flat battery. The only defence against that is to have logged on with the local rescue authority on the way out, giving them an idea where you are going and when you expect to return. That way, when you go overdue they can initiate a request for boats in the area to look out for you, and if enough time goes by they will come looking for you. Guess what? Only one in five boats passing under our local search and rescue tower bother to log on! People are just queuing up to die at sea.

Anyone who takes a small boat to sea must ensure that both the boat and skipper are sound. It is rare for well-informed locals to lose their boat and their life, but not so uncommon for ill-prepared boats with a good store of booze on board to go missing with all hands. The open sea is a place for sober and serious people, not drunken fools.

The travelling angler

It wasn't so long ago that 'travelling' in this country meant catching a train to a regular holiday resort not too far from home. The family car changed all that dramatically, and these days a lot of Australians are using aircraft the way our parents used motor cars to explore the most remote regions of this wonderful country.

When you travel by car you can hook up a trailer on the back and take everything, including the kitchen sink, with you. Instead of being selective with your tackle, you can just take the lot, which means you will never be caught without a particular item. You don't even have to worry about sorting it out – you can pile the lot into cardboard boxes and pick out what you want when you need it. It's just like fishing at home.

BOAT TRIPS

Extended boat trips put a little more pressure on the angler, as space is at a premium on most boats and you need to think about what you take, and how you take it. It is best to have a good planning session well ahead of time to see how much gear can be pooled, to avoid doubling up. You also need to be sensible about rods, unless you have a great deal of out-of-the-way storage, because nothing will ruin a boat trip quicker than a forest of rods sprouting up everywhere.

Big charter boats are another proposition altogether, and you need to check them out fairly carefully when you book, as they all work slightly different systems. The best system for many people is the one where they supply rods and reels you know are in good condition. Most work on a 'pay for what you lose' basis when you fish lures, so of course many anglers prefer to supply their own.

Charter boats were once a pretty risky business, as far as the quality of the tackle and service went, but the competition in Australia is quite stiff these days, and most companies now offer good service. In fact, be prepared for operators to take a great interest in your gear and the way you want to fish, and don't be offended if they suggest changes. It is in their interest to have you land fish, not lose them, as your success is good for business.

The same quality of service cannot be expected once you move outside Australia to fish some of the Pacific islands. Some skippers may try to use unacceptably out-of-date fishing techniques, so it's wise to take your own gear.

All of this raises the subject of just how much you should put yourself in the hands of any guide. That really depends on how experienced you are. Fishing with a guide is not some sort of exam where you have to prove yourself; the best guides will quietly try to find out just how much you know, then give you as much help as you need to catch fish. If you are right on top of your tackle and fishing techniques, they will put you where the fish are and leave you to it, but if you need to be shown how to fish, a good guide will do that too. Ask all the questions you want to ask and be ready to display your ignorance. A good guide will appreciate this, because it helps them sort you out. If you think you know a better technique than the one being used, ask if they ever fish the way you have in mind, or use the lure you want to try. Guides aren't gods, and sometimes the remoteness of their location cuts them off from new developments. Few of them are fools, though, so be diplomatic when you discuss options and alternatives.

TRAVELLING BY AIR

Nothing puts the angler to the test more than a trip involving air travel, especially when that trip involves light aircraft. People do not understand that the safety requirements for light aircraft operators are very strict indeed – they simply cannot overload a plane just to

please the angler who wants to take everything 'just in case'. Pilots also show a noticeable lack of enthusiasm for great heaps of fishing rods lying in the aisle. I have seen some very disappointed anglers heading off on holidays with most of their tackle remaining at the departure point. Check out your baggage allowance and stick to it. Fishing rods can be a real nuisance in an aircraft, mostly because of their length. Two metres in length tests the limitations of most light aircraft, and the patience of pilots and other passengers. Check very carefully with the airline involved regarding baggage limits before you pack.

The Great Northern Safari

Every angler wants to do the big trip up north where exotic species, and fish in general, abound. This is the home of the barramundi, queenfish, huge trevally, mackerel of all kinds, mangrove jack and a whole lot more.

Once considered the trip of a lifetime, it is becoming more common these days to find anglers cutting down on time spent fishing local waters in order to concentrate resources into one or two big northern trips per year.

Many take the do-it-yourself approach, driving to the Northern Territory or Cape York in their own four-wheel drive with a boat on the roof rack and a trailer full of camping gear tagging along behind. This is the cheapest way to do the trip, but it means that a lot of your holiday time is wasted on the road travelling. Arriving at the other end, anglers sometimes find that even in a fishing paradise you still need to know where to go fishing, and a lot more time is wasted sorting out where fish are to be found.

With leisure time seemingly harder and harder to come by these days, increasing numbers of anglers are opting to fly in and retain the services of professional fishing guides. Guided fishing can be anything from a one-man bush camp operation to lodges or mother ships, the top end of fishing packages. At the time of writing I have just returned from a week on the *Tropic Paradise*, a 19 m catamaran operating out of Bamaga on Cape York Peninsula. If I tell you a little about that trip you will understand why the tropical north is such a powerful magnet for anglers.

The boat itself is as comfortable as a fishing boat can get. Being a cat with a huge beam, it barely moves about at all as it skims over the water. It has two state-rooms with ensuite facilities, then four more cabins with double-decker bunks. The lounge/dining area is vast, and the cockpit is more or less a workstation for rigging and fish cleaning. Up top you have a big sun deck where pre-dinner drinks and sashimi are served every evening. The angler does nothing but fish for the entire trip – a full-time chef ensures that the meals are always in the gourmet class. And nobody ever goes hungry, with mud crab, barramundi, steaks and so on served every evening.

The mother ship steamed down the west coast to Port Musgrave on the first day, and anchored in the calm water of the Wenlock River. The trip to the fishing grounds allows the anglers to get to know one another, and it doesn't take long for all to be on a first-name basis.

The next morning anglers take to the 5.4 m fibreglass fishing boats – there is a guide in each boat – and head off over the flat calm sea, or into the river system.

That first morning, with all the guides doing their first trip for the season, the boats caught barramundi, fingermark, blue salmon, grunter, bream and groper. What's more, even the least experienced anglers caught good fish. With the area and tides sorted out, the next

One of the best mother shipping operations in the business, the 19 m *Tropic Paradise* offers comfortable accommodation, excellent cuisine, first-rate guides and solid fibreglass fishing dinghies on long-range operations around Cape York.

day saw us fishing mud drains on the turn of the tide. The baitfish were clustered around the shallow entrance, waiting for the tide to give them enough water to escape over the flats, where the barra would find it hard to get at them. In the meantime, the barra were almost as thick as the bait, and slamming any kind of lure that was thrown near them. In the middle of the barra bite I caught a 6 kg groper that really gave me a stretch on light tackle.

That night we steamed north to the mouth of the Jackson River, where the mud flats of the Wenlock gave way to beautiful yellow sand beaches and flats. We looked over the transom of the mother ship to find that two Queensland groper, both in the 100 kg range, had taken up station right at the back of the boat, obviously well aware that fishing boats meant easy pickings when fish were filleted at the end of the day.

Stepping down into our dinghy at the start of the day I had no idea that this would be one of the wildest days of fishing I had experienced in over 50 years of angling. It started out quietly enough, heading out over a smooth sea to try some small patches of reef just a couple of kilometres offshore. The reefs were dead, and with no sign of working birds anywhere on the horizon, we decided to head back into the river to try for barramundi. That's when we spotted a number of birds working bait in close to the beach.

As we approached it became obvious that this was a major bait school. It shimmered over a great area of clear water that was just a little over 1 metre deep. Then the whole surface erupted as thousands of baitfish took to the air to escape predators from below, making a noise as loud as heavy rain on a roof. Terns swooped on the hapless bait, then from below, big queenfish – over 1 metre long – exploded out of the water in great bursts of spray. The noise was incredible as the bait tried to flee and the feeding fish crashed back into the water. You could look straight down over the side of the boat and see metre-plus fish everywhere.

My companion cast a popper, and as he retrieved, the water boiled behind it time after time as big fish struck and missed the surface lure. Finally one connected, doing a headstand with the tail turning the water to froth until getting purchase and tearing away in an incredible run, terminating in a cartwheeling

A typical Cape York situation: on the right, about a metre of clear water over a yellow sand bottom. What looks like a stream of dark bluewater in the centre is a school of bait made up of many millions of tiny fish, and beyond that is clear blue sea. It won't be long before that bait will be hit hard by predators of all shapes and sizes.

jump. I cast, and a fish that must have been watching the lure coming down through the air engulfed it as it touched down. Now we had two big fish going berserk!

It went on and on like that, with the bait school at one time appearing as a dark, shimmering river some 5 metres wide by 30 or more metres long. Great and golden trevally moved in with the queenfish, along with sharks that ranged from teenagers to soberingly large specimens. I hooked the biggest queenfish I'd ever seen and he ran and jumped until I thought my arms must come loose from their sockets. Finally, long after he should have gone belly-up, he gave one last powerful surge and a series of leaps immediately ahead of a huge shark that engulfed him in one bite!

There came a time when we simply couldn't keep doing this. The big queenfish and trevally had given the light tackle a terrible hiding, and the drag in my reel sounded as if someone had thrown a handful of sand in there. It was time to take a lunch break back at the boat and allow the arms to recoup.

That afternoon we decided on a more leisurely approach to the fishing, heading way upstream to the point where the tidal salt water gave way to fresh water running off the flood plains. I have never seen a river as pretty as the Jackson, even though I have seen quite a lot of Australia's north now. Bank-side vegetation gave way to stands of Nepa palms that rattled in the breeze, brilliant green stands of reeds and waterlilies appeared, and sand beaches and bars sprinkled the banks and the main body of water.

In the fresh we started to cast to an abundance of snags and dark undercuts. This is critical fishing, with the lures landing within centimetres of cover to be engulfed by barra, saratoga, mangrove jack, tarpon and other assorted species, all intent on making it back into the tangled branches to break free.

A torrential tropical rainstorm drenched us at one point, but half an hour after it had passed we were bone dry again. In that heat, frozen bottles of water get you through the morning and afternoon fishing sessions, then there is the sheer bliss of a hot shower, a cold beer and a superb meal with excellent wine to prepare one for a night of blissful sleep.

Six days went by like that, with the fishing never slackening in pace. One day in the fresh, another on the tidal creek for barramundi, a session chasing big longtail tuna, then a frantic session on grey, narrow and broad-barred Spanish mackerel. It was on a school

of mackerel that I had my lure ready to lift from the water when a Spaniard came from below at speed, took the lure and kept on coming straight into the boat. You should have seen the fancy dancing going on as we dodged those razor-sharp teeth!

Greg Bethune, the skipper of *Tropic Paradise*, moves around the fishing boats all day with his video camera, catching the action. With dinner out of the way we would all sit back with a drink and watch the day's footage. At the end of the trip we were each presented with our own copy of the compiled tape, which was a lovely touch.

This operation caters for every kind of fishing, including baitfishing for those who are not up to speed with their casting, and saltwater fly for those who are expert in that art. The guides are excellent, tutoring and coaching those who need help, and at the end of the trip most of us came away better fishermen. I know

One angler's vision of paradise: on Cape York Peninsula, the top of the Jackson River where palm trees take over from mangroves. Freshwater barramundi, jacks and saratoga are all on the job in the snags.

The mother ship has attracted several groper between 100 and 150 kg in weight. Work experience guide Lee Hodgetts starts off with a large fish carcass and quickly finds himself clutching a small tail. That's Cape York for you.

some people who have taken trips like this for the coaching alone.

For an idea of the range of packages and services on offer, most of the fishing magazines now run a directory section where you will find advertising for a host of operators. If you would like to check this particular operation out, go to the website at www.seafaris.com, or phone (07) 4096 5632.

However you go about it, don't deny yourself the angling experience of a lifetime in the tropical north of Australia.

Further reading

For a handy reference to fish species, most highly recommended are *Sea Fishes of Southern Australia* by Barry Hutchins and Roger Swainston (Swainston Publishing, Perth, 1986), and *Marine Fishes of North Western Australia* by Gerald R. Allen and Roger Swainston (published by the West Australian Museum, 1988). Both books contain superb colour illustrations of all of the common – and many of the rare – Australian species, with a list of the dangerous fish and how to deal with the various stings and wounds they can inflict, along with advice on first aid when poisonous species have been consumed. Both are a must for any serious angler, as the great majority of the species dealt with are also common to the east coast.

For those heading for Western Australia, *Fishing the Wild West*, by Ross Cusack and Mike Roennfeldt (St George Books, Perth, 1987), is a superb reference on local methods and the Western Australian fishing grounds. Once again, because there is so much overlap of species, this is also a book from which east coast anglers can learn a lot.

L. & J. McEnally have produced an excellent book on baits and rigs, and if you really want to tie yourself in knots, check out the *Guide To Rigging Braid-Dacron and Gelspun Lines* and *Complete Book Of Fishing Knots & Rigs*, both by Geoff Wilson.

If you want to know more about sonar and GPS, my book for Lowrance Australia, *The Lowrance Book of Sonar & GPS* is a bit old now (published in 1996) but the principles are still solid. You can contact Lowrance Australia or *Freshwater Fishing Australia* magazine for it.

There are literally dozens of fishing books published in Australia every year, and a lot of imports come into the country. Most bookshops carry some, and tackle stores carry some. If you want to know everything that is available, buy a copy of *Freshwater Fishing Australia* or *Saltwater Sportfishing* magazine and check out their mail order service. If it's in print, they sell it.

Naturally, the Internet is also a great resource for anglers. In addition to dedicated fishing sites, you can go to Google (or your search engine of choice) and enter 'Articles on gelspun fishing line', or whatever you want to know about, and you will be hit with an avalanche of articles on the subject from around the world.

Glossary

back casting: A false cast to the rear to load the rod.

bail arm: A spring loaded wire arm on threadline reels, used to pick up or release line.

baitcaster: A small, overhead reel or short overhead rod.

Bait Runner: A type of threadline reel which includes a free-spool device

baitball: A term used to describe a tightly packed school of bait fish.

barrel sinker: A free-running sinker shaped like an elongated barrel

bean sinker: A free-running, bean-shaped sinker commonly used in estuary fishing.

berley: Fed into the water to produce a stream or slick designed to attract fish, berley may consist of grains, chicken laying pellets, weed, chopped or crushed fish frames or whole fish etc. Fish oil is often added to produce a surface slick. Sometimes called 'ground bait' when used in such a way as to be released on or near the bottom.

berley pot: A plastic or metal pot set on the back of a boat to dispense berley. The sides of the lower half of the pot are perforated with holes and a metal ram with teeth is used to crush the berley in the pot, allowing a stream of fine particles to escape through the holes. Plastic pots are preferred as they produce less noise than the metal pots.

bib: A stiff metal or plastic sheet projecting from the face of a lure, a bib causes the lure to wobble and produces a swimming action. The bib can also be used to make the lure dive, the length, shape and placement of the towing point on the bib determining how deep it will dive and run.

blank: The basic fibreglass or composite blank on which guides and winch mountings are placed to produce a fishing rod.

blob: A specialised wire or timber float designed to be packed with, and dispense berley. Normally associated with herring fishing.

blooper: A surface popping lure with a deep concave face in the head of the lure. Bloopers are the noisiest of the sonic lures and are usually worked with a sharp tug on the line that causes the lure to make a single loud 'pop' or 'bloop'.

bobby cork: Most commonly made from Polystyrene foam these days, bobby corks are a top-shaped running float, frequently used in rock fishing.

bomb: Berley bombs are normally made by mixing the berley in use with wet sand. This is then fashioned into a hard ball or 'bomb' which gradually breaks up as it descends to the bottom. Berley bombs are also used by anglers, usually shore based luderick anglers, who need to be able to throw the berley out some distance from the shore. Metal cages and jam tins used to get berley to the bottom before release are also sometimes referred to as bombs.

breaking strain: Breaking strain is a term used to define the strength of fishing line. It refers to the theoretical minimum weight that would break the line if suspended by it. Since this represents breaking strain under absolutely ideal conditions, which are automatically compromised when the first knot is tied in the line, anglers work on applying pressure of no more than one-third of the breaking strain to the line at any time.

bubble float: A ball-shaped clear plastic float that can be filled with water to negate buoyancy. Normally used in freshwater fishing.

bug: A type of running lead sinker, oblong in shape and slightly flattened.

butt: The lower part of a fishing rod below the reel seat fitting.

catch-and-release: Releasing fish caught unharmed, catch-and-release often includes tagging the fish for research purposes (also see tag).

centrepin reel: Any direct drive, un-geared reel where a simple spool rotates over a central axle.

ciguatera: A form of poisoning associated with some tropical and sub-tropical fish. Ciguatera poisoning may occur when a person eats a large quantity of an affected fish, or it can be an accumulative poison building up over a period of time when tropical fish are eaten very regularly. Barracuda, Chinaman-fish and red bass should never be eaten, and large specimens of Spanish mackerel and coral trout are potentially poisonous. The symptoms of ciguatera poisoning may occur within an hour or two of eating the meal, but they may also be delayed by as much as twenty-four hours and are always significantly increased if alcohol as been consumed. Muscle aches and a tingling sensation at the extremities of the limbs, nose, ears or lips are experienced. Nausea, vomiting and muscle weakness follow, with reversal of temperature sensation. Seek medical help immediately.

cleats: Serrated-edged metal plates fixed to the bottom of shoes to enable rock anglers to walk on slippery rock surfaces.

cliff gaff: A form of grappling gaff used by rock anglers to retrieve fish when fishing from high cliffs and ledges.

closed-face reel: A form of spinning reel where the spool is fitted with a cover allowing the line to emerge through a small hole located in the centre of the cover

countershading: The natural colour scheme of the great majority of fish where a dark or brightly coloured back graduates to lighter sides and usually white belly. The object is to make the fish difficult to sea when viewed from any angle.

crimping: Using a small metal tube in place of a knot when rigging with wire or heavy monofilament. The two lengths of line or wire used in the connection to hook, swivel or double are run through the crimp which is then compressed with a special crimping tool.

CRT: A cathode ray tube display, similar to a television screen, usually associated with echo sounders.

deep diver: A lure with a long and sometimes wide bib designed to dive quickly and run well below the surface of the water.

double-handed threadline: Any threadline rod requiring two hands to cast. Double-handed threadline rods may be short, but heavy and powerful rods, or long rods with a high reel seat position.

downrigger: A device used to set lures at a particular depth while trolling. The basic downrigger consists of a heavy lead ball on a cable and a winching device to raise and lower the cable. The rod is set behind the downrigger winch and the line is connected to the weight with a release clip with an appropriate length of line from the clip to the lure. Some downriggers have counters so that the operator can set the depth required, but in some cases the weight can be seen on a good echo sounder and this then can be set to match the depth of fish seen on the sounder. When a fish takes the lure the line is released from the clip and the fish is played on the rod in the normal fashion.

drag system: A clutch inside a fishing reel which can be pre-set to release line under pressure when a specified amount of pull is applied. It is normal practice to set the drag resistance at one-third the breaking strain of the line so that a reel loaded with 12 kg breaking strain line would have the drag set to release line when pressure at the reel exceeds 4 kg.

draw-and-sink: A method of working lures, flies or bait where the rod tip is used to draw the line inwards and upwards, then the rod tip is lowered to allow the lure or bait to sink back to the original depth. An ideal system to use when the fish may be found at varying depths.

dropper: This term is used to describe a short trace taken out at right angles from the main line to attach a hook or hooks, usually above a sinker in rigs used for deep sea bottom fishing. The term drop is also used to describe the length of line between rod tip and sinker or lure when casting.

dry flies: Freshwater flies that are tied or coated so that they float on the surface of the water.

ebb tide: The run-out tide also referred to as a falling tide.

echo sounder: A sonar device fitted to boats firing a sonic pulse to the bed of the sea. The signal bounces back and the sounder times the returning pulse to reproduce the bottom shape on a screen. Sounders are also capable of displaying fish and bait schools in the path of the signal.

feathering: Placing the thumb lightly on the flange of an overhead reel during a cast to prevent overrun.

fixed head gaff: Any gaff that has the hook permanently fixed to the shaft.

fizzer: A surface lure fitted with one or more small propellers that rotate to make a noise when the lure is moved forward through the water.

flat line: A line that is taken down from the rod tip and attached to a lower towing point on the boat. Elastic bands are often used to secure the line to the reel, deck cleats or towing eyes low on the transom of a boat.

float: Anything used to suspend a bait at a fixed depth.

floating bait: An unweighted bait that is allowed to sink slowly in a natural manner.

floating bodied lures: Lures with bodies that will float on the surface. Floating bodies are often used in conjunction with deep diving bibs to produce a lure that can be dived deep in the midst of a snag tangle, then allowed to float to the top to be worked slowly over obstacles directly in its path. Most poppers and fizzers are also floating bodied lures that can be left sitting quietly on the surface between rod tip movements.

fly: A fly is usually an imitation of an insect or bait that is made by tying materials directly onto a hook. Feathers, animal hair and a range of modern synthetic materials are used in the construction of flies. The smallest freshwater flies are the size of a match head while some of the saltwater flies used on game fish may be 15 cm or more in length. Popper flies and other specialised types are also used, but purists argue that these are lures and not true flies.

fly line: A special type of line used to cast flies which have little or no weight of their own. The line itself is manufactured to have sufficient bulk and density to be cast on its own delivering the fly on a series of tippets of descending weight tied to the end of the fly line. Fly lines are as short as 10 m in length and as long as 30 m, and are usually backed up with an appropriate length of dacron line. Fly lines come in floating and sinking types, and offer a range of tapers and weights to suit various rods and casting jobs.

fly lining: A term most commonly used in the United States to describe fishing with a free swimming bait on an unweighted line.

flying gaff: A type of gaff normally used in gamefishing where the gaff hook slides free from the pole. The hook has a length of rope attached to it and after the pole has been used to place the hook up against the fish, the rope is used to actually sink the gaff and hold the fish.

foregrip: The cork or hypalon hand grip located on a rod above the reel seat.

free spool: Refers to any reel being fished out of gear.

gaff: The basic gaff is a timber or aluminium handle with a large hook set in the end to facilitate the handling and landing of large fish. Some gaffs include a leather wrist strap in the end. Also see cliff and flying gaffs.

ganged hooks: Refers to the practice of running the point of one hook through the eye of the next to link a series of hooks. The rig is used to present whole fish baits with three to six hooks, and sometimes two hooks are rigged back-to-back for use with strip baits.

gape: The distance between the shaft and the point of a hook.

gear ratios: All geared reels state a ratio which determines the number of spool revolutions that occur with each turn of the handle. Care should be taken to note that the outside diameter of the reel spool has a considerable effect on retrieve speed achieved, and that a large reel geared at 4:1 may well be retrieving more line per turn of the handle than a small 6:1.

gimbal apron: A shield, normally heavy plastic, fitted with a free-moving gimbal device into which the base of a rod is slotted when fighting a fish. The apron is strapped around the angler's waist so that the shield covers the whole groin

and lower stomach area. The gimbal is fitted inside with a cross bar that locks the butt of the rod firmly into place.

gimbal fitting: A metal fitting fixed to the butt of a rod. This is designed with a cross-shaped receiver in the face which locks onto the bars located in gimbal aprons and the base of rod holders fitted to fishing boats. The idea of the fitting is to lock a rod firmly into place in a boat's rod holders so that the reel and guides are always on top of the rod. This is mainly to stop the rod rotating and allowing a tight line to rub on the frames of roller guides and become damaged. The gimbal apron came into use to protect anglers from the potential of a gimbal fitting to bruise the groin severely when fighting a fish.

GPS: GPS stands for Global Positioning System, a series of satellites put into orbit by the United States Defence Department to facilitate its 'Star Wars' programme. The system is also available to the civilian population. With a receiver and display terminal it is possible to fix position anywhere on the face of the earth with greater accuracy than can be achieved with any other navigation system available.

grinding ratio: Slang terminology for the lower gear ratio on reels offering low and high gearing.

guides: Rod guides are actually line guides, used to direct the line along the length of the rod and to distribute pressure evenly over the curve of the rod when fighting a fish. They may be as basic as an elongated 'S' shape used on the lightest fly rods, or as sophisticated as the very heavy-framed roller guides used on heavy game rods. Rod guides are generally judged by their ability to minimise friction on the contact surface. Friction can cause a build up of heat capable of causing damage to monofilament line, and can even cause the line to break. Ring guides are the type used on the majority of fishing rods, and these are generally manufactured with a metal foot and frame encompassing a ceramic inner liner of some kind.

handcaster: A simple plastic spool with a flattened lip on one side to facilitate casting a line by hand.

handline: Any fishing line that is not used with the aid of a rod or reel.

helmet sinker: A helmet shaped sinker used in surf fishing.

hot spot: Created when guides are incorrectly located on a rod, causing the line to cross the guide at a harsh angle causing friction. A hot spot is also a good fishing location.

jig: This term is normally reserved for lures that have no built-in action and rely entirely on rod tip movement to impart action to the lure. Almost any metal lure can be fished with a 'jigging' action, a useful technique when angling for bottom-dwelling species or fish that may be suspended in mid-waters. A broad range of metal casting lures are sometimes incorrectly termed jigs.

jig rod: A rod specially designed for bluewater jig fishing where sufficient tip power is required to impart lively action to large lures in very deep water Also often used for casting heavy lures.

lateral line: A line, often clearly seen as a hard ridge, running along the centre of the side of a fish. Sensitive to vibration, this lateral line allows the fish to build up a picture of movement in the water around it.

LCG: Stands for liquid crystal graph display on an echo sounder. LCD, liquid crystal display, is also sometimes used to describe the same thing.

lever drag: A lever operated cam system for applying pressure on a reel's drag system (also see star drag).

Loran-C: An American navigation system based on radio signals.

memory: Fishing line is said to have a strong memory when it retains the shape of the coil after being removed from the spool.

minnow: A small elongated bait fish. The term 'minnow' is used to describe all timber and plastic bodied lures based on the tapered cigar like body shape of the minnow.

monofilament: Material used to manufacture the great majority of fishing lines used in the world today.

mono trace: A trace made up from monofilament line.

neap tides: The period of the moon phase when tidal movement is at a minimum.

Overhead reel: Includes the entire family of reels that are fished on top of the rod, all of which are revolving spool types. Most of the smaller, lighter reels are casting models, and only the full gamefishing reels have no casting ability.

overrun: A tangle of line created when the speed of the reel spool exceeds the speed of the casting weight allowing line to bunch up in front of the reel without being carried away.

parabolic: The even curve described by a rod with uniform wall strength throughout the blank.

pelagic: Surface dwelling fish of the open sea.

picker's doom: Also known as channel sinker, the picker's doom is a free-running sinker designed with a big open channel down the centre to allow line to slide freely through without offering any resistance. Commonly employed in rigs used to fish fast running tidal waters.

plug caster: An American term used to describe baitcasting outfits, most commonly double-handed rods.

polaroids: Sunglasses using the polarising principle of sandwiching lens elements to almost completely eliminate surface glare on the water. This greatly enhances the angler's ability to see fish under the water.

popper: Any of the surface lures employing a concave or angled face to create noise and surface disturbance.

recovery speed: The speed at which a rod tip returns to the original position after having been deflected.

reel seat: The cylindrical fitting used to attach a reel to a rod. Reel seats, or winch fittings, are made of stainless steel, carbon fibre or aluminium, and usually have a fixed hood to receive one side of the reel foot, then a movable hood backed by threaded locking nuts to secure the other.

Rockhopper: Colloquialism for anglers who specialise in fishing from the rocks.

roller guide: A rod guide in which the line passes over a rolling wheel set inside a fixed frame, usually metal. Roller guides are used on gamefishing rods where extreme pressures on the line cause serious heat build-up pressures on anything other than a free rolling surface.

runner: Another word for rod guides.

running float: Any float that is tree to run along the line between the terminal rig and a stopper placed at the maximum depth to be fished.

running sinker: Sinkers designed with a hole through the centre allowing them to move freely along the line.

sheet lead: Favoured by float anglers, soft thin sheets of lead are cut to the required size then wrapped around the line. Sheet lead offers the advantage of being easily removed from the line to adjust weight.

shock trace: A length of single or double line heavier than the main line designed to withstand the stress of hard casts when heavy weights are being used. Shock traces are normally used by rock anglers casting lures over long distances with long rods, where enormous pressure, capable of repeatedly breaking the main line is generated right at the rod tip.

sidecast: One of the most commonly used reels for rock and beach fishing the sidecast reel is essentially a centrepin which is fitted with a locking device enabling the reel to be turned side on to cast in the same manner as a handcaster.

single-handed threadline: A spinning rod and reel outfit, light and short enough to be cast with one hand.

snapper lead: A bomb-shaped lead commonly used for long-range casting when shore-based anglers fish for snapper, and also popular with bluewater anglers where the shape enables the lure to sink very quickly.

snap swivel: A swivel fitted with a snap lock enabling quick connections to be made to other items of terminal tackle.

spinner: A term used to describe metal casting lures ranging from small trout lures that actually spin, through to all sorts of large metal bars and fish body shapes that do not spin. This confusing term may have originated with early lures that tended to spin, and stayed with us as the same basic shapes evolved into lures that have swimming actions without spinning

split ring: Metal rings enabling hooks to be attached by sliding the eye into the ring.

split shot: Small balls of lead that have been almost cut through the centre. The line is placed in the cut then the lead is squeezed shut on the line.

spool flange: The curved outer shoulder where a reel spool tucks into the inner side of the reel frame.

spoon: A lure originally fashioned from the bowl of a spoon, now a popular commercial style with freshwater anglers. The majority of spoons used these days have the spoon bowl shape elongated into a long tear shape.

spring tide: Relates to the moon phase when the greatest variations between high and low tides occur.

star drag: A system of operating a drag on overhead reels, where a star-like metal wheel is used to increase or decrease pressure on a series of drag washers.

stink bag: The berley bag used when catching beach worms.

stopper knot: Usually a separate length of line or wool used to create a knot around a fishing line to act as a stopper for a running float.

streamer: A range of saltwater flies typified by having tails that stream behind.

strip bait: Flesh baits cut into long thin strips.

Surfcaster: A term, almost redundant now, that was used to describe overhead reels designed for long-distance surf casting.

swivel: An item of terminal tackle designed to eliminate line twist. Swivels range from simple brass models with wire eyes through to sophisticated and expensive ball bearing models for gamefishing. The purpose of the swivel is to allow the terminal end of the rig to spin without twisting the main line above the swivel.

tag: A system for identifying fish for research purposes, fish tags are a small plastic spear with a barbed point, to which is attached a tag section bearing a number. When fish are captured, a card bearing the same number as the tag is filled out with information relating to the time and location of capture and the size of the fish. If recaptured later, the fish and tag are returned to the appropriate fisheries department which may then gain knowledge on movement, growth rate and so on.

taper: The taper is the shape of the rod from tip to butt which may be varied according to the amount of material used over the mandril on which the rod is rolled.

terminal rig: The terminal rig includes everything that is tied and attached to the end of the fishing line.

Terminal tackle: Includes hooks, sinkers, swivels, rings, traces, lures and floats.

threadline reel: Fixed spool reels using a rotating bail arm to recover line. Some threadlines are now available with a free spool system as well.

tidal run: The movement of water as a tide rises or fails.

trace: Any length of wire or monofilament added to the main fishing line. Traces are normally used when the angler chooses to present a bait to shy fish on a trace lighter than the main line, or when sharp toothed fish or a potential abrasion factor calls for a heavier material on the end of the line. These days when some anglers are using bright fluorescent colours in their lines, neutral traces are used to the lure or bait. Traces are also sometimes referred to as leaders.

transducer: A transducer is the device fitted to the bottom of the boat, or hung over the side or back of the boat, that sends and receives pulses from echo sounding equipment.

Triducer: A three-way device that includes a transducer, a speed measuring device and a water temperature sensor.

troll: Pulling lures behind a boat.

unlimited tackle: Refers to the gamefishing classification for lines of 60 kg breaking strain or more.

wet flies: Freshwater flies designed to be fished beneath the surface of the water.

wrist: The section of a fish's body between the tail and the second dorsal.

Appendix:

Sportfish profiles

A quick guide to Australia's most popular angling species

Without getting into the minefield of attempting a scientifically accurate reference to fish species, their distribution and habitat, all of which are covered in great depth in a number of excellent specialised publications, it seemed appropriate here to have a quick reference to our most important angling species. I have also included some reference to baitfish, as without them a lot of our sportfishing would never happen.

Maximum recorded sizes for each species are given wherever this is known, but this is done as a matter of interest rather than as a guide to the size of fish you can expect to catch. Record specimens are often freaks of nature rather than well-fed examples from the normal run of stocks.

AUSTRALIAN BASS

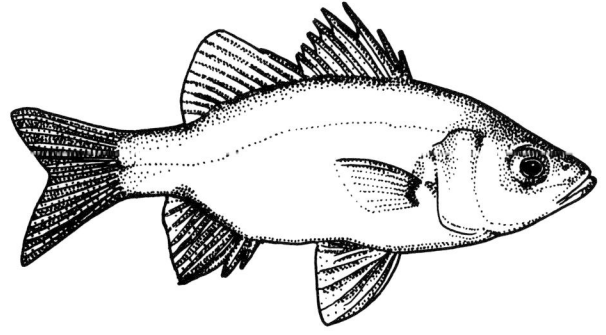

Many Australian anglers, particularly the older generation and a lot of country people, know this fish best as a 'perch', but this becomes confusing as we have other true perch in our waters.

The bass has quite limited distribution along the east coast of Australia from south-east Queensland through to the north-eastern corner of Victoria. The fish ranges from the fresh water through to brackish water as a rule, although large female specimens are sometimes taken well downstream in pure salt water.

A small fish, a 1 kg bass would be welcomed by most anglers, and a 2 kg bass is generally considered a very good capture, with the odd 3 kg fish turning up once in a while to make an angler's reputation.

The average bass is a dark bronze colour with darker back and white belly, but you can find them almost black on the back or very much lighter.

An ambusher by nature, the bass is normally associated with bank-side cover of some kind. Snag entanglements, rock shelves, reed beds and undercuts along the bank where the water is deep and dark are all favoured spots, although the fish move about quite a lot in open water under cover of darkness.

The bass is an opportunist, and it feeds on a variety of food from the land such as insects, small lizards and even mice if they happen to tumble into the water. It also feeds on the shrimps, prawns, worms and small fish found in both fresh water and salt water.

The bass tends to attract a dedicated breed of specialist anglers, who enjoy both the demands of fishing for bass with lures and the beautiful backwater streams in which the wild bass is to be found. Canoes and shallow-draught punts are usually employed to work upstream areas where the craft may have to be dragged over shallows and obstructions between the deeper holes.

Live insect baits, such as crickets, as well as live shrimp or peeled prawns, will usually attract a bass, but these days they are most often fished with lures cast close to bank-side cover.

When fishing with lures, baitcasting outfits are normally used by bass specialists. They take advantage of the outfit's great casting accuracy to place lures within centimetres of snags, and well in under overhanging branches that may leave only a few centimetres of clearance to the surface of the water. A basic bass-fishing tactic is to place a deep-diving lure right alongside a log or snag, then dive it hard right next to the cover so it can be seen by a bass hiding underneath. Floating deep divers are popular as they allow the lure to be fished through logs by diving in the clear areas, then floating to the top to be worked over shallow tangles, then dived again – a very effective tactic.

Probably one of our best freshwater fish to eat, the bass is normally pursued on a catch-and-release basis these days, as more and more anglers come to appreciate the rather fragile nature of the bass fishery.

If you have to handle them, take care of the sharp spines on the side and rear of the gill covers.

BARRACOUTA

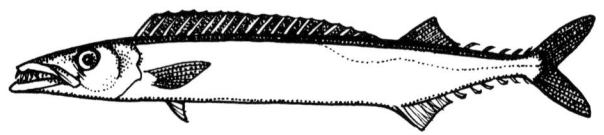

Not to be confused with the tropical barracuda, the barracouta is a fish of our cooler southern waters. An important species in Tasmania and Victoria, when cold currents from the south bring the couta well up into New South Wales, they are about as popular as the Grim Reaper at a birthday party, as the appearance of this species usually indicates the presence of cold water that will send the more popular species right off the bite.

A very long, shallow and compressed body terminates in a long mouth full of the most awful-looking needle-like teeth. The body is a mirror-silver, with dark back and scales so fine they come off when the body is touched.

Related to the deepwater gemfish which has become an important commercial species now, the barracouta is a voracious predator that will freely take fish baits and lures.

When making a film at one time, we had a huge school of barracouta under the boat, and after getting them stirred up with pilchards and poppers splashed on the surface, we were able to make one jump into the boat by holding baits right on the surface then snatching them away as the fish raced up after them. We went on to catch more on bare hooks jiggled in the water.

One of the few fish I have encountered that will actually try to swing around and bite a person holding it, these fish also have to be handled with some care because the gills are full of needle points.

A popular table fish in the south, they are generally shunned by northern anglers who often find worms in the stomach lining.

BARRACUDA

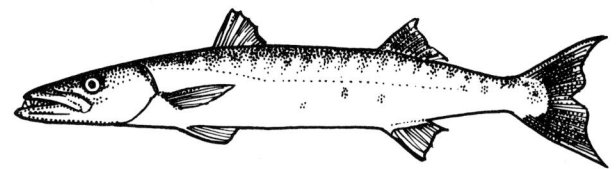

The barracuda is a tropical species found in estuaries and creeks, along beach and rock foreshores and over outcrops of reef. It is primarily a silver fish with a grey to black back and dark spots on the back half of the body, although young fish are often a brownish colour on the back. Striping of varying intensity is also evident.

Two species of barracuda, the great barracuda and the pickhandle, are found in our waters, but for the purpose of this exercise we will just deal with them as barracuda, other than to say that the world record for the great barracuda is a whopping 37.7 kg.

Barracuda are a schooling fish, but large fish tend to be loners or to work in smaller groups.

Barracuda have immense, dog-like jaws with a combination of teeth that includes quite long canine-type gripping teeth at the front backed by a long row of cutting teeth. They make a terrible mess of lures with these teeth and can effortlessly cut quite large fish in half.

Fishing from a small dinghy with my son off Lizard Island on Queensland's Great Barrier Reef, we had quite a large barracuda of 10 kg or so alongside the boat, when a second, larger one slid up from out of the depths and simply cut the middle right out of the fish without effort. Obviously, wire is required when fishing for them.

The fight of the barracuda varies a great deal, and I have seen a 20 kg fish wound straight up to the side of the boat and gaffed, while recently I fished a school of crazy barracuda that never stopped jumping and were incredibly dangerous to handle in the boat.

Barracuda are edible, but generally passed up because they are often found to have infestations of parasites in the stomach. They have also been known to have been involved in cases of ciguatera poisoning.

BARRAMUNDI

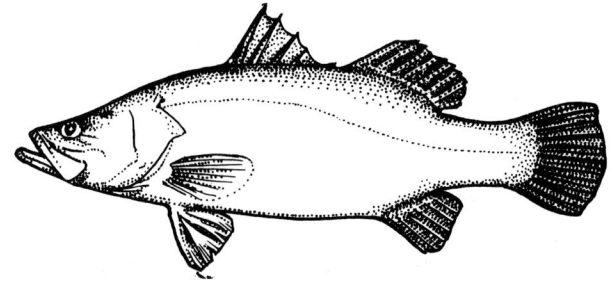

Perhaps our most prized sportfishing species, the barramundi is found in the oceans, rivers, streams and billabongs of the tropical north. Barramundi travel between fresh water and salt water with the annual northern wet season, when monsoon rains produce massive flooding that gives land-locked billabong fish access to the sea.

The barramundi is a beautiful fish, with a huge, cavernous mouth and large eyes located towards the top of the head. The eyes often show as bright red at night or from certain angles in sunlight. The muscular body and large paddle tail are there to deliver considerable power in short bursts – bursts that are used to great effect in the aerial fight of a hooked barramundi.

The colour of barramundi varies a great deal. In fresh water, particularly landlocked lagoons, the fish may be a very dark bronze with fins almost black. Saltwater barramundi, on the other hand, can be pure silver with great mirror-like scales and yellow touches in the fins. Between these two extremes barramundi differ greatly according to the habitat, but always with the common element that the colours will be unmistakably 'metallic'.

Like all fish with the potential to reach an impressive size, barramundi tend to be much larger in folklore than they ever are in real life. People who do a lot of fishing for barramundi consider a 'forty-pounder' (18 kg) to be an unusual and exceptional barra, and some of the top-gun anglers are rated according to the number of 'forty plus' fish they have to their credit. For most anglers a 'twenty-pounder' (9 kg) is considered an excellent, although not uncommon fish.

The barramundi is a carnivore, and the schooling mullet that are prolific in northern waters form a major part of the diet. The mullet spend a great deal of their time right at the surface of the water, and the barramundi, with its eyes perfectly located to monitor the area immediately to the front and above, is well equipped to hunt these fish. When feeding at the top, barramundi make quite a loud, explosive popping sound as they strike, which anglers refer to as 'chopping'.

A very aggressive fish as a rule, barramundi can be taken on a wide variety of lures including a range of minnow-like bodies that include surface runners, medium to deep divers, surface poppers and fizzers, and saltwater flies. Makes, models and colours of barramundi lures are subject to ever-changing fashion. Many of the best are the work of local backyard lure makers, but the Nilsmaster Invincible for casting, and the Nilsmaster Spearhead for trolling seem to have remained both popular and highly productive over the years.

Live baits are probably the most popular angling method and the best of these are live mullet and prawns.

Anglers fish for barramundi with lines ranging from as low as 2 kg breaking strain through to 15 kg, although 6 kg would be considered a good average size. Choice of line depends largely on the terrain being fished and the average size of fish running at the time. A short, heavy trace to the lure or hook is essential, and this would normally be made up of hard 30 kg breaking strain monofilament line, although some anglers do use wire.

Barramundi specialists normally fish with single-handed baitcasting outfits to facilitate accurate casting to snags, but there are quite a lot of double-handed outfits in use where the angler also does a lot of open-water sportfishing for light game fish. Double-handed threadlines are the tackle of choice for less skilled anglers and those who normally fish with live baits where accurate casting is not required.

There is a never-ending debate over the fighting qualities of the barramundi, but few would argue that the barra is not one of the most spectacular sportfishing species in this country. The sheer spectacle and noise of a big barramundi jumping in an otherwise silent backwater creek is not easily forgotten.

Because the barramundi delivers large fillets of moist white flesh, they are one of our most popular table fish, although the quality of the meat varies a great deal according to where the fish are taken. Landlocked billabong fish are almost inedible, while the sea-run barramundi are quite outstanding.

Some care needs to be taken when handling barramundi, especially when lures fitted with treble hooks are involved. The fish can suddenly explode into life after lying inert for some time, and sometimes the hooks are then transferred to the unwary angler. They also have some razor-sharp edges on the sides of the gill covers and substantial spines in the fins.

BILLFISH

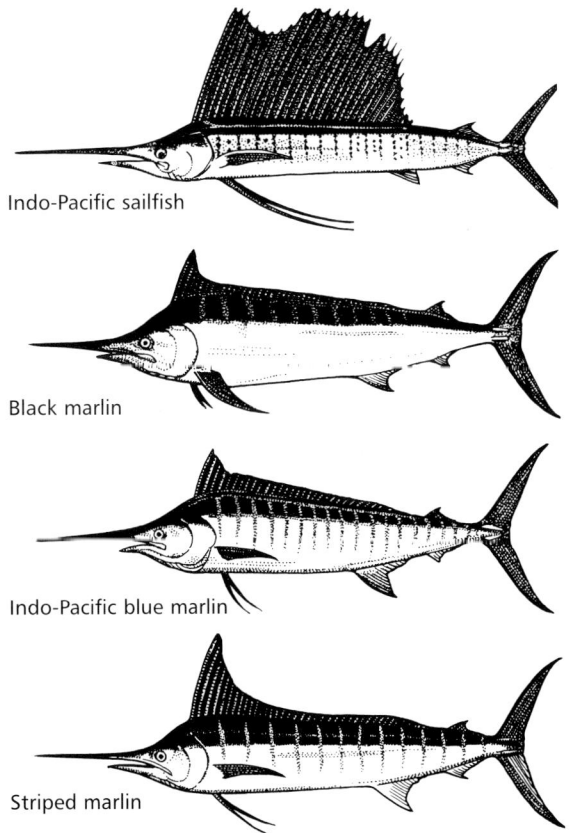

Indo-Pacific sailfish

Black marlin

Indo-Pacific blue marlin

Striped marlin

Four billfish figure prominently in the captures of game anglers in this country, and these are the Indo-Pacific sailfish, the black marlin, the blue marlin and the striped marlin.

The sailfish is a true tropical species with the odd straggler wandering well down into southern waters now and then. Possibly the most beautiful of the billfish, the distinctive feature of the sailfish is the sail-like dorsal that gives the fish its name. Standing over twice the depth of the body in height and running from just behind the head to two-thirds the length of the body, the sail is a brilliant blue with a scattering of blue and black spots. The back is a deep purple–blue extending into silver sides which carry a series of stripes formed from blue spots joined in a line. After capture the silver body may turn bronze to gold before all colour fades. Sailfish also 'light up' when checking out a lure or bait, and they may for a short time look quite a dark copper–brown or take on other colours. The world record stands at 100 kg, but a 50 kg fish would be considered a large specimen in our waters.

A slender fish known more for its aerobatics than any great strength or speed, the sail is a magical fish to watch as it tail-walks across the surface of the sea.

Sailfish are normally caught by trolling baits, usually garfish, or by casting live baits to fish sighted at the surface. It is a common practice for them to work together in small groups, quietly rounding up a school of bait into a tight ball, just like aquatic cowboys. Depending on the type of bait, they may simply quietly feed from the edges of the ball, or slash the fish with their bills and pick up the injured fish at leisure.

The black marlin has become a household name due to the exploits of well-known actors chasing the big breeding fish out of Cairns during the end-of-year season. They are found all the way around the country, but clearly favour tropical seas and are normally caught well offshore. Having said that, the not infrequent captures of marlin from the rock platforms of New South Wales always involve black marlin, which probably tells us that the juvenile fish do not share the mature fish's preference for deeper water.

Colour is not much help when identifying black and blue marlin, as the black will be a brilliant purple or blue across the back when fighting, sometimes showing distinct stripes on the silver sides. The infallible test is the pectoral fin, which is rigid in the black and cannot be folded down.

Black marlin are normally fished with trolled baits, although the smaller fish do take lures. The world record for black marlin stands at 707.6 kg, and this fish was caught in 1953. The Queensland record is 654 kg, and a lot of people think when the world record eventually changes hands, it will probably be a Queensland fish that does the job.

The blue marlin is a beautifully coloured fish with a cobalt blue back over silver–white sides. Side stripes are pale blue and these fade away after death. The pectoral fins on the blue marlin may be folded down against the body for positive identification from the black marlin. It has wide distribution in our waters, but with a more southern bias than the black marlin.

Blue marlin are much more enthusiastic about lures than the blacks, and much of the blue marlin fishing is done with lures these days. Blues are tremendous fighters, producing great aerial displays and very long runs, but their major weapon seems to be a use of depth that can really push an angler to the limit. Pumping a big, sulking blue marlin up out of the black depths of deep ocean waters soon sorts out the men from the boys.

Japanese long-liners are reputed to have reported blue marlin over 910 kg, and the world record stands at 624.14 kg for a Hawaiian fish and a 319 kg fish has been taken in Australia. We are probably still sorting out the blue marlin potential in this country and, in my opinion, are still to see the best of it.

The striped marlin is not all that different in colour to the blue, but it is a dark purple to blue on the back with more pronounced brilliant blue stripes that often remain after death. The dorsal is higher than the other two marlin, and is usually as long as the body is deep, sometimes longer. The striped marlin also shows a pronounced lateral line which is not readily evident on the blue. The fish is also more compressed in the body which makes a fish of any given length weigh less than other marlin.

The striped marlin is found right around Australia, although it may be more common on the east coast and in southern waters. The world record is for a 206.5 kg New Zealand fish, while the Australian record stands at 166 kg for a fish taken at Bermagui.

BREAM

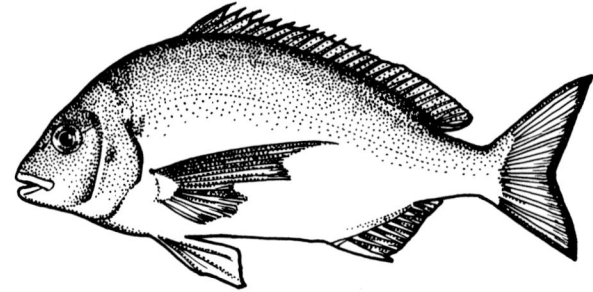

We have three significant bream, these being the black (illustrated here), the yellowfin and the pikey bream. All are slightly different in appearance, but sufficiently similar in behaviour and habitat to be covered here under the general heading of bream.

The pikey is a tropical species confined to the northern half of the country, the black or southern bream ranges from southern New South Wales across the bottom of the country and up to Shark Bay in Western Australia, and the yellowfin or silver bream ranges from central Queensland down into eastern Victoria. Maximum recorded sizes for each are 56 cm for the pikey, 66 cm for the yellowfin and 54 cm for the black, all of which are gigantic specimens of the species. Most bream are commonly caught in sizes ranging from ½ to 1 kg in weight.

The very backbone of estuary angling in most places where they occur, bream are found over sand flats, in deep channels, around weed beds, jetties, deep reef, wrecks, oyster leases and anything else that might produce food for them. They eat almost anything that will fit down their throats and to facilitate this they have rows of crushing teeth and bone over the entire mouth area.

Bream are also important to the beach and rock anglers, occurring in great numbers when they congregate outside the estuaries at spawning time.

Legendary areas for the bream enthusiast are spots like Jumpinpin in Southern Queensland, the Yamba walls in New South Wales and most of the east Gippsland rivers. Bream catches often resemble cricket scores in these places, although the bream specialist prepared to work intensively with berley can turn up cricket scores in spots where lesser anglers fail to catch a fish.

Bream can be berleyed with almost any fish waste, but wheat and chook laying pellets are hot favourites and always readily available. I knew a man once who lived near the water in an area not renowned for quality fishing. Every night he took the table scraps down to the water at exactly the same time and threw them in in exactly the same spot. Once a month, on the dark of the moon, he fished the spot and would take a bag of bream.

Having said that bream will eat anything, the same fish can be infuriatingly particular at times. Fresh or properly frozen prawns caught in the estuary where the fishing is done rarely miss out, and blood and beach worms along with live yabbies are also excellent baits, as are small crabs.

Many bream specialists prefer 'puddings' made to their own recipes, and these include bread, dough or pollard base with cheddar cheese, garlic sausage, ground sardine and all sorts of other smelly ingredients. Pudding can be tremendously effective at times, but few pudding enthusiasts will ever share their recipes with others.

Off the ocean rocks pilchards, garfish fillets and other fish baits work very well, as does white milk loaf bread, crabs and live yabbies. On the surf beaches pipis, beach worms, prawns and fish baits all work.

Light tackle, fine lines, the smallest lead that will do the job, plenty of slack line and very sharp hooks are the order of the day in many estuary situations where bream may be extremely shy. Even the hook size may prove important and a fine wire hook may take fish that are rejecting a heavier, bulkier pattern. The fish need to be given the opportunity to tug and pull at the bait, even take tentative runs, until they actually swallow the bait and move off before you try setting the hook. Other times they will simply swallow the lot and bolt.

On the beach and around the rocks bream are normally not at all shy unless the water is still and clear, and then you might need to go to light line and a small sinker.

Excellent eating fish with moist, well-flavoured white flesh, the bream are one of our most popular angling species.

COBIA

A most interesting fish, the cobia is a tropical pelagic species that wanders well down into southern waters from time to time, with the odd fish encountered at Jervis Bay on the east coast and Cape Naturaliste on the west coast.

With a suggestion of catfish in the body shape and a rather broad, flat head, the cobia has a shark-like appearance with a high triangular peak on the dorsal that looks very much like a shark fin in the water. It has a chocolate to dark grey–brown back with a pale band along the side, and a white underbelly.

Cobia travel in small groups, and have a habit of travelling with manta rays. They eat a wide range of food that includes items as small as prawns and tiny sand crabs. One of the names used for cobia overseas is crab eater, and you sometimes catch them full of the small red spot crabs commonly found right inside the surf line.

They will take most trolled lures, surface poppers, and can also be taken on deep jigs as well as almost any live bait.

The maximum length recorded in this country is 2.02 m, and fish in excess of 20 kg are not uncommon. Cobia are an acceptable table fish when skinned, filleted, then cut into thin steaks.

CORAL TROUT

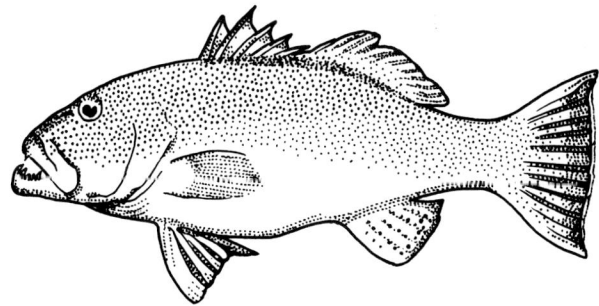

Although a tropical fish, coral trout can at times be found well down into subtropical regions. A 10 kg coral trout could be considered a large specimen.

Although usually quite spectacularly coloured, coral trout vary enough in colour schemes to confuse many people. Shallow-water fish may be predominantly a muddy green while those from deeper waters normally range from bright salmon pink through to a deep red. The spots are usually an electric blue. The 'trout' in the name may be a little misleading, as in appearance the fish is quite cod-like, with little rounded paddle-like pectoral fins.

Predominantly a bottom dweller associated with deep reef, coral trout are also commonly found inshore where they will feed right up to the surface at times. Carnivores, they feed mainly on other fish, and are well equipped with a large mouth to swallow quite big fish.

Coral trout are usually caught along with other species when baitfishing over deep reefs, but they also turn up frequently in the catches of sport anglers casting lures around shallow reefs and coral outcrops.

Although an excellent eating fish, coral trout figures prominently on the list of species that can cause ciguatera poisoning.

The advice is to stick to the small fish, and only eat small quantities off a large fish. It is always better to eat a small portion from a number of fish than to eat a lot off any one fish when unsure if the meat is safe.

As is the case with all reef-dwelling tropical species, you should avoid gripping the gills. Most tropical reef fish have rough or sharp areas in the gills that can injure fingers, with a good risk of infection occurring later.

DART

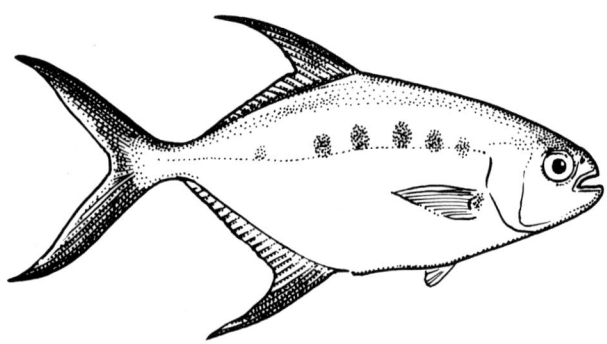

The southern swallowtail dart illustrated is a common fish in subtropical surf waters, and more often encountered than its relatives the snubnose and the northern dart.

A most beautifully proportioned little fish, the swallowtail's elegant lines belie its great speed and fighting ability when encountered by the angler. Recorded to a weight of 3 kg, the swallowtail is commonly taken in the ½ kg range.

Dart are usually incidental encounters when fishing with pipis, peeled prawns or worms for bream and whiting, but they can be found in good-sized schools.

The speed with which the line whips through the water is usually a good indication that a dart has arrived on the scene.

Like tailor and trevally, dart need to be cared for if they are to make it back to the table in good shape. If ice is not available, fish buried deep in moist, cool sand will usually make it home in adequate condition.

DOLPHINFISH

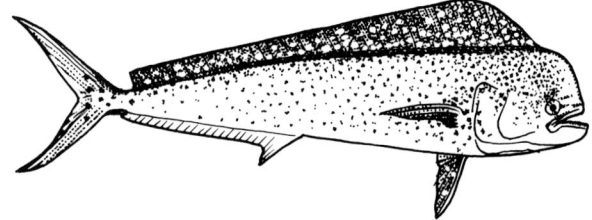

Once seen alive in the open sea, dolphinfish are never forgotten. Although a decidedly odd-shaped fish with their supercompressed bodies and head-to-tail dorsal, plus the high, flat forehead common to the male fish, the dolphinfish is one of the most spectacularly coloured fish in the sea.

The back is a neon blue, sometimes shot with metallic greens, and the sides are a brilliant gold. Spots scattered all over the body may be black, bright blue or yellow, and the dorsal is a deep blue to purple. Descriptions of the dolphinfish colours vary a lot, because the colour may change on the fish as it swims by. They light up like a neon sign when chasing a bait or lure and are like nothing more than a marine fireworks display when they take to the air. Sadly, these colours rapidly fade away when the fish is boated.

Also commonly known as mahi-mahi or dorado, they are a fish of the open sea. They love cover of any kind, and the first residents on the spot when a FAD (fish attracting device) is put down will be the dolphinfish. Almost any piece of flotsam or floating timber found at sea is worth checking out for dolphinfish, and sometimes a quite insignificant piece of log may have hundreds of dolphinfish associated with it.

Dolphinfish are found around the world, and in Australia they have an unusually wide range that extends from the tropics down as far as Montague Island on the east coast. The biggest fish recorded was 39.46 kg.

Dolphinfish are usually caught by game boats trolling lures or bait, or sport anglers casting lures or saltwater flies to fish associated with surface debris. They are an excellent fish to eat, but need to be bled soon after capture and kept on ice as the flesh does not handle all that well.

ESTUARY COD

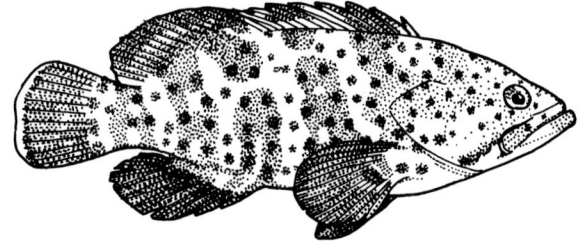

An incredibly aggressive fish, the estuary cod is normally an incidental catch when fishing for barramundi and mangrove jack. A very territorial fish, the estuary cod normally stations itself near cover of some kind, ambushing fish that swim by and monstering any lure that comes near its domain. Most anglers find them an annoying pest as they are very adept at bulldozing their way back into snags with an expensive lure in their mouth.

A pale to yellowish mottled brown, with distinctive red spots, the cod is quite handsome. An acceptable table fish, these cod are dismissed by anglers who expect to be landing barramundi or jack for the table.

FINGERMARK

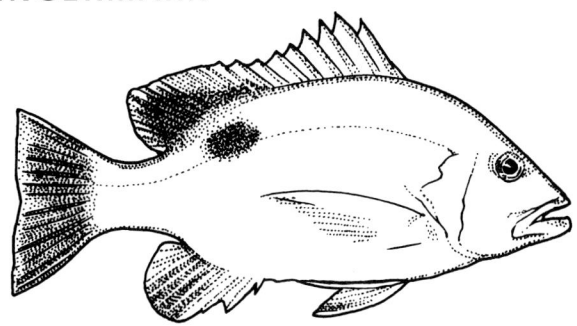

The fingermark is a tropical species known variously as spotted-scale sea perch or golden snapper.

The fingermark is a beautiful red–bronze colour with a clear dark spot immediately below the rear of the second dorsal fin. In common with the other lutjanids it has the sharp canine-like teeth that mark it as an active hunter. With a maximum weight in the range of 10 kg, the great majority of fish taken by anglers would be under 3 kg.

The fingermark occupies a similar niche to the mangrove jack in the tropical estuary scene, but out in the bays and over inshore reefs they sometimes school in large numbers.

In the creeks, fingermark are taken as an incidental catch by anglers casting lures to cover for barramundi and mangrove jack. In open waters they may be targeted by bait anglers using prawns or cut baits of fish or squid, and live bait can be employed by an angler looking for larger fish.

It would take an expert to pick the difference between the white moist flesh of the fingermark and that of the mangrove jack, and it is definitely in the top bracket of our best table fish.

FLATHEAD

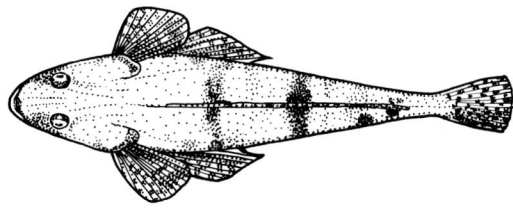

In one form or another, flathead may be found all around Australia, but they really only become a fish of any significance in the southern half and subtropical regions of the country.

Although a surprisingly varied family of fish, the most important flathead are the eastern dusky (illustrated here), the tiger or sand flathead and the western bar-tail. To the casual observer all three are identical except for the colouring.

The dusky is mainly confined to south-eastern estuaries and bays, and can be anything from a pale sandy colour through to almost solid black, depending on the nature of the bottom it is on at the time. It is one of our most common flathead and is also the largest, with a potential maximum length of 1.5 m.

The tiger is an offshore species and an important fish to offshore anglers and commercial operators. It is a sandy-coloured fish with reddish orange spots on the head and body. Maximum size would be around 65 cm.

The bar-tail is the common estuary flathead in Western Australia where it fills the same ecological niche as the dusky on the east coast. This is a brown fish with dark spots and yellow, black and white bars on the tail fin. The maximum potential length of this species would be around 1 m.

Those maximum lengths are a little misleading in a way, as western anglers rarely see a bar-tail over 2 kg, while eastern dusky specialists take fish over 8 kg. Flathead tend to put the weight on the head and shoulder area of the body as they grow, so you may only have a quite minor length variation in fish with quite different body weights.

The great majority of the flathead's food is taken from a position of ambush, the whole body of the fish concealed in the sand or mud bottom, with just the top of the head and eyes above the sand to watch for prey passing by. More like a snake than a fish in a way, flathead have an explosive burst of speed over a very short range, with the whole body from head to tail being involved in the swimming motion. They have a huge mouth and gill structure, and the gaping mouth is backed by suction from gills expelling water, producing a big vacuum-cleaner effect which sucks prey in. The teeth are very small and sharp, and are used only for gripping large creatures before swallowing them whole.

I have observed some situations where the use of a lot of berley has had flathead out and about, swimming and feeding freely in the berley trail, or moving about under a school of tailor chopping a school of bait, but the ambush role is the most common mode of operation.

Flathead will generally eat anything that will fit down their throats, and small ones also try hard to eat fish that will not fit down their throats. They are a very ambitious fish when it comes to feeding. Prawns make up a large part of the diet as do small fish of all kinds.

Tidal movement is very important to the inshore flatheads and they are normally associated with the channels used by small fish and prawns to move with the tide. Through the day they tend towards deep channels, but at night flathead will come into a few centimetres of water to hunt small mullet that hug the edge of the shallows for safety. There are times when, on the low tide, you can see the indentations left by flathead lined up along a sandy shore, all with the heads within a metre or so of the high-tide mark. In areas like this it has often occurred to me that it would be productive to approach from the back in a boat, and cast live baits right up onto the sand and retrieve them back into the shallows with plenty of splash. The run-off tide is the preferred time for flathead, and in addition to the deep channels they will also station themselves at the mouth of any small channel where water drains off a bar, and at the draining end of shallow beach gutters.

The majority of serious flathead fishing is done on the drift with live mullet or yellowtail fished on a large, but light hook. A trace of a metre or more is used with just enough weight to keep the bait at the bottom. A shore-based angler can simply cast a bait out and walk along the bank as it is taken along in the tide. Sometimes it helps to use a float when drifting a bait like this, as this does away with the problem of having a sinker rolling along the bottom twisting line.

Another method is to anchor up in a good tidal run and lay down a berley trail which is then fished either by casting baits well back down the trail and working them back to the boat, or by allowing a bait to swim down the trail then working it slowly towards the boat. Large, hardy baits such as yellowtail are the best for this style of fishing and they can be hooked through the upper lip to allow them to breathe and swim normally.

Flathead love pilchards and whitebait which can be fished on a flight of hooks with great effect.

There is a never-ending argument about whether heavy traces should be used when fishing for flathead, as they often appear to bite through the trace just when they are about to be landed. Flathead cannot bite through a trace with their tiny teeth, but they can saw through it and they do this when overanxious anglers try to drag them across the surface to a waiting net or simply lift them straight into the boat.

When they do this the line is stretched and the flathead only has to shake its head a few times to quickly saw through the line. The trick is to let the flathead swim and tire itself at the point of landing, allowing it to make as many last-minute bursts as it has in it without ever lifting its head from the water. Only swim it over a net when it is exhausted.

If you are land-based you also need to have the fish exhausted, then you lead it quietly towards a sloping edge of the water and accelerate it to the shore at the last possible moment, planing it up the bank. This is really an awful way to land a fish and you would be far better off carrying a belt gaff or net with you.

Flathead are a prized table fish delivering a sweet, moist white fillet which is bone-free at the tail end. Large fish tend to be very dry and the smaller specimens are by far the best to eat.

FLOUNDER

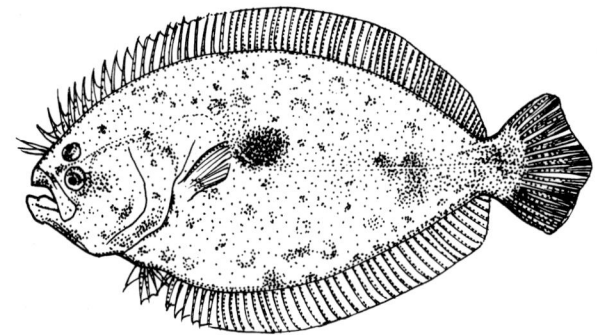

The flounders are found all around Australia in one form or another, and although there are a number of members of the family, they are all primarily estuary and bay fish with common behaviour patterns.

The example illustrated is the large or longtooth flounder which has distribution around much of Australia with the exception of the far south. Its near relative, the smalltooth flounder, has similar distribution but is more common in the west. As the names imply, the distinguishing feature is several large pointed teeth at the front of the mouth.

Colour varies enormously in the flounders as they are ambushers who rely on matching the colour of the bottom to conceal themselves. The general overall effect is a base of sandy yellow to brown with an array of blotches or spots to break up the outline. Preferred environments are sand to sandy mud bottoms and ribbon weed-sand mixes.

An extremely aggressive little hunter, flounder don't look much until you prise open the jaws and note just how large they are and how well they have been equipped with fine, sharp teeth. Prawns make up a large part of the diet along with small fish.

West Australian anglers have made quite an art out of catching flounder on tiny bucktail and soft plastic jigs.

Flounder are an excellent table fish but care needs to be taken not to overcook them.

GARFISH

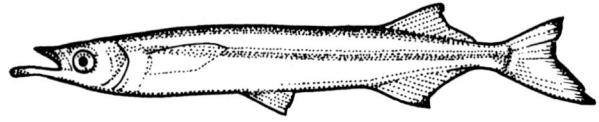

There are a number of varieties of garfish found around Australia, most having a long beak attached to the lower jaw. The exception is the snub-nosed garfish where a projecting lower jaw replaces the true beak.

All garfish are best categorised as baitfish in the broad scheme of things, but they are also a superb table fish.

The sea garfish is of special interest to anglers as it is a quite exceptional baitfish, whether fished alive under a float for game fish, or used as a fillet bait for almost anything that will eat a fish bait. While most other garfish are acceptable as bait, the sea garfish is in a class of its own.

The sea garfish is characterised by having a steel blue back and mirror-silver sides with black bars or spots down the side, and a red tip on the end of the beak. Most other garfish are quite green on the back.

A schooling fish, garfish move in or near the surface layers and are easily berleyed up with crushed Sao biscuits, bran or anything else that can be distributed largely at the surface. They often turn up in the slick from a berley pot.

Sometimes garfish will come right up to the boat, but you can normally spot them some distance off in calm water as they swim along with just the point of the beak breaking the surface.

The best bait for garfish is a small piece of green prawn, although they are also partial to maggots and bacon rind. Small, fine wire, long-shank hooks are used tied to a short, unweighted trace, fished under a little float. I like a quill float or just a small piece of stick as a float, and often simply attach this at one end so that it lies flat on the water then stands up as the fish takes the bait.

If you have 2 kg gear, catching sea garfish can be a lot of fun, but you can use any tackle at all as long as you have a light trace to the hook.

You can cook garfish almost any way, but the preferred method is to coat them in flour and fry them quickly in butter or a light oil. Some people roll them hard with a rolling pin or bottle, and this makes the flesh fall away from the bone when cooked, but you can easily pull the side of a garfish away with a knife blade or fork after cooking, or do what I do and pick them up and eat them off the bone like a cob of corn.

Garfish have a lot of fine bones, but most of these are digestible and too soft to do any damage if swallowed.

GROPER

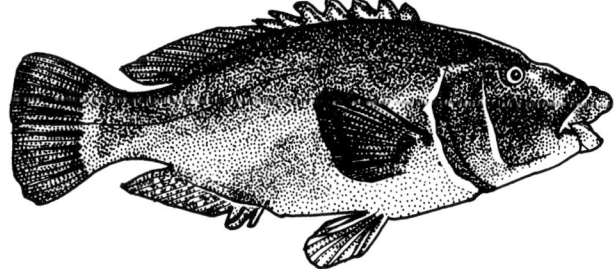

The blue groper is a member of a very extensive family of beautiful fish bundled under the general heading of wrasse. Beauty being in the eye of the beholder, not all people would agree with that after taking a close look at the features of such family members as the hump-headed maori wrasse, but there can be no argument that the family can boast some of the most extraordinary colour schemes in the kingdom of the sea.

Possibly the least colourful of the wrasse, the blue groper varies from a soft dark blue through to a startling electric blue. 1 have often found myself at a loss to understand the colouring of these fish when I see a blue groper, lit up like a neon sign, feeding on the top of a shallow reef in clear water. It seems to go against all the principles of fish colouration, but no doubt they have a good reason for it. Blue groper also have some beautifully coloured lines radiating out onto the cheeks from the eyes. Maximum growth potential is in excess of 50 kg.

Female blue groper vary in colour from a dull red through to a red–blue mix.

These are a very heavy bodied fish, with heavy-duty rubbery fins supported by thick spines and armour-like scales covered in slime. This tough, protected exterior allows the fish to work hard up against rock without damage, and they are also equipped with protruding leathery lips and powerful peg-like teeth backed by crushing plates in the back of the throat. The design allows them to tear shellfish from the reef and root out the crabs that they love to eat. Anything too tough to be dealt with by the teeth is consigned to the grinders at the back of the throat to be pulverised before entering the stomach.

Groper are inhabitants of inshore reefs and they like caves, shelves and other very broken ground. They are also common in the washes around the rocks. Once a popular angling species, they were decimated in the spearfishing boom of the 1960s when competitions were held based on a maximum weight of dead fish. This lead to a spear- and line-fishing ban that produced a quite remarkable comeback, even to the point where divers were once again able to fondle and handfeed the big fish.

Anglers never really recovered their pre-ban interest in groper and they are only occasionally fished for now. Small groper are often caught along with other fish when fishing with prawns and cunje from the rocks, but the big fish are so strong they need a specialised approach. Line of 15 to 30 kg is used with a powerful rod and sidecast reel, as groper are capable of stripping even heavy-duty gears. The hook needs to be extra strong and very sharp, able to retain its shape in the tug of war between heavy tackle and a powerful fish. Whole red crabs are normally fished as a floating bait or under a bobby cork, or sometimes rigged with the hook set quite high over a long trace to a bottom sinker. If it is at all possible, it is a big help if you can fish from a ledge that will get you as high above the spot as is practical, for the more leverage towards the surface the angler can achieve, the more chance he has of actually getting a groper clear of the bottom.

Small groper are quite nice to eat, but larger fish can be unpleasantly rubbery.

JAVELIN FISH

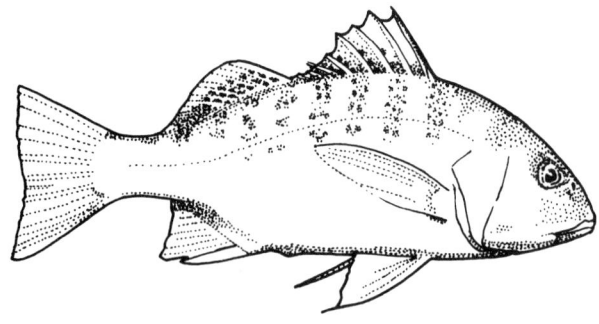

The javelin fish also commonly goes under the name grunter and is confined to the tropical regions. It is a very pretty fish with a metallic purple or green flush through a silver base and a combination of dark stripes and speckles. The majority of fish encountered are under the 2 kg mark with 6 kg representing an exceptionally large fish.

The javelin is an inshore fish found in bays and estuaries where it is most often associated with reef and gravel bottoms. Its diet includes small crustaceans, squid, octopus and small fish.

With a reputation for caution, javelin are normally fished for with light lines and weights and are considered to be an excellent fighting and table fish.

JEWFISH

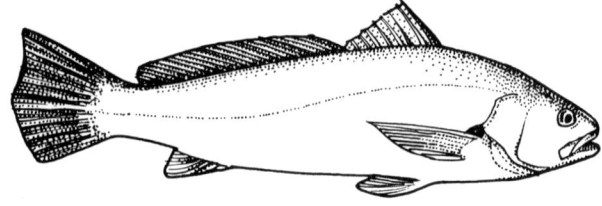

Although the southern fish is more correctly known as mulloway, and the tropical variety is a black jewfish, virtually no anglers at all ever use that name, and both the southern and northern variations are universally referred to as jewies. No angler considers himself complete until he has captured at least one big jewfish, and a lot of people specialise in them to the exclusion of everything else.

The southern jewfish has a distribution ranging from southern Queensland right around to Exmouth Gulf in Western Australia, and the black jewfish is exclusive to tropical regions.

The southern jewfish has a copper to copper–green back with bright silver sides and a row of distinctive spots down the side. The inside of the mouth is a bright yellow and the fish has been recorded at a maximum weight of 61 kg.

The black jewfish is a dark grey infused with bronze on the back and a silver cast carrying into the sides and belly. It

has dark blotches over the back, the sides of the head and the fins and there is also a dull purple cast on the cheeks of the fish.

The mulloway is a schooling fish, but lone fish often work the beaches and headland shallows at night. They are particularly fond of gutters and ledges in reefs where they sometimes congregate in great numbers, and there would be very few wrecks in our waters that are not attended by schools of jewfish. They also become very active offshore on the full moon. Inshore the dark of the moon is the time for big jewfish, suggesting that the fish are moving in and out with the moon, although the lesser tides associated with the dark of the moon would certainly suit a fish that prefers the slack water at the change of tide to feed.

Inshore, jewfish are commonly found along the training walls at river mouths, especially in flood time when they chop mullet at the surface. They also favour deep holes in estuaries and areas where pronounced outcrops from either the bank or bottom formations produce eddies. On the beaches they are found in holes and gutters running parallel to the beach, and off the rocks they also prefer deep holes and wash-outs formed behind rock outcrops. On the north coast of New South Wales where rock headlands are normally associated with sandy bottoms, it is sometimes possible to cast into a hole situated inside a wide sandbar where heavy surf is breaking, and these features are also happy hunting grounds for mulloway.

They can be caught on very fresh strips taken from dead fish, especially tailor, and on the beach they are particularly fond of a large bunch of beach worms on a hook if these can be kept away from bream. Fresh squid also has its appeal for the jewfish, but the fish are primarily interested in live baits and these will usually out-fish anything else wherever they can be used. Yellowtail, yellowtail pike, mullet, tailor and luderick are all excellent live baits.

Heavy handlines are normally used when fishing offshore for jewfish, and rods are employed in shallower water and from the beach and rocks. Jewfish are often fished with heavy tackle because their size potential is so great, and if there are rocks and reef nearby the jewfish will soon take advantage of these to cut the line. Stopping a rampaging 20 kg jewfish dead in his tracks takes a lot of doing.

There is a knack to hooking jewfish as they are in the habit of fooling around with a bait for a long time before swallowing it. Sometimes they will simply bolt it down and run, but more often than not they will mouth it, chew on it, run and then drop it and do all sorts of odd things before they actually get it down. There is also the problem that the fish have a very large mouth which means that they can easily expel anything that alarms them. Therefore, hooks need to be as sharp as you can get them and you need to take a lot of care when putting the bait on the hook.

The black jewfish shares all the characteristics of the mulloway, but has a much higher rating with anglers for its fighting qualities. Where the southern fish is considered to be powerful simply because it is a large fish, the black jewfish comes as quite a shock to those fishing them for the first time. They are far more powerful on a power-to-weight basis and an extremely difficult fish to capture around wrecks and jagged reefs where they tend to congregate.

Jewfish are an outstanding table fish, and made even more so by the fact that the big fillets and cutlets can be eaten without any problems with small bones. They tend to smell pretty bad when brought out of the water, but don't let that put you off – all jewfish smell that way.

JOHN DORY

There are three dory species in our southern waters, the John dory, mirror dory and silver dory. All are deepwater fish, but the John dory is of interest here because it does seasonally move inshore where it can be found over reefs and often around the pylons and wharves of marinas.

The John dory is a grey-to-silver fish, but can be a mottled yellow to brown when over sand and weed bottom. A deep, laterally compressed fish with eyes set right in the top of the head, the main identifying feature is a distinct dark blotch circled with white on the side of the body. John dory have been recorded to weights of over 4 kg, but the majority of fish encountered inshore would be less than 1 kg in weight.

The John dory, although slow moving, is a very active predator, and gets the jump on its prey by being able to extend its mouth for quite a surprising distance to suck in unsuspecting fish that probably think they are out of range at the time.

John dory are normally fished with live baits suspended just off the bottom. They are an excellent table fish, and many seafood lovers rate the delicate, white, and well-flavoured meat of the John dory the best fish of them all.

LEATHERJACKET

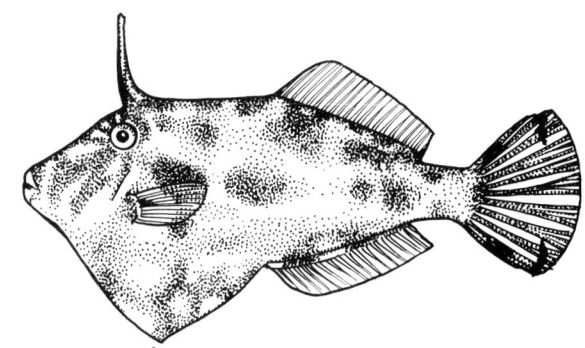

A large family of fish, leatherjacket of one kind or another are found right around the country. They inhabit waters ranging from coastal estuaries to the deep offshore reefs, and come in an incredible variety of shapes and sizes. The largest of the jackets is probably the tropical unicorn leatherjacket with a maximum growth potential of 76 cm, while the pygmy leatherjacket can only look forward to being 9 cm long when fully grown.

The southern waters rough leatherjacket was chosen for the illustration as it seems to represent something of a middle ground, or average appearance for the family. It has an unusually rough skin, but otherwise the leathery skin, 'centre-board' shape and the prominent dorsal spine are basic characteristics of all leatherjackets.

Free-swimming leatherjacket, such as the reef or Chinaman jacket, are smooth bodied, beautifully coloured and fairly conventional in terms of fin and tail shape. Others, such as the fan belly, have quite elaborate fin structures that may help them disappear into a weed or kelp background.

Small leatherjacket are bait-stealing pests, but the larger fish are commonly caught in great numbers by offshore anglers and frequently figure in the catches of estuary anglers, particularly those fishing off jetties.

With the exception of the coral reef-inhabiting scribbled leatherjacket, which is associated with ciguatera poisoning, all other leatherjackets are good to eat, and some could be classified excellent. I personally regard a plate of leatherjacket as something of a special treat.

Obviously, care needs to be taken when handling the fish not to get spiked by the dorsal spine, but care also needs to be taken when cleaning any number of leatherjacket. The fish are cleaned by cutting off the head, then peeling off the skin. The rough surface of the skin will leave the fingers quite badly scratched if gloves are not worn or pliers not used to pull the skin back.

LONGTOM

Longtom of one kind or another are found around much of the Australian coastline, generally inshore and often in creeks and rivers. The southern varieties are usually only a half metre or so long, but in the tropics longtom are often encountered well over a metre in length.

Many anglers refer to longtom as 'mini marlin' because of their habit of tail-walking across the surface of the water for quite long distances when hooked.

Virtually a giant version of the sea garfish in the body, the longtom is distinguished by having jaws the length of a garfish beak, but, unlike the garfish, these jaws are full of needle-like teeth.

The long, hard beak of the longtom and the abundance of teeth make it an incredibly difficult fish to hook. When these are coupled with the longtom's enthusiasm for hitting the same lure over and over again, you often see anglers boiling with frustration as they desperately try and get a solid hookup.

Mainly valuable as a source of entertainment when fishing for other species is a bit slow, longtom are edible but fairly ordinary as a table fish.

Spanish mackerel appear to be specially fond of longtom, and when they are about offshore, mackerel often provide anglers with a spectacular sight as they come from out of the depths at great speed, take the longtom right across the middle with their jaws, then continue straight on into the sky like a submarine-launched missile wearing a fish dinner.

LUDERICK

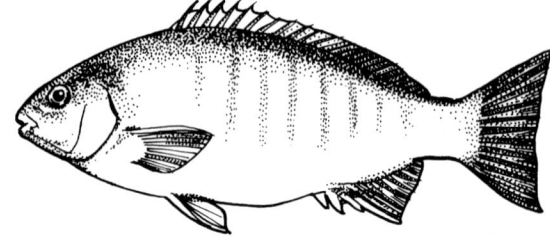

The luderick, more commonly known as the blackfish, is an east coast fish ranging from southern Queensland to northern Tasmania. An important species to sport and commercial fishing alike, they are abundant in the estuaries and around the ocean rocks.

Luderick vary a great deal in their colour according to habitat. At one end of the scale they can be a very pale grey with a mauve cast and only pale stripes, and at the other extreme they are quite black on the back with pronounced dark bars on the sides. Ocean-run fish are sometimes referred to as 'bronzies' because of the distinct bronze tone evident on the back. They are normally vegetarians feeding on cabbage weed on the ocean front and a variety of fine weeds in the estuaries. At times they will be found over clean sand and will take sand worms, and quite a few are taken from time to time on prawns. Anglers probably get more blackfish bites than they ever realise when fishing with worms and prawns, for the fish have tiny mouths and most of the hooks used in general estuary fishing would be too large for them.

Luderick are normally fished for with floats and light line, and they attract their own little army of specialised anglers who fish for nothing else.

Luderick have moist, fine-textured white meat with quite a sweet flavour, but they do vary greatly in quality. They do not keep well and need to be kept alive as long as possible then quickly iced down after cleaning. Many people complain of a weedy taste in blackfish, but this can usually be avoided by skinning the fish.

MANGROVE JACK

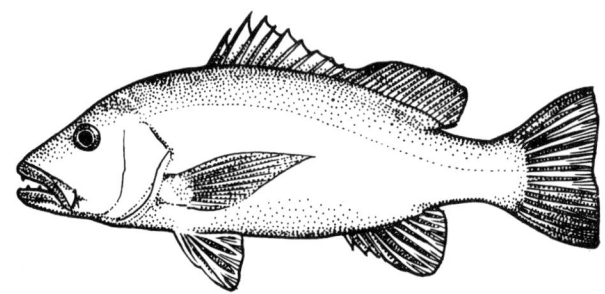

This tropical species is interesting in that odd specimens have turned up as far south as Shark Bay in Western Australia and Lake Illawarra on the New South Wales south coast. There are quite good populations as far south as the Gold Coast and in some northern New South Wales streams, but in tropical waters mangrove jack are a fairly abundant species.

Jack are found out over offshore reefs, but the great majority encountered by anglers are taken from rivers and creeks where they are associated with snags and shoreline cover. A bright brownish red with olive or green–blue undertones on parts of the body, jack are readily identified by their large dark eyes and fierce dog-like teeth. The dog theme can be taken a little further to add that they have the biting power of a doberman in their jaws, coupled with the aggressive nature of a psychopathic terrier. The largest mangrove jack recorded was an amazing 16 kg specimen, but a 5 kg fish would be regarded as a very big jack by anglers.

The fish are carnivores, feeding mainly on other small fish and prawns, although nothing would be safe that ventured within striking range of a jack.

Jack can be taken on live baits cast in close to cover, but the great majority of captures are made on lures cast close to shoreline cover. The jack hit these lures and return to cover so fast they demand lightning reflexes on the part of the angler, and the cost of even a moment's hesitation will be the loss of the lure. They are reputed to be great fighters, but most of the drama in jack fishing is restricted to the first moments of the encounter when the fish has to be kept out of the snags.

Baitcasting outfits are the preferred tools for jack fishing, and line from 6 to 10 kg breaking strain is used.

Mangrove jack are a great eating fish with delicate white, moist flesh.

MORWONG

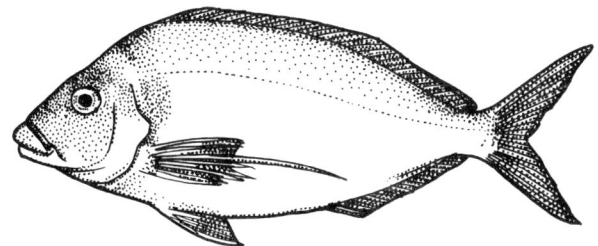

The morwong family is a reasonably large one, although only the blue (illustrated) and red morwong are of any importance to anglers. The red morwong is an incidental catch usually taken by rock anglers fishing with prawns for other species, but the blue morwong figures heavily in the catches of anglers working deep offshore reefs from southern Queensland right down to north-eastern Tasmania.

A silver–blue in colour with extended pectoral fins, the morwong has a protruding mouth with quite large lips. Growing to over 4 kg in weight, they take baits of prawn, squid and cut fish, and are always taken right on the bottom.

Morwong are underrated by many anglers, no doubt disappointed to find a morwong on the end of the line rather than a snapper, but they are an excellent table fish.

MULLET

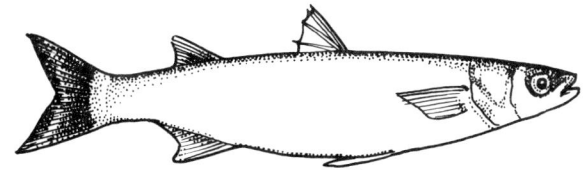

There are many different species of mullet in the family, but they are generally of interest to anglers only as a baitfish. Quite an important commercial fish, the sea mullet spend most of their time in estuaries but take to the ocean shoreline in great schools at spawning time. At this time they are often decimated by commercial netters and on more than one occasion I have seen mullet netted in great numbers, then buried on the beach when a market glut has reduced the price to the point where they are not worth taking to the co-op.

Children can have a lot of fun berleying mullet up with bread, then fishing for them with a tiny piece of crust or dough on a small hook under a float.

All mullet make superb live baits and they are a better dead and strip bait than they are often given credit for. In some states where the practice is allowed, mullet are caught using cast nets and elsewhere they are trapped in bottles or homemade traps made from wire, ice-cream cartons and all sorts of other things.

Mullet are a fairly dubious table fish and are only really acceptable when at sea or resident near the sandy mouths of estuaries. They need to be eaten very fresh and are best cooked on a fire wrapped in foil or a lot of wet newspaper.

Mullet have very sharp spines in the dorsal fin and care should be taken to fold this down when handling the fish.

MURRAY COD

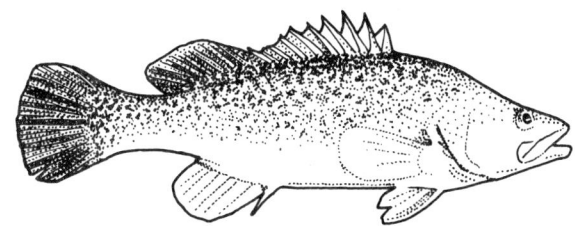

The Murray cod is the sort of fish about which legends are made. With the potential to run into weights up to 50 kg even now, Murray cod probably grew very much larger than that back in the days when our rivers were still relatively untouched. Huge Murray cod have figured in the work of countless bush writers and in the imaginations of most people who have fished the outback streams and dams of the south-eastern half of this continent.

For a time the Murray cod was fighting a losing battle against pollution, dam construction and overfishing, but these days the fish is enjoying a comeback in some of the newer impoundments and through successful stocking programs.

Although not a true cod, the Murray cod is more cod-like than anything else with its barrel body, paddle-shaped tail and gaping bucket mouth. The basic colour is a yellowish green back to yellow sides fading into white belly, with darker mottling over the back, but this can vary a great deal according to environment.

Murray cod can be found in clear, fast-flowing streams, mud brown holes of stagnant water in western rivers and in deepwater dams. Their preference is to work from cover, ambushing food with a quick lunge to the target, involving minimum expenditure of energy.

The diet of the Murray cod might be said to include anything that will pass down the throat. Small fish confine themselves to fish, yabbies, frogs, shrimps and so on, but larger fish will eat almost anything, although this probably has a great deal to do with the availability of food. A cod living in a dam well stocked with forage fish might be less inclined to take a waterbird off the surface than a large fish confined to a muddy river hole which has a limited food supply.

Angling techniques for cod have varied greatly over the years, and in the context of historical interest may prove to have included some of the crudest tackle and techniques ever employed in this country. Heavy set-lines used with a range of baits that included birds and rabbits made set cord lines baited with yabbies look like sporting tackle.

Cod were also probably one of the first species to be fished seriously with lures. The 'lures' were called aeroplane spinners, contraptions that could be made from fencing wire and tin sheet cut into the shape of blades and twisted to make the whole thing spin. It was common practice to 'roar the boat about the hole a bit' to 'wake the fish up' before trolling some of the holes in rivers. Although this all sounds unbelievably crude, if you consider the remote and untouched nature of our western rivers some 30 or more years ago when this was going on, and appreciate the extremely belligerent nature of a large territorial cod, it all makes sense. More refined versions of these spinners remain in use today.

Murray cod are still fished with handlines and yabby and bardy grub baits in the western rivers, but these days they are becoming an extremely popular fish with sport anglers casting lures to cover and working rock bars with deep-diving patterns. Their high profile in the booming impoundment fishery will probably do more than anything else to ensure a safe future for the species.

The cod is a rather bland, fatty fish that is edible without being in any way exciting. Availability and bulk alone have made it an important table fish in the west, but it is considered by sport anglers to be strictly a catch-and-release species.

NANNYGAI

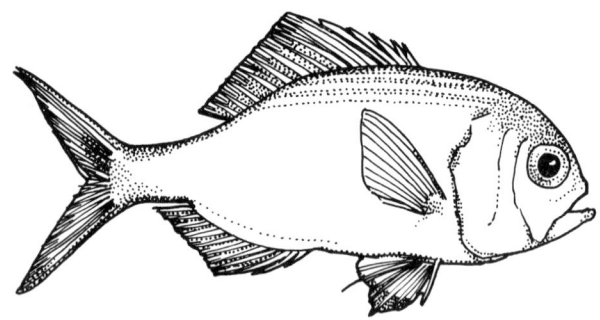

A fish of the southern half of the continent, nannygai school in deep offshore waters over hard bottom, reefs and wrecks. They are frequently called redfish which is confusing as a lot of people refer to snapper as 'reds'.

A bright orange–red, nannygai have the large eyes and huge mouth common to a lot of the deepwater fish. Their scales are extremely tough and have a slight metallic look and feel about them.

Although usually quite a small fish, nannygai have been taken to a length of 50 cm. They frequently occur in such vast, close-packed schools that an echo sounder shows them as a huge dark cloud suspended over the reef, sometimes extending for hundreds of metres.

Very few nannygai that take a bait, which they do with great enthusiasm, ever fail to find the hook, and anglers fishing deep reefs where it can take minutes to get a bait to the bottom, find it extremely frustrating to haul a weight all the way to the top only to find four nannygai hanging off their four hooks. Others take the view that the nannygai are a blessing in areas where snapper and morwong are getting hard to find.

If you can get them big enough to fillet or cook whole, nannygai are a good table fish. If you do find yourself over a school of fish big enough to be worth catching, it may pay to

use very large hooks on the line, as these will be much easier to retrieve from that large mouth than a small hook that will probably be swallowed.

PEARL PERCH

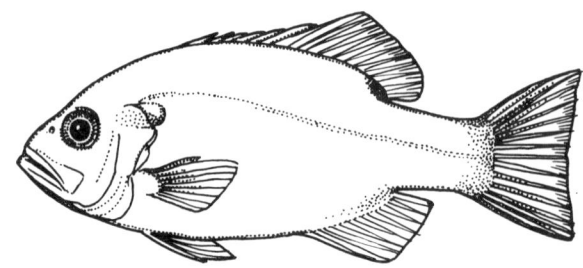

A close relative of the West Australian jewfish, the pearl perch is restricted in distribution to northern New South Wales and southern Queensland. It is a fish of the deep offshore reefs and is commonly referred to as a 'pearly'.

It is basically a silver fish with a faint purple cast through the body and a purplish back. Dark spots are usually apparent at the base of the dorsal and at the top of the gill cover. The maximum length is said to be 70 cm.

Pearl perch have a big mouth and large dark eyes, attributes common to deep water and nocturnal feeders. The odd one is taken in daylight hours, but the great majority of captures are made after dark.

My limited experience with this fish showed that they tend to feed up off the bottom, and in his *Fishes of Australia*, Ern Grant says that the fish rise away from the bottom as they feed, and that he marks a depth on his line by tying a knot on the line with a length of wool where fish are encountered. This is the sort of situation where good echo sounders start to pay for themselves.

The normal bottom-fishing rigs are used for pearl perch with cut fish baits, squid and prawns all being accepted by the fish.

While West Australian anglers claim that their Westralian jewfish is the finest eating fish in the sea, east coasters make the same claim for the pearl perch. The delicate flavour and moist, finely textured flesh takes a lot of beating.

PERCH, GOLDEN

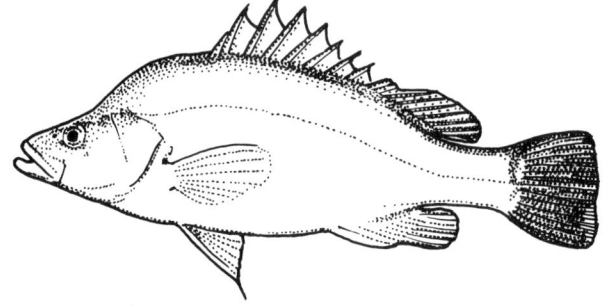

Traditionally known as yellowbelly, and in some areas as callop, the species is commonly referred to as golden perch in the fishing magazines and books of today, and this will probably become the common name within a few years.

Along with the Murray cod, the golden perch has formed the backbone of our inland fishery for native species. Widely distributed, the golden perch is found in Queensland, New South Wales and South Australia. In addition to its broad natural distribution, the golden perch is also well suited to stocking programs which will ensure its long-term survival and probably see it even more widely available than it is today.

Ideally suited to our country and climate, the golden perch can tolerate a wide range of temperature variations and environments. It prefers slow to still water, likes cover and will eat a wide variety of food.

Like all fish, the colour of the golden perch varies according to the quality of the water it is in at the time, and this ranges from a milky yellow through to deeper metallic tones with green inflections, to dark-backed fish that are almost black. A 4 kg golden perch would be considered a genuine trophy fish, and the majority of captures are half that size.

Although traditionally fished for with a variety of worms, grubs and yabby baits, golden perch are increasingly coming into focus as willing lure takers and worthwhile light tackle sportfish. As interest in impoundment, and freshwater fishing in general, continues to rise, the golden perch is occupying an increasingly important niche in our fishing scene, and it is not altogether out of the question to see a future where the yellowbelly creates an Australian equivalent of the American mid-western bass fishing scene.

Golden perch rate fairly highly as a table fish, and some who specialise in freshwater fish rate them as the best table fish of the lot.

Goldens should be handled with care as they have razor-sharp cutting edges on the gill covers and strong, sharp dorsal spines. A lower-lip grip with either thumb and forefinger or pliers is the way to go.

PERCH, MACQUARIE

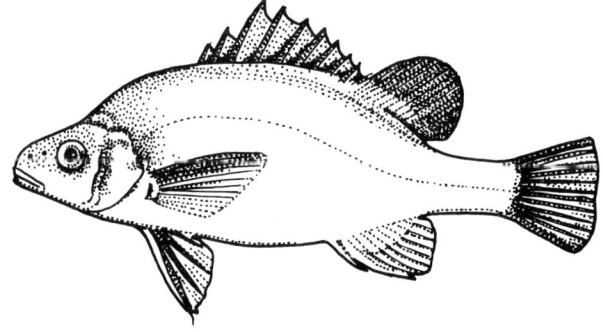

The Macquarie finds its way in here, not because it is a very significant fish in the overall scheme of things, but because quite a lot of anglers get caught up in the business of feeling that they need to catch just one Macquarie to round out their freshwater fishing experience.

One of our smaller native fish with a maximum recorded weight of 3.5 kg, distribution of Macquarie perch is quite limited. They are found in the upper reaches of the Murray–Darling system, and dams such as Burrinjuck, Cotter, Wyangala and Eildon.

The Macquarie prefers cooler water and is fond of running streams. Like most freshwater hunters they are normally associated with cover such as snags, boulders or shoreline overhangs.

Light tackle and very small lures are called for, and the lightest of single-handed threadline outfits are ideal for this sort of fishing. Baits, including mudeyes, earth worms, grasshoppers and crickets, should also be kept small and very lightly weighted.

Although considered a fine table fish, Macquarie perch are generally thought of as a fish to be released, because of their limited distribution and availability.

QUEENFISH

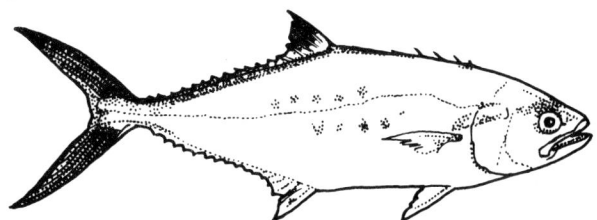

Also known as 'leathery' or 'skinny', the queenfish is unquestionably one of the most spectacular sportfish of our tropical regions.

A quite strange looking fish, the queenfish is remarkably compressed across the body – thus the name 'skinny'. The bones in the head appear to bulge out around the eyes giving them a popeyed look, which combines with the extremely wide, grinning mouth to produce a quite bizarre appearance. But having said that, in profile the queenfish is quite a handsome fish, looking like nothing more than a stretched trevally. The bright silver sides are marked with a series of dark spots.

Due to the lack of body bulk in the fish, there is not much to a queenfish in terms of weight, and it would take a very large and unusual specimen to weigh 10 kg.

Queenfish can be found well upstream in tropical rivers, in most mangrove creeks and well out to sea. They are normally associated with reefs, sand cays, rock outcrops or islands, but moving schools of fish are also frequently encountered out in open water.

A very active predator and surface feeder, queenfish may be taken on a range of baits and lures, but the real action is to be found fishing with surface lures. The most popular of these are the pencil poppers, basic cigar-bodied lures with the weight bias to the rear to enhance casting and only a very small cup in the face. When these are retrieved across the surface at speed, usually on medium threadline tackle, the queenfish turn on quite a spectacle as they rip through the water in pursuit of the lure. Normal blooper-style surface poppers also attract the queenfish. Once a school of queenies get worked up, almost any small jig, saltwater fly or small lure will find a willing taker.

Queenfish are spectacular jumpers, shaking their heads as they cartwheel across the surface. They are also a very strong fish, adept at turning side-on to the angler, using the flat profile and depth of the body to present maximum resistance to the pull of the lines.

When captured, they should be handled with some care, being mindful of two spines on the belly of the fish that can cause a nasty wound.

Like the trevallies, queenfish have reasonable white flesh, although it is a little on the dry side. The meat is firm enough to be well suited to raw-fish marinades.

There are times when a big school of queenfish will go absolutely berserk and the fish can be taken in the hundreds. In such situations it is a good idea to either file the barbs right off the hooks, or to flatten them with pliers. This makes it possible to easily release the fish over the water outside of the boat, which makes the fishing more enjoyable for the angler at the same time as it dramatically increases the survival rate of the fish released.

RED EMPEROR

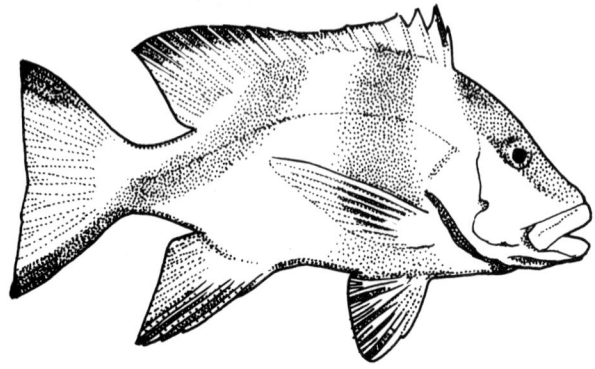

The red emperor is far and away the most popular of the emperor family of fish, and holds similar status in the tropical and subtropical regions of the country to that enjoyed by the southern snapper. They also inhabit similar terrain to the snapper, being associated with deep reefs and gravel bottoms in deep water.

A beautiful fish to look at, the base colour is pink with the striping a dark red. Both the body shape and colour are quite distinctive in younger fish and less distinctive in the largest specimens, although at any size a red emperor is still unmistakable. A fish of 20 kg would be considered unusually large, but night anglers commonly have runs of fish to 10 kg.

Crustaceans of all kinds, squid, cuttlefish and other fish all figure in the diet of the red emperor.

Almost exclusively caught by anglers bottom fishing in deep water, the best catches are usually taken after dark.

Possibly one of our best and most highly prized table fish.

REDFIN

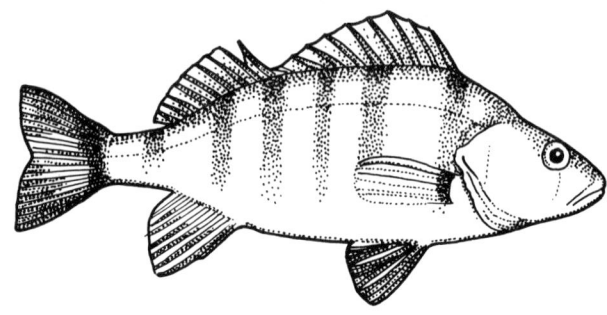

The redfin is variously known as English perch and redfin perch. It is an introduced species, cursed by some in areas where it competes with native fish for a limited food supply, blessed by others where it provides a relatively easy-to-catch fish in places where fishing opportunities had previously been limited.

Although recorded at much larger sizes, a 3 kg redfin would be considered an exceptional fish and they are most commonly encountered in numbers at much smaller sizes.

On the credit side of the ledger, redfin thrive in most subalpine waters and have spread widely throughout New South Wales and Victoria as well as Tasmania. They are also present in southern Western Australia and South Australia. On the debit side, redfin tend to overpopulate an area very quickly, and very soon the average size of the fish drops away to the point where fully mature adult fish are only 15 cm in length.

Redfin are voracious feeders and they will eat fish (including other redfin), shrimp, yabbies and insects.

Because they are a schooling fish, once redfin are located they tend to be found in large numbers. They can be caught on a wide range of baits including worms, shrimp and small live fish. They freely attack small-bladed spinners and spoons, jigs and tiny soft plastics as well as wet flies. Very light threadline tackle is usually required to cast the small lures to cover away from the bank, although it can be especially productive to lower lures and jigs down beside bank-side cover and simply jig the offering up and down with limited rod tip movement in the one place.

Although the majority of the fish offer only a small amount of meat, this is one of the very few species that all anglers are encouraged to catch and kill in the greatest numbers possible. It is not possible to overfish redfin, and even the worst excesses will only cause the remaining fish to grow and replace their numbers at a faster rate.

ROCK BLACKFISH

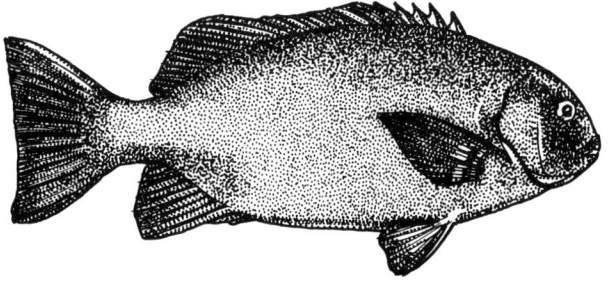

The rock blackfish is also called the black drummer or pig. Although the fish is almost never called a rock blackfish, it is closely related to the luderick and the comparatively uncommon bluefish, and not related to the true drummer.

An east coast fish with its range limited to New South Wales and the lower part of south Queensland, the rock blackfish inhabits the inshore reefs and coastline washes. It is almost always a very dark grey to black all over, with only a faint lightening on the underbelly of some fish. There are periods when the fish will leave the rocks for a short time and venture out over sand, and then they take on an oddly mottled appearance, but this is unusual. I was lucky enough to capture the largest drummer so far recorded, a fish of just over 9 kg.

Deep-bodied, powerful fish with heavy slime-coated scales, rubbery fins and tail supported by strong spines, they are well equipped to operate in the difficult terrain of wild white water and jagged reefs they love. Their diet includes cabbage weed and the fine red weed that grows on the rocks, as well as any crustaceans that inhabit the reef.

Rock blackfish are normally fished for with reasonably heavy sidecast tackle and lines ranging from 6 to 10 kg test, depending on the nature of the terrain being fished. If the bottom allows it, a tiny lead running straight down to the hook is a good way to fish in the wash, and bobby corks are often used where the reef bottom is impossibly hostile. Prawns, crab, cabbage weed, cunje and milk loaf bread are used for bait and the area is normally berleyed with laying pellets, bran, cabbage weed or bread.

These fish are incredibly powerful swimmers and fishing for them is a little like fishing for mangrove jack. They can never be allowed to have their head and must be kept out in clear water or they will quickly vanish into cover and cut the line. They are amongst the most challenging of the east coast species and much underrated as a sportfish.

Rock blackfish are considered by many, including myself, to be one of our best table fish. The flesh is made up of quite large flakes and is pure white and moist. They must be skinned before cooking and I also take the fillet excluding the meat over the rib cage.

SALMON

We have an eastern and a West Australian salmon, but the two fish are so close in appearance, the differences are not worth going into here. The most significant difference for the angler to note is that the western fish has a greater potential size, around 9 kg compared with 7 kg for the eastern fish.

It is also sometimes claimed that the Western Australian salmon feeds primarily on pilchards while the eastern salmon is predominantly a plankton feeder. This is a little hard to believe when you see eastern salmon carving up schools of baitfish, eating quite large lures with enthusiasm and freely taking pilchards cast on ganged hooks. Periodical obsession with plankton would, however, explain why the same fish can be sighted moving in large schools at times, treating the most tempting morsels placed under their nose with disdain.

Restricted to the southern half of the continent, salmon are also known on the east coast and in New Zealand as kahawai. They undertake long migrations at spawning time, and are usually found close inshore off beaches, rocky headlands, as well as in bays and estuaries, although it is unusual for the larger fish to be encountered away from the open sea. They are a steely blue to green on the back with white undersides and yellow or black speckles on the top half of the body.

Salmon are a very strong fish and great fighters on light tackle. They have speed and stamina, and will jump repeatedly when hooked. They will take pilchard baits with enthusiasm, and when in the surf will take worm, pipi and prawn baits. They can be caught on a wide range of lures, sometimes showing a distinct preference for silver lures with a patch of red.

They are also a great favourite with saltwater fly anglers.

Salmon once travelled our beaches in great schools that turned the water black as they passed, but overfishing for the canneries decimated stocks. They have made something of a comeback, but not in the numbers one might expect. I suspect that this is linked to the overfishing of bait stocks for the petfood industry.

Salmon fall into the 'desperation' class as a table fish, and even when used as a base for fishcakes and pies, the end result is fairly ordinary. They are best encountered, enjoyed, then released unharmed to get on with the business of making more salmon.

SALMON, THREADFIN

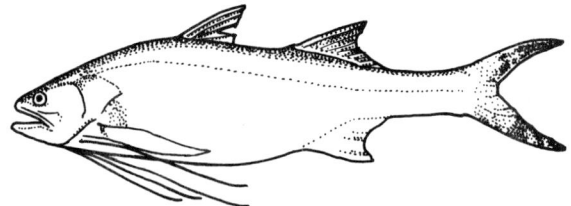

There are a few species of threadfin, the most common being the blue and the king threadfins.

A very distinctive and handsome fish in appearance, the threadfin are quite unusual in that they have a slightly overshot upper jaw. They also have long, trailing soft rays just below and ahead of the pectoral, which is probably the feature that gave them their name.

The blue threadfin has a blue back melting into silver then white underside, and the king is a basic blue–grey across the back, but with a golden or yellow undertone over the entire body. The blue is the smaller of the two fish, with a maximum recorded weight of 18 kg, while the king has been recorded at a massive 30 kg, although both fish are normally taken very much smaller than those weights. A good blue might be around 4 kg, while a king might weigh 10 kg.

A tropical species, they inhabit much the same areas as the barramundi, and are most often an incidental catch by people fishing for barramundi. Quite spectacular sportfish, the threadfin are high and frequent jumpers and the fight is characteristically a frantic one.

Opportunistic feeders, prawns play a large part in a diet that also includes a lot of small fish.

Quite an important commercial fish in some areas, all threadfin are very good to eat.

SARATOGA

The saratoga is a strange-looking, but most interesting tropical freshwater fish. The southern saratoga is restricted to the Fitzroy River system in southern Queensland, while the northern version occurs in northern Queensland, the Gulf of Carpentaria and the Northern Territory.

Both of these fish are identical in shape, with a narrow, compressed body, very large scales, a protruding lower jaw, eyes set well towards the top of the head and fins biased well back towards the tail.

The southern saratoga has an olive green back and silver sides, while the northern has a darker green back with the greenish tinge carrying right down over gold to silver sides. Both fish carry either a red spot or band on each scale.

With their jaws and eyes designed the way they are, saratoga are obvious surface feeders with frogs playing quite an important part in their diet. They like to get in under cover, and lily pads are a favourite haunt for these fish.

Saratoga have become a priority target for fly anglers in the north, and small popper flies produce some very spectacular action. Soft plastic double-tail lures worked through lily pads also draw fire, and although not commonly used in this country, some of the American weedless spinner baits are dynamite.

Fine jumpers, saratoga taken on light tackle close to cover, or a tangle of lilies, will test any sport angler as they use those large paddle tails and centreboard-style bodies to apply a great deal of pressure.

This is a 100 per cent sportfish with no value whatsoever on the table. The flesh is soft, tastes like mud and is full of fine bones. A fish to be seen, wondered at then carefully released.

SILVER DRUMMER

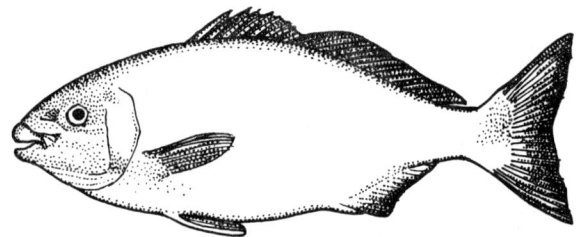

The silver drummer is a fish of southern waters, although it is rare in Victoria and Tasmania. It is sometimes called the buffalo bream, although there is a true buffalo bream which is common in Western Australia.

Silver drummer are most commonly encountered in offshore reefs where they sometimes combine in large schools, but at the same time they are not uncommon along the shoreline.

Not an especially attractive fish, they are deep-bodied and silver grey in colour with a slightly darker back. They have been recorded to 12 kg and big ones are a sensational fish on the end of a fishing line.

Considered inedible by the majority of anglers, silver drummer are normally only an accidental catch when fishing for something else.

SLIMY MACKEREL

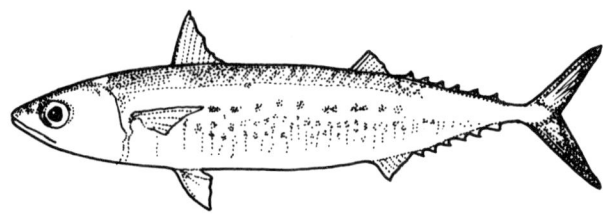

One of our most important bait species, the slimy mackerel occurs right around the southern half of the continent.

Schooling fish, they are generally encountered in great numbers, anywhere between the shoreline and the continental shelf.

A very handsome little fish with their cylindrical bodies, tuna-like fine forked tail and blue to blue–green back with darker bars, the great majority of fish caught are from 20 to 30 cm in length.

The flesh is a dark, bloody red, and the fish make excellent strip or live baits, although they are quite a big baitfish and can be difficult to keep alive in anything other than the largest live bait systems. Fillets keep very well when salted and they also keep well when brined if refrigeration is not available.

Mackerel are normally first berleyed up with fish, bread or bran mixed with tuna oil, then fished with light line and small, unweighted baits of fish flesh or prawn, or with multi-hook bait jigs.

Once the bite gets underway the little mackerel are usually caught at a breakneck pace, particularly when using the jig chains.

SNAPPER

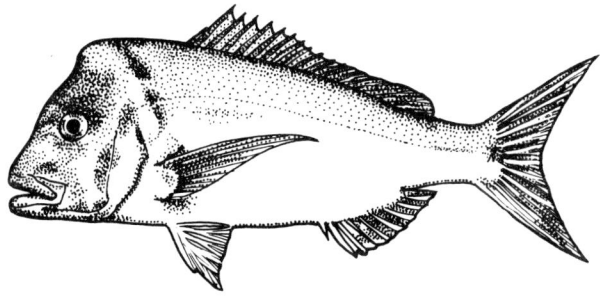

The snapper is widely distributed around Australia, from subtropical regions all the way down to Tasmania. The fish spawn inshore and the young make their way into mangroves, bays and estuaries. As they develop they gradually make their way offshore to the deep ocean reefs and gravel beds.

Snapper vary in colour from a pale but very bright pink through to a deep brick red on the upper body, then silver–white on the sides to the belly. Bright metallic blue spots are apparent on the sides, more so in the small fish than the larger specimens. The largest recorded snapper was a fish of 19.5 kg.

Some people like to use the names cockney bream, red bream, squire and then snapper to describe this fish through its various stages of growth, but a snapper is a snapper no matter how big it is.

Snapper are basically a scavenging fish and they will eat whatever is available – prawns and other shellfish, small squid, fish and so on.

The largest snapper are wanderers and they can be found inshore in quite shallow water as well as out on the deep sea reefs. I am tempted to believe that the fish become more predatory as they grow older and that these inshore forays are connected with availability of food supplies. The Victorian fish certainly come in to feed on scallops, and along the east

coast large snapper are usually inshore close to the rocks after a southerly gale, and when tailor are moving along the coast in numbers. Very large snapper are often caught by land-based and game anglers on live fish baits and blue pilchards, and they are most commonly encountered up towards the surface rather than down on the deep reef.

The great majority of snapper are taken by anglers fishing the bottom over very deep reef using baits of prawn, squid, pilchards and cut fish. Tuna meat is much appreciated by snapper.

In shallower offshore waters berley can be very effective, often bringing the fish right to the surface behind the boat. Many big-fish specialists believe that floating baits are the way to go for big snapper, and it certainly pays dividends to fish both bottom and floating baits when using berley.

Fishing from the shore anglers generally use floating pilchards on ganged hooks, but there are many recognised snapper grounds along the coast where big fish are regularly taken on the bottom. There are many areas along our coastline with 5 to 10 fathoms of water all the way in to the base of the shoreline rocks, and these will produce some level of snapper activity year-round. Many of the inshore spots require such a long cast to be made that bottom fishing is mandatory, and baits of octopus and squid are popular as they stay on the hook well during the cast and also resist the nagging attention of small pickers until a snapper comes along. Fishing white-water washes, crabs can be quite a lethal bait for snapper.

One of the great attractions of the snapper is the quality of the moist white flesh and the fact that quite large fish are almost as good to eat as the smaller fish. Snapper of 1 kg or so are one of the best table fish in our seas.

SOOTY GRUNTER

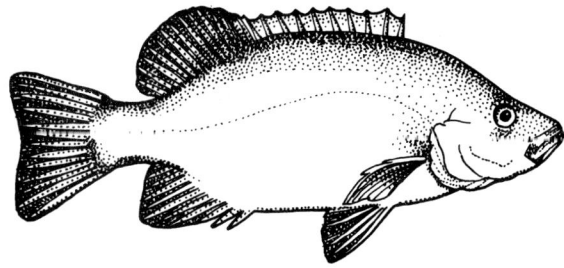

There are several members of this freshwater family, all similar enough in character to be lumped under the general name sooty grunter.

Inhabitants of the tropical north, they are found in streams, lakes, billabongs and dams.

The majority of sooty grunter encountered are grey to black, but others range through to a dark olive. The fish are characterised by a deep, chunky body and prominent rubbery lips.

The fish move about in schools and small groups and an average example would be half a kilogram in weight. A 2 kg fish would be an unusually large one.

Sooties are opportunistic feeders that will take advantage of almost anything the environment will offer. Their basic diet includes the usual shrimp, worms and small fish, but at the other extreme they have been known to eat fruit that has fallen into the water.

The normal freshwater baits of shrimp, yabbies and worms are all welcomed by sooty grunter, and their willingness to strike quite a wide range of lures makes them popular with sport anglers. A light, single-handed threadline outfit is ideal for casting the light lures required and is more than adequate for landing fish of this size.

The sooty grunter is generally regarded as being quite an acceptable table fish.

SPANGLED EMPEROR

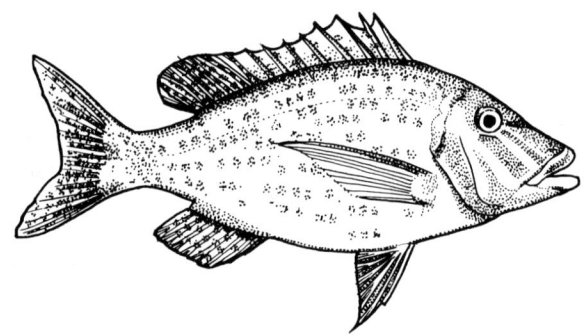

The spangled emperor, also commonly known as northwest snapper, is a tropical fish that is also found, on occasion, well down into subtropical zones.

It is difficult to describe the colours of the spangled emperor, but it is basically a blue to blue–grey fish with gold and green edges on the scales, although the bright blue is the more common tone. Bright blue bars radiate from the eyes down to the chin and the fins are all yellow with bright blue spots. They grow to around 10 kg in weight and are commonly caught at 2 to 3 kg.

A reef species, spangled emperor also come in over sand around beaches at night, and I have caught them spinning from the shore of Barrier Reef sand cays. They respond to baits of cut fish and squid and can be berleyed in close to the bottom in the same manner as snapper.

Opinion on the table quality of the fish varies quite a lot, but they are generally thought to be a good eating fish providing they are properly cared for after capture.

SPANISH MACKEREL

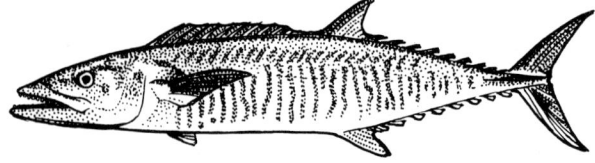

The narrow-barred Spanish mackerel ranges from the tropical north down as far as the north coast of New South Wales and Geographe Bay in Western Australia. It is an important commercial fish and a favourite with game and sport anglers alike. Commonly called a Spaniard, it is also given the name tanguigue.

A silver-bodied fish with striping that varies from a bright blue to a dark grey, Spanish mackerel are frequently encountered in large schools in the tropical north, but are often lone hunters at the southern extremity of their distribution. Maximum recorded size is over 60 kg, but fish of 25 to 30 kg are not uncommon and fish of this size are sometimes taken by land-based anglers.

Spaniards are high-speed surface hunters and they are equipped with close-set triangular teeth in a long, pointed jaw. The speed of attack and the rate at which the jaws work result in a lot of hooks being missed in a strike. They often attack their prey from below, spearing out through the surface and into fresh air for quite staggering distances before falling back into the water.

Spanish mackerel are usually an easy fish to catch, as they will attack a wide range of trolled or cast and retrieved lures with enthusiasm, and fresh and live fish baits are also effective. Blue pilchards are a hot favourite and it pays to anchor up and berley a current with these when the mackerel are about.

It is always necessary to use some wire when fishing mackerel as their teeth make short work of monofilament line. It is also important to use a reel with plenty of line on it, as the opening run of a big mackerel can account for 100 m in what seems to be the blink of an eye. More than one land-based angler has been introduced to the bare spool of the reel by a big Spaniard.

Spanish mackerel are an excellent table fish, although they do tend to be a little on the dry side. In tropical waters they can be affected by ciguatera and the usual warning stands that it is better to eat a little off a number of small fish than a lot off a big one.

Other important mackerel are the spotted mackerel and the shark mackerel. Both are fish with a much smaller growth potential than the Spanish mackerel, and the spotted mackerel is commonly found inshore in sandy bays.

TAILOR

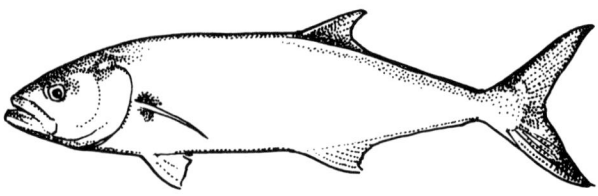

The tailor is an abundant fish throughout all of southern Australia, although these days not as prolific as in years gone by. Related to the kingfish and trevallies, the tailor has a potential growth to 1.2 m and a weight of 14.5 kg. Some West Australian locations are renowned for producing regular runs of 10 kg tailor, but such fish are nowhere near as common on the east coast, although they are not by any means unheard of.

Basically a silver fish, the tailor may have either a green or a blue back, and a similar cast over the upper half of the body. You will often hear it said that 'greenbacks' are tailor of a particular size, but 1 have seen enough big blueback tailor to be convinced that the colour reflects the environment the fish is in at the time, just as it does with every other fish.

The most distinctive feature of the tailor is the extended lower jaw and the mouthful of razor-sharp triangular teeth. Commonly referred to as choppers, tailor quite literally chop into their prey with jaws working at an incredible speed. It is not at all uncommon to remove what appears to be a whole fish from the stomach of a tailor, only to find that it has been neatly sliced into several pieces as if with a razor. The jaws open and close so fast in attack, striking at a tailor bite will give you a 50 per cent chance of ripping all of the hooks out of a wide-open mouth without making contact.

Tales of the tailor's voracity are legendary, and every tailor angler has taken tailor so full of food, the tail of the last fish they ate will be sticking out of the mouth next to that of the bait. The floor of any boat involved in a tailor session is usually carpeted in small whole fish, or bits of fish, that the tailor regurgitate when hooked.

The tailor's habit of simply slashing at fish when there is plenty of bait in the water means that they produce a cloud of berley wherever they go, and any bait that can find its way through a hot school of working tailor stands an excellent chance of finding a big snapper or bream working under the tailor to pick up the scraps.

The prolific numbers of tailor once found right around the southern part of the continent, coupled with the voracious nature of the fish, led to angling excesses that are embarrassing to recall today. In northern New South Wales and southern Queensland, tailor were killed until anglers could not find the strength to kill any more. These days, although still plentiful, our tailor stocks are a shadow of what they were 10 years ago, and studies are underway to try and find out why. At the greatest killing fields of them all on the southern side of Fraser Island, a closed season has been introduced to try and get the fishing pressure off the breeding season, but 1 am inclined to think that this is only a minor part of the problem. The tailor decline mirrors the boom in the canned petfood industry which consumes vast amounts of Australian baitfish every year. You can't take the bait out of the sea and still have it support vast numbers of a fish like the tailor.

Tailor can be caught on just about any fish bait, although the blue pilchard is the preferred bait of most anglers. Fished on a flight of ganged hooks the baits are cast out and slowly retrieved with either a rod tip lift and drop, or a slow retrieve on the reel handle. A tailor bite involves a preliminary sharp tap as he bites the tail off the fish to cripple it, then a staccato rapid-fire burst of bites as he chops his way down its length.

To hook a tailor you simply keep winding at the same speed and smoothly lift the rod tip. Needle-sharp hooks are a big asset.

Tailor will also eat just about any kind of lure, and they are great fun to catch on poppers as up to a dozen fish at a time will fall all over the surface trying to get to the popper first. In the bays where smaller tailor will often school in great numbers, you can stand well off a school in a boat and cast to them with small metal fish slugs such as the Stingsildas and Teeny Terrors. This is a far more effective method than trolling, which tends to put the fish down and break the schools up.

Tailor are a great beginner's fish and a real winner with kids. They fight very well, jump all over the place and are generally pretty easy to catch.

With soft flesh, slightly dark meat and poor keeping qualities, many anglers regard the tailor as a poor table fish, but others prefer the rather strong flavour to anything else. They must be bled and cleaned immediately and put on ice, and smart anglers take care in handling them in the boat to ensure minimum contact with hard, bruising surfaces. They can be greatly improved if they are frozen for a day or two before eating.

TERAGLIN

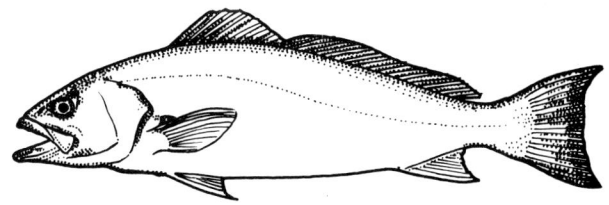

The teraglin has quite a limited distribution from around Fraser Island in southern Queensland to Montague Island in New South Wales.

Teraglin are so much like a mulloway, a lot of people can't tell them apart after death, but they can always be separated by the fact that the trailing edge of the trag's tail curves inward, while the mulloway's curves outward. When first caught the teraglin is a silver fish with a strong purple–blue colour on the back and the inside of the mouth is bright yellow.

Teraglin are an offshore fish and are always caught at night. They pack into tight schools and will usually be found over just one spot on a large area of reef. They tend to start the night deep and work their way up towards the surface, and will also rise to the surface with hooked fish. The trick to fishing them is to find the level at which the school is working and try never to lose one once hooked, as a lost fish will sometimes take the whole school away with him.

Teraglin are an excellent fish to eat, very much like a jewfish, and like jewfish they have a terrible smell when brought into the boat.

TOMMY ROUGH

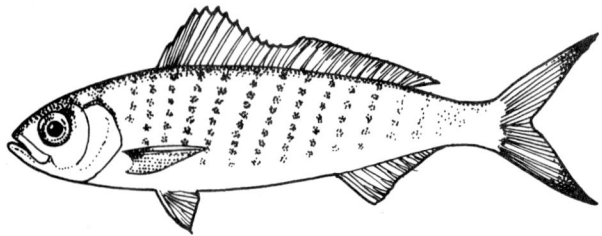

A fish of southern waters, the rough is found in lower Victorian waters, and is prolific in South Australia and southern Western Australia.

This small herring is usually caught to lengths of around 25 cm, but even at this relatively short length, the cylindrical little body of the fish delivers a quite substantial, well-flavoured fillet.

A very dark grey–green on the back with silver sides, the fish is notable for unusually large dark eyes. The scales are rough to the touch, which may be where the 'rough' part of the name comes in.

Northern anglers living beyond the range of the herring are a little puzzled by the great popularity of this little fish, and sometimes refer to them by the name 'Tommy rots'. However, you only need to observe the herring fishery first-hand to appreciate their great popularity. Sheer availability is the key to the fishery, and rough can be caught in quantity from just about any jetty, rock outcrop and beach without the need for complicated or expensive gear. They are a fish for experts, novices, old people, children and everyone else who wants to fish for them. When the herring are on, the expert will catch a lot of fish, but just about everyone seems to get something to take home.

Berley is a fairly essential ingredient when fishing for rough. The preferred berley is a mix of fish oil and pollard, which can be dispensed in conventional ways, or packed into a 'blob' float which will then shower berley down around the bait when it hits the water.

The best bait for herring is maggots, and most keen herring anglers breed their own. If maggots are not your thing, try whitebait or sardines on a flight of No. 6 Limerick hooks, or small cubes of squid. They will also readily take small lures, and bait jig strings fished into berley can be very effective at times.

Tommy rough have quite a strong taste, and much of it is in the skin. I prefer them grilled, but they also come up quite well when fried. A fish to appreciate every now and then rather than one you would eat in great quantities all the time.

TREVALLY

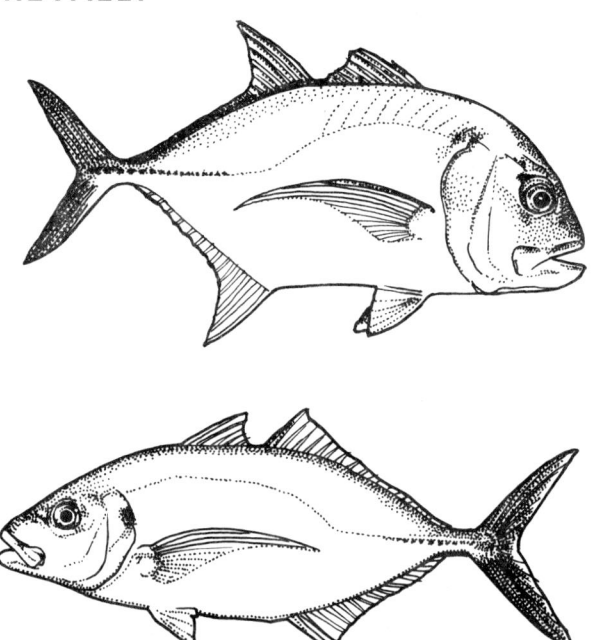

The trevally family is one of the world's largest groups of fish. They come in a great variety of shapes, sizes and colours, but all are great fighting fish. One of the toughest fish in the sea, all trevally are possessed of great speed when they run, incredible lugging power when they turn side-on to stonewall the angler, and staying power that often sees the light-tackle angler wishing he were somewhere else doing just about anything other than trying to subdue a trevally.

Typical of the heavyweights of the trevally world is the giant trevally, a tropical species recorded at 1.7 m long and a weight in excess of 50 kg. A truly belligerent-looking fish with an eye socket shape that gives it the appearance of scowling, it has an enormous set of crushing jaws. The great trevally is known to anglers as the GT.

GTs will take almost any lure from a deep runner to a surface popper, and their wild, boiling surface strikes and screaming initial runs are hair-raising stuff. They do roam about in open water, but are most often encountered close to reefs where they are incredibly difficult to stop before they dive back into cover and cut the line.

A muscular fish, the meat of the great trevally is rather dry and a little tough on the small fish, and large specimens are best left alone.

The silver trevally, on the other hand, is a smaller member of the family that is a common inshore fish. Anglers catch them in considerable numbers from $\frac{1}{2}$ kg to a little more than 1 kg in weight. Offshore they are commonly encountered up to 2 and 3 kg. Maximum size is said to be around the 10 kg mark.

The silver trevally has wide distribution around the southern half of Australia, where it is found from deep offshore reefs all the way into estuaries and bays. Inshore the fish are usually found in close to the rocks or over reef bottom of some kind. The fish is a basic silver colour with blue and green sometimes showing on the back, and on some specimens faint bars are evident on the sides. The fins and tail are tinged with yellow.

It is caught by bait anglers using prawn and cut fish baits and will readily take small lures and jigs. Like all trevally, it puts up a fight out of all proportion to its size and needs to be played with some care as there is an extensive soft membrane behind the lips of the fish from which a hook can easily tear free.

Silver trevally are quite good to eat and are much improved if skinned before cooking.

TROUT, BROWN

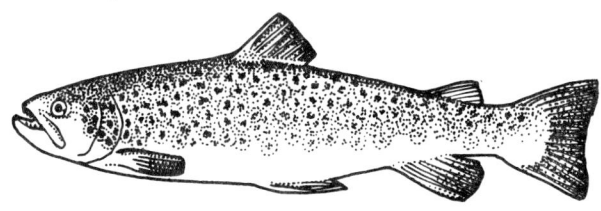

The introduced brown trout is limited to the cooler waters of alpine regions throughout Australia, and this includes New South Wales, Victoria, South Australia, the southern part of Western Australia and all of Tasmania.

The colour scheme of the brown trout is a rather complex one, with pronounced black and red spots that are haloed with a blue-to-white tinge. The back is brown to olive, fading to a yellow that carries well down to a white or cream underside. The fins and tail are normally a plain brown.

The fish are found in a range of environments from fast-running shallow streams to large impoundments and open lakes.

A 10 kg brown trout would be considered a monster, and most anglers would be celebrating the capture of a 5 kg fish.

In the streams brown trout rely largely on the available small aquatic life, insect larvae and any terrestrial insects that alight on or fall into the water. In the lakes and dams they are more likely to be feeding on shrimp and yabbies as well as other small fish.

Brown trout are considered to be more sensitive and cunning than the rainbow trout, and for this reason they are normally fished with the lightest tackle that will get the job done. They can be taken by all of the normal methods including baitfishing, spinning with lures and, of course, fly fishing.

For both bait and lure fishing very light threadline tackle is used. Threadlines spooled with no more than 2-3 kg breaking strain line, with fine diameter to breaking strain characteristics, are ideal for casting the very light weights involved in trout fishing.

Bubble floats are frequently employed to impart movement or keep baits of insects, worms or shrimp up off the bottom. As little lead as possible is used and hooks should be very sharp and as small as is practical for use with the bait involved.

The most commonly used lures are the Celta-style spinners in their many forms, and small spoons. When trolling from a boat the flatfish, Tassie devil and Baltic minnow all have their adherents.

There have probably been more books written on fly fishing for trout than on any other six angling subjects lumped together. The topic is complex, highly specialised and far beyond the essentially superficial scope of this condensed guide. I refer you to this abundant supply of literature with the warning that this is not something to be undertaken by a person with little time to spare, and you should also be warned that there is quite a high potential for chronic addiction associated with the subject.

Brown trout have a delicate flavour and are generally quite good to eat. The flesh may vary in colour from a pale pink to a definite red, which sometimes comes as a bit of a shock to those accustomed to the white flesh of saltwater fish.

TROUT, RAINBOW

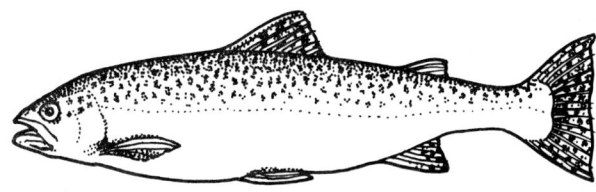

Not dissimilar in form from the brown trout, the rainbow is generally characterised by the range of colours in its camouflage.

Basically a silver-bodied fish, the rainbow may have a green–brown to blue back fading to a greenish tinge over silver, then often a bright pink stripe along the centre of the side and a pink patch on the gill cover. There is commonly a lot of dark green in the tail which is covered in black spots, with black spots liberally dotted over the upper two-thirds of the body. All of this colour can become greatly exaggerated in the mating season.

The rainbow trout are not quite as well suited to the marginal warmer waters tolerated by the brown, and thus their distribution is slightly reduced to the higher areas and cold water.

The rainbow has much in common with the brown trout, including diet, but it is generally thought of as being a less cautious fish, even a silly fish in the case of young rainbows. On the other side of the coin, fly anglers are well acquainted with periods of obsessive feeding when only a perfect match for the food in favour at the time will get a look from a free-feeding rainbow.

Generally speaking, the comments on angling and the table qualities of the brown trout apply equally to the rainbow.

TUNAS

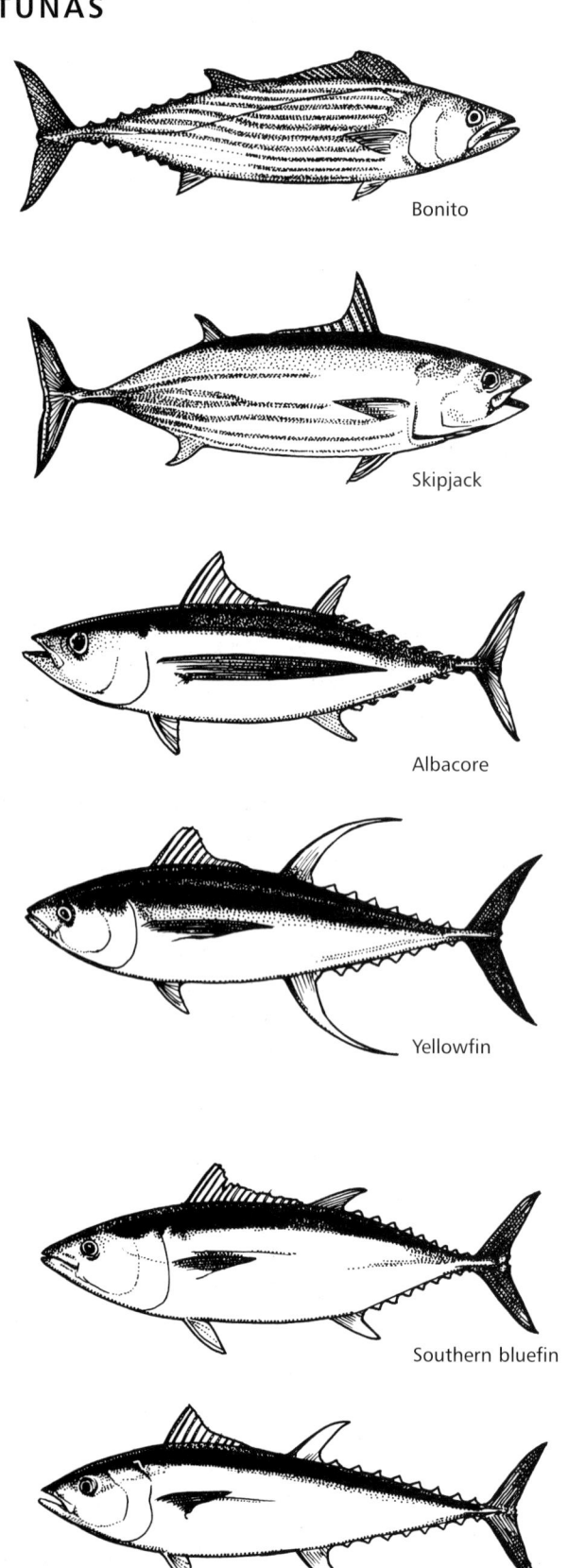

Bonito

Skipjack

Albacore

Yellowfin

Southern bluefin

Northern bluefin

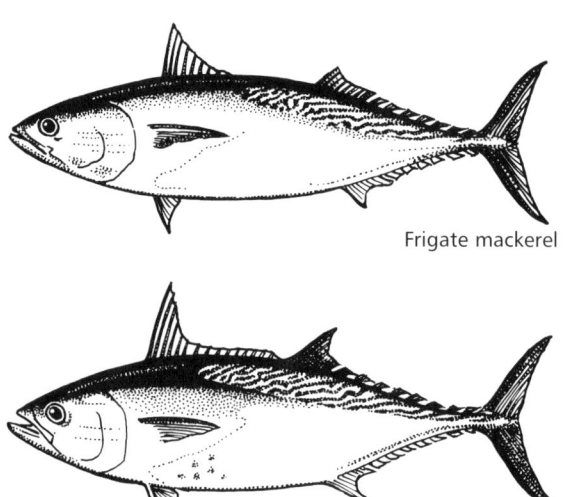

Frigate mackerel

Mackerel

There are many tunas in Australian waters, and for ease of handling in this book I have taken the liberty of grouping the important ones under the general heading of 'tunas' and dealing with them as fish that are primarily important either as bait or sporting species.

The frigate mackerel illustrated is a tuna and not a mackerel, and is also fairly commonly known as the leadenall for some reason. Frigates have become immensely popular as a live bait in recent years, especially with land-based game anglers, but they have been recognised as a top strip bait for jewfish and snapper for a long time, especially on the north coast of New South Wales. They are a small tuna with a maximum growth potential of 58 cm.

Bonito and skipjack tuna, also known as striped tuna, are also prime baitfish. The skipjack has dark red, bloody meat while the bonito has a much lighter meat and is also considered a reasonable table fish by some. Both fish provide great sport when taken on light tackle, particularly the striped tuna which are fast and possessed of great staying power. Both fish are caught either by trolling small lures or casting to schools working at the surface. Skipjack grow to a weight of 20 kg and bonito to a weight of 10 kg, but around 2 to 4 kg would cover the great majority of either fish taken by amateurs.

Tuna meat is fine if used for bait soon after capture, but after a time the skin becomes very hard and the flesh turns mushy, which makes it difficult to use. If it is to be kept, especially if it is to be frozen, sprinkle the meat with coarse salt first and this will keep it firm.

The last fish in this group is the mackerel tuna which is easily identified by the 'saddle' of dark mackerel patterning on the back and a series of black spots on the belly. Mackerel tuna will at times take large cast or trolled lures, but they have their seasons when they will feed obsessively on tiny bait and at these times they become difficult to catch. They can be very boat shy and at times can only be taken by casting long distances to them with small metal lures.

The next group of fish are the major sport and gamefishing species of tuna.

The albacore is the first of the group with a maximum growth potential of 1.5 m and a world record size of 40 kg, although it is normally encountered at a fraction of that size in our waters. Usually a schooling fish found well offshore, the albacore is characterised by a very long pectoral fin extending back beyond the second dorsal in adult fish. Taken when trolling lures, and with live baits, the albacore has quite light meat and is called 'chicken of the sea' in the United States.

The yellowfin tuna is easily our most important tuna from a sporting viewpoint. They are taken to over 170 kg in waters off Mexico where a lot of night fishing is done for them, and in Australia, where most of the fishing is done in daylight, the record stands at 102 kg.

Yellowfin are one of the most beautiful fish in the sea with a dark blue to black back, giving way to a mixture of metallic green, blue and gold below that, then turning to silver overlaid with mother-of-pearl on the underside with yellow and blue flecks back towards the tail. There are so many colours combining to make up the dominant shades in the yellowfin, ten people describing the fish would probably pick out ten different colour schemes. The fins and finlets are bright yellow, and in some adult fish both the second dorsal and anal fins grow to remarkable length in great curved sickles.

Yellowfin are found in all Australian waters and may be encountered from the continental shelf to the coastal rocks in areas where deep water is found close inshore. Nearly all of the pioneering work done on sportfishing for yellowfin occurred in the south of New South Wales, but more recent activity has focused on southern Queensland grounds. Reports of giant yellowfin working the prawn trawler wakes in northern New South Wales probably identifies great future potential between Coffs Harbour and Tweed Heads as well.

Yellowfin are always fished with full gamefishing tackle as their great stamina and speed demands reels with the very best drag systems and big line capacity. They are caught trolling lures and live baits of small tuna, and also by fishing live baits, cubes of tuna meat and pilchards into a berley trail.

The southern bluefin tuna stocks in our waters are said to be marginal after the species has been overfished by commercial operators worldwide, but there are still some very large fish to be found.

A fish of our southern oceans and usually encountered wide offshore, the southern bluefin has a potential weight of over 100 kg. It has a dark blue to black back and silver sides, with bright yellow lateral keels in younger fish, but these become dark in adults. There is some yellow in the second dorsal and tail.

Southern bluefin are subjected to concentrated fishing off Tasmania but further north the more abundant yellowfin tend to overshadow the bluefin.

The final tuna is the northern bluefin or longtail, a tropical species that is found as far down as the south coast of New South Wales and Geographe Bay on the west in the summer months.

The longtail is easily identified by the fact that the typical barrel tuna shape is confined to the forward third of the body, which then tapers steadily all the way back to the tail to give the fish a super-streamlined appearance. They are a dark-backed silver fish with only a small amount of yellow apparent on the finlets towards the tail.

Small longtails are commonly encountered in schools in the northern regions, but those found to the south are usually loners and quite large fish. The Australian record is 35.9 kg. Fish of 20 kg or so are often encountered by rock anglers fishing live baits, who need to work hard to get the fish back to the rocks before they simply go to the bottom. Northern bluefin have no swim bladder.

WAHOO

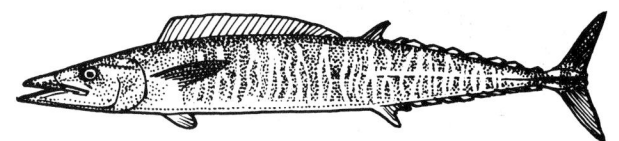

Very similar to the Spanish mackerel in a number of ways, the most distinctive difference is that the first dorsal is much more pronounced and often has a straight-line appearance to it. The jaws are more pointed and not as heavy as those of the mackerel, and where the mackerel has a deep fork to the tail, the wahoo has a small tail that is almost straight up and down. Beautifully marked with violet stripes in the water, these stripes fade to a universal dark grey colour after death. Wahoo range further south than the mackerel and are found down as far as Montague Island in the east and Exmouth Gulf in the west.

The wahoo is not classified as a schooling fish, but I have encountered them in great numbers in an area and it is pretty hard not to call it a school of fish when every lure behind the boat goes off at once to wahoo.

If Spanish mackerel are fast, then wahoo are snake-strike fast. After being brought to the boat at the end of an extraordinarily sustained opening run, a wahoo will again streak off so fast that the line actually hisses quite audibly through the surface of the water. A wahoo is also the only fish I have seen to cause the star drag washers in a reel to produce smoke within the first 100 m of a run. They are fast!

Wahoo are the all-time champions at slicing baits within millimetres of the hooks time after time, and many anglers who are not concerned with records rig their lures with a stinger, a treble hook that hangs back behind the lure or bait on wire. Wahoo is a very good table fish and not associated with ciguatera.

WEST AUSTRALIAN JEWFISH

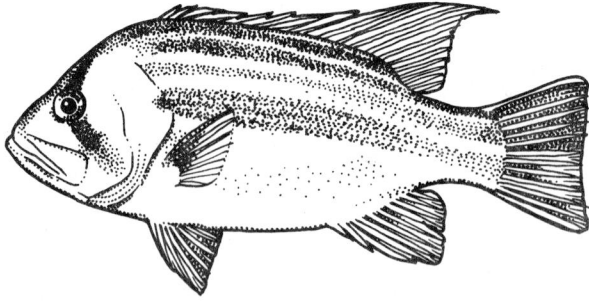

Most commonly called the Westralian jewfish, and often incorrectly called dhufish, this species is exclusive to the western side of the continent and occurs within a limited range from the Recherche Archipelago in the south to Shark Bay in the north.

The Westralian jewfish has nothing in common with the mulloway or jewfish, but it is a close relative of the eastern Australian pearl perch, and like the pearl perch is considered by anglers to be a prize capture. In the west it is thought the finest table fish of them all, and with a growth potential of 1.2 m and a top recorded weight of 30 kg, the fish has a great deal going for it. A fish over 7 kg would be considered a good catch by the average angler.

Found mostly over deep offshore reefs and broken bottom, the jewfish is a deep, heavy-bodied fish with a large mouth and big eyes. It is basically a silver fish with a purplish back. Younger specimens carry the dark back colour into stripes on the sides and a black eye stripe is also evident. Another identifying feature on larger fish is a long trailing filament on the rear of the dorsal fin.

When hauled up from the depths the swim bladder expands to choke the fish, so there is little in the way of a fight involved in the capture beyond the first rush after the hookup, when the fish will try to get into cover. From time to time jewfish will be encountered in shallower water inshore, and when this happens they are said to be a very strong fish capable of giving a good account of themselves on a line.

Pilchards, octopus and squid are considered top baits, as are live fish baits of almost any kind. It pays to be patient when the typical sucking bite of the jewfish is experienced, as the fish have a reputation for fiddling with baits before swallowing them.

WHITING

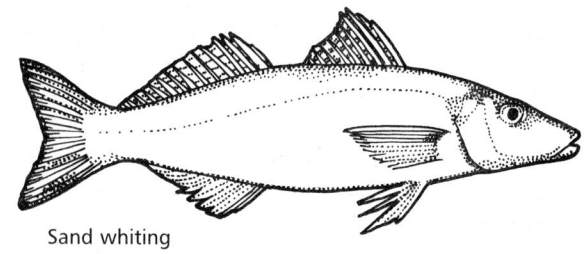

Sand whiting

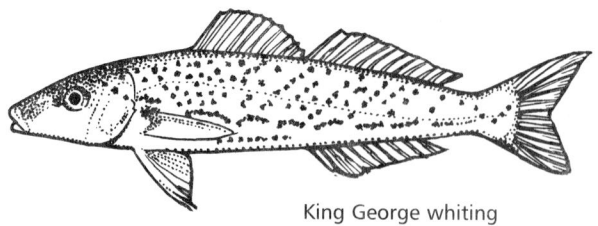

King George whiting

There are over a dozen different members of the whiting family distributed around southern Australia, and most of these share the common habitat of sandy bays, beaches and estuaries. The exception to this is the King George whiting, a very large whiting found only in the extreme southern parts of the country including Victoria, South Australia and the southern part of Western Australia.

The King George has a potential size of 4.5 kg and a length of 69 cm. Although young fish are found inshore in ribbon weed beds in shallow waters, the adult fish are normally found in water to 18.2 m, with sand gutters adjacent to reef being a popular haunt. The smaller fish school, but as they become larger they tend to move in small groups or become loners, frequently seen moving with groups of other species.

The King George has silver sides turning brown on the top of the body and characteristic black spots scattered over the body with the tail a clear yellow.

Live worms, shellfish and sometimes skinned squid are excellent baits for this member of the family which has a reputation as a great sporting fish on light tackle. River mouths and shallow bays are generally the places most anglers look for them in the summer months.

The sand whiting are more typical of the majority of the family, and these fish are found all the way up to subtropical regions. They are a silver fish with back colouring that may range from the palest sand tones through to a yellow–brown. Many of the whiting carry a strong yellow flash at the base of the pectoral fins and all have a quite distinct black pupil in an otherwise clear eye. Large sand whiting develop a bluish colouring around the nose, which accounts for the popular name 'bluenose whiting'. Potentially the largest of the rest of the whiting family, sand whiting have been recorded to 47 cm long, which is an enormous size for whiting.

Whiting are found over sand and ribbon weed in estuaries, bays and surf beaches where they travel in schools, often in great numbers. Soldier crabs, yabbies, worms and prawns play a major part in their diet, and in recent times anglers have had considerable success with large whiting using strips of salted pilchard and whitebait on gangs of tiny hooks. The whiting taken this way are usually an incidental catch when fishing for other species, but enough of them are taken to suggest that small fish may play a larger part in the whiting diet than had been previously thought.

Whiting are normally fished for with light threadline tackle or sidecast gear in the surf. The lines are kept as light as is practical under the circumstances, and fine wire, long-shank hooks appropriate to the run of fish are used with the lightest lead that will get the bait to the fish. Most anglers like to present a moving bait to whiting, and the usual system is to cast out, then slowly retrieve the bait with a series of haul-and-stop movements. The bite is like machine gun fire when it comes, and whiting are one of the few fish you actually need to strike at when they take the bait as they have a habit of not running, but seem to eat the bait on the spot.

While small whiting tend to have a kamikaze mentality that allows them to attack baits right next to the feet of a wading angler, the largest specimens can be incredibly fussy. Specialists go down to fine 2 kg line with split shot weights, fished over ultra-soft rods. Soldier crabs are a favourite bait, with several tiny crabs going on the hook and others crushed in sand being used as a bottom berley.

It has often been said that if whiting ever grew to the size of a small marlin, no tackle on earth would be strong enough to stop them. An overstatement no doubt, but a strong compliment is not out of place for these little fish that are surprisingly fast and strong, especially in the surf or on a shallow sand flat.

Amongst the very best of our table fish, all of the whiting have delicate white meat that is just as good raw as it is cooked.

YELLOWTAIL

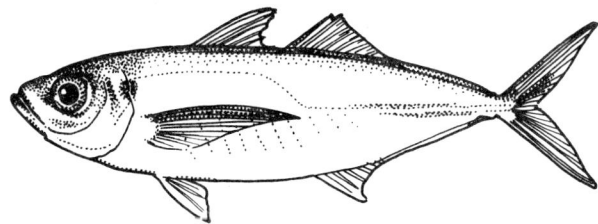

The yellowtail is a common baitfish in the southern half of the continent. It occurs in dense schools over inshore ocean reefs, around headlands, and is also found in numbers around jetties in estuaries.

The fish varies in colour from a golden brown on the back with cream belly when over reef, to a yellow back through to white belly when it is over clean sand. Yellowtail can change colour quite quickly, and for this reason a lot of anglers insist on using a white bait tank which causes them to turn a very pale colour, making them stand out for a short time after they are used for bait.

Yellowtail are normally berleyed up with fish scraps, bread or potato scraped on a grater, then caught on small pieces of fish or prawn. Multi-jig bait rigs are also a good method of taking the fish once they are feeding freely.

YELLOWTAIL KINGFISH

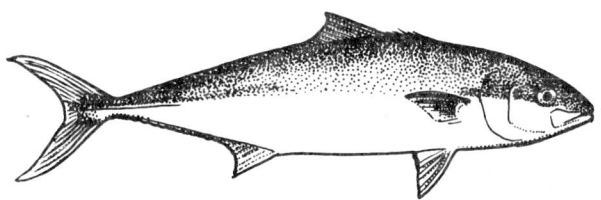

The yellowtail kingfish is one of the most highly prized sportfish of southern waters. Although found in South and Western Australia, yellowtail kings are most prolific on the east coast where they occur in great numbers.

A beautifully shaped fish with a perfectly smooth, scaleless body, the king may be blue–green to dark green on the back with silver white belly and sides, usually divided clearly by a yellow stripe down the side. The tail is a bright yellow. A 52 kg specimen has been recorded in New Zealand waters, and fish over the 40 kg mark are not uncommon, although extremely difficult to land.

The kingfish is most often encountered offshore where it is almost always associated with structure of some kind. Any reef, wreck, buoy or offshore island is well worth checking for kingfish. They also prowl deep drop-offs along rocky ocean shorelines and are particularly fond of areas where the rocks are undercut or contain ledges and caves. Juvenile kingfish also like cover but are found out in open water more frequently than the big fish and they also move into harbours and bays from time to time.

Yellowtail kings are a schooling fish, and although they are found over structure as a rule, the school could be located anywhere between the surface and the bottom. Sometimes the schools are so huge they actually do layer from top to bottom in very deep water.

Small fish and squid play a major role in the diet of the yellowtail king, and fresh squid or cuttlefish are a hot favourite that will rarely be rejected. Even a quite small piece of squid impaled on the hook of a lure will turn a lethargic kingfish right on.

They also find it hard to resist a live bait, and if they are a little slow reacting to the bait, clipping one lobe off the tail fin will change the swimming pattern and that is normally enough to induce a strike.

Kingfish have the curiosity of a cat, and when a fish is hooked in a deep-swimming school, the rest of the gang will often come to the surface with the hooked fish. Smart anglers always try to keep one hooked fish next to the boat to keep the school at the surface. To see the blue void below you start to turn green, then a bright yellow as hundreds of big kingfish rise to the surface, is one of the great experiences associated with offshore fishing.

They can also be attracted by holding a captive fish right on the surface to thrash about. Bonito and striped tuna, with their high-speed tail action, act very much like a dinner bell for any kings in the area. Big poppers will also bring the fish up and call them in from quite a distance away from a boat at times.

Whilst there is great excitement to be had from having a school of big, frantic kingfish tearing around just under the surface close to the boat, there are also very practical reasons for keeping them at the surface. Kingfish are masters at the art of taking a bait or lure as they turn to dive to the bottom, tearing line away from the reel at a blistering speed until they whip under a ledge or into a cave to cut the line off. The further you can get them away from the bottom to start the fight, the better your chances of landing the fish.

At Lord Howe Island, which is arguably one of the best kingfish grounds anywhere in the world, anglers commonly use 24 and 37 kg breaking strain line over powerful short stroker rods, and still get 'buried' in the reef by huge kingfish. Even when the initial rush is turned and line painfully won back onto the reel, these incredibly strong fish will still turn and try for the bottom time and time again.

As a table fish, yellowtail kingfish vary greatly from place to place. A parasite occurs in the fish in subtropical waters, and many Queenslanders consider the resulting soft, mushy flesh to be inedible. In southern waters they are a popular table fish, although not in the same class as our best high-quality fish. The fish taken at Lord Howe, on the other hand, are considered to be far superior to those taken close to the mainland and tourists often return raving about the superb fish meals served on the island.

Kingfish are best filleted and skinned with the blood line removed from the side. They can be grilled or fried in large fillets then, although a good way to break down the fibre in the flesh is to cut the meat into scallops by cutting thin slices with the knife angled back towards the tail section of the fillet.

Index